SHOULD PSYCHOLOGY BE A SCIENCE?

SHOULD PSYCHOLOGY BE A SCIENCE?

Pros and Cons

JOCK ABRA

Westport, Connecticut
London

Library of Congress Cataloging-in-Publication Data

Abra, Jock, 1939–
 Should psychology be a science? : pros and cons / Jock Abra.
  p. cm.
 Includes bibliographical references and indexes.
 ISBN 0–275–95476–5 (alk. paper)
 1. Science and psychology. 2. Science and psychology—History.
 3. Psychology—Methodology. 4. Psychology—Philosophy. I. Title.
BF64.A27 1998
150′.1—dc21   97–21853

British Library Cataloguing in Publication Data is available.

Library of Congress Catalog Card Number: 97–21853
ISBN: 0–275–95476–5

First published in 1998

Praeger Publishers, 88 Post Road West, Westport, CT 06881
An imprint of Greenwood Publishing Group, Inc.

Printed in the United States of America

The paper used in this book complies with the
Permanent Paper Standard issued by the National
Information Standards Organization (Z39.48–1984).

10 9 8 7 6 5 4 3 2

To Lynn and Nikki

Contents

Introduction   ix

Chapter 1: The Empirical Rule   1

Chapter 2: The Dark Side of Empiricism   30

Chapter 3: Generalization   51

Chapter 4: Generalization: Some Disclaimers   70

Chapter 5: Determinism in Science   98

Chapter 6: Psychological Determinism: Problems and Alternatives   120

Chapter 7: Analysis and Reductionism   153

Chapter 8: Conceptual Devices   179

Chapter 9: Conclusion and Epilogue   194

References   203

Name Index   229

Subject Index   235

Introduction

To deserve study, a topic must have at least one and ideally both of two qualities: It must be important and/or it must be interesting. On both counts, psychology qualifies in spades. If we define it loosely as the study of human beings, its importance is obvious. As Skinner (1971) pointed out, in the last analysis, most of the problems we face involve human behavior. Waging wars, polluting environments, and the like—these are things that *people do*. Fortunately, we are also capable of better. No mystery is more perplexing than this, that the same species that fostered the Inquisition and Auschwitz, also created the *Jupiter Symphony*, and a treatment for diabetes. Every advance, every stumbling step away from jungle law and survival of the fittest has come about because of what people at their best accomplish, so knowledge of how they do it and why may help inhibit events of the first kind and encourage those of the second. Studying psychology, then, is nothing less than a means to progress if not survival itself.

As for interest, can any other topic rival ourselves? If the human zoo was not a constant source of fascination, why would people-watching be such a favorite activity? Why would we so avidly eavesdrop on conversations or consume TV programs that showcase our foibles such as *America's Funniest Videos*? Psychology has a personal relevance matched by no other discipline; it hits us where we live. Indeed, when all is said and done many psychologists are little more than snoops or voyeurs, so bewitched by it all that they can't take their eyes and ears away from it, which puts them in the happy position of being paid for doing what they love. Certainly, in my objective, unbiased opinion, psychology is the most fun you can have with your clothes on! Moreover, many others seem to share my enthusiasm. In universities, introductory psychology course enrollments are among the highest of any offerings. There are several reasons, but one is certainly inherent interest. We educators are first of all in the entertainment business. This means, I hasten to add, that we must try at all costs not to be merely amusing or popular, but to be interesting and stimulating, because, in the entertainment business, the one unforgivable sin is to be boring. With psychology, given even a halfway decent presentation, no fear!

So psychology deserves study if anything does. But how? To answer, we must become more precise about its definition. Most people on the street believe that psychology does indeed focus on human beings, particularly on the "mind" and most particularly on its dramatic manifestations such as dreams, hypnotic states, and mental telepathy. Such beliefs are responsible for an experience that most psychologists sooner or later will have: Someone—perhaps the little old lady next to me on the plane—asks what I do. I grimace, knowing too well what will happen, and murmur, "I'm a psychologist." "Oh my goodness," she chortles, "I'd better watch what I say or you'll analyze me." No, I won't, lady! Not only am I not the least bit interested in doing so, I don't know how! I know less about such things than advice-to-the-lovelorn columnists. (But I've learned my lesson. Now, when asked about my job, I lie. Extensive research has revealed that one way to discourage more unwanted questions is to answer "I'm a pimp!")

Still, this popular belief is not entirely off base. In fact it jibes closely with the definition that, beginning with the ancient Greeks, reigned for centuries. The word "psychology" combines two Greek terms, *psyche* and *logos*. Roughly, the second means "the study of" and the first resembles our notions of "mind" or "soul," that presumed but unobservable entity that supposedly provides our essence and *consciousness*, or awareness. Thus taken literally, "psychology" has historically meant the study of the mind and as such formed one major area within philosophy, most of whose great figures from Plato and Aristotle down through Locke, Descartes, Kant, and others tackled topics that lie within psychology's domain, such as perception and memory. But around the turn of this century it suddenly acquired a very different meaning, so nowadays most psychologists, certainly most who reside in North American universities, define it as the scientific study of behavior, and their lectures and textbooks duly pass on this definition to those hordes of acolytes.

Psychology has therefore become a different ball game, because this change in definition implies a very different position on two fundamental matters. The first is subject matter. It is no longer mind but behavior, the things that organisms do. The second is the method of study. "Science" refers first of all to some rules of procedure that any discipline that calls itself a science must obey, and it also demands certain beliefs and practices and strongly encourages others. This abrupt change in direction has fostered a truism: psychology has a long history but a short past. The discipline goes back to time immemorial, but in its scientific guise it is still a youngster.

This brings us to this book's purposes and its inception. Its gestation has been longer than most. I was privileged to study with Benton Underwood, a prominent researcher into human learning and memory whose views of science (Underwood, 1957b, 1966) have strongly influenced those here, and for some years worked within the tradition he represented. However, I also had a second career as a singer and dancer and later stage director and choreographer, so I was playing two diverse roles, hard-nosed empirical scientist and creative artist. One can live with schizophrenia only so long, and eventually doubts began to intrude because the psychology I knew had no discernible connection to and little to tell me about my artistic side. This gap became increasingly vexing. Creativity is a defining human act and, as the source of everything called progress, an important one. How could a discipline that aimed for a complete account of human beings ignore what was an integral part of my own experience, and why did it do so? Wider reading, notably in existential philosophy, suggested the major culprit: the wholesale commitment to science. The result? Ever more disillusionment with that approach, a feeling that I now realize a growing number of professionals shared, for it was then, in the early 1970s, that the seeds of the grass-roots movement now known as the Cognitive Revolution were taking hold.

At any rate, my desire to release and understand these feelings led to a first version of this book, which largely rejected the approach as a dead end. In retrospect, I am heartily thankful that this version was never published, for it seems to me now a shrill polemic and an immature rejection of everything in my earlier background. I did not believe even then that the scientific approach had no merit whatsoever—after all, it had attracted me to psychology in the first place (it was even rumored that I slept with Kimble's, 1961, classic survey of rat-running behaviorism under my pillow)—and I certainly do not believe so now. Still, the book wouldn't leave me alone. I kept coming back to this nagging piece of unfinished business, because one thing you learn from artistic work is to go with your intuitions even when you don't quite understand them; they're trying to tell you something.

While seeking to understand how I felt, and why, about science and psychology, I learned a great deal about both. My aim, therefore, is to share this knowledge with both students and fellow professionals and to bring together, so far as I know for the first time, diverse objections and alternatives to the scientific approach, many of which have escaped notice. I would like to think this survey is encyclopaedic, but I came across many deserving candidates through accident or word of mouth, so others have no doubt been missed. *C'est la guerre*! Given that one way to grasp something is to consider its opposites (Rothenberg, 1979), I hope to help understanding of the scientific approach's virtues and limitations, and other approaches that might supplement it.

The first aim, then, is to consider not only the philosophy but the psychology and sociology of science. How does this mysterious beast really work? How do scientists think about things? These are not easy questions. The usual answer is that science is a set of methods for advancing knowledge, but Feyerabend (1993) claims that, if one examines examples of what is called "science," there are no such methods let alone outlooks or beliefs that clearly typify and distinguish sciences from other disciplines that are not sciences. In reality science is an anarchic enterprise in which anything goes (which Feyerabend sees as all to the good because every possible approach has both strengths and weaknesses). Nonetheless the questions must be asked because science's

influence is now so immense that no one should remain ignorant of its attributes, which leads most universities to require at least some exposure to it.
However, ingesting a course or two and memorizing some formulas and jargon
is not enough for awareness of these more basic matters to also seep in. Most
students and many professionals manage to remain woefully ignorant of the
advantages and especially the weaknesses of science as it actually works and
adamantly pursue it without realizing the implications. It seems worthwhile,
therefore, to show that, contrary to wide belief, science cannot do everything and
scientists are far from infallible.

The second purpose is to understand why psychology became a science and
what the results have been of this dramatic development. It is important to
realize that those who pioneered the new approach *borrowed* it from other
disciplines wherein it served very different purposes. Certainly it had yielded
immense benefits in both basic understanding and technology (precisely why
those pioneers found it so attractive), but because science worked well for
studying heavenly bodies, molecules, or lower organisms did not guarantee that
it would do the same for human beings, a rather different kettle of fish. Fortunately, the version those pioneers borrowed had some specific characteristics that
reflected science *as they thought it to be,* however inaccurately, and it is this
version that affected the discipline's subsequent directions, which makes
determining what science is a less foreboding task for us.

Thus the psychology-science marriage had a decided shotgun air about it. It
came about to salvage the reputation of the blushing bride, psychology, because
of difficulties in which she found herself. It was forged in undue haste, without
heeding the protagonists' possible incompatibilities, on that all too common
assumption that "Everything will be OK once we're married." Like most
metaphors, this one is not entirely accurate. For one thing, the marriage was
forced not because the bride was developing in unwanted ways, but because she
wasn't developing at all. So the intent was to stimulate, not legitimize, her
growth. Then too, most shotgun weddings are sad affairs wherein everyone tries
to put the best face on things. But this one was cause for celebration, at least
among the bride's relatives (the groom's, especially the older generation, were
more skeptical), because it heralded a fresh start. Have subsequent events, once
these nodding acquaintances were so abruptly brought together, borne out this
optimism? How did the marriage change them, and vice versa? Have they grown
together to live happily ever after? Coexisted in uneasy truce, to go their separate
ways while pretending togetherness? Or has the liaison proved so unworkable as
to warrant a trip to the divorce courts? Above all, what of the offspring that
resulted? Have they been the apples of every eye? Delinquent boors? Or, worst of
all, a stream of miscarriages and stillbirths, leaving little of lasting worth to
repay the hard work and passion that went into their making?

To serve these purposes, six of science's major characteristics will be examined, whether a rule, fundamental belief, or preferred tactic. I make no claim that
these exhaust science's traits, only that they have most influenced modern
psychology's development. Nor do I claim expertise in philosophy of science

that deals with these sorts of topics, but while my version of science may seem naive or outmoded, I think it reasonable to present it as a workaday psychologist such as myself has, rightly or not, conceived it, because it is grass roots beliefs such as these that have most influenced developments. Each characteristic's essential properties are first described at a general level, along with the reasons why every science includes it. Its manifestations in and effects on psychology are then discussed, along with several notable contributions that exemplify it, some bodies of knowledge gained through its implementation, and some difficulties that it brought about.

In discussing each characteristic, major emphasis is placed on eminent figures whose work exemplifies it and on the investigations their work spawned, the implications it raised, and other contributions that took issue with it. For these movers and shakers have most influenced psychology's directions and sometimes the very manner in which people think about themselves (had Freud never written, such art forms as painting, theater, and dance would have taken entirely different courses). These discussions also try to bring home why these people deserve to be called "great." In many sources, for example, Freud comes across as little more than a sex-obsessed, dirty old man who demands the reaction "Oh, come on! Get serious!" Why would any sensible person admire him? Freud does at times cause common sense to shudder, but it is his best ideas that matter. Everyone has bad ideas, but most people have no other kind. Einstein is supposed to have said that he would hate to go through life never having made a fool of himself, because this would indicate that he wasn't taking the risks that great achievement demands. If you go out on enough limbs, some are bound to break and deposit you unceremoniously in the mud!

This emphasis on the enduring extends also to empirical information; much of it is of less than recent vintage. Contributions that have withstood the test of time provide ultimate standards of achievement against which later entries are compared, so psychology's classic investigations deserve attention whatever their dates. Like the great figures, they represent the scientific approach at its best. In addition, they tackled important issues that too often were not so much resolved as swept under the rug, so reexamining those issues may encourage their long overdue resurrection. Also, this demonstrates how science works, because while specific issues come and go, the strategies used to resolve them do not.

Finally, another purpose is to understand how the psychology of the 1990s came to be. How and why did those major changes of a generation ago, labeled the cognitive revolution, come about? Answers require an understanding of where we were before, identifying the factors that induced that revolution as well as the antecedents that in retrospect formed its vanguard. Hull's theory, the sundry investigations it stimulated, and the issues it raised, is a case in point. Not so long ago it bestrode psychology like a colossus; Hull's influence rivaled Freud's. Yet many of today's students have never heard of him, and he receives at best only cursory mention in most textbooks. How the mighty have fallen! Here Hull is extensively scrutinized. His was arguably the most thorough attempt to fulfill the canons of what a truly scientific theory should be. Much of what psychology later became represented a reaction against Hull and his followers, so one way to grasp the psychology of the 1990s is through learning about their failings. Finally, Hull's ideas are far from a complete waste. Some proved unworkable, but others hold up well.

A disclaimer is in order, however, about the discussions of both some of the authorities such as Freud, Skinner, and Piaget, and classic studies. Since such material is familiar to many readers as staple content in standard texts and courses, extensive treatment would be redundant. Only enough detail is provided here to show how these matters exemplify certain science characteristics. However, it is hoped that senior undergraduate and graduate students, as well as professionals, will find the content edifying, so I seek a presentation that they can follow without undue hardship. When in doubt, therefore, I assume too little rather than too much of the reader, so professionals may find some parts elementary.

So this outlines our journey, but first each of science's properties will be introduced (other than empiricism, which is discussed in Chapter 1):

1) *Generalization* is a strategy that seeks similarities among individual phenomena. These are then grouped under a more general rubric, a scientific *law,* or observed regularity and consistency in nature, for example, the Boyle-Charles Law that describes the effect of varying temperature and pressure on the volume of gases.

2) *Determinism* is an article of faith that scientists invariably hold in some form. It sees the universe as not chaotic, but having order and law, so potentially it can be understood. Moreover, older versions of determinism also implied a belief in causality. No event just happens by chance; everything is caused, or determined, by other events.

3) *Analysis,* another common strategy, in some respects reverses generalization. Another way to understand phenomena is to take them apart and specify the components that make them up. Thus in chemistry, the example par excellence, physical matter is analyzed into its constituent compounds and these in turn into elements.

4) *Reductionism* attempts to understand and explain the phenomena of a more complex discipline such as psychology by referring to the phenomena or concepts of more fundamental ones such as physiology or biochemistry. Thus most sciences routinely borrow from what is in most opinions the most basic discipline of all, mathematics.

5) *Hypotheses and theories* are attempts to explain how and why events happen. Thus laws are not explanations but sets of observations that need explanation. Theories try to provide them.

A word about style. Excess in the cause of virtue may be no vice. Nonetheless, if insults to the English language are immoral, then ethical zeal has induced unethical behavior on the part of too many social scientists. The aim is beyond reproach, to avoid distressing anyone, so seemingly pejorative labels such as "retarded" are replaced by others hopefully more neutral such as "intellectually challenged." Unfortunately, such terms, besides being stylistic monstrosities, ignore the fact that no linguistic cosmetics can hide a painful truth, for example, that some people are intellectually deficient, and substituting a euphemism only insures that it too will soon become pejorative. Similarly, the latest APA manual decrees that those who serve in experiments are to be labeled participants, not subjects. However, once they have agreed to serve, are they not subjected to manipulations chosen by the experimenter? Is not portraying the interaction as one between equals therefore misinforming? Since the cardinal sin in today's newspeak is to call a spade a spade, if these practices suggest an aging reactionary, let me be called instead chronologically and progressively challenged! Finally, it has become de rigueur to use "he or she" when a singular third-person pronoun is required. In the absence of a satisfactory gender neutral alternative (my nominee would be "id"), I prefer to avoid this clumsy literary hiccup and alternate its two components more or less randomly.

ACKNOWLEDGMENTS

It is both a duty and pleasure to acknowledge others who have contributed to this project. They have helped improve it beyond measure while being in no way to blame for its deficiencies, for which the author alone is responsible. I am particularly grateful to my colleagues Mike Boyes, Rod Cooper, Charles Costello, Keith Dobson, John Ellard, Otto Haller, Bart Hicks, Bill McElheran, Tim Rogers, Hank Stam, Cam Teskey, and Bob Weyant for helpful discussions, information, and suggestions about sources to consult, and my heads of department, Don Kline and Brian Bland, for their unflagging support for my work, despite its unconventional aura. Gord Abra, Bruce Coulombe, and Linda Plotkins deserve thanks for contributing to the background research that an enterprise of this kind demands. I would also like to thank Alison Wiigs and Deborah Whitford for their capable and conscientious work during the production phase. Finally, a special thank-you to my wife Lynn and our cat Nikki, who provided needed support, diversion, and contact comfort when spirit and motivation flagged.

The Empirical Rule

OPERATIONAL DEFINITIONS AND
HYPOTHESIZED ENTITIES

Science, in some ways, resembles a game (Agnew & Pike, 1969) with nature providing the opposition. Like any game it has rules, and one of these provides its first characteristic—*empiricism*, that is, every science has as its subject matter events that can be measured, preferably along a scale such as temperature or size. Furthermore, the version of the rule adopted by most psychologists owes much to *logical positivism*, a system of philosophy espoused by the Vienna circle under Comte's influence (Boring, 1957), and to physicist P. W. Bridgman's (1927) *operationism*. In this version every term must be given an *operational definition* that specifies the procedures, or operations, used to measure it. Thus in psychology, intelligence might be defined informally as mental ability, but became legitimate scientifically only when tests were developed that claimed to measure it.

We use operational definitions every day, since such terms as temperature or body weight at base refer to readings on thermometers or bathroom scales, and in fact we grow so accustomed to some that their modification may be extremely irritating. Some years ago the Canadian government, showing the sensitivity typical of such bodies, decreed that we would "go metric," so we then heard the temperature, for example, in Celsius, not Fahrenheit. We knew what 80° F. meant, but does 22° C call for cut-offs or long underwear? Also, Celsius temperatures in western Canada remain below 0° for half the year, and -5° sounds colder than the Fahrenheit equivalent, +20°. Outrage over conversion to the metric system helped bring about the demise of that government in the next election. So by insisting on operational definitions, science simply formalizes a common practice, for they possess several advantages. Their clarity and precision helps communication, understanding, and decisions about a purportedly new concept. Is it genuinely new or merely old wine in a new bottle? Comparing its measuring procedures to those of already existing concepts tells the tale—a God-send in an era inundated by impressive sounding but trivial buzzwords.

Measurable concepts usually have other properties as well. First, most are *empirical*, observable by our senses, and thus qualify as *data*, which, in scientific circles, are synonymous with facts or results of measurements. Second, most are *objective* or publicly available, so unlike subjective phenomena, such as mental experiences or feelings, one person's observations can be checked by others and shown to be *reliable* or repeatable—a considerable advantage, given the frequency with which some phenomena are overlooked and others imagined. Finally, most measurable commodities are *variables*, that is, they can take on more than one value along a scale of measurement. Some variables have a finite number of possible values, for example, dichotomous ones offer only two—as the saying goes, you can't be a little bit pregnant—whereas others are continuous, so their scales of measurement have no discontinuity between gradations and offer infi-nite possibilities.

Still, not all measurable concepts possess these other properties. Sciences also include *hypothetical constructs*, entities potentially but not yet open to observation (Hilgard, 1956). Harvey, in suggesting that blood circulated through the body, inferred the existence of capillaries to complete the circuit, but they were located only later by Malpighi. Because of inexplicable deviations in Ura-nus's orbit, another planet was hypothesized, but Neptune had yet to be discov-ered. Psychological concepts, such as intelligence and motivation, part company even further from observation. The existence of these *intervening variables*, or hypothesized states of the organism, may never be verified because they defy direct observation. Although hypothetical constructs and intervening variables do differ (MacCorquodale & Meehl, 1948), they are here grouped together for sim-plicity as *hypothesized entities*.

Such terms raise several questions. One is, Why use them? Don't they risk ambiguity and, more seriously, by violating the empirical rule, open a Pandora's box? Fortunately, these dangers can be avoided by insisting that even terms such as these be given operational definitions, so the demand for measurement is really the rule's sine qua non. If this demand is met, most scientists find such educated guesses useful tools, as they can guide searches for undiscovered possi-bilities and help understand data. Without them, a lot of behavior would be unfa-thomable. Why do some children excel in school? One possibility is that they possess more of something called intelligence that affects the tasks school involves, although it can only be surmised indirectly from behavior in situations where it supposedly comes into play.

Another implication of the empirical commitment involves theories. As attempts to explain events, theories resemble beliefs and opinions, but here again scientists accept data's priority: Any theory is evaluated by its ability to handle the facts, and if it flies in their face, it must be modified or jettisoned, regardless of its intuitive, aesthetic, or other attractions. This priority also extends to resolving controversies among theories. Scientists ideally do not argue about facts, about what happened; if reliable, they are assumed to be accurate. But attempts to explain them often conflict, since these are limited only by ingenuity. Everyone agrees that the sun's position changes, but is this because the earth revolves around it, or vice versa? As things once stood, each explanation was viable, yet mutually exclusive, so Copernicus invoked the empirical rule: that which best accounted for the data won the day.

But what if several conflicting theories do equally well? The preferred strategy is to devise a *critical experiment* in which the theories make different predictions, and to the victor go the spoils, even if it is not the theory that fashion or common sense prefers—common sense once knew beyond question that the earth was flat and the center of the universe! Einstein stimulated one famous critical experiment. It had been assumed that light traveled only in straight lines, but relativity's prediction that in certain circumstances it should bend led some intrepid scientists to journey to the Crimea, where an eclipse would allow them to observe the light from stars as it passed the sun. Lo and behold, it did bend (Clark, 1972). In fact a case can be made that, whereas routine contributions predict what is already suspected and so yield no surprises, groundbreakers suggest the not obvious, which observations verify. They thus give the lie to common sense, the main way by which science produces progress.

THE SCIENTIFIC ATTITUDE

Science is conducted not by robots in lab coats but by human beings, making it a more fallible but also far more interesting enterprise, so discussing the psychology of scientists, notably some outlooks that influence their work, seems appropriate.

What Motivates the Scientist?

The answer may help satisfy taxpayers who question supporting this sometimes expensive pursuit when they encounter seemingly pointless investigations of, say, the visual system of the frog. United States Senator Proxmire's Order of the Golden Fleece, shaped like a shovel, sarcastically recognized projects that he felt had most effectively bilked the public purse. We must first distinguish between *pure* and *applied science*. The latter needs little justification, being the kind that seeks cures for cancer, tougher brands of concrete, or hardier wheat strains. However, solving practical problems has never been science's sole aim; in fact prevalent beliefs that it should be seem relatively recent, probably originating during the Industrial Revolution with the increasing emphasis on technology (which is related to science but not at all the same) and its many payoffs in warfare, medicine, and so on.

Pure science, on the other hand, goes back at least to ancient Egypt and "all (it) wants to do is understand the world" (Underwood, 1957b, p. 9). It is this kind that gets people's backs up. Why not tackle matters more worthwhile? There are several answers. First, we humans are relentlessly curious. We want to know about anything and everything, regardless of practical importance, so investigating something for intrinsic interest has always been deemed worthwhile. What could be more useless than studying stars and planets, yet it is the irresistible fascination they exert that has made astronomy so long-lived a science. Moreover, the ceaseless questioning about everything, relevant or not, with which youngsters bombard their parents suggests that this insatiable desire for answers is natural. Still, it can have less desirable aspects. Many Canadians were infuriated when capital punishment was abolished. Numerous arguments and statistics indicate its ineffectiveness as a deterrent and the infamous Donald Marshall case warned that innocent persons might be executed, but some people don't want facts or reason. They want answers, however horrifying, for what seems to be an alarming increase in violent crime. String 'em up!

Fromm (1960) points out that, because several once inviolate assumptions have been overturned, doubt runs rampant. A Reformation destroys confidence in cherished beliefs, a French Revolution, in one's place in the social order. Many people find such insecurity intolerable and in exchange for the security that certainty provides will willingly sacrifice personal freedom, which, for Fromm, explains the attraction of totalitarian systems, such as fascism—they give comforting albeit simplistic answers to complex questions. So everyone has the human desire to make sense of things, but scientists part company with the answers at any price crowd in finding unsolved problems stimulating, not threatening. Getzels and Csikszentmihalyi (1976) suggest that creative people are distinguished less by their ability to solve than to find problems, by their desire to seek them out, and Barron (1965) found that creative people, unlike the less creative, evince *tolerance for ambiguity*, preferring vague perceptual figures over clearcut alternatives such as circles or triangles.

In the same vein, most of us enjoy hobbies, sports, or cultural pursuits. Why? What use are they? The questions seem silly, because such activities don't need defending. Like virtue, they are their own reward. It is enough that they are enjoyable or fun. In short, curiosity may have killed the cat, but it helps keep people psychologically alive. Science too demands hard work and dedication, but for devotees it is first and foremost a hobby, a point wonderfully expressed by Tolman (1959). Looking back over his long, distinguished career, he wrote, "[My theory] may well not stand up to any final canons of scientific procedure. But I do not much care. I have liked to think about psychology in ways that have proved congenial to me. . . . The best that any individual scientist . . . can do [is] to follow his own gleam and his own bent, however inadequate they may be. . . . In the end, the only sure criterion is to have fun. And I have had fun" (p. 152). A better epitaph is hard to imagine!

However, our economic system demands production, so scientists who confine themselves to questions that no one wants answered would soon be out of business. Those tax dollars need other justifications. History provides them. Time and again seemingly useless work has had unforeseen, practical spinoffs, such as those from the space program, begun largely for the purest of motives— because "it's there." So beware of dismissing any scientific activity as useless! In fact the most efficient way to solve a pressing problem may be to set scientific busybodies loose to sniff out whatever questions catch their interest. Blind alleys, sound and fury signifying not very much there will undoubtedly be. But eventually, without any real intent, they may provide helpful answers. Cures for cancer and AIDS will probably come from those simply pursuing problems that interest them, not from the I Want To Help The Suffering contingent, because, laudable as such desires may be, they can limit vision, causing hidden possibilities to be overlooked. As canny old Polonius advised, "By indirections, find directions out."

Two other attributes of the scientific attitude follow from the empirical rule and the priority given to data in making decisions.

The Subject-Object Split

William James (1907), a founding father of North American psychology, distinguished between *tough-minded* and *tender-minded* temperaments. The latter believe in mind's power to discover validities, but the tough-minded camp, where scientists usually pitch their tents (Stevens, 1963), avows a mind separate from the objects it knows (R. Watson, 1963), a dichotomy between knower and known. Even sensory experiences, the main source of knowledge, are seen as detached from oneself. Thus Stevens asserts, "What becomes acceptable psychology accrues only when all observations, including those which a psychologist makes upon himself, are treated as though made upon 'the other one.' Thus, we make explicit the distinction between the experimenter and the thing observed. This distinction is obvious in physics; *in psychology it is equally valid*" (p. 53, italics added).

It is this outlook that underlies many attributes scientists are encouraged to develop: to be detached, aloof, and above all, objective. Concerns with how things should or might be should never intrude, since these might interfere with discovering how things *are*. This explains central casting's stereotypic scientist, the depersonalized humanoid, who peers unblinkingly at the world from which he, she, or it is separate, on the obligatory clipboard recording observations of "the other"—which is everything and everybody else—and allowing no feelings of empathy for same, whether living or not, to threaten objectivity. It says here!

I'm From Missouri—Show Me!: Skepticism

The other attribute, is that scientists should not be close-minded or inflexible, but, like Doubting Thomas who remained skeptical about Christ's resurrection, demand convincing data before changing their minds. One good reason to include science in education is to implant this attitude. When demagogues of the Oral Roberts–Jerry Falwell variety market their simplistic generalizations and unfounded assertions so effectively through mass media, it is crucial to throw them the curveball: "Prove it! Where's your data?" The effect is the same as that of any pin thrust into a bag of hot air.

The attitude that data has priority, however, is far from universally accepted. It became common only during the seventeenth century's Enlightenment, whereas the *dogmatic* attitude that prevailed before, and still has many adherents, assumes that some final, inviolate authority, such as, the Bible or established religion rules on a belief's accuracy. If the latter contradicts prevailing dogma it is certifiably wrong, even if it handles the facts more capably. Furthermore, that final authority also takes precedence over facts, so should the two collide, the latter must be wrong as well; a dogma is a theory that defies disproof. Galileo fell afoul of this attitude. His observations of Jupiter's moons, using the recently invented telescope, supported Copernicus' claim that the earth revolved around the sun, but Holy Scripture apparently portrayed the earth as the center of the universe, so Galileo's scientific outlook conflicted with the dogmatic one held by Church authorities and scions of the Inquisition. To them, he was automatically wrong, and the telescope was therefore an instrument contrived by the devil to lead mortals into heresy. Galileo had to recant his belief or be burnt at the stake, to teach him to be more careful. Yet he was privately unrepentant, reportedly muttering as he left his hearing, "Yet it [the earth] does move!" No dogma could change what was.

Dogma may begin with empirical evidence (that life exists led to the version of creation presented in Genesis), but once ingrained it is extraordinarily invulnerable to disproof. Evidence that life has evolved and been around for millions of years indicates that Genesis is incorrect at least in details, yet the 1923 Scopes "monkey trial" that placed the two accounts at odds revealed the fervor with which fundamentalists cling to its authenticity. So skepticism's main benefit may lie in its resistance to fanaticism, because from the Romans, down through the Crusades, to Hitler and the Ayatollah, most of history's abominations have stemmed from People Who Knew They Were Right. One result of scientists' skepticism follows directly: they favor freedom of expression and deplore censorship. Every notion deserves its day in court before "the right honorable judge data." If in error, sooner or later it will be found out, but it is just possible that it might have merit, so eliminating it by arbitrary fiat simply because it is politically "incorrect" or offends sensibilities is unacceptable. Because scientists are out to understand the world not as they would like it to be but as it *is*, and the two may not always coincide. All of which explains why the relationship between scientific and totalitarian communities, be they religious, political, or some other, is invariably strained. The latter need scientists, especially for military purposes, but know too well that those who take pleasure in rocking theoretical boats may also capsize dictatorial ships of state.

Skepticism offers other benefits. We might think of history as a great experiment that compares the effectiveness of dogmatic and scientific outlooks, since at different times each has held sway. Since science came to the fore during the Enlightenment, we seem to have made great strides in understanding the myriad mysteries around us. The proof is in the pudding. Science seems to work better, because inviolate authority's explanations for natural phenomena tend to be more awkward or implausible than those based on and answerable to those phenomena. As a result, in western industrial nations, at least, science is now widely accepted as the better road to travel, not only by professionals but by many lay persons (although the laity are probably more impressed by its technological than theoretical achievements). In fact it may now fulfill needs that religion once met. I suggested elsewhere that

[Since modern] science arose when religious orthodoxy was on the wane . . . perhaps its underlying faith in reason, order and logic, together with its unambiguous criteria for making decisions, provide the same comforts and defence mechanisms that religions once did. Note the similarities. Science substitutes the inviolate dogma of "the fact" for that of Holy Writ. Its Nobel Prize winners and the like become canonized Saints who deserve our unthinking reverence. It uses foreign languages (mathematics and computerese) as The Church once used Latin, to discourage laypeople's understanding, thus denying them admittance to the inner sanctum because they are insufficiently knowledgeable. They must take the enlightened minority's decrees "on faith" without question. The Church sold indulgences to smooth the path to eternal bliss. So too telethons and door-to-door blitzes convince the public that their largesse to science will keep those modern devils, cancer, heart disease and AIDS from their doors. Our cure for all ills and comfort for all distress, is science, perchance, the new opium of the people? (Abra, 1988a, pp. 105–106)

I do not wish to imply, however, that scientists' priorities make their lives easier. They may face public antipathy should they advance unpopular ideas, however soundly based on data; witness Galileo and Darwin's tribulations. Moreover, data may demand interpretations that they themselves find repugnant. Consider Kepler. Post-Copernican belief had it that planetary orbits must be circular, having been devised by God who would surely employ this most perfect geometric form. However, by Kepler's calculations the orbits had to be elliptical. Deeply religious, he was horrified, but as a conscientious scientist he had to follow their dictates. He reportedly lamented that he had left behind a carload of dung (Koestler, 1970). Of course skepticism is sometimes inappropriate, notably when a controversy concerns beliefs that by their very nature cannot be tested empirically. For example God, by definition, defies observation so we cannot establish His, Her, or Its existence let alone characteristics. What happens when fervent believers confront avowed atheists? Because both beliefs must be based on faith rather than data, they argue indefinitely, with the last word going to those with more stamina or louder voices. Such episodes help one appreciate the empirical rule. By restricting themselves to measurables, scientists save energy that might otherwise be wasted on fruitless arguments.

COMPLICATIONS

Empiricism so far has been idealized, portrayed as it was understood by psychology's science pioneers. Realism must now intrude because, influenced as this borrowed version was by logical positivism and operationism, it was atypical of general science from the outset and some revolutionary changes in science and its philosophy have made this version downright misleading about science's actual characteristics. Yet ironically, as Koch (1964, 1981) has noted, no other science has equaled psychology's concerns about doing it right by the supposed book, however anachronistic; natural scientists are far less concerned with slavishly following the empirical rule and canons of methodology. Why this obsession? One reason no doubt is the greater enthusiasm that new converts so often show for any religion's tenets, but the usual explanation is that psychologists were riddled with guilt about their mentalistic heritage and well aware that many natural scientists saw their attempts to study such content scientifically as ridiculous. Therefore they felt they had to outscience the sciences, to show them, like a little brother tagging along after the big guys and trying to impress them with his swaggering toughness. (Why psychologists have been so concerned with what physicists thought of them I do not pretend to know!)

We turn now to some realities with which all modern sciences must cope, that in practice, reduce the empirical rule's effectiveness. We begin, however, with one unique to psychology, because it insures that in this domain these realities have so great an impact that ignoring them becomes especially suspect.

The Problem of Intimacy

The human mind poses a quandary: Can something understand itself? Thus in psychology, the topic of study and those who do the studying (experimenter and subject) are not separate. Psychologists seek knowledge about people, a category to which they belong, producing an unparalleled intimacy between body of and seeker after knowledge. The implication? Demanding objectivity or detachment is both hopeless and ridiculous; amateurs and professionals alike will react to content subjectively and emotionally in a manner foreign to other sciences. This is not always the case. Few have strong opinions about physiological functions or psychological processes of subhuman species, such as, the ever-popular rat (so objectivity's most enthusiastic proponents tend to be investigators of these sorts of topics), but these exceptions aside, psychologists will, and should, evaluate ideas, theories, even neutral facts, in light of their own experience. On that level, do these matters help understand it? If the answer is in the negative, the commodity will carry little weight, its scientific merit notwithstanding.

Instructors of beginning psychology courses routinely face one result. In contrast to other sciences, students possess strong conceptions, both pre- and mis-, about what they expect to learn—ideas relevant to their own lives—and are disappointed when not enough are forthcoming. Few laypeople would claim expertise about the natural sciences, but everyone thinks themselves an expert about psychology, and in a real sense they are. Yet suppose that rocks could receive information and communicate and that a geologist had cause to inform them as to his discipline's knowledge about rocks. Suppose too that they replied, "What you've told us is all very interesting so far as it goes, but there's a lot more to rocks than that. We know! We're rocks!" Should this not give that geologist pause?

The History of Science: Thomas Kuhn

By classic scenarios, science progresses gradually, accumulating ever more empirical observations from which ever better theories emerge by the *method of induction*. For Kuhn (1962), this portrait is inaccurate. Instead, at one point in time a discipline's practitioners share a set of beliefs called a *paradigm*, for example, Newtonian views that for so long dominated physics and physicists. It determines the kinds of questions asked, investigations conducted, data deemed important, the interpretations of those data, even the types of theories found acceptable. Paradigms are not theories as such, but are more panoramic, theories about theories, but whatever they are (Kuhn's usage is inconsistent) they affect a discipline's every aspect and ultimately its body of knowledge. In other words, most scientists are as prone as everyone else to dogma and the whims of fashion. But not all. In Kuhn's view the vast majority do work within a prevailing paradigm, while only dimly recognizing its suppositions. They thus carry on *normal science*, a *problem-solving activity* like crosswords or jigsaws in which every puzzle has a potential solution on whose merit everyone agrees (Abra, 1988a), except that now it is the shared paradigm that renders correctness reliable. Thus a theory's legitimacy is accepted only if it conforms to current canons of what theories should be like. So normal scientists go their merry way, their data and theories by all appearances driving the discipline forward. However some evidence always lurks that does not fit the paradigm and calls it into question, for example, the Michelson-Morley results (Clark, 1972) that contradicted Newtonian views and set Einstein to musing. Playing by the rule of data's priority, these *anomalies* should cause the paradigm's overthrow but they don't, at least not at first. Scientists, acting like the humans they are, simply ignore these dangers to the status quo, just as Freud claims we all suppress threatening events.

Eventually, however, too many anomalies accumulate, the sense of progress is replaced by one of wheels being spun, and the discipline is ripe for a *scientific revolution*, the replacement of an outmoded paradigm with a new one, as when Einstein supplanted Newton. Since a new paradigm is advanced largely to account for anomalies, they are no longer ignored but brought front and center. Even previously commonplace facts are reinterpreted in light of the new outlook so that a revolution in a real sense causes the world to change and to be perceived very differently, just as one's underlying biases affect one's interpretations of Rorschach ink blots. Thus normal scientists leap on the bandwagon and once more set to work with a revitalized sense of progress, and the cycle begins again. But for Kuhn, revolutionary science, involving genuine creativity rather than problem solving, is closer to art than to normal science, because new paradigms are preferred more for aesthetic than empirical reasons. They seem more beautiful, elegant, and enlightening, so in practice subjective criteria affect science enormously.

Do revolutions represent progress or returns to square one? The possibility that science sometimes goes backward may seem silly, but let us not confuse science with technology. We have more inventions and cures for disease than the Greeks did, but do we understand the world any better? It is a moot point because understanding at base refers to how one feels about things and we have more things we are puzzled about. Then too, a new paradigm may handle embarrassing anomalies better and seem to be an improvement, but its predecessor may have better accounted for other phenomena which in the rush onto the new bandwagon now become suppressed anomalies. Kuhn seems to believe that on balance progress does result, but he has certainly changed its connotation from gradual, inevitable growth to sudden leaps followed by slower gains, and then stasis. Also, by advancing some novel beliefs that have themselves achieved virtual paradigmatic status, he exemplifies his own theory. Together with other contributions of recent vintage (notably J. D. Watson's, 1968, portrait, warts and all, of how DNA's structure was discovered), he has caused prevailing views about science's realities to change substantially and stimulated interest in how psychological factors, such as perceptions and attitudes, affect it.

Above all, he implies that paradigms strikingly resemble religious systems in that they too can foster that dogma to which scientists are supposedly immune. Consider his claim that a new paradigm will gain few converts among the obdurate old guard, so their influence must wane before it can claim victory. Perhaps old scientists, like old soldiers, never die, they just lose their paradigms! Einstein for one was vulnerable. Convinced of relativity's validity, he dismissed contradictory data, later put forward, as due to flaws in experimentation or measurement (Holton, 1988). Pasteur (Geison, 1995) was even more susceptible. For example, he adamantly opposed the notion that spontaneous generation of life from nonliving matter was possible; less than 10 percent of the data he obtained on this matter supported his view, yet he admitted such results alone as "acceptable," being unsurpassed in his ability to find reasons for rejecting findings that were less comforting. Nor was he above machinations of questionable morality or that bordered on fraud, to "prove" ideas that seemed to him well founded.

Quarrels between creationists and evolutionists make the same point, when some of the latter assert that evolution has become not merely a powerful theory—which it is—but self-evident truth—which it is not and can never be. Hume and Popper's (1972) arguments to be presented later show that no theory however appealing can be proven true, only false. Yet, evolution's dogmatists bluster, anyone who questions this gospel perforce stamps himself as a modern heretic who should be charred on a Bunsen burner in the city square. They too, it seems, share the need for security that dogma provides! (In my view creationism should be taught in schools. These are seminal ideas in our culture with which every young person should be familiar. I would insist, however, that they be presented not as an inviolate truth but as a theory like any other, with due consideration for pros and cons—precisely the approach that dogmatic creationists reject.)

Finally, within psychology's domain, the phenomena of *parapsychology*, such as extrasensory perception (ESP) and mental telepathy, also reveal how susceptible some purported scientists are to dogma. To be skeptical about such phenomena is not only desirable but mandatory, given the prevalence of charlatanry and unsubstantiated claims, for example the seemingly amazing "psychic" Uri Geller, who was later shown to be a hoax (Randi, 1980), and the willingness of proponents to uncritically accept anecdotal reports that have simpler explanations. For instance, Aunt Abigail dreamt about a plane crash and lo and behold one occurred in Irkutsk *the very next week.* After a myriad other similar dreams, nothing happened. Some people just worry a lot. Still, attempts have been made to evaluate these hypothesized phenomena empirically (Rhine, 1953), notably studies of mental telepathy (Honorton, 1985) using *ganzfelds*, unchanging sensory environments in which the person receiving the message is denied ordinary sensory input by eye shades, headphones presenting white noise and the like. The sender then views a stimulus such as a videotape, after which the receiver is shown four stimuli including the appropriate one and asked to identify it. Whereas the hit rate by chance would be 25 percent, over several studies it averaged an impressive 38 percent. Nonetheless, Wagner and Monnet (1979) found that the proportion of professors who rejected ESP as either an accepted fact or possibility was among natural scientists, 34 percent, those in the arts, humanities, and education, 23 percent and psychologists, 66 percent (so their empirical mindset again surpasses their natural science counterparts). Such seemingly unempirical phenomena may lie beyond science's pale, but to therefore dismiss them out of hand as bogus is mere superstition. These dogmatists should recall another Humian point, that it can never be conclusively proven that something does not exist. Even if not observed so far, it is always possible that one day it will be, because all conceivable observations or experiments can never be performed. To verify that "there ain't no gold in them thar hills," you would have to dig up every inch of ground in them!

Data Is in the Eye of the Beholder

Here is the first consideration that troubles every science. The empirical rule seemed to insure that scientific topics would be reliable and objective. In practice, not so! As Polanyi (1959) points out, we observe the data with our sensory receptors, making the observer's personal or *tacit* experience integral determinants of her responses to them, and, following Kuhn, scientists too differ in their biases and therefore interpretations. Thus supposedly reliable data become as ambiguous as a Rorschach ink blot, which calls into question the supposition that they protect science from irresolvable arguments. Consider those supposed paragons of objectivity, operational definitions. As regards temperature, for example, with apologies to Gertrude Stein, 22° is not necessarily 22° is not 22°. I learned this some years ago while visiting South Africa, which is very hot, and not just politically. Although it was winter, the daytime temperature hovered around the 22° mark (roughly 70° F, for the unmetricated). The South Africans and I could agree on this; we could see it on thermometers. However, our interpretations apparently differed because our actions certainly did. Running around in sweaters, heaters turned up to the full, they complained about a new ice age, while the same 22° found this native of western Canada wherein the lyrics to *Home On the Range* would read to the effect that therein the reindeer and polar bear play, that seldom is heard an unfrostbitten word, and the ice crystals dangle all day, in a bathing suit soaking up rays and risks of melanoma be damned. They thought I was crazy. I thought they were. (Why waste beautiful weather? It might snow tomorrow!)

Furthermore, Polanyi continues, even if we could restrict ourselves to objective phenomena we wouldn't want to, because the resulting knowledge would be trivial. A worthwhile topic always includes a large tacit aspect because this is a major component of our responses to both the world and ourselves. Thus intuitions, gut reactions and leaps of imagination greatly influence science, although they cannot be explained logically or verbally. Einstein (1952) often relied on visual or even "muscular" thinking, along with colorful images and metaphors supposedly more typical of artists or mystics. Final products, such as published papers and mathematical proofs suggest more logical processes, but to him they misrepresent reality. No productive person, he asserted, thinks in such a "paper" fashion (Wertheimer, 1959). Similarly, the mathematician Gauss avowed that he had his solutions long before he knew how to get to them (Koestler, 1970). Even language usage involves much more than the formal meanings of words. How often do we know something that we cannot express verbally, or use a word correctly that we cannot precisely define? In fact poetry's effects depend primarily on tacit communication.

Which Data Are "The Data"?

As another source of subjectivity, a vast array of stimuli from what James (1890) called the blooming, buzzing confusion, most of which we ignore, constantly bombard our sensory receptors. But testing a theory requires decisions about which of these data deserve attention, and on this score arguments are endless. Consider operational definitions. For a given concept it is possible to devise any number, and the choice among them boils down to a matter of opinion. Why are there so many intelligence tests available? Profit is one motive, since producing them can be lucrative, but cynicism aside, "intelligence" has many connotations, so different tests stress different abilities. To compound the problem in psychology, Harré (1985) points out, physical concepts, such as time, possess universally accepted standards that represent their ultimate measurement, such as a perfectly calibrated clock in some bureau of measurement. All other clocks, then, are regulated against this standard and any departures from it or variations among other clocks, by definition, reflect measurement error. However, many psychological concepts, notably hypothesized entities such as intelligence, have no universal standards because people disagree about what is being measured and therefore about how to measure it. Even if we compare abilities to predict, there is disagreement about what measures should predict, so different criteria will be advocated. The fact that intelligence tests correlate only moderately may indicate not error but differences in what is being measured, so maximizing correlations may not be possible or desirable—in theory, there could be as many tests as there are psychologists to invent them. In short, operationism, far from helping eliminate redundant concepts, often has the reverse effect.

Also, consider experiments. Thousands are published annually and most fulfill the basic canons of methodology and empiricism. Yet while the vast majority soon sink into oblivion, a few come to be recognized as classics and stimulate a host of followups, textbook and classroom discussions, and so on. But what distinguishes classics? Certainly not their superior fulfillment of science's canons. By these criteria they are no more, and sometimes less, admirable than humdrum entries. Finally, consider theoretical controversies. Suppose theories A and B provide alternative explanations of a phenomenon. Data is invoked to arbitrate. Theorist A undoubtedly advances observations M, N, and O, which fit her account but embarrass theory B. Says she, "Explain them apples, B?" Playing by the book, the latter should surrender like a good sport, "Yes, the facts clearly show your account is better. Darn! And I had my Nobel speech all prepared and my tuxedo rented!" Actually, B does nothing of the kind, but counters, with facts X, Y, and Z, that his theory handles better, so it again comes down to the data deemed more important. The result? The very sort of endless debates that empiricism supposedly prevents. Thus a theoretical article by, say, Went, Dent, and Malcontent, invariably elicits "Reply to Went et al.," by Haversack and Featherbed, "Response to the reply of Haversack and Featherbed," "Note on the heresies of Went et al.," on and on, ad infinitum. Perhaps the combatants eventually adjourn to the field of honor to settle their differences via reprints at twenty paces! A cynic might blame such episodes on desires to vivify comatose publication records, but, naive optimist that I am, I prefer to see them as honest disagreements about matters that defy empirical resolution.

In short, we choose among facts, experiments, and theories much as we do among works of art, that is, on aesthetic grounds, preferring those that seem more elegant, beautiful, or personally valid. Natural scientists have long recognized the role of the subjective in science—Einstein admitted and rejoiced in it (Clark, 1972), as did Poincaré (1952). Even operationism's guiding light, Bridgman, observed, "[Explanation] consists in reducing a situation to elements with which we are so familiar that we accept them as a matter of course, so that our curiosity rests" (quoted in Stevens, 1963, p. 50). At what point does curiosity rest? People differ. Dickens's *Hard Times* wonderfully satirizes arch-empiricists in the person of Mr. Gradgrind, who firmly believed that focusing exclusively on "fact" and avoiding interpretive bias would inevitably lead to truth, and indeed many a nineteenth century scientist evidently believed that facts could be gathered like rosebuds. But few nowadays are similarly deluded for, as Bertrand Russell (1969) observed, people without biases do not exist. And in psychology, these considerations are still more profound because of intimacy. Introspection must render our opinions about commodities such as personality that we ourselves possess even more intense. Yet ironically, Mr. Gradgrinds still lurk here in profusion.

This Changing World

The natural sciences have also come to realize that observations are not completely informative about the external world. According to the Heisenberg principle, phenomena change when observed or measured, which complicates determining their everyday properties. This problem particularly troubles psychology, because if electrons change their behavior when observed, this is even more true for people. Witness attitude surveys. If residents of a neighborhood are asked about a minority group, responses indicate that prejudice doesn't exist. "Some of my best friends are _____". Yet should members of that minority move in, the convulsions of bigotry suggest that those residents expressed ideal not actual beliefs. This problem even bedevils supposedly controlled studies in laboratories. Human subjects have preconceived beliefs about what is being studied, and suspect ESP, repressed sexual desires or some such. That actual purposes may be more mundane is beside the point, because their knowledge that they are in an experiment and being observed are likely to have an effect. Nor do subterfuges such as one-way mirrors or misinforming cover stories avoid the difficulty. Merely placing subjects in an artificial environment changes things. Some may want to cooperate and do what they believe the experimenter wants, while others, out of resentment at this waste of time, do the opposite. Either way, due to these *demand characteristics* (Aronson, Ellsworth, Carlsmith & Gonzales, 1990) their behaviors must differ from those that would ordinarily occur.

Moreover, the Heisenberg difficulty is compounded in psychology because experimenters are also human. They too have expectations, about the data they should obtain, and so more often than not obtain them. In Rosenthal and Jacobsen's (1968) exhibition of *experimenter bias*, students were each to train a rat to traverse a maze; half were told that their rats were bright, bred for learning mazes, the others, that theirs might prove slow. In reality, all rats came from the same litter and should have learned equally well, but the supposedly brighter acolytes on average did in fact excel. How such expectations were communicated to rats was by no means apparent—so far as could be determined, experimenters tried to be "objective"—yet somehow they were, and the danger must be even greater with human subjects. Hence it can happen that two conflicting theorists who each conduct that seemingly ideal test, a critical experiment, each obtain results they predict. Therefore, experiments such as double blind ones are now common, wherein an experimenter who actually runs subjects is kept unaware of the group to which they belong and of underlying expectations.

What *Really* Motivates Scientists?

Stressing curiosity and enjoyment was not misinforming—these motives certainly operate—but scientists, subject to the same foibles as everyone, also evince others less lofty. Motives that drive creative work of all kinds have been discussed elsewhere (Abra, 1996), so only a few need be reiterated. First, diverse motives probably impel not only different people but the same person at different times, so Samuel Johnson's opinion that no one but a blockhead ever wrote except for money (Bate, 1979) seems an overgeneralization. Still, crass materialism no doubt influences many, including scientists. Profits can be made, if not in such ethereal pursuits as astronomy then certainly in technological and medical research, and if investigators cared not a whit about such things, why bother with patents?

We may prefer to think of scientists as selflessly pursuing knowledge, with the discovery being all that matters and never mind who makes it. Hogwash! Egos are heavily involved. Far and away their most powerful motivators, as they themselves admit (Mitroff, 1974), are professional reputation and peer respect. Nobel prizes are sought not for the financial reward but because they represent ultimate prestige. Hence those *priority disputes* that dot history (Merton, 1983). Surprisingly often, several people have independently advanced the same idea— Newton and Leibniz of calculus and Darwin and Wallace of evolution. Who thought of it first? If scientists were so selfless no one would care, but since fame is a powerful consideration, and in these races the winner gets it, these disputes can become extremely nasty. As a result, another prime motive is *competition*, the desire to get there firstest with the mostest. James Watson (1968) candidly admitted to seeking DNA's structure because of the Nobel that awaited, so he saw the enterprise as a race against others in the hunt (although his partner Crick evidently did not: Judson, 1979). For Watson (1977), competition is a highly effective spur and indeed many scientists have shown highly combative streaks (Mitroff, 1974), Newton being but one (Westfall, 1980).

EMPIRICISM AND PSYCHOLOGY

The empirical rule's effects on the development of psychology have been enormous. By specifying what may and by implication may not be studied, empiricism decided its very subject matter. That newfound definition established this as behavior, and it came about to fulfill the rule and thus earn psychology scientific status.

The Coming of Science: Wundt and Watson

The late nineteenth century revered science even more than we do now. Demonstrations of its less desirable results, notably at Hiroshima and in the environment still lay ahead, and its awesome contributions to both understanding and technology led some to expect that it would soon solve every problem of note, leaving only a few details to be mopped up. However, psychology was still mired in philosophy's bogs, tackling the same age-old problems with little discernible progress, so a growing number of people hoped to place it on a scientific footing. Wilhelm Wundt provided an early attempt. In essence, his problem was that mental experience is subjective and immune to reliability checks, but he felt that consciousness could be made empirically legitimate if the experiencing person communicated its contents to others, and to this end he resurrected Socrates' *method of introspection*, (R. Watson, 1963). Subjects were exposed to situations such as flashing lights and asked to examine and then describe their various experiences. The method's failings soon became apparent. One is revealed by that phrase so often used in the face of intense experiences: "Words fail me!" They certainly do. Every description seems woefully inadequate. As Malagrida (quoted in Stendahl, 1953, p. 152) sardonically observed, "Language has been given to man to *hide* his thoughts" (italics added). Similarly, several subjects placed in the same situation might produce different reports, such as having seen a "blazing light" versus "fiery glow." Did this indicate differences in experience or in the words chosen to describe it? Alternatively, do similar words suggest similar experiences, as witness that age-old question, does my experience of "orange" resemble yours? Such questions are ultimately unanswerable because no one can know another's experience and because "We are tied down to a language which makes up in obscurity what it lacks in style" (Stoppard, 1967, p. 77).

The introspective method also trips over the Heisenberg principle. When we examine our own consciousness and become aware of being aware, our consciousness no doubt differs from when we are thinking about something else, so even accurate descriptions may be atypical. In addition, assuming that Freud's notion that mind includes an unconscious has some merit, how can introspection be accurate if so crucial a component is largely inaccessible? In support, Nisbett and Wilson (1977) cite several lines of evidence to indicate that people are simply not very good at introspecting, remaining blissfully unaware of such things as their reasons for doing something or of factors that have demonstrably influenced a behavior, such as, solving a puzzle. Wundt tried to overcome this problem by training his subjects to introspect. He was concerned, rightly, that since reliability checks were impossible, their biases might color their reports, so they were told to observe their experience as if it was someone else's. A lofty but hopeless ideal, and such training raises the objection that it could suggest, however unintentionally, the experiences subjects should observe if they were introspecting correctly—the sort expected by Wundt's theories. Psychologists' reluctance to admit what other sciences now recognize, that data usage is inevitably subjective, is another of Wundt et al.'s bequests (Riegel, 1978).

But the bottom line that did in this admirable but doomed attempt was that Wundt's methods simply didn't work! The torrents of windy introspections dutifully published noticeably depleted timber resources and increased library holdings but added precious little to knowledge. James expressed the growing disdain: "[The approach] could hardly have arisen in a country where natives could be *bored*" (quoted in R. Watson, 1963, p. 326). Thus psychology was ripe for another change, and John B. Watson (1913, 1929) was more than willing to oblige. He realized full well that a science-consciousness union was unworkable; one or the other would have to go, and science seemed the more likely victim. Psychology had always studied mind, so if the scientific method proved unsuitable, surely another must be adopted. Thus Wittgenstein (1958) believed that since psychology meant the study of such phenomena, a scientific version was impossible. Such overt activities as believing or remembering, while they have a mentalistic ring, cannot be tied conclusively to and therefore cannot be taken as indicants of inner processes or structures (this potentially devastating critique of attempts at a scientific cognitive psychology is discussed later; H. Gardner, 1985; M. Williams, 1985). But Watson preferred the more radical alternative. If consciousness could not be so studied, substitute another topic that could. Nor in retrospect is this choice surprising, given the mood of the day. On one point at least Watson and Wundt were in complete agreement: after several millennia of bumbling around in philosophy's bramble bushes, psychology had at last got itself on its proper, scientific track. It needed not a derailing but more modern equipment.

However if consciousness was to be abandoned, what should replace it? Watson answered that behaviors are ideal subjects for objective and experimental methods. To him, actions did speak louder than words! Behaviors are legitimate empirical phenomena, because if someone, say, lifts her arm, this act, unlike the lifter's thoughts or emotions while performing it, can be observed by others and measured. Moreover, in Watson's view behaviors should be studied as ends in themselves, not as means to assess any presumed hypothesized entities from which they might stem. But what of those subjective aspects of experience? Were these, psychology's historic concerns, henceforth to be ignored? Not to Watson's way of thinking(!). He saw these too as at base behaviors, differing from others only in quantity, being more difficult to observe. Thought, for example, is merely implicit speech—talking to oneself, as it were—and sooner or later technology was sure to provide sufficiently sensitive devices to operationally define the *psyche*'s most private, subtle constituents. And since what once seemed hopelessly subjective phenomena can now be assessed using technology such as lie detectors, Watson's faith was not entirely misplaced.

What are the sources of emitted behaviors? Watson exploited Aristotle's concept of the *association*, a presumed connection or link formed between several events, so one tends to evoke the other; virtually everyone asked to free associate to "table" responds with "chair." The British empiricist philosophers such as Locke, Berkeley and Hume also stressed this concept. Mental life supposedly consisted of a neverending flow of individual elements or *ideas* in what James (1890) would later call *the stream of consciousness*. Presumably one idea, A, led to B rather than C (or for schizophrenics, XYZ) because B's association is stronger. Thus understanding how associations were acquired became tantamount to understanding mind and the favored explanation invoked empirical events. Locke's view was typical. At birth the mind is a tabula rasa or blank sheet on which neither ideas nor knowledge is inscribed; rather, sensory experience provides them. Likewise, associations between ideas depend on *contiguity*, being jointly experienced in time or place.

Watson's similar explanation began with the concept of the *stimulus* (S)—any event that causes a behavior to occur, the most obvious stimuli being environmental events. That a stimulus evokes a particular response (R) suggests that an association, S-R, exists between them and that one acquires a *habit*, when S occurs, to respond with R. Thus explanations for any behavior of interest must specify the antecedent stimuli to which it is associated. As for the origins of our myriad S-R associations, Watson again followed his empiricist forefathers. Aside from a few inborn reflexes, they are bequeathed by that great teacher, experience. How? Here Watson leaned on Pavlov's recent demonstrations. A stimulus such as a bell, when presented repeatedly in contiguity with another, such as food in a dog's mouth, came to elicit a particular response that initially it did not—in this case, salivation. Thus subjects acquired new habits. This *classical conditioning* suggested a method for forming associations and in turn an operational definition for this heretofore mentalistic concept. Which brings us back to the empirical rule. Among the S-R conception's attractions was that since both components were laudably objective, focusing on them would satisfy that rule. Furthermore, stressing stimuli as the presumed causes of behaviors, rather than mental events, consigned these mysticisms at long last to their proper place: psychology's scrap heap.

So it is to Watson that we owe that modern definition. His revolutionary approach found immediate favor, even though a change of this magnitude, in the very subject matter, was akin to botanists suddenly discovering that henceforth they would no longer study plants but hair styles. Within a generation his "behaviorism" had become the preeminent brand of psychology in North America, and its obsession with empirical knowledge also dominated Britain's Oxbridge axis until the 1950s (Hudson, 1976). Which again reveals the mood of the day. Clearly many others were dissatisfied with the way things weren't going and were looking for greener pastures. We also learn something about Watson himself. He was an immensely colorful personality, a textbook revolutionary as dogmatic and outspoken as any Lenin and contemptuous of opponents and prevailing opinion, at which he openly thumbed his nose. A later liaison with his student Rosalie Rayner led to what was at that time intolerable, divorce, and the scandal was compounded when the lovers married with unseemly haste (Viney, 1993). Watson had to resign from Johns Hopkins University, but while he retained his interest in and wrote about psychology, it is ironic that one of psychology's preeminent figures spent his later years working very successfully not in it but in advertising!

Do the Wundt and Watson episodes fit Kuhn's scenario? Especially the latter certainly seems to, but for Kuhn the social sciences, because no one outlook is shared by every worker, are in the *preparadigmatic* state that characterized the natural sciences when these were less developed. Whether a closed system such as a dominant paradigm signifies maturity is open to debate, but in any case behaviorism was certainly not the only influential brand of psychology in Watson's day or now; psychoanalysis was and is another. However, within North American academia at least, it approached paradigm status, if by a behaviorist one means, as I do, anyone who accepts Watson's definition of psychology as the scientific study of behavior, regardless of whether they go along with his other views. (Skinner, for example, another archetypal behaviorist, found S-R explanations unappealing.)

The Mind-Body Problem

This problem, a persistent one in psychology's history, concerns the relationship between our spiritual/ mental and physical/corporeal sides. Do they affect one another? If so, how? Of the several answers put forward, none are conclusive (see R. Watson, 1963, or Boring, 1957), but one notability provides a sense of its complexities and implications. For Descartes, mind and body were independent, so the properties of one could not be inferred from the other. Lordly mind exists above and is impervious to influence by the crassly physical, whereas body, composed of matter, is ruled by cause and effect, so Descartes equated it with a machine, a category to which animals, lacking mind, therefore belonged. This dualistic view faces immediate difficulties. How could mind affect body and thus down-to-earth existence in any important manner? If it doesn't, why postulate it at all? Descartes therefore hedged on total independence, claiming mind and body do interact somewhat in the brain's pineal gland. Yet this position is also unsatisfactory. If they differ so substantially, how could they influence one another, and would dallying in reality not compromise mind's purity?

Examples of Empiricism

Emotional Behaviors and Phobias. Although Watson believed that our behaviors in the main reflected classical conditioning, examples of everyday ones acquired in this way are rather few. Few phenomena seem more resistant to empirical study than those definitively subjective experiences, the emotions or affective states. Behaviorists counter that we also produce postures or facial expressions that typify each emotion, so that happiness and depression are characterized by laughter and smiling or lethargy and crying, respectively, and it is these observable behaviors, not hypothesized inner entities, that provide the proper focus.

Furthermore, Watson himself, collaborating again with Rayner (Watson & Rayner, 1920) but now in a manner more socially acceptable, exploited the talents of psychology's most renowned infant, Baby Albert, to show that *phobias*, exaggerated fears of specific stimuli, could be acquired by classical conditioning. Albert initially emitted responses suggesting fear, such as crying and trembling, to loud noises but not to small furry animals. The experimenters, following Pavlov's recipe, paired the two stimuli in contiguity, and Albert soon had a raging phobia for rabbits. (The moral aspects of thus burdening his young *psyche* were apparently ignored). Phobias certainly can be acquired in this way, but that all are is unlikely. What of people who have never experienced the stimuli they fear, such as those afraid of flying? We might invoke (Watson would not) *vicarious conditioning*, that is, having heard about crashes, they imagine and imitate the terror of victims. I would go still further and suggest that some phobias are inborn. Snake phobias rarely reflect personal traumas but are extremely common. There may just be something about snakes! In our distant past such fears would be highly adaptive and might, like physical structures of proven evolutionary utility, be handed down in a shared, collective psyche as a species memory (Jung, 1966). The behaviorist would dismiss such notions as mysticism. That doesn't mean they are off base.

Watson's principles have been extended to other emotions. Amsel (1958) hypothesized a response of frustration, r_f, which is unobservable but supposedly occurs in situations that seem conducive to this feeling, such as when an anticipated reward is not forthcoming. Thus a phenomenon usually described as an emotion is again recast as a behavior, albeit one implied rather than manifest. Besides holding out the possibility that it too can be associated through classical conditioning to other stimuli, this gambit also allows otherwise unempirical concepts to gain legitimacy. Consider that most unforgettable of emotions called *love*. The unromantic behaviorist, ever eager to reduce the intangible to the concrete, would see this as nothing more than a set of reflexes elicited automatically by a beloved stimulus, among them palpitations, dryness in the throat, acute stammering and verbal utterances such as "What's your sign?" that effectively hide any intelligence one might possess. (The greatest mystery of all, why this one stimulus should evoke these reflexes while countless similar others do not remains unexplained, but behaviorists rarely tackle these deeper questions). In the extreme, a Watson-Pavlov scenario yields phenomena that can only be called bizarre. A character in *My Fair Lady* extols in song the enchantment to be found on the street where his beloved lives, presumably because (the lyrics put it more romantically) this thoroughfare, having frequently occurred in contiguity with the object of his afflictions, now elicits similar behaviors. Someone who has a thing for concrete has got problems and let us not even think about asphalt!

Verbal Learning and Transfer: Ebbinghaus and Functionalism. Studies of associations between verbal units represent another application of S-R principles. Animals can acquire a rudimentary language (Gardner & Gardner, 1969; Premack & Premack, 1972), but our abilities in this regard are infinitely more sophisticated, our most marked departure from them. But in order to use words and understand their meanings we form many associations, both to events to which they refer and to other words (dictionary definitions, for example, merely provide other associates). The experimental study of verbal learning was begun in Wundt's time by another German, Hermann Ebbinghaus (1885). Suspecting that a frequently used word would already possess many associations and wishing to study their acquisition de novo, he therefore invented the *nonsense syllable*, a sequence of letters, such as *zep*, that doesn't form a word (except for scions of the government or military with their fondness for that monstrous modern linguistic invention, the acronym). He assumed that such structures should have no associations to muddy the empirical waters (in this he was later shown to be mistaken). Ebbinghaus served as his own subject, acquiring numerous lists of such syllables via *serial learning*, wherein one studies a series of items in a constant order (as in learning the alphabet) until able, upon glancing at each, to anticipate the next. Showing laudable dedication to science—to say nothing of sheer persistence bordering on compulsion—Ebbinghaus tackled several such lists every day for some years.

His approach was soon taken up by the movement known as *functionalism*. Its first generation, located at the University of Chicago and featuring John Dewey and James Angell, voiced within psychology that distinctively American philosophy known as *pragmatism*. Functionalists wished not only to describe and explain psychological phenomena but also, showing Darwin's influence, to specify the functions they served for well being and survival. Early functionalism also had a decided Wundtian aspect in that it encouraged introspection and the study of subjective phenomena, so that although Watson himself had trained under Angell at Chicago, functionalism later became another target for his wrath. However, its next generation, ironically, practiced Watson's preaching more faithfully than did so-called behaviorists such as Hull and Tolman, who routinely resorted to the unthinkable, assessing hypothetical entities from behavior, to concoct grandiose theories of learning whose squabbles and testings dominated psychology between the wars. Archetypal functionalists of the day such as McGeogh (1942) remained aloof from the fray. Behaviorists in all but name, specifying the stimuli that controlled a behavior was all the explanation they sought. Manipulate stimulus conditions, systematically observe the effects on the response, then express this S–R relationship as a *functional relationship* having the form $R = f(S)$, to show how R varies as S does, as demonstrated by the data. Thus "functionalist" acquired another connotation, someone who mainly seeks out functional relationships and has no interest in abstract theorizing or, skeptics suspected, in using his imagination. That most functionalists resided in the drought-ridden Midwest, that they tortured subjects with boring tasks such as memorizing lists of syllables by rote, and, like Sergeant Friday of the old TV program *Dragnet*, wanted "just the facts, ma'am," led to a less flattering label: Dust Bowl Empiricism. Functionalism seemed as dry as the landscape from which it sprung.

Their pragmatic priorities led functionalists, pre- and post-Watson both, to promote another of his pet concerns: psychology's practical applications, especially to education (where Dewey's influence has been immense). Hence the many studies of *transfer*, the effects of previous learning on subsequent learning. Since education is cumulative, discovering conditions that maximize positive transfer benefits everyone involved. However curricula had long been based on the *doctrine of formal discipline*, which assumed that the brain, like a muscle, needs rigorous exercise to develop, and the best means for this were disciplines such as mathematics, philosophy, and classical languages, although their similarity to real-life learning situations was minimal. Thorndike (1903) called this doctrine into question by showing that positive transfer requires that tasks share *identical elements*, that similar specific associations be learned again. Education's watchword has been "relevance" ever since. Classroom learning that has no apparent overlap with "real life" matters is, supposedly, pointless.

As an unrepentant classicist I remain unswayed. Perhaps formal discipline's lack of empirical support indicates only that the appropriate experiments have yet to be performed. Freud warned, regarding ideas that felt right, that one must not be misled by the data (Holton, 1988), and Harlow's (1949) studies of *learning to learn* give my suspicion credibility. Discrimination tasks present several similar stimuli, such as a circle and a triangle, and one must learn to choose the rewarded alternative. Monkeys, given several hundred such tasks, each with different stimuli for six trials each, found the first ones enormously difficult but gradually improved. With enough tasks, they eventually became so adept that a single exposure to a new stimulus set produced errorless performance thereafter. Learning to learn is problematic for S–R accounts that stress identical elements. Because the stimuli change on each task, associations learned on one should not help the next, so positive transfer should not occur.

It will be useful to examine a lively controversy that arose over serial learning in the 1960s. In forming associations therein, what is the *functional stimulus* that subjects actually use as opposed to the *nominal stimulus* they supposedly use? The ingenious studies the issue engendered nicely demonstrate how critical experiments are used in resolving controversies, and also, understanding serial learning has implications tantamount to understanding how any complex behavior is mastered. Swinging golf clubs, driving cars, or performing music, all consist of a series of components occurring in sequence. Another standard method for instilling associations, *paired-associate learning* is also relevant here. It features that presumed sine qua non for association, contiguity, since subjects receive a series of verbal pairs, such as "keg-surplus," and must link each pair however they wish, so on a subsequent test they can produce the second, response member when given the first, or stimulus member, alone; usually order of pairs changes on successive trials to prevent serial learning of responses.

It had long been assumed that in learning sequences, each item is linked to its predecessor, the so-called *chaining hypothesis* (because a chain of separate S–R associations would thereby result, with every item except the first and last serving two functions, as a response to the preceding item and stimulus for the next). However Young's (1962) elegant experiments suggested otherwise. Consider a serial list, A-B-C-D, and so on, and a paired-associate list constructed so that items adjacent in this serial list become members of the same pair, that is, A-B, B-C, C-D, and so on. If the serial list is learned by chaining, then having learned it should produce positive transfer to the paired-associates; the same associations can be used. Young however found none and therefore concluded that serial learning's functional stimulus could not be the preceding item. What other candidates are there? Perhaps the serial position an item occupies; we might learn the alphabet by A is first, B second and so on. Thus the issue was joined and two critical experiments will be described that tackled it.

Young's (1962) subjects acquired a serial list and then a second list with the same items in which the position of every alternate one was changed, while the intervening ones remained where they had been; thus if List 1 had the form A-B-C-D-E-F-G-H then List 2 might be A-H-C-B-E-D-G-F etc., with A, C, E and G being unchanged items. The serial position notion expects unchanged items to be acquired more readily in Task 2 than changed items (the same associations being required). From the chaining standpoint, changing alternate items disrupts every association between adjacent items, so changed and unchanged items should not be differentially advantaged. Results verified the serial position hypothesis.

Young, Hakes and Hicks (1965) studied transfer from a Task 1 serial list to a second paired-associates one. Each item from the former became the response for one pair in the latter, with its corresponding stimulus being a number representing its position in the serial list. Thus if A, B, and C had been items 1–3 in Task 1, their Task 2 paired-associate stimuli were the actual numbers 1, 2, and 3, respectively. Regarding this group's Task 2 performance in comparison to a control not receiving the serial list, the theories again generate different predictions. If items are associated to position, positive transfer should result, but chaining would produce associations irrelevant or perhaps detrimental to Task 2 learning and, hence, negative transfer. Examining Task 2 performance for each individual pair as a function of its response member's position in the prior serial list (see Figure 1.1) put yet another face on the matter. Serial position is supported for items that came from its ends—there is positive transfer—but chaining is supported for those that had been in the middle. Moreover, with hindsight this finding makes sense. To use serial position, one must first determine what it is. This is easily done for end items—in the alphabet, A obviously comes first, B second, and Z last. But what is the eighteenth letter? For middle items in lengthy sequences such determinations are difficult, so subjects, ever ingenious, may fall back on the predecessor. In short, serial learning's functional stimulus may not be an either-or matter; subjects may use any of several possibilities, depending on the circumstances.

Unfortunately, these experiments, however cunning in design and intriguing in results, did not provide the last word. The functional stimulus and, by implication, what is actually learned in a serial task remained unclear, which called its usefulness for understanding associative mechanisms into question. As a result, paired-associates learning gradually replaced it as the preferred method (Postman, 1971). Besides more distinctly separating the associations to be learned (each item serves as only stimulus or response whereas, according to chaining at least, in serial tasks most play a dual role), the stimulus is more apparent. Admittedly, it was later shown that it does not always exactly replicate the one presented, but in the last analysis subjects must surely in some sense use this if they are to succeed on the test.

Figure 1.1
Young, Hakes, and Hicks's 1965 Results

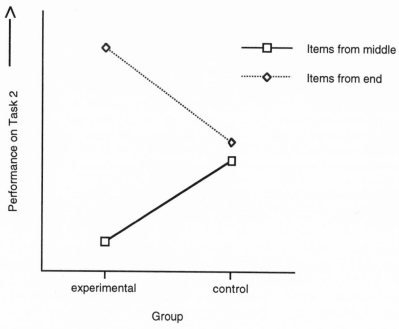

Source: Adapted from data reported by Young (1968), p. 141, with permission of the author.

Individual Differences: Hypothesized Entities Resurface. This content area also epitomizes empirical priorities at work. In the early nineteenth century (Boring, 1957), England's Astronomer Royal and his assistant both measured the movements of certain stars, but despite using the same instrument, their observations differed. The assistant was dismissed as incompetent (as every executive knows, infallibility always increases with hierarchical rank), but it was later shown that no measurement technique could eliminate *personal equations*, or differences among observers, so these had to be taken into account. Thus was born the study of individual differences, which for most psychologists reflect differences in an entity such as intelligence or personality as assessed by tests, the operational definitions that give it scientific legitimacy. Still, testing won only slow acceptance by post–Wundt psychology, no doubt in part because to study such differences goes against the scientific grain, due to the tendency to generalize and seek similarities among phenomena. As well, the testing movement openly confronted such practical problems as retardation, and while Watson promoted such concerns, most academics including the still influential Wundt preferred purer realms.

However, things have changed. Psychological tests are now a prominent, some would say epidemic, feature of modern life. To touch on a few highlights of their development (Anastasi, 1988, provides a fuller discussion), the pioneer in assessing mental abilities was Sir Francis Galton, one of those insatiably curious gentleman/scholars whom the fortunes of inheritance leave free to delve into whatever they wish. And delve Galton did, widely, among other things initiating the study of mental imagery and statistical methods. Related to and influenced by Darwin, his first priority was to increase humanity's chances for survival. Hence his landmark studies of genius (Galton, 1869), which showed that it tends to run in families (his own kinship with Darwin and other notables is exemplary, as is in music the Bach family). This phenomenon could reflect the enriched environments such families would provide, but Galton took it to mean that genius is inherited and therefore devised tests to identify those who had it, so they could be convinced to interbreed and improve the species. Evidently sharing a prevalent belief that talented persons are more sensitive, he emphasized abilities to detect subtle stimuli; thus his "Galton whistle" presented very high-pitched sounds for identification (while also attracting any bats that might be lurking in the vicinity).

Galton shared not only Watson's practical priorities but also his attitude that only behavior per se, in this case on tests, matters and should not be used to assess hypothesized entities. Therefore, his approach found favor with early behaviorists in North America. But just as Watson's belief on this score was soon compromised, Galton met a similar fate at the hands of the testing movement's next key figure, Alfred Binet. The instruments Binet and Simon invented to identify feebleminded children, so they could receive special schooling, assessed abilities to define words, remember strings of digits, and the like, which the authors felt better measured higher mental entities, such as, memory and attention, than did Galton's sensory items. Ever since, major intelligence tests such as the Stanford-Binet (Terman & Merrill, 1973) and Wechsler Adult Intelligence Scale (WAIS) (Wechsler, 1958) have featured items of this kind.

Are such tests effective predictors? For some abilities, yes. Terman's famous longitudinal study begun in the 1920s and carried on by his successors (e.g., Oden, 1968; Sears, 1977; Terman & Oden, 1947, 1959) identified some 1,500 children deemed gifted by their Stanford-Binet IQ scores (over 135) and followed them through life. By any standard the prognosis was verified; they were far more likely to graduate from university, obtain graduate degrees, publish books or articles, realize patents on inventions, and the like. Moreover, in contrast to prevailing stereotypes, they also turned out to be superior in less intellectual respects, such as physical and mental health. Virtually the only cautionary note is that not one in this large sample seems likely to attain genuine immortality (Tannenbaum, 1986), suggesting that IQ scores may not reveal creative ability, a point to which we shall return.

Another inviting target for testing, personality, also reveals empirical purposes. First, one assumption that has influenced the design of tests for many characteristics including intelligence (Wechsler, 1958) is that as measured, personality should remain fixed regardless of changes in age or environment, which suggests that it must be in large part innate (e.g., Eysenck, 1965). Thus one popular approach to testing personality focuses on presumed *traits*, relatively enduring ways in which individuals differ (Guilford, 1970), and "personality" then becomes a collection of traits such as aggressiveness or compassion, as measured on some scale. Eysenck's (1965) influential example exploited two personality types proposed by Jung (1923) that have entered common jargon. *Extraverts* (E), affected by the external world and other people, are outgoing, impulsive, and optimistic, whereas *introverts* (I) are withdrawn, detached loners. Eysenck first pays lip service to the obvious objection that real people, infinitely diverse, rarely fall neatly into any such pigeonhole. But, he answers, these types should be thought of as extremes on a dimension that is continuous, as are most traits (Guilford, 1967), so individuals can vary greatly in E-I with most clustering around moderation. Eysenck's second dimension, *neuroticism*, ranges between extremes of emotional stability and instability, so four quadrants are posited (Eysenck & Rachman, 1965) whose types correspond to Hippocrates' four temperaments (see Figure 1.2). The continuity assumption also allows the two dimensions to be quantified by a set of items identified by factor analysis (Eysenck, 1960). In addition, Eysenck's claim that E-I tendencies are determined by the autonomic nervous system holds out the prospect that other indicants controlled by it, such as heart rate or blood pressure, might also reveal such tendencies. Finally, he asserts that extraverts are, for complex reasons, less affected by experience and internalize social norms less effectively, so accident prone persons and criminals, for example, tend to fall into this category, with psychopaths, who lack any moral sensibility whatever, representing its extreme. While these hypotheses are undeniably intriguing, their viability remains uncertain.

Factor analytic techniques now available, however, suggest that Eysenck's two dimensions oversimplify matters, and yet proposing many dimensions, as did Cattell (1986), needlessly complicates them. By growing consensus, the so-called Big Five (Digman & Inouye, 1986) dimensions—extroversion-introversion; neuroticism-placidity; agreeableness-antagonism; conscientiousness-undirectedness; openness-nonopenness—can account for virtually all variation. Nonetheless, the broader question remains, whether *any* trait approach is viable, because several objections can be raised to the stasis they imply. For developmental psychologists, such as Piaget, profound change not only over the life span but during childhood is the rule. Also, someone's behavior in different situations displays as much variability as consistency (Mischel, 1968, 1984). If we were as stable as trait approaches suggest, how boring we would be! Still, people may vary in tendency to be consistent in traits such as friendliness (Bem & Allen, 1974), some being veritable chameleons with the changing winds of circumstance, others not. Two types of actors illustrate this difference. One, epitomized by Olivier (Spoto, 1992) and Peter Sellers, favors becoming the character, so in various roles these actors are well nigh unrecognizable, and by anecdotal reports, in personal demeanor they may be rather colorless—perhaps, only taking on distinctive traits when pretending to be someone else. Other actors, so-called, such as John Wayne or Clint Eastwood, present the same persona regardless of era or plot, and become veritable icons.

Figure 1.2
Eysenck's Four Quadrants

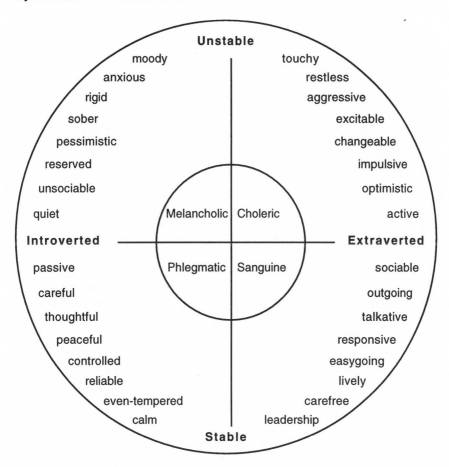

Source: Eysenck and Rachman (1965), p. 16. Used with permission of H. J. Eysenck and EDITS, Publishers.

Another trait approach also deserves mention: to infer personality from physical appearance. Sheldon (1940, 1942) designated three physical types, each reflecting one of the fetal primary germ layers that give rise to specific body tissues; thus in the *endomorph*, *mesomorph*, and *ectomorph*, fatty, skeletal-muscular, and nervous tissue, respectively, predominate. Based on various measurements, a subject's propensity for each type is rated on a seven-point scale and then probable traits predicted, for example, predominant endomorphs should be jolly, mesomorphs aggressive and competitive, and ectomorphs nervous and high strung. Supporting evidence is meager, but lest this approach be dismissed out of hand, the basic premise at least seems sound. Personality is powerfully influenced by the responses of others, which affect one's self-concept and thus traits, such as, confidence and assertiveness. Is physical appearance not a major determinant of those responses? An irritating driver who resembles an ectomorphic Casper Milquetoast, someone to accounting born, receives honking horns and vertically pointed fingers, while a textbook mesomorph returning from football practice garners only sheepish waves.

Which raises a general point. An approach's apparent validity is beside the point. The key question is whether it works. If measuring the big toe can accurately reveal intelligence, so be it! But intelligence tests are facing mounting criticism precisely because of their seeming inability to serve some purposes to which they are put (Wallach, 1985). The best do predict school grades effectively, but these predict only other grades, not later success, as measured by any number of economic, psychological, and sociological criteria. Guilford's (1950) comments in this regard greatly encouraged the study of *creativity*. Although its importance is evident, most scientific psychologists, when they discussed creativity at all, equated it with giftedness and assumed that IQ tests predicted it. But Guilford showed this not to be the case. It now appears (Dellas & Gaier, 1970) that IQ and creativity are not completely independent: below IQs of about 120, they do covary (those of low IQ are rarely creative) but thereafter part company; IQs of 120 or 180 are equally likely to accompany greatness. Guilford (1967) therefore devised special tests to measure creativity via such supposedly relevant traits as *divergent thinking* (the ability to consider a broad range of ideas), but it is doubtful that either his tests or others (Mednick, 1962; Torrance, 1962) are able to predict it much better (Amabile, 1983). It may be time therefore to consider alternatives to the higher mental abilities that since Binet have carried the testing day. Galton's sensory measures at one time seemed unable to identify creative individuals, but versions now available may prove more effective (Eysenck, 1967), suggesting that such people's supposed sensitivity may be as much a physical as mental commodity (Greenacre, 1971).

Unfortunately, a bleaker prospect also looms. Identifying talent early is obviously desirable, so it can receive the training needed for fulfillment. However, Bloom (1985), after studying high achievers from many fields, concluded that they usually progressed through the same several stages of skill development and that these stages differed considerably in the abilities they required for success. As a result, individuals who excel initially may not be those who ultimately will, which in turn, Bloom intimates, makes early identification unlikely. Happily, other indicants suggest otherwise. As mentioned, Getzels and Csikszentmihalyi (1976) stressed the creative person's ability for problem finding, sensing things to be puzzled about. Einstein asserted: "The formulation of a problem is often more essential than its solution. . . . To raise new questions, new problems requires creative imagination and marks real advance in science" (Einstein & Infeld, 1938, p. 92). They therefore showed art students diverse objects that were to be sketched, but whose precise usage was not specified, so before setting to work subjects handled them and tried various arrangements. A *problem finding score* was based on the amount of this behavior. As this increased, so did not only drawing quality (as judged by staff members) but likelihood of later success as an artist.

2

The Dark Side of Empiricism

The several drawbacks to the empirical rule all grow from one truth: it decides the content with which scientific disciplines can be concerned.

SINS OF COMMISSION

The common theme in this section is that insisting on measurement may lead to inappropriate uses.

Procrustean Methods in Psychology

A feature of modern academic life introduces the first such theme. Since it involves the criteria used to evaluate professors, it affects every discipline including psychology. Professors are in essence lifelong students, for, as supposed experts in a field, they must keep abreast of developments. However, the material they must ingest nowadays has several unsavory aspects. One is quantity; the journals, articles, and books come forth and multiply in abundance. A second is mediocrity; every science is inundated by trivia which is for the most part methodologically and empirically sound, but whose main beneficiaries are the printing, pulp, and paper industries. Increased quantity has not produced comparable gains in quality. This means that meaningful contributions may be overlooked, because keeping up has become so mind-numbing an activity, especially when so little is worth remembering, that many have given up.

In the publish or perish syndrome that now dominates universities, professors are expected to publish scholarly work, frequently, because quantity has become the main indicant of quality. Those who do not have regular ejaculations of literacy are unlikely to find jobs (prospective employers look first at the length of publication lists) or keep them, their salaries stagnate, they are assigned 8 A.M. lectures and offices next to the skunk labs, and the ultimate incentive, peer recognition, plummets. We might dismiss the situation as merely silly were it not for its consequences. The first victim is scholarly activity itself. It is the publish or perish syndrome that is most responsible for those torrents of mediocrity. As J. Spence warned, "After a certain point, high levels of productivity can be sustained only at the expense of quality. We may inadvertently be training young scholars to produce the superficial, the flashy, and the quick . . . causing them to become disillusioned and cynical about the purpose of research" (1985, p. 1293). Petersdorf (described by Spence) mentions another fortunately still rare possibility. Since available outlets have not kept pace with the numbers wishing to publish, it is an increasingly competitive business and the pressures may induce a few to doctor their findings to make them more impressive or to invent some outright. Such frauds, notably the infamous Sir Cyril Burtt,[1] seriously wound science.

Another effect is that professors must devote more effort to publishing they might better spend elsewhere, notably teaching. All universities pay lip service to teaching's importance and its weight in determining rank, salary, and so on. With the public finally demanding accountability for their huge investment in higher education, there are signs that this lip service may one day be matched with deeds, but anyone who believes they are at present must also possess several deeds to the Brooklyn Bridge. In practice, universities regard teaching by professors as they do character building by coaches: a nice bonus if it happens, but when push comes to shove, professors must publish and coaches must win or Goodbye, Charlie. Scholarly work should certainly provide one criterion of performance. A university is not solely a teaching institution, and those who do not keep up nor feel a need to contribute to their fields will stagnate to the detriment of their teaching. But it is quality of scholarship, not quantity, that should matter. Most of us have but a few good ideas in us. Einstein reportedly expressed amazement at a younger colleague's incredible productivity on grounds that he, Einstein, didn't have that many ideas worth writing down (Gruber, 1994). We should be allowed to hold back until we have something worthwhile to say.

Still along these lines, let me tilt at another educational windmill that reflects empirical priorities, one of which psychology programs are especially fond, multiple choice examinations (MCEs), wherein one selects a question's best answer from an array of alternatives. They admirably suit those priorities; being computer scored they are objective, reliable, and, as a bonus, avoid another numbing task, grading essays. However, even allowing that MCE grades correlate well with others, I view them as inventions of the devil, only to be countenanced when alternatives are unworkable. The main purpose of exams should not be to evaluate but motivate, to master whatever is deemed desirable.

---

1. Burtt's studies of identical twins influenced views about the role of inherited factors in intelligence, but after his death, Kamin (1974) showed major errors in his analyses. Whether these reflected conscious fraud or shoddy workmanship is unclear but either way, neither the data nor the conclusions can be relied on.

But students take away from courses that use MCEs very different and, to me, less deserving content, too often diverse bits of information useful only in Trivial Pursuit. As well, no MCE I know of encourages one to learn to express ideas in clear, well organized, and (if the gods are unusually benevolent) stylish prose, which is still, let us hope, one mark of that mysterious beast, the educated person.

These bizarre practices all reflect an insistence on reliable measurement even when this interferes with *validity*, that is, a device's ability to measure what it claims to measure. The doctrinaire empiricist objects: How can tests be useful and therefore valid if not reliable? My answer: some phenomena such as quality, value, and beauty are by their nature matters of opinion; they provoke endless disagreement. As the sayings go, "one man's meat is another's poison" and "nothing is either good nor bad but thinking makes it so." This explains why value judgements are anathema to orthodox empiricists, and, more to the point, why these phenomena can only be validly assessed if it is not done reliably. Insisting on this exemplifies Procrustean methods, by which phenomena are made to fit an approach even when it is unsuitable, which in turn changes them beyond all recognition, to the detriment of validity. Publish or perish and MCEs exemplify the fallacy. Publications for example can be counted, so frequency, it is assumed, indicates someone's worth more precisely than does their quality, let alone the calibre of lectures or contributions to the institution's intellectual life. Admittedly, great creators do produce more in quantity than lesser lights (Simonton, 1984) (which may explain their success, since it increases chances of periodic quality), but it does not necessarily follow that those producing more will routinely achieve higher quality. Yet publish or perish rests on this assumption.

Unfortunately, psychology provides other examples of this fallacy. *Experimental aesthetics* (Berlyne, 1959) sought to operationally define beauty, quality, and so forth, by manipulating properties of stimuli, such as novelty and complexity, and measuring effects on indicants, such as heart rate. In essence, picture A was better than B it if it produced faster palpitations. The attempt was doomed from the outset. To repeat, operational definitions to be accepted must have face validity and many would regard experimental aesthetics as an oxymoron of the first water. In matters such as these, the only recourse is to take the bull by the horns, assume that some judgments are worth more and allow them to carry the day, as is done in the arts with those intriguing beasts called *critics* (Abra, in press). Certainly they can be wrong and often are, but, as presumably unusually enlightened experts, their opinions should carry more weight than those who know nothing about art, but know what they like. And the alternative, stressing agreement and majority rules, that is, reliability, is worse, because the result is a catering to the lowest common denominator; witness commercial television. Democracy has no place in evaluation! In a similar vein, anyone who grades essays admits that it is a subjective business. Others may disagree with your judgments, so may you yourself at another time, but to resort to MCEs is even less palatable. Arnheim's comment on the psychology of art provides the coup de grace: "I do not see how one can hope to proceed . . . without trusting one's own intuitive judgement. . . . Pretending exactness (through measurement) . . . means nothing more than *being objective about nonobjective decisions*" (1966, p. 20, italics added). Amen!

The remaining examples involve hypothesized entities whose use in common parlance has given them connotations that behavior measures cannot capture, so using such measures probably misrepresents them. Watson avoided this trap, albeit for the wrong reasons: to him, there was no point in studying behavior to understand such entities because they were fictitious, but many followers who disagreed on this point fell in. For example. Boring's (1923, cited in Lefrancois, 1983) claim that intelligence is what an intelligence test measures exemplified adamant operationism. But the score such tests provide, the famed IQ, has come under increasing criticism (R. Sternberg, 1985), because it predicts some common connotations of the word "intelligence" such as school grades, but not others such as creativity, mechanical aptitude and street smarts.

Learning, defined as a relatively permanent change in behavior as a result of experience, like other hypothesized entities, defies observation. However, it is routinely supposed that by assessing behaviors it presumably affects, learning can be measured indirectly. Yet consider students' frequent and sometimes accurate response to disappointing exam results: "I don't know why I did so poorly. I knew my stuff!" Unfortunately, performance depends not only on learning but on motivation, communication skills, and a host of other factors. Overt behavior, our sole measure of learning, can be misinforming, because these other factors also come into play. A *learning-performance distinction* is necessary. Learning probably sets an upper limit that performance cannot surpass but may well fall beneath. *Latent learning experiments* (Tolman & Honzik, 1930) bring home this distinction. In one version, one group of rats were rewarded for correct responses in a maze, another only received equal opportunities to explore it. Correct responses increased only in the first group (see Figure 2.1, left panel), which might suggest that they alone had learned. But if so, when the second group was later rewarded as well, their initial performance should have resembled that of their colleagues on Trial 1, improving at the same rate. In fact (see the right panel), it soon drew equal, so they too must have been learning all along but failed to show it, having no reason to do so. (What did they learn? Perhaps the responses that can be made in a maze, so if one of these is later rewarded, it can be more efficiently invoked.)

Nowhere is the behavior–hypothesized entity distinction more evident than in the emotions. Do we not all wear masks that disguise inner feelings? Doesn't an old song moan about laughing on the outside, crying on the inside, because I'm still in love with you, and Hamlet snarl that one may smile, and smile, and smile, and be a villain? That staple device of modern society, the cocktail party, could not function without hypocrisy regarding feelings about others, and, as Molière's *The Misanthrope* brings home, those who refuse to practice discretion at least in moderation become veritable outcasts. Yet few topics in psychology are more deserving of study than the emotions, so how to proceed? Perhaps by

Figure 2.1
Latent Learning

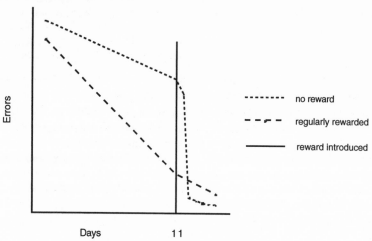

Errors

.... no reward

－ － ⌐ － regularly rewarded

——— reward introduced

Days   1 1

Source: Adapted from Tolman & Honzik (1930). Introduction and removal of reward.

admitting that sources besides the empirical can be informative, notably works of art, since artists have always placed a high priority on their portrayal. For Wordsworth (1952, p. 83), poetry was "emotion recollected in tranquillity," and "the spontaneous overflow of powerful feelings," and for Langer (1951), art reflects desires to release emotions deeply felt but too ambiguous to capture in words.

Good Answers to Poor Questions

That scholar of yore, Horatio, sounded this second variation when, upon wondering what Hamlet had learned from the ghost, he was informed, "There's ne'er a villain dwelling in all Denmark/ But he's an arrant knave." Horatio retorted, reasonably enough, "There needs no ghost, my lord, come from the grave/ To tell us this." Too much that is dignified by the magic label "research," certainly in psychology, involves mighty labor to bring forth conflagrations of mice, both literally (in the species so omnipresent in its labs) and metaphorically. Let us first distinguish good answers to poor questions from poor answers to good questions. The first category encompasses puzzles that can be readily investigated empirically and about which precise conclusions can be drawn, but that hardly anyone wanted solved in the first place. Good questions, on the other hand, involve matters that concern everyone, notably the enduring riddles of existence. Almost inevitably, attacks on them come up short, certainly by empirical criteria, yet they are the stuff of genuinely meaningful inquiry. So as Maslow observed, "What isn't worth doing, isn't worth doing well. . . [and] What needs doing, is worth doing, even though *not* very well" (1966, p. 14).

One of the empirical rule's nefarious results has been to encourage the first type of investigation, because investigators tend to ask first about possible topics, not "Is it worthwhile?" but "Can I measure it?" Hence those torrents of mediocrities. Furthermore, because young investigators trying to win their academic spurs are especially under the gun to publish, they are most susceptible to these misplaced priorities (J. Spence, 1985). In most contexts it is young people who more willingly take the risks that provide exciting new developments, but the modern climate encourages them to play it safe and do clean, that is empirically sound, research, to the detriment of both psychology and them. We must always beware of too hastily dismissing seemingly puerile investigations, as unforeseen payoffs are always possible, but a strong case can be made that over seventy-five years of scientific psychology has yielded relatively little. Hence, Cooper (1982), for one, has concluded that psychology is dead, because, in contrast to the natural sciences, it has done nothing comparable to eliminating smallpox or putting people on the moon. In my view, Cooper overemphasizes technology as opposed to pure knowledge as indicating progress, and I certainly do not accept his solution that psychology become still more narrowly scientific, devoted exclusively to biological approaches, but it is difficult to reject his criticisms completely.

The empirical work reported in the *Journal of Experimental Psychology* is by consensus as good as it gets, but perusing random volumes from earlier eras is both humbling and depressing. Most studies had little impact even at the time, and, of those that did have their proverbial fifteen minutes of fame, precious few have left a lasting mark. If this is the impression given by top sources, what of the countless lesser ones, the books, conference proceedings, symposia, and poster sessions beyond number? At some point one begins to wonder, "To what purpose?" To compound the problem, as studies of a topic continue to tumble forth, the usual result is not to clarify but to befuddle. That omnipresent concluding sentence, "More research is needed on this question" is not only a cliché that belabors the obvious (any worthwhile study raises as many questions as it answers), it also may be inaccurate. To obtain better understanding, sometimes less research is needed.

Indeed, one might wonder whether data gathering ever conclusively answers questions. At first new topics are vigorously attacked, but as unforeseen methodological problems, other variables that complicate effects and conflicting findings emerge, the picture too often becomes ever muddier. For example, Goldberg (1968) had several judges evaluate the same article, but its purported author's name at one time implied a female (Joan Smith), at another a male (John Smith). Judgments of quality were consistently lower in the first instance, especially when judges themselves were women. By any standard an important finding with a seemingly straightforward interpretation: sexist biases. Unfortunately, later work uncovered a host of possibly confounding factors, for example, various names may imply different ages or social class, (Kasof, 1995) that might affect ratings, so the reasons for the effect became increasingly obscure. To place the matter in a Kuhnian context, the sense of stasis that precedes revolutions supposedly reflects growing awareness of anomalies at odds with the prevailing paradigm. But perhaps available findings on a topic become so complex that workers can no longer make head nor tail of them, see the matter as increasingly intractable, and are ready to move on to something else. If problems are not so much solved as dropped one must ask whether all this data gathering produces progress. More facts we have. But more understanding?

To explain the lack of progress, committed scientists answer first that psychology is a young science, of extraordinary difficulty, so to ask for quick miracles is unfair. While this answer has some validity, and real contributions have been made, it sounds increasingly like an excuse. Seventy-five years is a long time, especially given the massive investments of resources and talent involved. The natural sciences after equal opportunities to show their wares had more to offer. Scientists also answer, "The fault, dear Brutus, lies not in empiricism, but in ourselves." If measures for phenomena of interest are inadequate, if most studies deserve only oblivion, this reflects not on the empirical rule but on the investigators. With sufficient ingenuity, seemingly vapid topics can be made interesting and vague entities measurable. Consider memory, a deserving topic by any standard, as anyone who has mangled an exam or forgotten an anniversary will agree. Until recently, however, most studies used verbal materials (Kausler, 1974), which is only one kind of memory, and the findings may not generalize to others. Why so few studies of memory for films, or music, or tastes, such as buttered popcorn? It is because these topics resist measurement. Retention of, say, a picture must be demonstrated via a behavior, but if drawing is used, does poor performance reflect inability to remember or to render what is remembered, since many people cannot draw well? And how is performance to be quantified? In contrast, most people can produce verbal materials, if they remember them at all, and the number retained can be counted. Fortunately, recognition tests wherein subjects choose among alternatives have allowed memory for something seemingly so vague as smells to be assessed, and ingenuity has also surmounted other problems (Schab, 1991). Moral? Beware of assuming prematurely that a phenomenon cannot be attacked empirically. However, for all practical purposes some phenomena do seem immune, so if this approach is insisted on, psychology's content must remain forever incomplete.

BREVITY IS NOT ALWAYS THE SOUL OF WIT: SINS OF OMISSION

All the sections to come arise from behaviorists' stumbling attempts to deal with the mind-body problem. Neither Descartes nor anyone else has resolved it satisfactorily, so behaviorists prefer to finesse it away. Criticism of Watson's gambit, that it was of no consequence because mind did not exist, will be deferred, but another more moderate answer merely dismisses the problem as a pseudo-issue that lies outside science's concerns because it cannot be resolved by acceptable procedures. Let us limit ourselves, it holds, to physical phenomena that can and not worry about mind's relationship to them or whether it exists at all. This position does follow Watson's preference for getting on with tasks at hand rather than debating philosophical niceties, but a problem swept under the rug may be out of sight but not out of mind—in every sense. Refusing to take a stand on this issue is itself a stand; it implies that all deserving topics can be tackled empirically, ergo, the mind's influence is minimal. What is in question then is Watson's certainty that every significant consideration can be measured. That he should stand accused of narrowing psychology is ironic, since one of his aims was to broaden it (Hilgard, 1980). So long as consciousness was its subject matter and introspection its method, subjects unable to introspect, such as animals and infants, would not be studied. In hindsight, Watson may have been better advised to found a new discipline, perhaps labeled behaviorology, not change one that had a long-established content. Behavior unquestionably deserves study, but in his haste to rid psychology of its mentalistic demons, he threw some very comely babies out with the bathwater. Several examples follow.

The Facts of Introspection

By a fact, Deese (1969) means "any observation available to ordinary experience" (p. 515). Unfortunately, for the dogged empiricist, psychology's intimacy means that these arise not only from externals but from what Skinner (1971) belittled as the world within the skin, that is, mental life. Of special concern to Deese are cognitive experiences, such as understanding of things such as linguistic structures or experiences, and interpretation, as when we classify bits of information into categories. Because these abilities lead to no behavior in particular, they cannot be studied by referring to it and so have been avoided. Deese's qualifications as an empirical psychologist are impeccable, nonetheless, he concludes that "the characteristic emphasis of the psychological laboratory on the measurable response. . . is responsible for the sterility of the study of thought. . . . The model of experimenting taken from the physical sciences. . . no longer belongs in the center of psychology" (p. 522).

Nonlinear Thought and Altered States of Consciousness

Ornstein (1972) distinguishes two types of thought. The first is *linear*, wherein mental experience seems to flow from one thought to the next to give a sense of time passing. The content of such thought routinely occurs in and is readily expressed in words. In fact language relies heavily on it, as does logical reasoning, understanding cause-effect relationships, and thus science itself. However, another type comes to the fore in phenomena such as hunches, intuitions, and knowledge that words cannot express. Its components are typically experienced not in sequence but simultaneously, so the sense of time passing is less acute. Ornstein labels such thought *nonlinear*.

He presents several lines of evidence that, in right-handed people at least, linear and nonlinear thought are located respectively in the cerebral cortex's left and right hemispheres. First, during linear activities, such as reading, EEG recordings of the right hemisphere manifest slow alpha waves characteristic of relaxed states, suggesting that it is largely uninvolved, whereas nonlinear activities, such as viewing pictures, produce alphas in the left hemisphere. As well, although findings are less clear-cut than they once seemed (H. Gardner, 1982), those who have suffered damage to the left or right hemispheres show diminished linear and nonlinear abilities, respectively (Milner, 1965). *Split brain studies* (Sperry, 1964; Gazzaninga, 1967) provide the most telling support for hemispheric specialization. The various connections between the hemispheres are cut, usually to treat severe epilepsy, which isolates them from one another and allows, under contrived circumstances (for the effects on ordinary functioning are surprisingly minor), each to be observed separately. By all appearances, patients are left with two separate minds and spheres of consciousness. For example, when an embarrassing or obscene stimulus is presented to the right hemisphere alone, subjects giggle but cannot explain why (Galin, 1974). However, it is Ornstein's conclusions that are most germane. Science, resting on linear thought, is suited for studying linear processes but not the nonlinear, so a psychology that allows only this type of inquiry must ignore an important aspect of thought and, as it were, 50 percent of the brain. Ornstein's solution? Include the methods used by the *esoteric psychologies* of the East, such as Buddhism and Sufism, that have evolved to induce and understand those definitively nonlinear episodes, *altered states of consciousness* (Tart, 1969), that supposedly lead to enlightenment. Such methods can supplement and overcome a scientific approach's limitations.

The purported elimination of nonlinear thought is ironic. It resembles tacit knowledge which is so indispensable to science (Polanyi, 1981), as it seeks solutions to problems and ultimately that hidden reality that by another article of faith it assumes exists. Scientists cannot as yet clearly picture this end result because if they could their searches would be over. Like those vague visions or *endocepts* (Arieti (1976) in the mind's eye that artists are driven to express, it is at first seen only indirectly, as through a glass darkly. Thus the paradox: how can scientists search for something without knowing what it is? Polanyi answers that intuition gradually senses it ever more clearly through a *gradient of deepening coherence* and guides the search itself, since although the process may not know precisely where it is going, it knows full well where it isn't going; many potential blind alleys are rejected without being tried. Indeed, a good part of scientific ability lies in sensing where worthwhile problems and likely solutions lie. Where is the irony? Since the seminal role that psychological processes play in science is now widely recognized, surely these must be elucidated for it to be understood and improved (Singer, 1971). If tacit knowing is critical—and Polanyi's arguments seem incontrovertible—yet is downplayed because of empirical priorities, psychology's accounts must prove invalid. In short, a psychology of science must include aspects discomforting to a science of psychology.

Creativity, Quality, and Value

Besides importance, creativity also possesses that other sine qua non of deserving topics, fascination. The achievements of George Eliot evoke the same wonder as all mysteries do. How did she do it? Nonetheless, it too has been largely ignored by mainstream psychology and again the empirical rule is mainly to blame. To many, "creativity" implies a mentalistic phenomenon, but the main problem lies in its very meaning: producing works of value or quality as well as originality. The latter property can in theory be determined objectively by, say, frequency counts and is in practice also reliable, since most will agree about the amount a product contains. But since value and other such characteristics are inherently subjective matters, scientists who play by the book are suspicious of judgments about them and therefore avoid topics that involve them. To render creativity more acceptable, questionable gambits have been tried, such as experimental aesthetics or equating it with originality, which the term has always implied (Williams, 1983), to eliminate the value connotation. Unfortunately, originality is in most views a necessary but not sufficient attribute; the term "creative" usually connotes approval—who is offended if so described?—which many highly original products do not deserve, for example, paintings by a psychotic (unless he is named van Gogh!). At any rate, value considerations are unavoidable.

The droll title of Pirsig's (1974) *Zen and the Art of Motorcycle Maintenance* masks a contribution that is both intensely moving and philosophically provocative, and it enlarges on the difficulties that result. He first distinguishes two approaches to gaining knowledge that resemble the linear and nonlinear kinds, and deplores the former's domination of Western thought through its offspring, science, because it rejects questions about quality. When studies cannot ask which things we prefer, and why, they must have little connection to reality, because among the predominant impressions we gain from phenomena is their quality. Do we not reflexively evaluate everything we encounter, be it films, hamburgers, or other people? Value-free perception is not in our repertoires! Truly, everyone's a critic! Thus Keats' *Ode on a Grecian Urn:*

Beauty is truth, truth beauty—that is all
Ye know on earth, and all ye need to know.

Now to the difficulties. A puzzled onlooker reportedly asked Count Basie, "If jazz has to swing, what is swing? I don't understand." Basie is said to have replied, "If you don't know, I can't tell you!" As Pirsig puts it "Some things *are* better than others, that is, they have more quality. But when you try to say what the quality is, apart from the things that have it, it all goes *poof. . . .* Because definitions are a product of rigid, formal thinking, quality cannot be defined (i.e., at least in linear terms) but *we still know what quality is*" (1974, pp. 178, 22, italics added). So while Pirsig agrees that quality is nonlinear, he denies that it is arbitrary. In fact, it is neither subjective nor objective, because it resides neither in an object nor in our minds alone but emerges from both, when observer and object interact. Therefore linear definitions, by only capturing its objective aspects, oversimplify it. Which may explain why those valiant attempts (Guilford, 1967; Torrance, 1962) to produce tests that predict creativity have fallen short (Amabile, 1983). Although some (Runco, 1988) are still hopeful of reaching this goal, it may be that trying to operationalize this concept is a contradiction in terms.

Should so subjective a matter be ignored by science merely because we cannot define it acceptably? Not according to Pirsig or Amabile's (1983) *consensus definition*, which claims that although we cannot define the term precisely, we know it when we see it. Her subjects produce, say, a collage or poem under varied circumstances and several experts then independently judge the amount of creativity it displays. Indicatively, although their reasons for their conclusions may vary greatly, they almost always agree. History forces one to question whether this comforting state of affairs always holds, for disagreements have been rife. The premiere of the Stravinsky/Nijinsky *Le Sacre du Printemps* provides only one of many examples. Now regarded as a landmark, its daring musical and choreographic innovations provoked a full-scale riot, cancellation of the performance, and at least one duel (Nijinsky, 1954)! Could it not then be said of creative works, as it is of horse races, that it is differences of opinion that make them?

Still and all, recognizing that in practice science too features value judgments may solve the problem. As Einstein pointed out, and most scientists now accept (Holton, 1988; Kuhn, 1962), when evaluating an idea, they ask not only whether it fulfills empirical canons but whether it has elegance, beauty, and the like. Similarly, Poincaré (1952) held that mathematical ideas originate in the unconscious mind, which acts as a sort of filter, trying out possible solutions and eliminating unacceptable ones without bothering the conscious about them. And even in so supposedly rigorous a pursuit as mathematics, to pass muster, ideas must be interesting, beautiful and able to affect one's emotions. Pirsig certainly feels that quality judgments belong in any science worthy of the name. An attitude that "whatever is, is good" is unacceptable when science faces so many formidable moral dilemmas—nuclear power, genetic engineering and mushrooming powers for invading privacy to name but a few. If value-free scientists ever existed, they are now obsolete.

Incidentally, Sternberg and Lubart (1996) also attribute creativity's neglect to psychology's scientific priorities. However, they advocate not compromising them but instead making creativity more palatable via a multidisciplinary, or *confluence, strategy* that employs a variety of approaches acceptable to science. Apart from the inherent Procrustean dangers, in my view this strategy does not go far enough. My eclectic approach (Abra, 1989, 1996; Abra & Valentine-French, 1991) tackles problems such as creativity's motivation or sex difference by adopting a variety of perspectives and determining the answer each provides, in the belief that each provides part of the story; thus they are complementary rather than contradictory. However, this approach includes contributions from such traditions as psychoanalysis and existentialism whose scientific credentials are dubious, but nonetheless have much to offer.

The Unconscious Mind

Disciples of the psychoanalytic tradition differ on many details but all assume an unconscious mind whose contents remain largely hidden but powerfully affect psychological and behavioral life. For Freud (1953a), of course, most such content was repugnant, usually a sexual product of personal experience that, being too traumatic to be faced, had been repressed. Jung (1959), however, maintained that we also possess a *collective unconscious*. Shared by everyone as a sort of race memory, its contents, notably the *archetypes* or universal, primordial images, have been handed down from our ancestors just as have our anatomical structures. Finally, for Adler (Ansbacher & Ansbacher, 1956), the unconscious centered around *fictional goals*, particularly the image of an *ideal self* that one hopes to become. One's prevailing approach to living, or *style of life,* was then influenced more by these future goals than past experience.

In essence, Freud *en suite* faced the same dilemma as did Watson's followers: to find adequate indicants for hypothesized entities, but of a more surreptitious kind. Thus dreams or free associations supposedly reveal the unconscious just as, say, maze performance does learning. For Freud (1953b), works of art provided still another outlet for the unconscious via the defence mechanism of *sublimation,* the expression of socially unacceptable desires in socially acceptable ways. Interpreting works of art should, therefore, offer another royal road to an artist's unconscious. Freud's (1947) attempt to unravel Leonardo da Vinci's art set the precedent, and by now almost every work ever concocted has undergone that decidedly mixed blessing, psychoanalytic scrutiny. Here again, Jung parted company. Great art reveals collective and archetypal, not personal, matters and provides another means to their understanding. It is great because it "[rises] above the personal and [speaks] from the mind and heart of the poet to the mind and heart of mankind" (Jung, 1966, p. 101), which gives it its defining properties, universal appeal, and staying power. If it merely expressed personal hang-ups, as Freud claimed, it would interest only the artist and her therapist.

Unfortunately, assessing unconscious entities becomes even more problematic than assessing those that behaviorists accept. First, reliability must suffer. Events such as dreams defy quantification, and, in any case, the primary interest is not in their amount but meaning, and interpretations can vary appreciably across observers. Witness the current controversy about recovered memories of supposed childhood traumas, such as incest, which are increasingly reported, to devastating effect on the families involved. Freud's own conclusion, that such memories are invariably imaginary, inspired the key notion that wish fulfillment is a cardinal factor in unconscious life, but it is now apparent that here he erred (Masson, 1984). Still, most authorities not driven by political agendas agree that not all memories are genuine (Loftus, 1993), and since too often the only evidence available is the testimonies of purported victim and accused, many decisions about accuracy come down to credibility. To compound the difficulties, it is usually assumed that unconscious events are not directly revealed, because their traumatic aspects might prove devastating, but are expressed subtly in symbols; hence Freud's (1953a) distinction between manifest and latent content of dreams. Therefore, the hidden message must be decoded, an exercise that in most views (although not Freud's) is hopelessly subjective, there being no ultimate criteria against which to validate interpretations. Finally, few would question that maze performance is partially influenced by learning. However, the assumption that dreams, say, have any connection whatsoever to and manifest presumed entities, such as archetypes, is open to dispute.

The main point is that psychoanalytic accounts are anathema to committed empiricists, and Freud's persistent claim that psychoanalysis is a science seems to them ludicrous. Such hypothesized entities as the unconscious, archetypes and fictional goals by definition defy measurement or observation. Admittedly, recent studies of *implicit memories* suggest that ingenuity may one day give the lie to this assertion also (Roedigger III, 1990). Learned materials that cannot be recalled, nonetheless influence transfer performance, and methods concocted to show this may help study other unconscious matters. Nevertheless, those in psychology obsessed with scientific respectability see psychoanalysts' claim to part of the territory as an embarrassment, another indication to revered physics that it can not rid itself of its mentalistic demons.

Still, for others less dogmatic, some psychoanalytic hypotheses are worth considering, as they are compelling on introspective grounds (how often are we at a loss to explain why we did something?) and offer intriguing speculations about deserving phenomena that empiricists simply ignore. Which raises the same irony as did tacit knowledge. Recall Poincaré's (1952) assertion that creative thinking in mathematics relies heavily on unconscious processes, which filter out unpromising alternatives so "all goes on as if the inventor were an examiner for the second degree who would only have to question the candidates who had passed a previous examination" (Poincaré, 1952, p. 36). Thus, once again, supposed scientific priorities limit discussion of processes that seem integral to scientific thinking.

Symbolization

Both Freud and Jung attached considerable importance to symbols as indicators of unconscious content, while disagreeing, as usual, on details. For Freud a given symbol always had the same, usually sexual meaning; thus long narrow objects such as pencils represented the male organ. But for Jung (1956) this confused symbols with *signs*. Symbols, inherently *multileveled* (Kreitler & Kreitler, 1972), provide a plethora of interpretations, including the ineffable. Thus Jungians do not dictate a particular meaning for dreams but suggest possibilities, leaving the symbol's producer to choose by a kind of gut reaction that which "feels right."

However, Langer's (1951, 1953) discussions are most relevant here. She first notes that most scientists share rarely expressed attitudes called *generative ideas* (cf. Kuhn's concept of the paradigm, 1962), and one is the belief that empirical data provide the penultimate road to knowledge. The success of this idea in the natural sciences is beyond dispute, but to her it has wreaked havoc on the human ones:

Even in psychology, where the study of stimulus and reaction has been carried to elaborate lengths, no true science has resulted. . . . We move further and further away from the problems which we ought to be approaching. The generative idea which gave rise to physics and chemistry . . . does not engender leading questions and excite a constructive imagination. . . . Instead of a method, it inspires a militant methodology. (1951, p. 32)

Koch (1964, 1981) has reiterated the last sentence's sentiments, but Langer adds that familiar irony, that dogmatic empiricism still dominated psychology long after it had been dismissed by the natural sciences. Many of them now deal with little direct data (at least in the classic sense), since their presumed sources will never be directly observed. Consider a star in a distant galaxy. Irregular tracings on recordings or blemishes on sensitive plates provide the sole sensory experience of it, the energy that presumably induced that experience was emitted eons ago and, by now, its source has no doubt changed beyond measure, if it is not extinct. In short, the facts with which many modern scientists are concerned are not direct perceptions of empirical events nor objects that give rise to these recordings, but the recordings themselves; whereas an operational definition once stated how a phenomenon was to be studied, many have become the phenomenon.

All this represents a huge step away from empiricism. Data must now be interpreted by trained observers; for others, vague blemishes on photographs such as those taken of outer space have no meaning. Also, observers differ about what data indicate, so reliability can no longer be taken for granted. Hence the gist of Langer's argument: data of this kind are *symbols*; empirical events still but of a kind that only indirectly represent a more shadowy realm and they must be interpreted. In turn, symbolization provides the new generative idea that the mental sciences need to free themselves from the pseudo-empirical mire and again attack the topics that had been theirs prior to the behaviorist blitzkrieg. To symbolically transform experience is our most notable departure from lower animals, underlying our most distinctive activities such as language, religious ritual, and art. Whereas animals use sense data exclusively as signs to indicate something else, we routinely translate them into symbols that represent things absent or outright imaginary, and we cannot be understood without recognizing this truth. Why has this not happened? Because symbols do not lend themselves to empirical study. We use them less to communicate than to capture in tangible form otherwise inexpressible feelings, especially nonlinear ones, that, like itches that must be scratched, demand release. Indicatively, for Housman (1952) poetry is a "secretion" and for Langer herself the arts create forms symbolic of human feelings.

She mentions too our love of talk, chatter, and gossip. Contrary to rumor, these like all symbolic activities aim first not at communication, which is at best an incidental, albeit extremely useful byproduct. Eavesdrop on conversations in public places. Note how participants talk past rather than to one another and how each while resting does not so much listen as wait, for the current speaker to finish so they can resume; how toddlers chatter away even when no listeners are around; how most emissions communicate precious little information, as when someone notes on a -30° morning, "Sure is cold out!", as if it might have escaped our notice! Much of the dialogue in Harold Pinter's plays, such as *The Caretaker*, is inane, replete with repetitions ad nauseum of a few points and irrelevant observations. Yet what is striking is that it seems a painfully accurate depiction of real conversation. But if symbols are produced for expressive purposes, then interpreting them in linear terms, as critics do, is contradictory, an exercise that Langer calls vicious. We use symbols when words fail us. Bronowski (1965) agrees that data usage involves symbol interpretation but, unlike Langer, believes that this has always been the case, that symbols and metaphors are as integral to science as to poetry. Even for Newton and Galileo, raw empiricism was less fact than fiction; only a few systems of philosophy, such as logical positivism, have seen symbols as disreputable. Unfortunately, these are the very systems on which modern psychology built.

In any event, symbolization's importance means that ignoring it is indefensible. It may also be dangerous. May (1969) has described some neuroses characteristic of modern life: apathy, listlessness, and a lost sense of meaning. Might these reflect our industrialized/computerized/Watsonized tendency to downplay our symbolic side? J. Campbell (1988) has warned that a society devoid of symbol usage—rituals, myths and so on—that provides a sense of tradition treads on perilously thin psychological ice. How is psychology to study symbols? According to Langer, the answer lies beneath its very nose, in that other major, much disparaged by behaviorists, modern movement—psychoanalysis. It did not uncritically borrow a methodology perhaps unsuited to psychology's unique content, so it might provide one that serves rather than dominates that content. Langer here ignores her own advice to forego interpreting symbols, since this is standard practice in psychoanalysis, but otherwise, hers are telling arguments.

Religion

If empirical psychology has downplayed symbols, it is not surprising that religion, shot through as it is with them, represents another omission (Beit-Hallahmi, 1984). No one more fervently advocated science for psychology than James (1890), but he realized that it could not encompass all of the latter's appropriate concerns, notably the psychology of religion (James, 1902). Later events bore him out, because post-Watson the topic foundered, apart from a few studies of certain behaviors and of religious peoples' attitudes and characteristics (Beit-Hallahmi, 1984). While useful, these are but pale reflections of the real thing.

Must an empirical discipline deny room at its inn to religious experiences, to the unknowable and/or supernatural? Actually, quasi-religious outlooks occupy many of its best rooms. Witness determinism, that faith in the universe's order. History provides empirical justification for it—science should not have proved so effective if built on a fake foundation—but in the last analysis the belief cannot be verified empirically but must be accepted on faith. It is then but a small step to affirm some Master Planner who/which devised such a glorious system, so the prevalent notion that scientists must be atheists is dead wrong. A few, such as Freud and Darwin, were, but Newton (Westfall, 1980) was anything but, and Einstein too saw science as a means to understand what the Creator had wrought and, in turn, that Creator Him/Her/Itself: "I believe in Spinoza's God who reveals himself in the orderly harmony of what exists. What we strive for . . . is just to draw his lines after Him. . . . I want to know His thoughts, the rest are details" (quoted in Clark, 1972, p. 502). It was this deep religiosity that fostered his distaste for Bohr et al.'s *indeterminism*, which held that subatomic phenomena could be explained only statistically, within the limits of probability. The implication, that the Guiding Hand had similarly waffled, evoked Einstein's cryptic retort: God does not play dice with the universe! Scientists also resemble the religious in their emotions (M. Gardner, 1984) of wonder and awe at the universe's marvels. So those detached robots devoid of feeling that behaviorism commanded psychologists to imitate are found only in B-movies.

Maslow (1966, 1970), another outspoken advocate for broadening empirical psychology, also saw scientists and the religious as similar breeds and deplored the separation of the two pursuits. To him, diverse activities, including creativity, sports, and religion, all elicit moments of ecstasy, or *peak experiences* during which we supposedly reach our maximum potential, become most alive, and come to understand intuitively what being human means. Still, Maslow found that, strangely, not everyone reports having peaks and was forced to conclude that some find them intimidating and suppress them. Therefore, to encourage a science-religion rapprochement, he advocated distinguishing not between the two activities but between the two types of persons who surface in each: "peakers," who enjoy and frequently have such experiences, and "nonpeakers," who do not. In every organized religion then, mystics, prophets, and the intensely involved coexist in uneasy truce with those who prefer their religion dished up casually, one morning a week, so for Maslow, organized religions are one means to communicate peak experiences to nonpeakers.

Thus Ivan Karamazov imagines Christ Himself facing a nonpeaking embodiment of formalized religion, The Grand Inquisitor, to whom Christ is a threat. Were He to return, the very Church dedicated to promoting His teachings would be forced to burn Him for heresy! And these two types, Maslow adds, also appear in science. It provides peaks and personal fulfillment when it strikes daringly into the unknown, but when it stresses control and neatness it supplies the timid with a security blanket. (Maslow mischievously observes that at times science seems like a device to help nonpeakers have peaks). Reading between Kuhn's lines suggests that to him revolutionary and normal scientists might provide peakers and nonpeakers, respectively, but he has often been accused of underestimating the normal kind as unimaginative plodders (H. Stam, personal communication, September, 1995). Working within a paradigm can still yield great dividends; arguably the greatest advance in modern biology, Watson and Crick's discovery of DNA's molecular structure, in essence was a matter of solving a problem.

Death

One of religion's purposes, through beliefs in afterlife, forgiveness for sins, and the like, is to provide comfort for this otherwise terrifying fact. That empirical psychology has ignored taxation is forgivable, since economics has this market cornered, but its silence regarding life's other great certainty, Becker (1973) contends, is not. He first points out a bizarre paradox that humans display: capable of boundless flights of fantasy, of nostalgias and longings, we house this spiritual life within an earthbound body that must perform base functions—imbibe and ooze, feed and excrete—to survive. Even Socrates had to expel wastes, and the smell from his saintly mentor's corpse traumatizes Alyosha, the mystic Karamazov brother. Most distasteful of all, our physical side must ultimately feed the worms. "Lads and lasses and everyone must/ Like chimney sweepers, come to dust" says the doggerel and to increase our delight, we alone of all animals know this to be our fate. Surely, Becker asserts, this must color our lives. Thus people may create, in part, to deal with death (Abra, 1997).

Still, for Becker, this Ultimate Truth is so threatening that we cannot face it, and, therefore, as Freudian doctrine claims we do for any trauma, we repress it. But Becker holds that the trauma that most affects psychological life is not sex, but death. Furthermore, unlike the two-backed monster, this one cannot be worked through, death being inevitable, so any comforts must be superficial. Becker then levels his artillery against behaviorism for its silence on this score: "The Watsons, the Skinners, the Pavlovians—all have their formulas for smoothing things out. . . . [But] somehow they don't take life seriously enough. . . . Whatever man does on this planet has to be done in the lived truth of the terror of creation, of the grotesque" (1973, p. 284). Viewing ourselves in a manner acceptable to empiricism, then, could enhance security by downplaying mortality, but accuracy would suffer.

Yet perhaps psychology can be forgiven for this, since according to May (1969), modern Western society in general has done the same. If, as Freud contends, neuroses reflect repression of sexuality due to a puritan outlook, then in this less uptight era they should be rare. They aren't. Loneliness and apathy are different neuroses than those treated in Victorian times but are every bit as debilitating. May maintains that where once we denied sex, we have become obsessed with it. Now guilt descends not if we do, but if we don't (this claim predated the AIDS pandemic, which changed matters considerably). However, this obsession expresses the *new puritanism* which denies other facts of existence with which Victorians dealt openly. Thus sex, once repression's main target, now keeps other unmentionables repressed. We are less liberated, it seems, than *Playboy* et al. would have us believe! And one prime victim of the new puritanism is death. No age has surpassed our Dorian Gray–like searches for eternal youth and sexiness. We no longer care for the aged or terminally ill at home but ship them off to institutions where, apart from occasional visits, we can forget them, along with the fact that one day we may suffer the same fate.

Values and Morality

Here are other topics common in religious contexts that empiricism has repressed. One can assess beliefs about such questions as capital punishment and abortion by scientifically legitimate methods, such as surveys, but problems arise when one wonders what people ought to do. As matters of opinion, must these too be ruled out? Maslow (1966), in answering, comes not to bury science but to broaden it, because in his view it provides the only guarantee that we have truth. However, a new brand of science that recognizes differences between people and other topics is needed. People, unlike, say, sulfuric acid frequently object to being studied, and experimenters observing others cannot avoid feeling empathy toward or judging them. Fortunately, these difficulties can be turned to advantage by a *Taoistic science* that is less manipulative and more accepting, that gains more experiential knowledge about us. Thus Maslow's commitment to induction goes beyond behaviorism's, for he admits as data not only easily measured phenomena but others less definite, such as nonlinear consciousness, and broadens the scope of methods to include, such as introspection. Finally, he welcomes studies of values and morality. Humanists, perhaps because many were either children of or themselves clergymen (Maddi & Costa, 1972), have readily offered opinions about such matters (Rogers, 1973), and Maslow deplored scientists' refusal to follow suit as harmful to both religion and science.

Must science be value free? According to Bronowski (1965), this belief too reflects the version of science that behaviorism borrowed. Hiroshima led him to wonder if science had become primarily a force for destruction, for if it had, it then is a vanguard lemming leading us to our doom. If so, is this due to its moral neutrality? Fortunately, this dismal scenario overlooks values both admirable and practical that scientists share. As recurring debates about genetic engineering, environmental damage, and the like confirm, the belief that science is value free confuses its findings (which are) with its activities (which avowedly are not). The supreme scientific value is to search for understanding and truth, but others arise from the primary means to this end, empiricism. The first is *independence*, to take no belief on faith or authority but to make up one's own mind. Others follow: *originality* (revolutionary ideas verify that one has acted independently), *dissent* (the duty to disagree with prevailing views when data demands it), and *tolerance*, respecting opinions that oppose one's own so long as evidence supports them. Thus scientists actually live by the creed, "I disagree with what you say, but will defend to the death your right to say it." In addition, science allows no arbitrary censorship of ideas no matter how repugnant or ridiculous they seem. Therefore, it values *freedom*, the right to untrammeled inquiry, as well as *democracy*, in the sense that all opinions deserve equal consideration, and it is the data summoned in support, not their advocates' track records, reputations, or power that carry the day.

It was for this reason, incidentally, that Popper (Magee, 1973) saw science as being a not only more admirable but more effective system than totalitarianism. Some assume that dictatorships must prevail because their centralized decision making is more efficient. Yet since such systems brook little dissent, overthrowing erroneous dogmas is extraordinarily difficult. Lacking flexibility, they must eventually become obsolete; only a genuinely free society can find better alternatives. The collapses of Hitler's predicted Thousand Year Reich after only twelve and more recently of Europe's communist states both vindicate this analysis. At any rate, Howard (1985) describes other *epistemic values* that help choose among theories. An attractive one has not only empirical success but *internal coherence* (it "hangs together"), *unifying power* (it brings together previously unrelated fragments), and *fertility* (it provides many testable predictions). I would add that the belief that theories that handle the data more adequately are superior is itself a value judgment, as is advocating objectivity or subject-object separation.

Bevan (1980, 1982) identified still more values that current realities have forced scientists to accept, specifically that the division between pure and applied science is narrow. It was once assumed that laypeople were to act as unquestioning patrons of pure science who provided funds without expecting material returns, whereas applied science, more answerable, had to deliver tangible goods. However, pure science is no longer immune to applied criteria. World Wars I and II forged more intimate science-technology partnerships, epitomized by the Manhattan project, and psychology was not exempt. Placement tests were developed and used for placing large numbers of personnel, and sophisticated weaponry fostered *human engineering*, the science of designing systems, such as aircraft cockpits, that take into account operators' psychological characteristics. As another humbling force, because modern science is expensive and needs private and public largesse, pure scientists must now defend their activities to laypeople, few of whom care much about the sheer pursuit of knowledge. They want more "bang for their bucks" (figuratively if not literally).

How does all this affect scientific values? According to Bevan, both pure and applied modern scientists must accept evaluation by lay standards, become politically and socially involved, and value *professional patriotism*, accepting responsibilities to lobby for funds and educate the public about their enterprise. Their values, so incontestable to themselves, may not be so to others who, nonetheless, as investors rightly claim that they should be kept informed. Moreover, if scientists believe, as surely they must, that their work is in society's best interests, do they not have a duty to insure that it is supported and properly used? Still, they must beware overselling the possibilities lest, come next budget, the chickens of disappointment come home to roost. There is a warning here for psychology. Its technologies have, Bevan intimates, delivered nothing like the successes it once promised if given generous support for such things as social services. Problems such as crime are as prevalent as ever and "we're still a young science" no longer washes, if it ever did. Too many pure psychologists take a "let them eat cake" attitude toward educating the public (however one regards his specific proposals, Skinner [1971] is in this respect a refreshing exception, asserting that not to extend possible applied benefits is both inefficient and immoral). Psychology's house may not have so many rooms as God the Father's, but it has quite a few, and its pure and applied wings must begin to share the same postal service.

Finally, Howard (1985) notes that since people are psychology's subject matter, it more than any science must concern itself with values. G. Miller (cited in Bevan, 1982) sees psychology as a revolutionary science in that the implications of realizing its stated goals would far outrun those of, say, atomic energy. Psychologists who ignore ethical questions are therefore acting unethically because knowledge gained could affect people's views of themselves and in turn their behaviors in the future (thus G. Miller's [1969] concern about the psychology we give away to the public at large, notably through courses we teach). So if psychologists are, as Howard puts it, agents in forming human beings, they must constantly ask how people should behave.

Psychology's involvement with people also raises moral questions regarding experimentation that natural sciences do not face. The empirical rule requires that this is one means by which ideas are pursued, and it often involves studying human subjects. As a result, many studies that might be desirable in terms of knowledge gained are unacceptable on moral grounds. Some classic studies in social psychology are exemplary. Despite their justified renown on grounds of intrinsic interest, fertility and such, they prompted doubts that their results justified the means used to obtain them, especially in the postwar years when memories of the horrifying research in concentration camps were still fresh.

To study conformity, Asch (1955) grouped his subjects with several others who in fact were confederates and who, when asked to judge which of several lines was longest, chose incorrectly, although the answer was obvious. Most actual subjects then did the same. The infamous case of Kitty Genovese, whose rape and torture was witnessed by many others, none of whom so much as called the police, inspired Darley and Latané's (1968) studies of *bystander apathy*. Subjects encountered bogus emergencies such as smoke coming out of an air duct. If alone, they were more likely to take action than when others were present, suggesting that bystanders are not so much apathetic as prone whenever possible to "letting George do it." Finally, Milgram (1974) assigned two subjects seemingly at random to be teacher or pupil in a learning experiment. In fact the actual subject always became the teacher, who was to teach the pupil (actually a confederate) a list of words and, whenever a mistake was made, deliver an electric shock; moreover, dosage was to be increased with more errors (no shock was actually delivered, or confederates would have been hard to come by). Despite agonizing screams from pupils and pleas to stop, most teachers continued to deliver shocks to what they thought were lethal levels. They found the experience extremely stressful, but few considered disobeying authority by refusing to continue.

Worthwhile studies all, by any standard, but by deceiving subjects about purposes, they probably invaded privacy and Milgram's in particular also exposed subjects to appreciable stress, which debriefing them afterwards, that it had all been faked, probably did not alleviate. Someone who has voluntarily delivered shock, real or imaginary, has learned something unpleasant about themselves. Ring (1967) adds another dimension to these objections. Because many social psychology studies feature hierarchical relationships wherein the experimenter stands dominant, subjects must endure ludicrous "games," such as embarrassing procedures that seem intended more to have fun at their expense than to provide useful information. This contradicts science's preferred image as seriously pursuing knowledge for knowledge's sake.

A still greater dilemma concerns data obtained by certifiably repugnant methods, notably the concentration camp experiments. Once such data are available, should they be used? To do so would seem to give these abominations a legitimacy they do not deserve. On the other hand, the data could never be obtained under ordinary circumstances and not to use them might be seen as a disservice to those who suffered so horribly to provide them, by making their ordeals on top of everything else pointless. The debate is largely academic since most of these studies can be rejected purely because of their shoddy methodology, but what if this were not so? I have heard the matter debated by sensitive people who clearly couldn't decide. Nor can I.

In any event, due to increasing concern about treatment of subjects, the American Psychological Association (APA) (1990) has developed a code of ethics, and most universities and granting agencies now require ethical approval for studies that use humans to prevent psychological or physical danger. As well, it was once routine to require undergraduate students to serve as subjects on grounds that they would thereby learn something about research. However, some institutions have recognized that this is a questionable assumption at best and so rely on volunteers, and those institutions that continue the old ways offer alternatives to serving, such as writing essays, that are more likely to provide educational benefits.

Since this topic has ended on an ethical note, it is fitting that it be summarized with a Bunyanesque morality tale. The landlord Science, his vicious watchdog Empiricism straining at the leash, has evicted the poor widow Mind and her many offspring such as Subjective Experience, Creativity, and Religion, from the domicile Psychology. She's not The Right Sort Of Person and those brats of hers are nothing but trouble—messy, uncontrollable and worse, often invisible. Turf them out, or there goes the neighborhood!

3

Generalization

This tactic seeks similarities among phenomena and statements that apply to all of them, so the properties of one are of interest only insofar as they exemplify a broader principle. While folkwisdom has it that every snowflake is different (although verifying this empirically would be challenging to say the least), all snowflakes also have properties in common and it is these that concern the scientist interested in snowflakes; for example that each and all, whatever its idiosyncrasies, helps clog up one's driveway. In its fondness for similarities, Bronowski (1965) points out, science resembles art. For Coleridge, the quest for beauty was a search for the unity in the variety of experiences that sensation provides, and for Bronowski and many others (e.g., Poincaré, 1952; Mednick, 1962) creative inspiration in any sphere involves what Koestler (1970) called *bisociation*, connecting several previously unrelated ideas. Similarly, compelling connections form the gist of metaphors, those devices so vital to effective artistry, as when life becomes a poor player that struts and bellows his hour upon the stage.

How do scientists discover similarities? One popular tactic (Tweney, Doherty & Mynatt, 1981), the *method of induction*, was reportedly invented by Socrates (R. Watson, 1963) and promoted by Francis Bacon. One first observes many individual phenomena and then asks what all have in common, so one works from the particular to the general. But as each item is contemplated, Bacon warned against various *Idols of the Mind,* or preconceptions about possible connections, which might affect the items selected for examination and result in an invalid generalization. Darwin is routinely cited as a quintessential practitioner of induction. During his voyage to the Galápagos Islands, he gathered innumerable flora and fauna, supposedly indiscriminately. Then later, as he reread Malthus about overpopulation's destructive effects, inspiration suddenly dawned: overpopulation could also advantage a species by offering more alternatives for Nature to select the fittest, a general principle that could explain the origins of every species.

The commitment to induction also suggests that science is *cumulative.* Since each generation adds more empirical observations, generalizations should become ever more accurate approximations of some final truth. Witness an uncharacteristically humble Newton: "If I have been able to see farther than others, it was because I stood on the shoulders of giants" (quoted in Koestler, 1970, p. 124). Another common supposition (Morison, 1963) follows—the *principle of gradualness.* Because time is needed to gather enough facts for induction, overly hasty generalizations that leapfrog over gaps in empirical knowledge risk falling flat. Pavlov's attitude is typical: "What can I wish to the youth of my country who devote themselves to science? Firstly, gradualness [about which] . . . I never can speak without emotion. Gradualness, gradualness . . . severe gradualness in the accumulation of knowledge" (quoted in Morison, 1963, p. 287). Finally, the preference for working from particular to general also explains why many scientists study simple, albeit artificial situations before taking on larger ones. As Morison told an audience of psychologists,

Three decades of the most painstaking and intelligent observation by the best minds in psychology [had provided only] . . . the foggiest notion of what goes on in the [brain] between the moment a monkey sees a peanut covered by a small tin can and the time he reaches for it 30 seconds later. . . . Let us think on this before we set forth to tell mothers how to bring up their children . . . [or] social workers how to abolish delinquency. (1963, p. 287)

However generalizations also enter science through the *method of deduction.* The term is loosely used, but in science it refers to the reverse of induction. It begins with a generalization, usually in the form of a theoretical proposition, and the specific instances that follow from it are then determined. The proposition's merit may then be tested by determining whether those instances actually occur, but strictly speaking this is not required. Where does an initial statement come from? In pure deduction it is a truth so self-evident that it needs no verification, for example, the axioms of geometry, or the one idea Descartes felt he could accept with complete confidence, "Cogito, ergo sum" (I think, therefore I am), from which he was able to deduce to his own satisfaction that, among other things, God exists. But pure deduction is rare. Most hunches grow from preliminary evidence, so induction is also involved, for generalizations simply plucked out of the air might well prove invalid, as would systems built upon them.

Scientific generalizations may be stated in several ways. Similarities among objects suggest *classification systems,* such as Linnaeus's taxonomy, which places the plant and animal kingdoms in descending hierarchies (phylum, class, order, and so on), with lower categories having more similarities among members and stricter criteria for inclusion, and Mendeleev's periodic table, which indicates various families of elements whose members all display certain common properties. Similarities among events, on the other hand, are stated as scientific *laws*, or statements of regular, predictable relationships among empirical variables (Marx, 1963b). However, a genuine scientific law specifies the conditions under which it does or does not apply (Turner, 1968). Discovering the latter does not disprove it—laws are never wrong, since they merely express what happens—but only establishes its limits. Here is a reef on which sweeping generalizations such as "You can't trust city hall" and Murphy's famous first law "Anything that can go wrong, will go wrong" founder. Although they may seem beyond reproach, no limits are mentioned so they imply that events always conform when in reality they do not. Such pseudolaws *over*generalize—which is precisely what makes them amusing—whereas a prototypic scientific one, such as the Boyle-Charles law, specifies that the stated effects of temperature and pressure on gas volume only hold in intermediate ranges.

Why do scientists stress generalizing? Probably because it simplifies things, and in this they manifest a prevailing human tendency. Do we not all group the stimuli we experience that have common properties, be they lawnmowers, or hamburgers, and, even though no two are completely alike, respond to them similarly? For regarding every event as unique would eliminate past experience as a guide to responding. Children acquiring language reveal how ingrained this tendency is. A word such as "cat" labels various, sometimes very diverse stimuli—Siamese, Cheshires, Garfield—yet a child readily grasps the concept of "catness" (although typically unable to state its necessary properties) and decides whether a novel event qualifies. If anything, we generalize too frequently and ignore differences among phenomena. One repugnant example is *stereotyping*, the pretense that all members of a given group possess certain, invariably undesirable characteristics. Thus generalization has provided not only scientific laws but an abominations such as the Aryan myth that certain races are inherently superior, a basic doctrine of National Socialism.

The scientist also generalizes for simplicity, for classifying more situations under a common principle makes Nature seem more comprehensible. This preference for simplicity also affects the type of theories he favors. The *law of parsimony* (known in other variations as Morgan's Canon and Occam's Razor) holds that explanation should account for the greatest number of facts or observations with the fewest number of principles (Underwood, 1957b). Parsimony is not a law in the strict sense, but an attitude about the kinds of explanations that are preferable. It by no means invalidates complicated or imaginative ones, but only those more complicated than is necessary to handle the data, because things will become involved enough as it is. But laws also serve other purposes. First, they provide a type of explanation for exemplary phenomena. When an overheated pot boils over, we can sigh, "It's the Boyle-Charles law" and feel slightly better as we mop up, because we understand. Second, a law helps predict events, if it clearly applies to the situation. Third, it may suggest phenomena to seek out; the periodic table indicated as yet undiscovered elements of specified atomic number and properties that were later discovered.

However, this presentation downplays some complications. A perfectly rational investigator could perhaps avoid Idols of the Mind, but no scientist and, because of intimacy, certainly no psychologist can, so pure induction is impossible to carry off. Darwin, that supposed exemplar, was nothing of the kind. His private diaries and notebooks reveal that he was a convinced evolutionist before ever setting foot on HMS *Beagle*, and he consciously collected his data to provide support for a theory of this kind (Gruber, 1974). He later adopted the pretense that he was reluctantly driven to these views by the sheer weight of evidence to try to ward of the storm of controversy that he knew would follow. Furthermore, even were induction possible it would not be desirable. Selection of examples not guided by considering possible relationships among them would yield so helter-skelter a heterogeneity as to defy any attempt to find such relationships, and how could one ever be sure that they had gathered enough examples to begin that attempt?

Finally, induction and generalization rest on another of those articles of faith from which science is supposedly exempt. Extending a relationship uncovered in one time and place to others assumes that the universe possesses uniformity and permanence. But, as Hume pointed out, these presumptions are shaky because they cannot be verified by empirical means, the only ones science supposedly accepts. Evolving general principles from specific observations assumes that those observations will be repeated, but the fact that something has always happened does not guarantee that it will happen again. A leap of faith is required. Russell summarizes the quandary: "Pure empiricism is not a sufficient basis for science. . . . Induction is an independent logical principle, incapable of being inferred either from experience or from other logical principles, and . . . without this principle science is impossible" (quoted in Magee, 1973, p. 21). The best we can say is that as we uncover more evidence of laws, assuming uniformity and permanence becomes ever more reasonable.

GENERALIZATION IN PSYCHOLOGY

According to its current definition, psychology seeks laws that describe the behaviors of organisms, especially laws that, in the interests of parsimony, apply universally. Only if phenomena demand it are these supplemented with others that apply to more specific groups, such as human beings. These *nomothetic* investigations (Marx, 1963a) of large numbers of subjects are not the only possibilities. An *idiographic approach* intensively studies the attributes of an individual, biographies being ready examples. Most scientists find this approach less appealing, but there are those who prefer it. Skinner (1963), as committed to science as anyone, felt that any truly fundamental principle should be discernible in every individual and therefore compared behaviors produced by one at different times and conditions; thus his methods were idiographic, his aims avowedly nomothetic. It is not surprising that uncovering behavioral laws is difficult, for it flies in the face of the valued cliché that everyone is different, and this one like most contains an element of truth. Are psychologists therefore pursuing ghosts? While readily acknowledging individual differences, they think not, because it is also apparent that in many ways everyone is alike. Food tastes may differ, with one person preferring steak, another borscht and still another pasta, but we all need nourishment of some kind to live.

Still, individual differences are facts of life, so a complete scientific psychology must show how general laws can account for them. Suppose that five variables in total affect a phenomenon such as memory, and suppose too that each variable has three possible values. Should subjects differ in even one of these variables, so will their memories. Moreover, even this simple example provides 243 (3^5) possibilities, so for behaviors affected by many variables (as memory certainly is, to say nothing of personality), the number of possibilities borders on infinity. It follows that an individual is completely described by the values she possesses on all influential variables or (to use the language of trait approaches) by her position on each dimension. So stating that "the unique individual is simply the point of intersection of a number of variables" (Eysenck, 1952, p. 18) says, in scientific terms, that everyone is different. It follows too that if we could specify every variable that affects a given behavior, and someone's specific value on each, we could predict their behavior perfectly. Even the simplest of behaviors, of course, have so far defied this utopian prospect. Some would say "Thank goodness!"

The Evolutionary Bias: Comparative Psychology

The attempt to generalize fostered one much ridiculed (e.g., Koestler, 1970) characteristic of modern psychology, its predilection for studying lower animals and by implication ignoring people. The pet species has been the rat, to the point that in behaviorism's heyday the discipline was sometimes called Rodentology. Still, there are good reasons for the practice. First, psychology's definition states that it studies behavior, not human behavior, making any organism fair game. As well, any inherently interesting topic is legitimate and animal behavior certainly qualifies, as the popularity of zoos attests. Then too, it is generally accepted that animals may be subjected to procedures, if these seem promising, that are unacceptable with humans. One of many animal studies that may have practical benefits (see N. Miller, 1985) investigated lesions in the medial (central) section of the brain's hypothalamus, which cause rats to overeat until their body weight reaches several times the normal, whereas damage to the lateral section causes animals to starve even with food close at hand (Hetherington & Ranson, 1942); stimulation through electrodes inserted in these areas has the opposite effects (Anand & Brobeck, 1951). All of this suggests that the medial and lateral areas initiate satiation and hunger, respectively, findings that apart from their intrinsic interest, might help explain (although to my knowledge the possibilities remain conjectural) the eating disorders anorexia nervosa and bulimia.

The most compelling defense for using animals, however, stems from evolutionary theory. If we and they do not differ in kind, then similar behavioral laws should apply, and many do. Consider *reinforcement*, here defined as any event whose occurrence depends on a specified behavior occurring first and which increases the frequency of that behavior. Rats learn to press a lever to gain a pellet of food (Ferster & Skinner, 1957), and we acquire behaviors for pay. Everyone is in part governed by their food pellets, real or symbolic. Or consider *partial reinforcement*. Behaviors not reinforced on every occasion are far more persistent than those that are (Kimble, 1961). The effect is surprising (intuitively, less frequent reinforcement should produce weaker responses) and has a host of explanations (see Houston, 1991), but it is the effect itself, not the reasons for it, that is relevant here. Gambling involves partial reinforcement, and it is evident to even a casual observer in Las Vegas that such behaviors are extraordinarily persistent. In fact gambling addictions, especially when bingo, lotteries, and so on are taken into account, are so common that they probably affect far more lives adversely than do the more publicized ones of alcohol or drugs. Statistics gathered by the University of Alberta indicate that in this province alone there are about 60,000 compulsive gamblers—about 3 percent of the population (*Calgary Herald*, September 9, 1993). Much as it may offend our sense of human uniqueness, animal studies can be very informative about laws of human behavior. With that in mind, we turn to several examples of generalization.

THE LAWS OF PSYCHOPHYSICS

These have historic interest because one was apparently the first scientific law in psychology. Weber presented a series of paired stimuli such as weights. One member, the *standard*, remained constant while the other was systematically varied, and subjects judged whether each pair was identical or different, with the matter of interest being the *just noticeable difference* (jnd), the least change necessary to yield the "different" judgment. The result was *Weber's Law*, that the ratio of the jnd to standard stimulus is a constant, with the corollary that as the standard increases, so must the jnd proportionately. For instance, a glass of water produces a discernible increase when poured into a small pail of liquid but not when dumped into the ocean, and the luminescence of trilite lamps apparently increases more from 50 to 100 than from 100 to 150 watts, although the absolute change is identical (Underwood, 1966). I would add another disheartening one, that as we age time seems to pass more rapidly; three weeks until Christmas for a child of six is an eternity, but not for someone in their twilight years. Weber's Law does however have limits; it generally holds up well in intermediate ranges, but not at extremes (R. Watson, 1963).

Fechner's firm belief that body and mind were not separate but aspects of the same led him to borrow Weber's work for a very different purpose, "the scientific investigation of the functional relations of dependency between body and mind," or *psychophysics* (quoted in R. Watson, 1963, p. 211). Thus this laudably empirical approach became a means to psychological ends—to assess mental sensations as revealed by judgments and relate them quantitatively, via an equation, to bodily stimulation. Assuming that all jnds along a given dimension are subjectively equal, allowed him to rephrase Weber's relationship in what became known as *Fechner's Law*, $S = k \log I$, where I refers to physical stimulus intensity, S to sensation in jnd units, and k to a constant.

Stevens's (1961) later studies using the method of magnitude estimation led to another formulation. As each stimulus in a series was presented, subjects assigned it a number proportional to their experience; thus if one weight seemed four times heavier than another, the number given the former was to be four times greater as well. Sensation measured this way did grow proportionately with stimulation as Stevens's predecessors had claimed, but the rate of growth differed across the senses, being slower for brightness, for example, than for pain. Therefore *Stevens's Power Law* states that $S = kI^n$, where n is another constant that depends on the dimension. The law that best handles the data at last report remains undecided, but it is the attempts to discover lawful statements of relationships between physical and psychological events that are noteworthy.

B. F. SKINNER AND OPERANT CONDITIONING

Skinner (1971, 1974), that most controversial of recent psychologists, like many others attributed all behaviors to the two great determinants, heredity and environment. However, he added that both work through the same mechanism, the *contingencies*, or consequences, of a behavior that decide whether it will flourish or disappear. More specifically, Skinner builds on the supposition that species must adapt to their environment to survive. Inherited behaviors, therefore, like other genetic traits might occur as novel mutations, but if they prove adaptive they would be selected for survival because members who possess these tendencies are more likely to thrive, so they eventually become part of the species' repertoire. Thus such behaviors depend on *contingencies of survival*. Learned behaviors on the other hand are ruled by *contingencies of reinforcement*. Whether consequences qualify as reinforcers is determined by their effects on a behavior, that is, they must by definition increase it. Since their involvement in classical conditioning is unclear (Kimble, 1961), we discuss them within the context of *instrumental* or *operant conditioning*. First, reinforcers may be *positive* or *negative*, but in either case their occurrence depends on the subject first producing a designated behavior. Relevant situations allow a variety of responses (limited only by factors such as subjects' abilities) that are mutually exclusive—subjects at choice points in a maze, for example, can produce only one at a time—so the correct, that is reinforced, response must be discovered by trial and error. Behavior is therefore at first unpredictable but becomes more consistent as a reinforced option gains dominance.

By empirical observation, Skinner identified a set of principles to promote learning, so in essence he provided a technology. Moreover, these principles were already well known, but he formalized them and specified conditions to maximize their efficiency. First, minimize delay of reinforcement after a desired behavior. Even short delays impede acquisition (Grice, 1948), presumably by reducing behavior–reinforcer contiguity and thus chances that subjects will make the connection. As well, use secondary reinforcers, those that have acquired their properties by being associated with primary ones such as food (Skinner favored a click sound). The quick delivery possible with the secondary kind lessens delay and a primary reinforcer is only effective if subjects have been deprived of it— food requires hungry animals—whereas powerful secondary reinforcers, such as the textbook example, money, never lose value.

Several other principles aim to surmount a difficulty specific to operant circumstances. Classical conditioning subjects invariably produce the requisite response since it is a reflex under control of the unconditioned stimulus (UCS), but in operant conditions the experimenter is in a real sense at the subjects' mercy. If they cannot or will not produce that response, reinforcers cannot be delivered to encourage repetition. Suppose one wants to train a pigeon to peck out *God Save the Queen* on a piano (perhaps to entertain Britain's embattled Royal Family, who these days need all the amusement they can get). One will have a long wait before most subjects emit such a behavior spontaneously, yet this is only one of the many unlikely behaviors that Skinner (1951) managed to instill. How? Operant subjects learning a task must discover a response that works, and the more responses possible, the less likely this becomes. Therefore, the first principle is to design the environment to minimize this number. Here lies the peculiar genius of the notorious Skinner box. Apart from its levers to press or discs to peck, it is barren, there isn't much else to do, so chances are good that before long these responses will occur. Furthermore Skinner, never one not to practice what he preached, raised his own daughter in a Skinner box of a sort, from which experience she reportedly emerged unscathed.

Another principle, *shaping* or *successive approximations*, at first reinforces any responses that remotely resemble the one wanted, but once these become frequent, now demands others of closer proximity, so subjects work up through a series of steps until achieving the goal behavior. These techniques cannot instill responses beyond an organism's biological capabilities—no one to my knowledge has shaped monkeys to warble *Melancholy Baby,* even when inebriated, or earthworms to dance *Swan Lake*—but otherwise, if skillfully applied they work amazingly well.

To return to generalization, Skinner (1971), a thoroughgoing evolutionist, saw these principles as applicable to all animals including the human and to everyday as much as contrived laboratory circumstances. Any differences between these variations on his themes are trivial; the lever-pressing rat provides a model for all learned behaviors. Not even creative achievements are exempt (Skinner, 1968, 1976). Mozart also indulged in trial and error (his much-touted ability [Perkins, 1981] to produce flawless first drafts presumably indicates only that he emitted his errors surreptitiously). On occasion, quite by accident, he produced *behavioral mutations*, novelties that others found attractive and reinforced, so such tendencies became more frequent. Thus he required no special talent or genius but was simply a product of his *history of reinforcement,* raised by a doting father who reinforced and shaped successful attempts, residing in a designed environment, Vienna, the city of musicians (he actually grew up in a provincial backwater, Salzburg, but good Skinnerians overlook such niggling difficulties). Given similar circumstances, anyone supposedly could achieve as much. No one is immune to these implacable laws. Skinner did pay lip service to individual differences, but when pressed to the wall invariably saw them as only differences of quantity. Some may learn a behavior more rapidly than others. However one views these analyses, one must admire Skinner's eternal optimism about human potential. Everyone can learn any behavior of which their species is capable, so failure is never the individual's fault. Follow the recipe and acquisition should be both effortless and faultless. Thus students, far from deploring Skinner, should revere him. Their shortcomings are due to someone else's—probably the incompetent behind the lectern.

As the label *radical behaviorism* implies, Skinner lay firmly in Watson's tradition. His first concern also was to describe behavioral laws and never mind their explanation. His distaste for theories, especially any that invoked hypothetical entities such as mind or cognition, was adamant (Skinner, 1963, 1971). Unlike Watson he did admit that such mentalisms occur; he simply denied that they influence behavior. The actual determinants, such as reinforcement, are external and so can be investigated empirically. Why do certain events work as reinforcers while others do not? Does what is learned differ in classical as opposed to operant conditioning? Does the latter perhaps require two associations: (1) S-R, between the situation and the correct response, as in "in this situation, I should do this," and (2) R-S, that expresses the contingency, as in "if I do this, this will happen?" Skinner eschewed such theoretical questions as distractions from the first priority: behavioral laws. For example, whether a certain event is effective as a reinforcer is an empirical question, to by answered by trying it out.

Applications

Since these principles supposedly affect all behaviors, they would be expected to have many applications, but Skinner's (1948) utopian novel, *Walden II* is the ultimate one, for it describes an entire society that follows these principles to maximize happiness and security; moreover actual communities, some quite successful, have been established along its lines (L. Miller, 1976). Skinner at one time wanted to be writer (Viney, 1993), but soon saw the light—fortunately, because however one feels about *Walden II*'s underlying ideas, its characterizations, style, and so on indicate that, by gaining a brilliant psychologist, we lost a mediocre writer.

Education. For Skinner (1968), the deficiencies of that most inviting target for criticism, the modern classroom, occur because it breaks every rule for effective learning. Rarely is shaping employed and reinforcement, when delivered at all, is fatally delayed, that is, by the time assignments are returned, students can barely remember doing them. In addition, Skinner holds that we learn through success, by emitting correct responses and having them reinforced, not by passively absorbing information or making errors and having them corrected, that is, punished. Yet these procedures are usually favored, so education becomes tedious, frustrating, and soon aversive, not the fulfilling adventure it should be. Skinner would therefore mechanize it via the teaching machine. This device now wears a computer guise, but it still poses questions for which students must compose answers. If correct, the question is replaced by another, if not it must be answered again, so question removal provides immediate reinforcement that one has responded correctly. Furthermore, one cannot leave a question until responding correctly, because this is how we learn. Finally, the sequence of questions presents increasingly complex versions of a concept, to shape one toward ever higher achievement.

Doesn't the system smack of depersonalized mechanization, of which we already have more than enough? As the first rejoinder, in this context surely what matters is not depersonalization but whether the system works. Modern surgery treats patients as little more than meat on a slab, causing some to mourn yesteryear's storied benevolent physicians with their acclaimed bedside manner. But medicine is now far more effective, so if depersonalization is the price to be paid for getting better, I for one will gladly pay it. Skinner presents other compelling defenses. His system should surpass even the most sympathetic human instructor, who cannot possibly monitor and immediately reinforce every correct response emitted by a roomful of students. His situations are also far less depersonalizing than some currently in vogue, notably huge lecture theaters wherein students watch monitors showing the flickering image of an instructor whose immediacy rivals events in galaxies long ago and far away. Skinner attains the ideal of one instructor per student, and an unusually patient instructor that does not play favorites, become angry at mistakes, or go either too fast or too slow, and is never anything but encouraging, rewards success, and, by exploiting the various principles, maximizes its frequency, all of which increases self-esteem. That instructor just happens to be a machine.

Attitudes. Beliefs that determine reactions to events, other people, and groups are presumably learned; it taxes credulity to assert that one's stance on abortion or capital punishment might be endowed by one's genes. As a song from *South Pacific* opines regarding prejudice, you've got to be carefully taught, and the same learning principles probably operate here as elsewhere. Furthermore, a self-perpetuating cycle typically results, because according to the principle of *belief congruence* (Rokeach & Mezei, 1966), we like better and therefore prefer to associate with others who share our attitudes, who tend to reinforce and thus strengthen them. Not surprisingly, the empirical literature emphasizes methods to change attitudes. Some are dangerous or undesirable, and powerful economic interests have a stake in this; advertising's raison d'être is to sway attitudes about products. On the face of it, since attitudes are learned, an efficient application of learning principles should insure success, but, once ingrained, attitudes become an integral part of one's self-concept, determine the people and groups with whom/which one is involved (Lambert & Lambert,

1973), and have intense emotional aspects. For all these reasons, they can be very difficult to modify.

Also, from a behaviorist angle attitudes connote mentalisms, not behaviors as such. We examine his position in this regard later, but in essence Skinner (1971) held that such things may seem to influence behavior because the two events accompany one another, but in fact both are controlled by the same factor, reinforcement. So behaviorists focus on changing not attitudes, but attitudinal behaviors, believing that whether private beliefs remain steadfast is irrelevant so long as one learns to act differently (although one could object that if changed contingencies modify a behavior, the underlying attitude should also change, if it too is ruled by them).

Several techniques exemplify this approach. The *brainwashing* procedures used during the Korean War at first rewarded prisoners of war with better food and privileges for small departures from their standard beliefs, such as expressing some sympathy for Communist doctrine. Then these rewards required more severe changes so that by war's end those prisoners should have become shaped to the party line, ready to overthrow Wall and Bay Streets, mom's apple pie and hockey night in Canada. Similarly, the *foot-in-the-door* technique (Beamon, Cole, Preston, Klentz & Stebloy, 1983) resembles shaping by first encouraging actions only slightly at odds with preferences, by requesting such things as signing petitions supporting traffic safety. Most people will agree if only to seem cooperative. Then larger requests to place a sign saying Drive Safely on one's lawn are more likely to be accepted. Finally, participants in the *role-playing* technique perform fictional scenarios that conflict with their beliefs. For example, smokers who had no intention of quitting became patients who had just learned they had cancer and acted out their feelings while waiting for surgery to be arranged (Janis & Mann, 1965). Actors reported lower cigarette consumption eighteen months after a single one-hour session than did controls who listened to a tape of the session, so actually emitting the behavior was indeed crucial.

The Definition and Treatment of Psychopathology. What criteria distinguish the psychologically healthy from the afflicted, so that those who need therapy can be reliably identified? What forms should such therapy take? Answers have practical as well as academic importance, and two approaches from different traditions vie for priority. The longer-standing alternative comes from medicine wherein its success is a matter of record. Overt deviations from health, such as fever or nausea, are viewed as symptoms of underlying, organic diseases; while one symptom may suggest several maladies, presumably an array is unique for each. The surreptitious culprit supposedly induced the symptoms, defines the disease, and is the primary target for therapy, for it is assumed that treating symptoms is no cure; diseases, like dandelions, must be cut off at the root or they will reappear. Since the presence of the causal agent is an either/or matter, it should clearly distinguish those who have from those who don't have that disease—you either have a malignancy or you don't—and also various diseases, because although their symptoms may overlap, each disease should stem from a distinctive source.

Psychology's *medical model* of disturbed behaviors adopts a similar position because many do reflect physical abnormalities. Brain damage or disease can produce amnesia, inadequate contact with reality, retardation, and any number of antisocial or criminal activities. The symptoms of advanced syphilis closely resemble those of psychosis, and the behavioral tragedies wrought by the physical ravages of alcohol or drug addictions are well known. The model's ardent proponents therefore assume, as a virtual article of faith, that every disturbance, be it anxiety, depression or whatever, must have a physical basis that will eventually be identified. Moreover, in the psychoanalytic tradition, disturbed behaviors remain symptoms, but of psychological rather than physical events; therapies aim to attack these and so fit the medical model. Freud himself was, first, a practicing physician treating the afflicted and his theory, including the more contentious aspects, evolved from those experiences. His belief, often expressed, was that all disturbances ultimately had organic bases, but until these were identified, therapy should focus on the presumed psychological determinants, unconscious traumas. Thus his method of *psychoanalysis*, in line with the medical philosophy, used several devices, such as free association and dream interpretations, to restore these presumed causes to consciousness so the patient could gain *insight* into them and work them through. Hence Freud frequently referred to himself as an archaeologist of the mind delving beneath the surface of things to lay bare significant remnants.

However, insight methods have met with less than overwhelming success. The prognosis for schizophrenics for example is bleak and overall, improvement rates may be no better than for those receiving no treatment whatever (Eysenck, 1960, 1965). One reason may be a faulty basic premise. As the adage Let sleeping dogs lie warns, discovering occurrences so threatening as to need repressing in the first place might be more harmful than beneficial. Freud foresaw this conundrum, but on balance subscribed to another adage, Know thyself. Still, he might have recalled that it was this very desire that led Oedipus to the realization that he had unknowingly killed his father and married his mother, and hence to his doom. But it was other premises of psychoanalysis that faced the main attacks (e.g., Wolpe, 1958). In the last analysis, it was argued, one is labeled as disturbed because one's behaviors are unacceptable. These could be seen, then, not as symptoms but as the illness itself, which, once alleviated, would justify the patient's being called "cured."

The second set of approaches, the *behavior therapies*, all share these attitudes. How does disturbed behavior come about? Therapists of this persuasion downplay the question. Ever pragmatic, their first concern is its removal, so they focus on the future more than the past, showing little interest in case histories. Still, although their philosophy does not demand it, most assume that such behavior is in large part learned through the same mechanisms that govern all acquisition. Thus Baby Albert's dastardly experiences supposedly demonstrated a standard scenario for producing phobias. Likewise, emitting depressed behaviors may produce payoffs in sympathy and attention from others, especially if suicide threats are included. Seligman's (1968) more elaborate account of depression is based on *learned helplessness*. Operant responses can be acquired to avoid an aversive event such as shock if produced not to the event itself but to a warning stimulus such as a light that consistently precedes it. Indicatively, avoidance learning is remarkably rapid and resistant to extinction (Solomon & Wynne, 1954). However, Overmier and Seligman (1967) first administered repeated shock that occurred regardless of behavior, and when subjects could later learn to avoid shock they did not do so because they did not indulge in trial and error, but simply cowered in resignation. Apparently they had learned that their behavior had no effect and that the world is a cruel place. Clinical depression also features such helpless, apathetic behavior.

If disturbed behaviors are learned, it should be possible to unlearn them and/or institute others more desirable by judiciously applying learning principles. Hence the *token economies* (Ayllon & Azrin, 1965; Kazdin, 1988) now common in treatment and correctional institutions reinforce appropriate behaviors with tokens that inmates can exchange for items such as cigarettes. A particularly effective means to eliminate behaviors is *counterconditioning*, wherein competing alternatives in the same situation are positively reinforced, on grounds that one cannot do A while also doing B. Thus a pioneering behavior therapy, *desensitization* (Wolpe, 1974), substitutes relaxation for fear responses to phobic stimuli. Subjects first list versions of the stimulus in order of the fear they evoke and are then taught exercises, perhaps under hypnosis, to induce relaxation. Next, a mild form of the stimulus is presented—subjects afraid of heights might mount the first step of a ladder—while they try to remain relaxed; should fear intrude, the stimulus is forthwith removed lest contiguity strengthen the association. Once calm is restored, the first approximation is reintroduced until relaxation can be maintained in its presence. The procedure is repeated with the next approximation, for example, mounting the second step, until eventually even severe versions can be faced with equanimity. Desensitization has been used with varying effectiveness for snake phobias (Brady, 1971), fears of social interaction and agoraphobia, for test, dental, and speech anxieties, asthma (Turner, DiTomasso & Deluty, 1985), female sexual dysfunction (Segraves, 1981) and sexual anxiety generally (Reynolds, 1981), and can also be effective when feared stimuli are not presented but only imagined by subjects (Deffenbacher & Suinn, 1988).

Possible causes of and treatments for homosexuality also exemplify behavioral principles at work. However, the attitudes of yesteryear that such behavior is neurotic, let alone perverse or sinful, attitudes that led to playwright Oscar Wilde's tragic demise (Ellman, 1988), are no longer appropriate, so the question arises, if there is nothing wrong with being gay, why is therapy needed? Still, since the lifestyle has its disadvantages, some gays prefer alternatives, so the simple rejoinder is that a service is being offered to those who wish to use it. Why do some have this orientation? Bieber's (1962) answer has a psychoanalytic but also behavioristic ring. Many male homosexuals, he noted, have a *close-*

binding mother, overly protective, intimate, even seductive, suggesting she may unconsciously desire her son sexually, so he is kept tied to the maternal apron strings. One unfortunate was still sleeping with his mother when he was eighteen! Due to these unconscious desires, such a mother might, Bieber surmised, discourage anything other than platonic interactions with girls and instill an incapacitating fear of the opposite sex—in effect, a phobia—forcing the boy to seek homosexual outlets which, if they brought pleasure, would be reinforced.

If homosexual behaviors are thus acquired, behavior therapies should be able to alleviate them, and Feldman and MacCullough's (1965) counterconditioning technique ingeniously exploits avoidance learning as well as many learning principles, such as shaping. Medical model advocates routinely object that by treating only symptoms not (presumed) underlying causes, behavior therapies must have but transitory effects. Avoidance learning was used, then, precisely because responses so learned vigorously resist extinction. Similarly, such principles as partial and secondary reinforcement and stimulus generalization were also incorporated to this end. All these applications, however insightful, are beside the point if the procedure proves ineffective, but early returns suggested otherwise. Of twenty-six patients, eighteen showed a marked and quite lasting trend toward heterosexuality in both overt practice and in fantasy life (Feldman, 1966).

CLASSIFICATION OF PSYCHOPATHOLOGIES: THE DSMS

Generalization is manifest not only in laws but also in systems that classify phenomena sharing common characteristics. Relatively few have been proposed for psychological phenomena, but abnormalities are one exception. Kraepelin's early attempt was followed by the various *Diagnostic and Statistical Manual of Mental Disorders* (DSMs) proposed by the American Psychiatric Association, with DSM I appearing in 1952, succeeded by DSM II, 1968, DSM III, 1980 (revised in 1987), and DSM IV, 1994. They too owe much to medicine, which identified various diseases, to introduce some order into what would otherwise be a chaos of individual cases, in the exercise of diagnosis. Placing a case in a specific category such as measles offers several benefits. Previous experience with other similar cases suggests therapies that have proved helpful and a prognosis of likely future events. As well, classification can guide research, since underlying causes and effective treatments should differ among diseases, and facilitates communication.

In keeping with the medical model, categories in DSM I and II were routinely viewed as diseases, and their specific descriptions and names were heavily influenced by Freudian outlooks (Kendall & Harmen, 1995). In addition, these early versions implied a multilevel hierarchy (see Figure 3.1). It was clearly assumed that at the most general level mental illness and health were separate. The illness category's ten subgroups included psychosis, under which was

Figure 3.1
Portions of a DSM Hierarchy

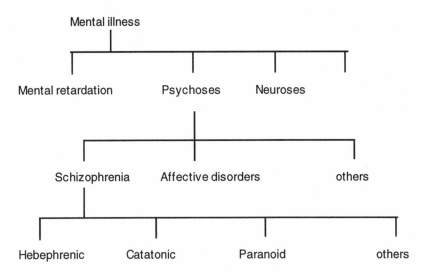

Source: Generated by author.

schizophrenia, among others, and which itself contained several still more specific possibilities.

Since these early systems emerged not from empirical evidence but were imposed by fiat, it is not surprising that they were less than resounding successes. The reliability of diagnosis was low (Costello, 1970) and doubts grew about their validity, such as whether conditions such as hysterical neurosis existed at all. DSM III, therefore, replaced the multilevel hierarchy with five separate *axes*, each with separable categories. For example, Axis 2 included various personality disorders, such as antisocial tendencies, and Axis 3, medical conditions, such as diabetes. An individual case now is no longer slotted into one category but placed in one or more along each axis, which in theory should more accurately describe actual cases. In addition, the older categories' defining characteristics, while clear enough in textbooks, were in practice unworkably vague, so to improve reliability the new ones were based on more precise physical and/or overt behavioral criteria. In effect, a *prototype* or definitive example established the features essential for placement in a category and also others that might or might not be present. Thus cases grouped together could vary appreciably while still sharing certain common characteristics. Finally, both DSM III and IV had extensive field trials, especially to test reliability. DSM III, while substantially bettering its predecessors (Spitzer, Forman & Nee, 1979), still left something to be desired (Garfield, 1993), a major reason for DSM IV's development. Whether it continues the improvement remains to be seen.

VERBAL LEARNING AND MEMORY:
THE LAWS OF INTERFERENCE

Functionalism provides the third example of generalization. Although re-membering is generally deemed desirable, Freud reminds us that there are some things such as embarrassing faux pas that are better forgotten; as someone said, the secrets to happiness are good health and a poor memory. Be that as it may, retention decreases as the *retention interval*, the time after learning before it is tested, increases. Why? The first culprit that springs to mind, the sheer passage of time, was discredited by Jenkins and Dallenbach (1924). Two groups learned the same verbal materials and were tested after an equal interval, but one spent that time awake going about their undergraduate duties, the other slept. That the latter remembered more shows that other events correlated with the passage of time are to blame.

What might these be? One plausible candidate is other learning, since it too would ordinarily increase with the retention interval and be reduced by sleep. A paired-associate learning experiment (see the top panel of Figure 3.2) demon-strates that such *interference* is a viable explanation. Three groups acquire the same list of associations called *critical learning* (CL) because its retention is later assessed. The control group learns only CL while the second, *retroactive inhibition* (RI), group acquires another list after CL, which in the most common format uses the same stimuli again but these are paired with new responses; thus the two lists form an A-B, A-C relationship. Comparing this group's retention with the control operationally defines RI, forgetting due to interpolated learning. RI is the most obvious source of interference, but the latter might also stem from events prior to CL. Therefore, a third, *proactive inhibition* (PI), group also learns the A-C list but before CL; comparing them to the control measures interference due to prior learning, or PI. On the retention test the RI and PI groups must produce, respectively, the first or second response learned for each stimulus. As a further complexity, the retention interval is varied. For some members of each group it is short (about fifteen minutes) for others long, perhaps twenty-four hours.

Figure 3.2's bottom panel shows the typical results (G. Briggs, 1954; Un-derwood, 1948). First, the control outperforms the PI and RI groups, so while forgetting varies substantially with other factors such as degree of learning (Keppel, 1968), interfering learning certainly produces memory loss. As a second principle, however, the amount depends on the similarity of the associations formed in the competing tasks (McGovern, 1964). The A-B, A-C relationship used here produces far more than others such as A-B, C-D (unrelated stimuli and responses). Returning to Figure 3.2, what one might suspect intuitively, that RI is more detrimental than PI, is confirmed at the short but not the longer interval, where their effects are equal; thus the amount of PI reliably increases over time while RI remains constant or decreases (Keppel, 1968). Therefore PI's effects develop more gradually but—another blow to common sense—at a longer interval (which most memory in practice involves) are at least as great.

Figure 3.2
Experiment on Interference and Typical Results

Group	Prior Learning (PL)	Critical Learning (CL)	Interpolated Learning (IL)	Retention Test of CL
Control	—	A–B	—	A–B
RI	—	A–B	A–C	A–B
PI	A–C	A–B	—	A–B
			<——RETENTION INTERVAL——>	

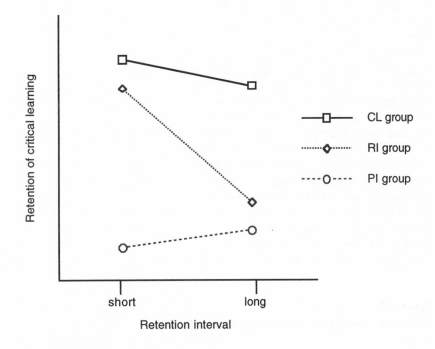

Note: RI = retroactive inhibition; *PI* = proactive inhibition; *A–C, A–B* = paired-associate relationships.

Source: Data adapted from Underwood (1948).

In fact, Underwood (1957a) persuasively argued, PI is probably the main cause of everyday forgetting. Control subjects from a plethora of previous experiments, those who had learned and later been tested on single lists, were classified as either naive or practiced based on whether they had or had not previously served in other verbal-learning experiments. Since degrees of learning, materials, and such differed across studies, retention was examined as a percentage of the amount originally learned. The results were startling. After twenty-four hours, naive subjects remembered about 80 percent, practiced subjects only 20 percent, so the prior learning of the latter produced a truly immense increase in forgetting. Moreover, it is if anything probably underestimated, since a practiced subject has the benefit of learning to learn. There are other reasons also to emphasize PI. Even a retention interval of several months allows only that amount of opportunity for retroactively interfering learning to occur, whereas prior learning spans a lifetime, so it stands to reason that interference should come mainly from this source. Furthermore (the final nail in RI's coffin), prior learning should increase and thus memory decline with age, and, while the effect depends on other considerations, such as the retention test used (Schonfield & Robertson, 1966), in principle it certainly does (Craik, 1977). In a real sense, the elderly know too much and suffer accordingly.

UNIVERSAL STAGES OF DEVELOPMENT: PIAGET, ERIKSON, AND KOHLBERG

These contributions all describe supposedly inevitable stages through which everyone passes as a characteristic matures. Since they try to explain facts of development, they might be called theories, but in the view of advocates they describe lawful events on which one can rely. Nowadays, only Freud rivals Piaget's influence on child psychology, but Piaget's main interest was in how knowledge is acquired (Ginsburg & Opper, 1969). His central notion is of a prevailing cognitive outlook that determines how the child interprets and responds to every experience, because each successive stage features a unique outlook that differs fundamentally from others. Thus those in earlier stages do not interpret comparable experiences as do the more mature. Piaget's many ingenious tests try to discover how each outlook conceives the world by presenting problems to be solved and focusing more on the responses made than on their accuracy. He views children not as passive internalizers of experience akin to tape recorders, but as active problem solvers who want to understand it. Thus a *conservation problem* presents a stimulus and then, while the child watches, changes one attribute—a beaker of water might be poured into another of different shape—and asks whether another attribute, such as volume, has also changed. A *preoperational stage* child (typically ages three to seven) is fooled, but one who has advanced to *concrete operations* is not.

All children regardless of experiences supposedly go through the same stages in the same order, which suggests a genetic influence; they differ only in their rate of progress. Thus the prevailing outlook sets a potential for mastering certain kinds of knowledge, so if requisite experiences occur too early, it will be acquired inefficiently at best. (Compare ethology's notion of *critical periods in development* [Hess, 1959; Lorenz, 1962]). It is therefore crucial that educators discover the stage that a child is in; Piaget's tests assist this aim.

What causes progress from one stage to the next? They themselves may be inevitable but such a transition is emphatically triggered by experiences, albeit of a kind so universal that such progress is guaranteed. We supposedly seek a sense of *equilibrium* between our cognitive structure and our experiences, so the latter seem comprehensible. However, children periodically encounter incomprehensible novelties or anomalies that cause tension. They are driven to reduce it by using either of two tactics: (1) *assimilation*, to reinterpret the anomaly to fit the prevailing structure, or (2) *accommodation*, to modify the structure itself to make the anomaly coherent by viewing it from another standpoint. It is accommodation that induces the transition to the outlook of the next stage, which is irreversible. It follows that to encourage progress, moderate anomalies should be introduced that the child will try to accommodate (too much novelty will simply be assimilated). Thus Piaget, unlike Skinner, sees not a one-way street running from environmental to mental events but a mutual give and take. Still, he agrees that children learn best not by observing but by doing and discovering the results of their actions.

The child was Piaget's main focus, and he certainly implied that, at least in terms of stage changes, development ends with *formal operations* in the early teens. In contrast, Erikson's (1950) eight psychosocial stages encompass the entire life span. Each presents a dilemma between conflicting alternatives, such as autonomy *vs.* doubt or identity *vs.* role confusion, and the choice made seminally influences personality development and choices. So here again one senses inevitable and universal stages, but the sequence is more flexible than Piaget's. One issue may dominate a certain period, as generativity *vs.* self-absorption—whether to live for others or oneself—dominates the late middle years, but predecessors continue to arise, so invariant sequence and irreversibility are less pronounced.

Kohlberg's (1984) stages of moral development reiterate the inflexibility of Piaget's. His main departure is that in this domain, unlike cognition, the most mature stage is eventually achieved by only a small minority. Methods for determining someone's stage also recall Piaget. Again a dilemma is posed, now of a moral kind, for example, should a man whose wife has cancer and who cannot afford needed drugs steal to obtain them, with the main interest being not the position taken but reasons for taking it. The mechanisms thought to underlie transitions are similar, too. Disequilibrium results from information at odds with the prevailing outlook and this input, if only moderately contradictory so it cannot be ignored or explained away, may induce a more sophisticated alternative.

4

Generalization:
Some Disclaimers

These more negative views begin with a nineteenth-century movement that influenced every art form in Europe and, by denying virtually everything for which science stands, anticipated many objections to come. *Romanticism* appeared first in literature, notably in the poetry of England, from Wordsworth, Keats, Coleridge and others. Beethoven's *Eroica* Symphony announced its arrival in music, to be furthered by Chopin, Schumann, and Wagner among others, while its adherents in visual art included Goya, Delacroix, and Turner. It explicitly rejected the Enlightenment of the eighteenth century, which had promoted reason and science as the roads to truth and was also a genuinely new artistic movement (Furst, 1969). For, unlike most others it did not simply reopen old wine in new bottles. Thus it is that nowadays it is assumed that creative achievements must involve originality, but prior to the romantic era this was by no means a given, and in other cultures it still is not (Abra, 1988c). Attitudes more than style or technique reveal a genuine romantic (Abercrombie, 1926), and the first of these relates directly to generalization. Truth comes from the individual, from personal experience rather than objective observation. This belief clearly demands abundant egos, so a typical romantic such as Wagner (R. Taylor, 1979) related to others with high-handed arrogance. More to the point, the romantic's credo was thou shalt not generalize, not about people at least.

A second supposition, the *imagination*, was a presumed psychological faculty that was thought to mediate between sensations and resulting experience, enriching them with images and symbols. Thus mind actively interprets rather than passively receives, or even withdraws entirely into an inner reality that is, well, imaginary. Furthermore, imagination was thought to distinguish the artist from ordinary folk, so generalizing from one to the other was inappropriate. Since the artist was different she must be alienated from society—misunderstood, unappreciated, starving in garrets, and no doubt dying young. In a word, artists had to suffer. Finally, imagination instilled unusual sensitivity, so the artist was probably emotionally disturbed as well. It is evident, then, how enormously romanticism has influenced modern stereotypes about artists, notably in perhaps its most important bequest (which it almost literally invented), the imagination itself. Its seminal role in creativity is now taken largely for granted but previously it had rarely been mentioned (Engell, 1981).

Romanticism's hallmark belief, in the uninhibited expression of emotion, follows from the emphasis on the individual. Feelings are more personal and therefore seem more trustworthy than reason or empirical evidence. Although emotional expression in art was hardly unprecedented, it was promoted as never before, supplanting the classical restraint of Mozart or Haydn that Enlightenment attitudes had encouraged. Now the mind gave way to the heart and philosophy to poetry (Abercrombie, 1926), which for Wordsworth (1952) could become no less than the spontaneous overflow of powerful feelings. Which brings us to generalization's deficiencies, because while humanistic psychologists (Maslow, 1962; Rogers, 1977) raised many of these, the themes are so reminiscent that humanists may be called neo-romantics (Abra, 1988a), to add to the several labels they already have (Goble, 1974).

METHODOLOGICAL PROBLEMS WITH GENERALIZATION

Idiographic Approaches

Allport (1969) almost single-handedly called aspects of scientific psychology into question when to do so bordered on heresy, and his promotion of in-depth studies of individuals was part of that campaign. The psychometric tradition has helped describe individual differences, but the reasons for and means to lessen them comprise one of psychology's largest gaps. Subjects exposed to purportedly identical situations will vary in their behaviors, and the proportion of this within-group variance accounted for by known variables is typically unimpressive. Statistical terminology refers to it as error, which suggests one reason why a scientific approach may not be helpful. Strictly speaking, this means only that this variance is due to as yet unidentified or uncontrolled variables, but it also implies that it is wrong. Subjects are not behaving as they should: all alike. In the best of all worlds, this irritating individuality would vanish. Putting it differently, it goes against a scientist's grain to even wonder about individual cases and therefore tacitly admit that general laws might not completely describe subjects. Therefore regarding a topic such as memory, apart from a few tentative beginnings (Gagne, 1967), the question is rarely asked.

Science may also fall short here if the basic premise that a unique individual can be fully described by his values on all relevant variables is faulty. Quite apart from the fact that all those values can probably never be determined, it too reflects Watson's questionable belief that all human properties can be measured. In addition, Allport (1961) pointed out, to determine an individual's specific values, we must compare him to someone else and express their values in relative terms. Thus as regards intelligence and assertiveness, we might determine that John has more of one but less of the other than Walter. But this does not reveal whether these attributes affect one another, whether they interact. Allport contends that only idiographic studies can reveal how John's intelligence relates to his dominance, conscience, and everything else in his personality, questions that baffle a science of universals. To state that the person is nothing more than the point of intersection of a number of variables is to assume that these are independent when they probably aren't. Scientists approach the individual as do actuaries, predicting a phenomenon in terms of a probability after examining its frequency in groups. To borrow Allport's example, nomothetic evidence predicts the proportion of males in Peter's age group who will die next year, and that is all an actuary cares about, but it is not what Peter cares about, which is whether he will. The recurring criticisms Allport faced (e.g., Leeper, 1963) for advocating idiographic approaches are not convincing. Far from seeking to replace the nomothetic with the idiographic, Allport saw both as necessary; attention should shift from particular to general and back again, because what we learn from any one person advances knowledge about people in general and vice versa. To argue (Marx, 1963a) that idiographic methods are incompatible with a scientific study of human beings is entirely beside the point. Science is not a sacred cow but a means to an end, and if it cannot do the job by itself, it should be supplemented.

Consider two approaches to studying great achievers. Simonton (1984, 1990) identifies large numbers from a specified group, such as painters, and teases out facts that apply to most. The most eminent produce not only better but also more work than do the lesser; they begin earlier, produce more per year, and continue longer. His *constant probability of success model* holds therefore that the likelihood of any one work being judged great is constant across creators, with the corollary that more works increase chances that some will have quality; similarly, according to statistical lore, an infinite number of monkeys pecking away at typewriters for infinite time would eventually, by chance, produce all the great books. Thus Picasso's greatness stems from his having brought forth no less than 20,000 works of art over his lifetime, but Simonton mentions specific examples such as this more to edify a general principle. The bottom line is whether for a given hypothesis the sample's positive instances outnumber the negatives.

On the other hand, Gruber's (1980, 1988) *evolving systems approach* is avowedly idiographic. Since any creative work is by definition unique, so too, he argues, must be the processes and the person that give rise to it, and these can only be revealed by studying the creator engaged in the process. The result is a theory of that individual, one that it may not be legitimate to generalize even to her other work, let alone to other persons. Gruber, showing Piaget's influence, views the process as an evolving one, so his main interest is to describe the development from an idea's first inklings to final result, to get inside a creator's head and relive those experiences. To study Darwin, therefore, Gruber (1974) pored over the notebooks and diaries that spanned the decades during which evolutionary theory was being refined. I share Gruber's doubts regarding generalizing about creativity. Every creator must find their own way to work. My skepticism about universal "right answers" fostered that eclectic approach wherein for a question such as creativity's motivation (Abra, 1997) the answers provided by diverse theories are each determined, and it is assumed that each hypothesis has validity for some of the people some of the time if not for one person at different times. However in the present context the key point is that while Simonton and Gruber prefer opposite methods, they do not compete with but complement one another in advancing understanding.

The Principle of Gradualness

Following from the commitment to induction, gradualness aims to answer small questions first while leaving larger ones until there is enough data. However, people tend to be impatient for solutions to psychological problems and wonder how long they must wait, while researchers stew over the factors that induce dogs to slobber. It is small comfort to someone whose child has a learning disability to be told that research will in the long run surely one day find a cure, because, as John Maynard Keynes (cited in Morison, 1963) aptly put it, in the long run we are all dead! Psychology's continuing failure to deliver promised payoffs has generated increasing dissatisfaction, and recent events suggest that the excuse of being a young science in need of time—and, of course, more money—will no longer suffice.

Once upon a time pure research stood master of all it surveyed, dominated course curricula, and persons of this persuasion dominated presidency of the APA, the ultimate indication of respect from the profession. But now the pendulum has swung toward applied areas such as clinical and counseling psychology. Their hold over such organizations as the APA is now unchallenged, as is their greater attraction for students, including most of the brightest. This reflects the perception not only that that this is where the jobs are but where the meaningful work is being done. It was because of pure researchers' new peripheral status that a group of them formed the American Psychological Society (APS) as an alternative to APA. Whether applied psychology can deliver the goods more effectively remains to be seen, but for the moment the lay public seems willing to give it the benefit of the doubt. Note that standard comment in the media that criminals or troubled children need treatment. Apparently faith remains intact that psychology can help. In sum, gradualness may over the long term be most sciences' best strategy, but psychology's special persona may render it impractical.

Subject Populations: Of Mice and Men and Overmen

That there are many similarities between animals and ourselves and that their study can be informative is undeniable. That said, laypeople are correct: generalizing has been far too cavalier and has ridden roughshod over important differences (although archetypal behaviorists here prefer unidirectionality, routinely generalizing from animals to ourselves while deploring the reverse, anthromorphism). The most notable difference is our more sophisticated communication system. While chimpanzees can acquire a language (Gardner & Gardner, 1969; Premack & Premack, 1972), our far more effective use of it has immense ramifications, notably in our ability to share knowledge, which is basic to progress. Perhaps a brilliant aardvark once conceived relativity, but her inability to enlighten her colleagues insured that the notion would die with her. Also, our greater propensities for abstract thought (Lorenz, 1966) and symbol usage (Langer, 1951) induce uniquely human activities such as religion. Then too, while we can never be sure, we alone seem aware that we are aware and sense our ultimate fate. Do rats know they will die? If so, do they wonder What is the meaning of life? and does this therefore affect them? They certainly haven't written any books about it, whereas these recurring questions haunt us. Allport reflected on our differences as follows:

A colleague . . . challenged me to name a single psychological problem not referable to rats for its solution. Considerably startled, I murmured something, I think, about the psychology of reading disability. But to my mind came flooding the historical problems of the aesthetic, humorous, religious, and cultural behavior of men. I thought how men build clavichords and cathedrals, how they write books, and how they laugh uproariously at Mickey Mouse; how they plan their lives five, ten, or twenty years ahead. . . . I thought of poetry and puns, of propaganda and revolution, of stock markets and suicide, and of man's despairing hope for peace. (1940, pp. 14–15)

Why then did psychologists persist at studying animals to the virtual exclusion of people? Perhaps because they realized that animals are different, so knowledge gained from them could seem less relevant and the problem of intimacy would be sidestepped, allowing the objectivity that they believed science demanded (no one is more determined to be scientific than the archetypal rat runner or pigeon shaper). But overgeneralizing has been rife even within the range of human subjects. For decades, college sophomores were routinely studied and findings uncritically extended to other populations on the assumption that this group would reveal all important principles. Happily this tendency has abated, due in large part to Piaget, who in other respects exemplified generalization. If children are not miniature adults but on different wave lengths, then one cannot reveal much about the other. Likewise, the growing population of the aged has caused increasing interest in gerontology, and it is generally accepted that the elderly themselves must be studied. Furthermore, one must be particularly cautious about generalizing about them, since the variance and diversity of many behaviors increase with age (Birren & Schroots, 1996). Finally, whereas the sexes were once treated indiscriminately, the rise in feminism has fostered doubts that the same principles apply to both, and has stimulated interest in their differences (Lips, 1988).

The issue of appropriate subject populations also arises as regards creativity. Philosophy's exemplary romantic, Nietzsche, personifying his own belief that "everything decisive arises as the result of opposition" (1952, p. 202), aimed above all to refute Darwin and the alleged continuity between ourselves and animals (W. Kaufmann, 1974). He had to admit that this held true for most of us, but not all. The best and brightest, the estimable triumvirate of philosophers, artists, and saints, constitute the Overmen (often translated misleadingly as "Supermen"), a special minority who are qualitatively superior to both animals and other people. It was Nietzsche's misfortune to have his beliefs bastardized by the Nazis as the Aryan myth, giving it racist and nationalistic aspects that he did not intend. For him, no group had a corner on excellence. Most romantics believed the elite's differences to be inherent, but in Nietzsche's view Overmanhood can be attained by anyone who strives to become the best person they can be. However few accomplish this because it requires self-overcoming, resisting our too prevalent propensities for sloth. Thus Overpersons demonstrate how to live as humans as opposed to existing as animals; sadly, as Martha Graham (1957) said in the film *A Dancer's World*, "Everyone is born a genius, but in most people it only lasts a few minutes!"

Those modern romantics, the humanists, have reiterated these themes. They too reacted against the overly rational and scientific approaches of twentieth century psychology's two dominant streams, behaviorism and psychoanalysis, and one of their objections concerned subjects. While behaviorists, arch-Darwinians all, were convinced that animals could reveal all, humanists noted our unique aspects, which demand that people too be studied. Psychoanalysis did venture this far, but by and large restricted itself to the disturbed. Hence Maslow (1954) observed that Freud's is a theory of sickness that treats health as if it were no more than an absence of the same, but it is more than that. He therefore scrutinized preeminently healthy, *self-actualized people* who, by reaching their maximum potential, or real self, personify humanity at its best. These *Overpersons* were set apart, he found, by greater accuracy in perceiving reality, acceptance of themselves and others, warts and all, and spontaneity, autonomy and independence, among other things. They also displayed less desirable features. Someone who strives for self-actualization puts their own needs first, which can foster propensities for boredom, impatience, and ruthlessness. Because "getting in touch with yourself" (one of pop psychology's dubious catchphrases) requires time alone, such people tend to be private if not reclusive, although the friendships they do develop are deep. But self-actualizers are also more creative, less in forging great achievements than in their approach to living. If each person's essence is by definition unique, those who fulfill its potential must have lives that are unique as well. Creativity in this sense, then, lies within everyone's reach.

Humanists are not alone in this belief, even in regards to great achievement. Authorities so diverse as Guilford (1967), Skinner (1971, 1974), and D. Campbell (1960) have professed it, and Weisberg (1986, 1993) has been especially outspoken. Any differences between a Beethoven or George Eliot and the rest of us are only quantitative. Therefore, to answer such deserving questions as the environments that best foster greatness, any subject population can be studied, including, for Skinner, subhuman ones. Others, however, including Freud (1947, 1961) Jung (1966), and Gruber adopt a more elitist stance, and I too firmly reside in this camp. My reasons have been presented elsewhere (Abra, 1988b, 1995), but essentially I think it incontestable that the great creators are a breed apart, endowed with a mysterious gift (curse?) called talent or genius. It follows that to understand genius, one must study those who possess it, as Gruber and his fellows have done (Wallace & Gruber, 1989). Information from species *collegium sophomorus* may be more convenient to obtain but irrelevant if not misleading about the genuine article.

For example, studies of general populations indicate that "hothouse" environments that maximize positive experiences while minimizing failure and frustration are more likely to induce creativity of a kind (Maddi, 1975). In Amabile's (1983) ingenious studies, subjects actually produced products such as poems or collages whose "creativity" was then judged by several experts. Reliably, it is augmented by *intrinsic motivation*, creating for sheer enjoyment of the activity itself, as opposed to *extrinsic motivation*, creating as a means to another end, be it financial reward or impressing experts. And yet, many great achievers, for instance, Beethoven, Eugene O'Neill and Virginia Woolf, endured domestic environments that were anything but positive (Ochse, 1990); such traumas as parental bereavement and severely dysfunctional families were rife. The suspicion that adverse rather than hothouse circumstances may be more fertile for such persons extends to Amabile's findings. They were by and large obtained from children and college students, but for professional creators extrinsic motivation is a fact of life. They must work at least in part for material compensation if they enjoy eating now and then, and they will certainly be judged, sometimes harshly, by critics, editors, and the public. Those who cannot function under these conditions do not last long. In short, in the absence of data to the contrary, one must wonder whether Amabile's results can be replicated with populations of professional creators.

The Laboratory: A World Apart

Most scientists ultimately want to understand phenomena that occur in everyday circumstances, but retreat to the lab to study them because of the greater rigor, precision of measurement, and control it offers. By the same token, it is unavoidably artificial, which means that investigators must walk a tightrope to gain the advantages without losing relevance, because phenomena that arise only under contrived conditions are of little interest. So one mark of experimenters' ingenuity is their ability to simulate natural situations. Unfortunately, others lack Skinner's confidence that lab–real-life differences are minor and wholesale generalization legitimate, for example, ethologists (Lorenz, 1962; Tinbergen, 1951) insist that to understand animal behavior it must be studied in its natural setting. Several lines of evidence have been criticized as lacking *ecological validity*, relevance to real-life circumstances, and one involves a key Skinner principle, reinforcement.

In the last analysis, subjects themselves decide whether an event qualifies as a reinforcer. By definition it must increase a behavior on which it is contingent, so they must value it sufficiently to either approach or avoid it. Given the control possible under contrived conditions, the effectiveness of certain events can be virtually guaranteed, for example, animals denied food will do whatever is necessary, be it press a lever or execute a triple lutz, to obtain it. However, in natural circumstances, as the saying "One man's meat is another man's poison" verifies, subjects routinely disagree about what they value. *Masochists* provide the definitive example: they treat as positive and act to obtain psychological or physical events that others view as negative. In turn this raises problems for would-be modifiers of behavior such as educators, therapists, and harried parents. They cannot predict in advance but must discover through trial-and-error the reinforcers that work for each subject.

The criticism of ecological validity can also be leveled against interference effects in memory. Their reliability in lab situations led to a theory that explained them (Postman, 1961b) and predictions about some effects in everyday forgetting. One property of a verbal unit is *meaningfulness* (M), which increases with, among other things, the number of associates it reminds one of (Underwood & Schulz, 1960); thus TABLE has more M than GUP. It seemed evident, then, that associations acquired in the lab between high M units, for example TABLE–CHURCH should face more interference from these language habits and so show more rapid forgetting (assuming that low and high M associations were learned equally well; Underwood, 1964a). However, several studies (e.g., Postman, 1961a) found no relationship whatever between M and forgetting, which led Underwood and Ekstrand (1966) to note that a language association has two distinctive properties. It is learned to a very high degree and, unlike most laboratory learning, under *distributed practice* that has a lengthy time span between successive presentations. They therefore presented a standard A-B, A-C situation wherein the first associations were learned under these conditions. In contrast to the usual results, such associations did not affect and were not affected by the second ones; retention tests showed no interference either way. The implication? Laws that govern forgetting laboratory associations do not apply to the language variety.

In a similar vein, Slamecka (1966) showed that retention of a common language association such as CHAIR to TABLE is undiminished when the stimulus member is used as a stimulus in a paired-associate list with a previously unrelated word such as SURPLUS associated to it. Nor did this reflect a *ceiling effect*, wherein the absolute level of retention is so high as to mask inferiority to controls given no laboratory learning; scores were well below maximum, and response time, presumably a more sensitive measure, showed no differences either. One explanation (not Slamecka's) is that associations acquired outside the lab are immune to interference. Linton's (1975) study of *autobiographical memories*, for events in life such as one's first kiss suggests the same conclusion. Each day for six years she recorded two events she experienced and once a month tested her retention, like Ebbinghaus, serving as her own subject and showing a commitment to science far beyond the call of duty. What is noteworthy is that whereas Ebbinghaus' memory for nonsense syllables declined to about 25 percent within days, Linton's for her experiences bordered on 100% after a year and above 70 percent after six years. Allowing for differences in methods of measurement, despite comparable potential for interference, everyday as compared to laboratory memories are far better retained, as are those of a less personal kind, such as for high school classmates (Bahrich, Bahrich & Wittlinger, 1975) and odors (Schab, 1991).

Underwood and Postman were deeply involved in developing interference theory and had considerable effort and presumably ego invested in it, yet they collected much of the data that led to its demise. Every scientist pays lip service to data's priority over theory, but in practice most cling fervently to their beliefs and are at pains to protect them rather than provide contradictory evidence. Thus Underwood and Postman exemplify another all too rare scientific value, *integrity*, a genuine commitment to empirical priorities even when the implications are unpalatable. Functionalism's much ridiculed atheoretical outlook had its virtues!

That said, Neisser (1982, Neisser, & Winograd, 1988) has chastised memory studies' lack of ecological validity on the grounds that situations such as paired-associate learning have little relevance to everyday ones. He advocates focusing instead on examples of the latter, such as *flashbulb memories* for dramatic experiences, such as where you were when you heard about Kennedy's assassination. Brown and Kulik (1982) questioned people about such events and found, not surprisingly, that whether memories gained this status depended on their importance to the person. Thus the Kennedy assassination qualified for people everywhere, whereas Paul Henderson's winning goal in the historic 1972 hockey series with the Soviets certainly would qualify for older Canadians but probably not for readers south of the border. Gruneberg, Morris and Sykes (1978), Neisser (1982) and Neisser and Winograd (1988) provide surveys of many other studies of this kind, but I want to interject a cautionary note: As inherently interesting as they are, too many have been content to demonstrate a phenomenon without attempting to explain it or offer insight into influential variables. Worthwhile studies raise as many questions as they answer. Fortunately, not all such studies deserve this criticism. Brown and McNeill (1966) explored the all too common *tip-of-the-tongue-phenomenon* where one knows they know something but cannot for the moment recall it. When subjects given dictionary definitions and asked for the corresponding word reported being in a tip-of-the-tongue state, they could often recall such properties as its first letter and number of syllables. A substantial literature has since accumulated regarding this fascinating phenomenon (A. Brown, 1991).

In a similar vein, the so-called *crisis in social psychology* (Jones, 1985) was initiated when some heretofore inviolate presumptions came into question, and one of these was the relevance of laboratory findings. For example, Wortman,

Abbey, Holland, Silver, and Janoff-Bulman (1980) set out to test several competing explanations, including learned helplessness, for reactions to uncontrollable negative life experiences such as being told one has cancer or having a rock drummer move in next door. A number of attempted experimental simulations foundered due to problems such as demand characteristics and the necessity that outcomes be relatively minor and only last for short durations. As a result the investigators had to turn to more informative naturalistic situations.

Finally, purported studies of collaboration in creative work face the same criticism (Abra, 1994). Although we tend to think of creative work as being solitary, as in poetry or painting, much of it, notably in the sciences and in filmmaking, involves teamwork, which brings a host of interpersonal factors into play. Many studies have claimed to investigate such situations, including that famed, pioneering attempt to improve creativity, Osborn's (1963) *brainstorming*. However, in most cases virtual strangers were brought together to solve a few problems for a few hours, so findings probably have little relevance to long-term collaborations such as between Gilbert and Sullivan or Watson and Crick, which may involve considerable stress, personal animosity, professional reputations, and money. In all likelihood, therefore, it's a different ball game, and the few comments on brainstorming I have come across (Amabile, 1983; Taylor, Berry & Block, 1957, summarized in Stein & Heinze, 1960, pp. 407–408) give the impression that it is ineffective in real-life contexts.

LIMITATIONS ON PURPORTED LAWS OF BEHAVIOR

Skinner's Principles and Applications

We will now survey specific criticisms of each attempt at generalization presented in Chapter 3, beginning with this one. As Mazur (1994) observed, early learning research assumed general laws that did not depend on the biological makeup of the species studied, but various *constraints on learning* have called this into question. As Mazur's extensive review of this literature shows, biology establishes a range of possibilities within which learning can operate, so its efficiency depends in good part on whether the potential is built in for the required response. Thus rats effectively learn an avoidance response that conforms to a *species-specific defense reaction* such as jumping or running that they reflexively emit in the presence of danger, but training them to bar press in such situations is difficult because a tendency to do this when a predator looms would be wildly maladaptive (Bolles, 1970). Nor is this because bar pressing is more difficult per se, since it is readily learned for positive reinforcers. Breland and Breland's (1961) well-known work exemplifies the constraint phenomenon. As card-carrying Skinnerians, they set out to train animals for commercial purposes, in one instance, a pig to deposit coins in a piggy bank for a food reward. The pig at first happily obliged, but once it had associated coins with food it treated them as food, by sniffing and rooting. The upshot? Despite efficient application of reinforcement principles, the desired response became less frequent as naturally dominant tendencies took over.

Comparable difficulties arise in classical conditioning. Saccharin-flavored water paired with nausea-producing injections later elicits aversion even when the interval between the conditioned and unconditioned stimulus exceeds one hour (Garcia, Ervin & Koelling, 1966). Thus another well-worn principle, that associations require contiguity, apparently does not hold if they conform with inborn tendencies, and an ability to connect illness with what one has eaten, even some time before, would be adaptive. In the same vein, Ohman, Dimberg and Ost (1985) claim that phobias to potentially harmful conditioned stimuli such as snakes and spiders are acquired more efficiently and are more difficult to extinguish than phobias to innocuous ones such as flowers (although Mazur finds the evidence on this point to be mixed). The personality types that Eysenck (1967) emphasized, the introvert and extravert, presumably reflect innate tendencies, and, if introverts are as he claims more affected by experiences, then once again what is learned depends on biological propensities. Still, this is not necessarily devastating for attempts to generalize about learning. Although Eysenck presents evidence in abundance to support his notions, studies by more detached investigators are few (C. Costello, personal communication, 1996), which raises the specter of experimenter bias, and Buss (1966), while providing no references, hints at some controversy about the actual support. Mazur cites recent indications that biological constraints actually support such generalizations, so the wheel may have come full circle. Certainly Skinner himself, far from denying nature's importance, was at pains to stress it, although the impression remains that when pushed to the wall he would avow that, under ideal conditions, anyone can learn any response of which they are physically capable; constraints render this extreme position untenable.

As for his recommendations vis-à-vis education, one objection will suffice. The ultimate question is whether they produce better educated people, but what exactly does this mean? Shaping and such are most efficiently used when target behaviors are clearly defined and when their achievement is reliably apparent, so agents know when to deliver reinforcers, making Skinner's system difficult to gainsay when precise behaviors like spelling or grammar are the goal. However, the higher one ascends the educational ladder the more vague the criteria become. Surely the truly educated have acquired not only precise informational knowledge of the sort emphasized by TV quiz shows but abilities to learn, to ask meaningful questions, produce ingenious solutions and, above all perhaps, the distinctive attitude that learning is inherently worthwhile, so it becomes a lifetime hobby that does not end with school. I remain to be convinced that Skinner's system can instill commodities such as this.

Concerning attitude change, Skinnerian-influenced techniques seem to work better in theory than practice. Beamon, Cole, Preston, Klentz and Stebloy's (1983) meta-analysis of many studies concluded that the foot-in-the-door technique had little or no effect on compliance. Similarly, brainwashing produced few genuine converts (Lambert & Lambert, 1973), and most of them were poorly committed to North American values to begin with. Likewise, while role-playing has sometimes had an impact, underlying beliefs at odds with a role are often left unaffected. If this were not so, every actor who received raves for his Hamlet would contemplate suicide and killing his uncles! The brainwashing studies verify this point. Prisoners emitted seemingly appropriate behaviors such as relentlessly chanting Maoist slogans, but in such a way as to subvert the entire enterprise, for example, a "study group" member from Brooklyn read slogans in a southern accent, the humor of which would escape his Chinese supervisor but not his compatriots. Behavioristically speaking, producing behaviors and having them reinforced should result in attitude changes; that it did not calls into question the underlying premise that the same contingencies govern both. Unless underlying attitudes change, the impact on overt behavior may be short-lived.

A well-known study by Festinger (1957) confirms this suspicion. Subjects, after participating in an extremely boring experiment, were asked to tell the next subject that it had been fun, a lie that earned either a one or twenty dollar reward. When attitudes toward the experiment were later assessed, they had changed more markedly toward the favorable after the smaller reward. The results appear to discomfort a behavioristic account—behavior strength usually increases with reinforcer magnitude (Kimble, 1961)—but vindicate Festinger's theory of *cognitive dissonance*. This hypothesized state of tension results from a perceived inconsistency between one's attitudes and behaviors, that is, when we believe we should do one thing but do another, as when smokers view the noxious weed as evil but still indulge. This state is presumably unpleasant, so one is driven to reduce it by changing either attitude or behavior to bring them into line. Thus one way to change an attitude should be to induce actions contrary to it. But there is a hedge. Such change requires that dissonance develop, and it won't if people can blame their inconsistent acts on extenuating factors. Thus those offered twenty dollars, at the time a substantial reward, could retort: "Who wouldn't lie for twenty dollars?," but more poorly compensated colleagues had less justification and therefore more dissonance, so their attitudes had to give. For Skinner, beliefs, as by-products of reinforcement, should always change. Some later studies confirmed learning, others dissonance expectations (Goldstein, 1980), but indiscriminately applying Skinner's principles to any and all situations is certainly called into question.

Regarding the final application of those principles, although some behavior therapists are as confident as the most doctrinaire Freudian that they can alleviate every enduring problem of existence, and although such therapies are demonstrably superior to others for many conditions (Rachman & Wilson, 1980), limitations have come to light. First, token economies are now less common in institutions (Glynn, 1990) because they are slow to take effect, and therefore often impractical when lengths of stay are declining, and require staff trained to apply them effectively and willing to constantly monitor inmate behavior. As a further restriction, since Skinner's techniques work best with clearly defined target behaviors, their effectiveness with phobias is to be expected, but problems such as free-floating anxiety about nothing in particular have proven less malleable. Yet Frankl (1984), May (1969), and Fromm (1960) all hold that the most pervasive afflictions nowadays are of this kind. People feel alienated from an increasingly impersonal society, undervalued as individuals, and lack that cornerstone of health, a sense that life has meaning. Not only is behavior therapy ill equipped to deal with such problems, according to Woolfolk and Richardson (1984) it may actually exacerbate them because it uses a fixed technology that treats one patient like every other and exemplifies modern priorities: technology, intellect and cold rationality over emotion, and a refusal to provide guidance about what one should do. Giving troubled people tokens whenever they assert that life has meaning may modify their verbal utterances while leaving their underlying distress intact.

In any therapy, what matters most is effectiveness, and with behaviorist methods, it is not always impressive. Token economies do temporarily improve many behaviors, but backsliding to former tendencies often occurs after release (Rachman & Wilson, 1980), and many clearly defined behaviors that would seem ideal targets, for example smoking, alcohol dependence, and obesity, have proved intractable for this reason. Likewise, notwithstanding Feldman's (1966) promising data, Adams & Sturgis' (1977) survey of behavior therapies for homosexuality, including those of an avoidance kind, was less optimistic. Follow-ups of smokers show that long-term abstinence rates are no better than for other therapies (Leventhal & Cleary, 1980), so that old-fashioned will power may be as effective as therapy, since a desire to quit is one effective predictor of success. While this will not surprise the layperson, strict Skinnerians neither include such mentalistic concepts in their lexicon nor recognize them as influencing reinforcer effectiveness.

Difficulties with Disturbance Classification

These have become apparent in the sweeping changes in DSM's recent versions. However, advocates remain hopeful that a useful system can develop from fine-tuning current ones, and the reduction of tenuous reliability of diagnosis (Costello, 1970) justifies this optimism. In earlier versions the defining symptoms of "diseases" were so vague and overlapping that one physician's schizophrenic might be another's manic-depressive and a third's nominee for the hospital board of governors! Schizophrenia especially became a grab-bag category that allowed diverse cases to be given a label of some kind. DSM III unquestionably achieved improvement on this situation, although it remains debatable whether categories are yet completely distinct (Dobson & Pusch, 1994). A major advantage of diagnosis, to suggest specific therapies, is also now more often realized. Formerly, when few even minimally effective ones were available, physicians tended to apply them to any and all cases or they might differ in those prescribed for cases similarly diagnosed (Costello, 1970). But recent discoveries, notably of helpful pharmaceutical agents, have improved the situation, at least for some categories. Lithium is now routinely prescribed for bipolar mood disorder (formerly manic-depression), prozac for depression, and the phenothiazines for schizophrenia. Also, electroconvulsive shock, once administered indiscriminately (Costello, Belton, Abra, & Dunn, 1970), is now used in less traumatic forms and only for severe depression (G. Smith, personal communication, 1985).

Validity was another concern. If a "disease" labeled schizophrenia does not represent an actual physical condition or names not one condition but several, then researchers seeking causes and therapies might be led down unproductive garden paths. Still, several medical conditions—cancer comes to mind—may also subsume several conditions that need different treatment. Insisting that categories emerge from and answer to the data lessens dangers of their being imaginary. Finally, there has been a laudable decrease in needless jargon. Another of medicine's dubious bequests was its penchant in naming categories to never use one syllable if five were possible. Why is this profession so fond of pretentious bombast? Is it because it strengthens one's credentials as an expert not to be trifled with—those whom we cannot understand, we tend to believe, must know what they're talking about? Because of that pervasive belief that naming something, especially jargonistically, also explains it? A third hypothesis, that since impressive sounding but meaningless verbiage is a mark of schizophrenia, it must be rampant in medical circles, does not bear thinking about! Whatever the purpose, sonorous psychobabble such as "hebephrenic schizophrenic with paranoid and catatonic inclinations," also seeks it. Attempts to explain disturbances display the same tendency. Kris, a psychoanalytically oriented creativity theorist, states, "Aggressive thoughts . . . [have] disturbed the pathognomic activity and turned it into parapthognomy. The topography and dynamics of the process are easily discernible; it is a matter of pathognomic parapraxis" (1952, p. 218). The process is only easily discernible to the rare bird who can decode the message.

So there has been progress, which may explain why, apart from the odd heretic such as Szasz (1966), few have questioned classification in principle. Yet problems remain; the exercise has provided nothing like the benefits realized by medicine, let alone chemistry or biology, wherein the Mendeleev and Linnaeus systems have needed elaboration but not fundamental revision. Skeptics may well ask whether this is the direction to go since some new problems arise from the very business of classification and others have actually worsened. First, unless precise physical criteria define conditions to make them diseases in the medical sense, cultural norms decide whether they are deviant and hence legitimate targets for therapy. Few deny that cancer deserves treatment but whether homosexuality does is a matter of changing opinion, so DSM IV, unlike its predecessors, excludes it as a disease category.

On the other hand, new categories have been added, such as nicotine dependence, which reflects the growing distaste for smoking. Unfortunately, this introduces the danger of instilling the impression that psychological problems are increasing, which provides the media with another item with which to panic the populace, when it may only be that more people are being classified as disturbed. Smokers have been around for years! The usual recourse to counteract such subjectivity is to rely on *statistical definitions*, that is, a disturbance is that which is rare. Such definitions can potentially be verified by frequencies and are also practical, since most of us view strange behavior as also undesirable, but they also suggest that whether homosexuality warrants treatment depends on whether it occurs in San Francisco or Wichita, Kansas, or in a law firm or in certain branches of the arts. Adding more categories, while improving diagnosis, may also sacrifice some of classification's benefits. Any system must choose its poison. A system that offers too few categories will ride roughshod over important differences, whereas with too many, the array of possible descriptions becomes too numerous and the cases grouped together too few to be helpful. Five axes that each offer a number of alternatives poses the second danger.

The most basic question of all concerns the assumption on which any system rests, that there is a discrete separation between categories. Its legitimacy as regards medical conditions is beyond dispute—one either has measles or one hasn't—but conditions such as depression or paranoia only exaggerate tendencies found in everyone. Who does not have their down days or worry about what others think of them? Psychologically normal people exist only in textbooks and would be bores to boot, since it is their quirks as much as anything that make people so fascinating. Unfortunately, the point at which these quirks are severe enough to warrant treatment becomes a matter of degree rather than kind and therefore more arbitrary. Since Eysenck (1952) has criticized classification on these very grounds, let us revisit his system in this context. It posits several independent dimensions, such as introversion-extroversion, and describes a person not by categorical labels but their placement along each dimension, with the extremes at each end representing different forms of dysfunction. Thus, as it did for the Greeks, virtue lies in moderation, not excess.

Notwithstanding changes in nomenclature and approach, however, the newest DSMs still express the medical model in that their categories are in practice thought of as diseases (K. Dobson, personal communication, November, 1995). Although psychology had more input into their design than on their predecessors, they were still produced by the psychiatric profession, which like other branches of medicine tends to emphasize diagnosis and prescribing treatment over the factors that led to the complaint. Whereas for a psychologist, social and environmental considerations are of equal concern as possible underlying causes that must also be dealt with, so classification may be for him irrelevant. Thus some in Canada, if the health-care system does not demand a diagnosis before providing funding, forego the exercise entirely (B. McElheran, personal communication, November, 1995). What lurks here is that eternal struggle, in clinical settings, between psychiatry and psychology. The reverence in which doctors have historically been held once insured the psychiatrist's preeminence and allowed her to impose her outlooks unencumbered, and she still holds certain exclusive rights, such as, prescribing drugs. However, this supremacy no longer goes unchallenged, which in my admittedly biased opinion is all to the good. A brief exposure to medical training before migrating to greener pastures implanted a suspicion in me that psychology's infinitely broader horizons provide a far better background for understanding the complexities of behavior, including the disturbed kind. Be that as it may, let us conclude on a general note. To dismiss the classification strategy for psychology out of hand would be premature, since it has rarely been tried, but the difficulties faced by the main attempt so far are not encouraging.

MORAL ISSUES

The Darwinian Doublethink

Concerns about the treatment of subjects in experiments reveal a paradoxical attitude in the behaviorist. On the one hand, he avowed that lower animals are our brethren and, on the other, that they could be exposed to treatments unacceptable for ourselves. I shall not try to resolve this Orwellian outlook, but simply point out that antivivisection, far from being worthy only of proverbial little old people in tennis shoes, is from a strict Darwinian point of view quite reasonable. Today's researchers seem to agree. While accepting that animals offer the only means to carry out some investigations, they stress minimizing their suffering and only countenance it when it serves deserving goals.

Self-Fulfilling Prophecies

A psychology we give away that stresses similarities among people and downplays their differences could have catastrophic results, for that growing audience could come to believe that uniqueness is imaginary. Arthur Miller (Evans, 1969) expressed this concern, and attention should be paid to someone perceptive enough about our condition to have written *Death of a Salesman*. He contends that we must feel important or life seems pointless. In fact, he suggests that Willy Loman, the salesman, suffered for precisely this reason. As long as Willy believed that he was well liked and needed by his firm he could manage, but discovering that his supposed significance was merely a manifestation of economic function destroyed him. To conceive of ourselves as individuals, Miller suggests, is an act of will that a self-concept imposed by others that assumes otherwise can wipe out. We must hold on to this belief not because it can be proven but because it is needed.

Which may explain laypeople's defensiveness toward psychologists. Their suspicions that we have them slotted into neat categories are not groundless, given our fondness for generalization and classification. Their distaste for being *rubricized* (Maslow, 1962) manifests a pride that goeth not before a fall but is necessary if they are to reach their individual potentials. Why so? One reason is the danger of *self-fulfilling prophecies*, that people act in ways that fulfill beliefs they hold about themselves and by doing so affirm their accuracy. One potent source of such prophecies is labels that others impose on us, because by adopting them into our self-concepts and then trying to live up to them to avoid guilt, we legitimize them. Sartre (1981) maintains that this happened to him when his precociousness caused adults to label him a child prodigy: "[Grandfather's] commandments were sewn into my skin; if I go a day without writing, the scar burns me. . . . [Writers] are all galley slaves, we're all tattooed" (p. 164). Similarly Orson Welles (Leaming, 1986), author of arguably the greatest film ever made, *Citizen Kane,* claimed that hearing "prodigy" whispered in his ear from infancy fueled that obsessive labor so typical of great achievers. Rosenthal and Jacobsen (1968) demonstrated the power of such mechanisms. At term's commencement, teachers were informed of some children, actually randomly selected, who should, based on test results, show unusual improvement. All test scores improved but theirs far more, probably because of the teachers' expectations.

To compound the problem, since human acts can be variously interpreted depending on one's biases, once others impose a label on someone, they tend to see the latter's every act as fitting it, thereby strengthening their belief in its accuracy. Thus the labelee is trapped in a vicious circle. Rosenhan (1973) had "normal" subjects gain voluntary admission to a hospital on grounds that they were hearing voices, which presumably caused staff to label them schizophrenic or some such. They thereafter adopted their everyday demeanor yet, records verified, the circle took effect. Several who dutifully recorded their experiences were described as indulging in writing behavior, as if only the demented would do this. Ironically, although staff never caught on to the interlopers, legitimate patients soon did. Sometimes it is only the insane who seem sane!

In deploring the entire practice of psychiatric classification, Szasz (1966) points out that people, unlike animals or things, are affected by being categorized. Such exercises, he argues, reflect a need to gain control, in this case over nature, so in the psychological context they convert people into slavish "things" with the psychiatrist as master who limits their possibilities. The effect is more debilitating than in medical diagnosis because psychiatric categories, by defining identity, may initiate self-fulfilling prophecies, causing the diagnosis to also become the prognosis. Szasz would therefore categorize not patients but psychiatrists as offering certain services (psychoanalytic, behavioral and so on), and allow patients to choose those they think will best meet their needs and set therapy goals themselves. These are provocative arguments, but there are valid objections. To allow patients to choose is all well and good if they are capable of rational decision making, but can this be safely assumed for the seriously disturbed? Should someone who wants to blow up airplanes be allowed to set his own therapeutic goals so he can do it more effectively? Furthermore, Eisenberg (1966) notes, Szasz seems to advocate a right to be sick, whereas psychiatric diagnosis and therapy seeks not control of but increased psychological freedom for the patient. Although diagnostic labels can have undesirable effects, few psychologists cynically use them to gain power.

Moral Problems with Disturbance Definitions and Therapies

How can we identify behaviors that are sufficiently unacceptable to deserve treatment? One criterion has been intimated: a belief by patients or their loved ones that they hinder everyday functioning, so therapists simply offer a service, and this (supposedly) morally neutral attitude most behavior therapists adopt (Woolfolk & Richardson, 1984). But it assumes, at times unrealistically, the rationality of those involved. Unfortunately, clear reductionistic criteria are available for only a few psychopathologies, and refusing to take a stand on an ethical dilemma is itself a moral stand, so behavior therapists when pushed must fall back on statistical definitions, defining a behavior as disturbed if it is rare. In addition to the difficulties raised earlier, these definitions also imply majority rule, yet some unusual behaviors, such as creative ones, far from warranting elimination, work for the common good. Furthermore, such definitions could sanction therapy that forces conformity to the virtuous mean, to improve *adjustment*. Maslow rightly objected to this concept of health because it assumes that prevailing cultural practices are desirable. Consider two concentration camp guards, one suffering from severe depression, the other happy in his work. Which one is in need of therapy?

Any therapy system involves ethical decisions about what is best for the patient, but to question most medical treatments such as eliminating tumors on such grounds would be nitpickingly pedantic. Decisions about behaviors, on the other hand, are less clear-cut because morality is here an arbitrary business. An objection that I reject deplores any technique, such as aversive conditioning, that uses unpleasant stimuli, especially when administered without subject consent. Eysenck (1965) answers that many acceptable medical therapies such as surgery are also discomforting; as always the first concern should be effectiveness. As well, do we not impose discomforts, such as imprisonment, without consent against those who transgress our norms? Surely therapies using, say, nauseating drugs can be countenanced if they discourage sexual deviants from attacking the defenseless. The concern here is the possible use of therapies for outright immoral purposes. In any society, conflicts arise between the rights of an individual to pursue his destinies untrammeled and the duty of society to protect the collective good. Which should have priority? Overemphasizing the former can foster the jungle "look out for number one" morality that Ayn Rand's sophomoric novels promote; in a modern urbanized society we all must be our brother's keepers. Yet excessive social control can be equally repugnant, especially if, as in Orwell's *1984* it serves only collective interests.

Several modern novels express concerns about psychology's possibilities in this regard. In Huxley's *Brave New World*, genetic engineering gives newborns the characteristics they need to fulfill their predesignated role in society and Pavlovian conditioning teaches them to relish it. No unhappy round pegs in square holes. The best of all possible worlds? Not to most eyes. In Burgess's *A Clockwork Orange*, the protagonist Alex's sadistic propensities are eliminated by associating them with a nausea-inducing drug, but this also curtails positive qualities, such as his love for Beethoven and ability to freely choose evil or good, and, Burgess suggests, those who cannot so choose are no longer human. Because the retarded Charlie Gordon of Keyes's *Flowers for Algernon* wants to "get smart," he volunteers for a new operation that rapidly renders him a genius. Was it justified? Is intelligence always desirable? The new Charlie remains a misfit, albeit a superior one, but now beset by anxieties (for he realizes his status) and resented by others, whereas, the old innocent Charlie was in a real sense "happy." Like Adam, he ate of the fruit of enlightenment with decidedly mixed results. Several other novels have expressed similar concerns, notably Kesey's *One Flew Over the Cuckoo's Nest* and Orwell's *1984*, which suggests that this problem has worried many writers, and May (1969) asserts that artists are the "antennae of the race" whose higher consciousness often senses conflicts that will later concern others. Should we alleviate retardation? Modify antisocial behavior? Affirmative answers seem obvious, until we encounter a Charlie or Alex. Presumably Keyes and the others did not wish to question the need for control in principle but to point out the complexities involved.

It might be objected that these are works of fiction and certainly until recently the very ineffectiveness of available therapies such as psychoanalysis protected psychology from such ethical quandaries. However, behavior therapies do work. 1984 has arrived and not only on the calendar: there is a drug, *anectine,* that reportedly simulates the experience of dying; recipients cannot breathe and their limbs are paralyzed, yet they remain conscious. The experiences are short-lived, but so horrifying that victims will do anything to avoid a repetition. In some American prisons, anectine was administered to troublemakers in contiguity with shouted commands such as "Do what you're told!"; thus classical conditioning was used to make them models of obedience (Sage, 1974). The ability to control behavior can be a boon to alleviate suffering and promote welfare, but also a threat to cherished rights. How should it be used? Which behaviors should be encouraged? Who should decide? No easy answers to these difficult issues are offered here, but the first step is for psychologists to face them and some still refuse to do so. Scientists who insist on remaining neutral about the moral implications of knowledge they provide became anachronisms when Hiroshima was destroyed.

LIMITATIONS ON INTERFERENCE

We have seen that the basic laws of interference, so robust for laboratory associations, may not extend to the everyday kind. To make matters worse, even in the lab they may hold only for verbal ones. Within these confines, they are manifest with diverse tasks and materials (McGeogh & Irion, 1952), including sentences (Slamecka, 1960) and simple facts such as "Julius Caesar was left-handed" (Peterson & Potts, 1982). Furthermore, despite assertions (J. Brown, 1958) that decay diminishes short-term memory as measured in seconds, interference operates here as well (Keppel & Underwood, 1962). But do these laws hold good elsewhere? Recent opinions range from Houston's (1991), that they encompass a variety of situations verbal and otherwise, to Ashcroft's (1994) suspicion that they may apply only to paired-associate tasks involving nonsense syllables. The second position is untenable, but the former, I will now argue, may be so as well. This is not the place for an exhaustive survey of interference in every conceivable situation, and studies using the classic paradigms and concepts have become virtually extinct, forcing one to rely on methodologically unsatisfactory predecessors, so I rely instead on a few suggestive studies as well as informal impressions to buttress this claim.

To begin on a positive note, however, there are indications of broader applicability. Dess and Overmier (1989) demonstrated proactive interference in classical conditioning of dogs (albeit with learning a subsequent task, not with later retention), and McGeogh and Irion (1952) report that in psychophysical situations, inserting an extraneous stimulus between two to be compared along either acoustic or weight dimensions decreases accuracy; moreover, interference increases, as it should, when that stimulus lies on the same modality. As well, although appropriate controls are lacking, the tendency for successive drawings of visual stimuli to become more symmetrical and recognizable may be due to forms experienced in life. Finally, interference is also manifest in motor learning tasks such as pursuit rotor, although this finding too is ambiguous. Retention is high even after very long intervals—you never forget how to ride a bicycle—which suggests little interference from everyday learning. In any event, McGeogh and Irion echo Houston regarding interference's ubiquity. Yet other evidence hints at a less happy state of affairs.

As was mentioned, memories involving other modalities have received little attention and those few studies of changes in interference with similarity or time—for example, see Schab, 1991 regarding odors—are only suggestive, since they usually involve short-term memory. However a few studies of *mnemonic devices* are relevant. Some of these demonstrably effective strategies for improving memory convert experiences into visual images and/or associate them with familiar scenes visualized in the minds eye, as in the method of loci, a favorite tactic since ancient times (Yates, 1966). Bugelski's (1968) subjects first learned a *peg-word system* wherein numbers one to ten each were associated with a concrete and therefore easily imaged noun that rhymed with it, as in "one is a bun, two is a shoe, three is a tree," and so on. They were then given a list of ten words and instructed to form an image for each with the corresponding noun in the jingle, so the first word would be imaged with a bun, and so on. Recall was markedly superior to a control not using the jingle, but what is noteworthy is that subjects used it effectively for six lists. Yet, if one image was indeed used repeatedly, then this should have been a prototypic A-B, A-C situation. A tenacious apologist for interference might blame the lack of proactive inhibition on the short retention interval, but a final test of all six lists gives little hint of retroactive inhibition either. For some reason, having visual rather than verbal stimuli made all the difference. In a similar vein, Charness (1976) had chess players visualize a display of pieces which, after thirty seconds, they tried to reproduce. Various interpolated tasks caused little interference and similarity had no effect (although it did influence response latencies). Paivio (1969, 1971) gives a theoretical frame to these findings by distinguishing two memory systems, separate but not entirely independent, that store material in verbal and visual form, respectively. That which can be stored in both should be better remembered—hence, a superiority of concrete over abstract nouns—but it is the innuendo that the systems may obey different laws that is notable.

Tulving's (1972) distinction between *episodic* and *semantic memory* implies a second limitation. Episodic memory involves events related to a particular time and place, such as the dinner I had last night or film I saw last week. How often do we say to someone, "I know you, but I can't place you," which suggests that we must locate them in the circumstances of meeting to remember them. Semantic memories, on the other hand, involve grammar and spelling skills, word meanings, and the like that we just know, that have lost or never had episodic status. In addition, Tulving (1985) has since postulated a third, *procedural memory*, which involves automatically performed skills, typically of a motor kind, such as tying shoelaces or shaving. Why are these distinctions necessary? First, there is little correspondence between one's competence at episodic and semantic memory tasks (Underwood, Boruch & Malmi, 1978). As well, some variables affect them differently. Episodic memories are debilitated by amnesia, but victims do not forget language, motor skills (Baddeley, 1990; Hirst, 1982), or, for that matter, implicit memories (Roediger, 1990). Above all, Tulving pointed out that most investigations of memory have focused on the episodic kind. A list of words such as "frog" and "table" does not test semantic memory. They reside therein before and after the experiment and so need not be learned at all but only temporarily transferred to the episode of the list, so subjects can recall that, of all the words they know, these ones were in it. Unrecalled items undoubtedly remain in semantic memory; only their presence in that episode has been forgotten. Researchers seem to have taken Tulving's point to heart, because studies of semantic memory have since come forth in profusion, but, unfortunately the key question for us, whether the laws of interference apply to it, so far as I know remains unanswered. My overriding suspicion, however, is that by and large the answer is negative, not only regarding similarity or time changes but that memory should generally decline with the retention interval.

Consider anecdotal reports that strongly imply that episodic but not semantic memory declines with age. Many seniors, whose linguistic abilities are impeccable and who indeed have never forgotten how to ride bicycles as long as physical capability allows it, cannot recall where they left their glasses ten minutes ago.[1] Semantic memories likely have advantages in degree of learning,

---

1. My father, now well into his eighties, tells of a little old lady who answers her doorbell to find that familiar figure carrying pamphlets and Bible who wishes to tell her about the hereafter. She answers, "Oh, I know all about the hereafter, I experience it all the time." "You do?," responds the astounded would-be missionary. "Oh yes! Whenever I go upstairs I have to stop and think, 'Now what did I come up hereafter!' "

partly because of having been learned early on (the main reason for the overall decline in memory with age is poorer learning [Craik, 1996]; my brain, once a veritable sponge for items such as baseball statistics, is now more akin to a brick wall off which information gleefully bounces). Still and all, their superiority is striking in view of the far longer retention intervals they must surmount. Although in fairness, the dominant current view (Hultsch & Dixon, 1990) has semantic memory suffering equally from age; if this is so, it further verifies actress Bette Davis's reputed observation, "Getting old isn't for sissies!"

In general, then, it may be that, while interference operates widely, the specific laws pinpointed by so much research effort of yesteryear hold only for verbal materials, only for episodic tasks, and only laboratory ones at that. Any scientific law has limits, but if these become too narrow, we must at some point ask whether it is a generalization or mere curiosity.

BEYOND UNIVERSALS IN DEVELOPMENT

At the outset it bears repeating that as age increases, generalization becomes ever more tenuous in view of the greater variance shown by a number of behaviors (Birren & Schroots, 1996). Our major focus, however, is on stage accounts. First, H. Gardner's (1983, 1993b) preference for these reveals his Piagetian lineage, but it is his departures that are relevant here. Piaget's stages imply universality. Everyone goes through the same ones in the same order, the structure that prevails in each dominates every aspect of cognition and interpretation of every experience, and when a stage transition occurs, the entire cognitive apparatus moves as one, in lockstep (D. Feldman, 1980). One cannot therefore be in more than one stage at a time. Gardner, however, posits seven independent fields of knowledge, a few being mathematical/logical, musical and bodily/kinesthetic. Each field, or *frame of mind*, has its own symbolic system for expressing knowledge, localization in the brain (depending on the location, brain damage affects some abilities adversely but spares others; H. Gardner, 1982), and, while each matures through a set sequence of inevitable stages à la Piaget, their specific stages differ. It follows that, since fields are independent, attributes such as intelligence and creativity are field specific; therefore a talent is not general but for something—a brilliant mathematician may be lacking in other domains such as the interpersonal.

It follows too that in contrast to the lockstep position, someone may be more advanced in one field than another, a contention that D. Feldman's (1982) estimable studies of *child prodigies* strongly support. Such children, exemplified by Mozart and Bobby Fischer, are remarkably proficient for their ages in one field (usually chess, music, or mathematics; prodigies are rare in visual art, almost nonexistent in literary pursuits). Feldman's subjects displayed high but not stratospheric IQs (typically 120–160) and in other activities were likewise not extraordinary, but in their field of talent they resembled adults in proficiency and commitment. In short, they were ahead not only of other children but, more important, of themselves, which is understandable from a Gardnerian but not

Piagetian perspective. Since Gardner's outlook restricts sweeping generalizations about development, it is fitting that he should use idiographic methods to study seven seminally influential twentieth century figures, each personifying one of the mind frames, for example, Stravinsky for music and Martha Graham for dance (H. Gardner, 1993a). While he is more inclined than, say, Gruber to seek commonalities among them, he nonetheless tacitly accepts considerable idiosyncrasy. However, his are hardly the last words on these matters. Lubinski and Benbow's (1995) review of Gardner (1993b) found his views more impressive on conceptual and literary than empirical grounds. In particular, they maintain, general intelligence as shown by standard IQ tests accounts for more individual variance in intellectual occupations than he admits. They feel a systematic empirical evaluation of his hypotheses is badly needed in view of their profound implications for and influence on education.

It was Kohlberg's distaste for the cultural relativism so evident at the Nuremberg trials in the standard defense, "I was only obeying orders," that evoked his main priority: to describe a universal, objective moral system (M. Boyes, personal communication, October 1995). Actions that are moral within a culture are nonetheless immoral if the culture itself is immoral. His hierarchy deems certain reasons for actions as inherently more sophisticated, and "better," regardless of culture. Unfortunately, it implies, no doubt inevitably, his own values, in that higher stages evince distinctively North American values such as personal independence and resistance to authority. However, other cultures, such as Asian ones, differ in these matters (Hwang, 1986; Vasudef & Hummel, 1987). There was some evidence of progress from Kohlberg's lower to higher stages with maturity, which suggests a universal sequence, but also considerable cultural specificity. Gilligan (1982) also criticized Kohlberg's system for reflecting masculine attitudes; women tend to emphasize less self-centered motives, which he portrays as less sophisticated. In sum, his attempt to tackle morality in a scientifically acceptable manner was a laudable exception to modern psychology's neglect of it, but as these criticisms indicate, he too may have been trying to be objective about a nonobjective matter.

CONCEPTUAL PROBLEMS

Are Psychological Laws Attainable?

Although a negative answer to this most basic question results in a definitively romantic position, some have reached it via the very rational means that stalwart romantics distrust. Harré (1985) chastised operationism for trivializing the discipline, partly because of the limitations it imposed on content, but also because defining a concept by a set of procedures means that any change in these, no matter how minuscule, implies a different concept. Therefore, intelligence tests that part company in specific items must each be measuring a different entity, since correlations are never perfect. The upshot is ironic. One supposed virtue of the operational definition is that its clarity promotes parsimony, since overlap among concepts is immediately apparent. In practice, however, its effect is the opposite, to open the door to innumerable similar but not identical concepts. Nor is this consideration merely academic; witness the flood of intelligence tests, each claiming its share of the limelight (and considerable profits). Furthermore, choices among them based on effectiveness must be subjective and inconclusive. Everyone has their own beliefs about what intelligence is and how and where it manifests itself, so there are no universally accepted standards, such as a perfect clock, against which the validity of each can be assessed.

As for generalization, Harré notes the faith on which it rests: observations are reliable, unaffected by changes in time and place. Is this valid for psychology? No instrument or test is perfectly reliable, so it is never certain whether changes in observations reflect its failings or the phenomenon's inherent instability. Consider possible changes in intelligence with age. The WAIS (Wechsler, 1958) determines IQ by the rank of one's test score compared to others of similar age, for example, a score one standard deviation above the mean yields an IQ of 115. Although someone's raw score changes appreciably over their life, their rank compared to age mates ordinarily should not—those in the top 5 percent at ten should still be roughly so at sixty—so the technique virtually guarantees IQs that remain fairly constant. As indeed they do, but this does not mean that the same holds for intelligence itself. In fact, Piagetian perspectives jeopardize the entire notion of such consistent traits, certainly as predictors. If each stage involves diverse outlooks, children most adept in one may not be so in another. Recall Bloom's (1985) interviews with high achievers in the arts, sciences, sports, and so on, which suggested that in developing their talents, most had progressed through three unique stages in the dedication and abilities displayed. If these stages are as inevitable as their ubiquity across fields indicates, then the abilities needed to excel in each may undermine early attempts to predict, and informal observation does suggest that those who ultimately excel at, say, a sport, are often not those who stood out as children.

As another aspect of the problem, not everyone evinces even the most reliable phenomena. Some subjects exposed to conditions highly conducive to interference retain as well as controls and by no means does everyone subjected to partial reinforcement become a gambling addict. Every law has boundaries, but the scientific variety state precisely in advance the conditions under which they hold. Unfortunately, we can rarely identify before the fact those persons who will display a given psychological phenomenon. Behaviors are so situation specific that even minor changes in conditions have pronounced effects (Bem & Allen, 1974). As Cronbach (1975) points out, most are influenced by a host of variables including intrasubject ones which, to make matters worse, often interact, so the effect of one depends on the level of others. As a result, generalizations are subject to so many considerations that circumstances to which they apply are severely restricted, even in lab contexts, where many of these factors can be controlled. Cronbach shows that even so pervasive a principle as Weber's Law can break down as a result of unanticipated considerations, so one cannot assume its applicability until this is verified empirically. In short, a major benefit that laws are supposed to provide, precise prediction, goes by the boards for psychological phenomena—if not for comparisons of groups, certainly of individuals. Too often psychologists must fall back on that dissatisfying disclaimer, It depends!

Gergen (1976) raises other difficulties. In contrast to natural science, in social psychology (and by implication elsewhere) facts change markedly over time, so many purported laws are written not in stone but disappearing ink. Witness for example the reliable evidence (Flynn, 1987) that IQ scores are steadily increasing, worldwide, at a rate of about 3 IQ points per decade. As usual, a plethora of plausible explanations can be advanced (Neisser, Boodoo, et al., 1996), but the possibility that people of today do indeed have more intelligence than their forefathers, let alone that it might differ entirely, as suggested by a Gardnerian perspective, introduces a host of complications. Likewise, Hudson (1996) wonders whether our changing world is causing dreams to change or perhaps disappear entirely. Film and TV provide the same shifting, ambivalent visual images, and, if dreams do stem, as Freud maintains, from repression of sex, violence, and the like, then the open and frequent depiction of these matters would also be detrimental. As would psychology's fondness in recent times for descriptions, notably those arising from behaviorism and computer metaphors, that stress our rational aspects. For these encourage us to downplay or view as suspect those activities that suggest a more irrational side, which dreams certainly do.

For reasons such as these, Gergen (1976, p. 16) asserts, "knowledge cannot accumulate in the usual scientific sense because (it) does not generally transcend its historical boundaries." In addition, experimenters receive messages from their subjects and in turn communicate these to a broader audience, which is rapidly expanding, making findings widely known. Moreover, however much such knowledge is presented in a pseudo-objective manner, it often suggests value judgments. Studies of authoritarian personalities or conformity, for example, imply hereabouts that these attributes are best avoided and in trying to do so, people may render findings obsolete. So, too, with a myriad other possibilities mooted about, for example, that women are more persuadable or that bystanders in the company of others are less likely to act in emergencies. Might not someone aware of reinforcement's machinations try, out of sheer cussedness perhaps, to react against it and thereby call another purported law into question?

As another complication, it is well known that many supposed behavioral laws vary across cultures (Matsumoto, 1994); the orient values conformity and respect for authority more than the west does and concepts such as the self differ markedly as well. As the pièce de résistance, laws differ in their tendency to vary across time or place; determining their resilience therefore is by no means an easy matter. Advocates of generalization could retort that historical epochs and cultures are boundary conditions, so such determinations are as always an empirical matter. But this, too, is challenging if these factors are both prevalent and whimsical, another obstacle to laws' facilitating prediction. Indeed, Gergen sees these sudden variations in such things as what is thought to be good as serious difficulties for attempts to reduce psychological phenomena entirely to physical entities. How can brain function explain such things? What all this adds up to, he claims, is that psychology is essentially an historical undertaking, an account of the human being here and now. One implication is to enhance applied research's credibility. It is often criticized as being time and place specific and so less conducive to generalization and prediction. However, the same can now be said, it seems, about pure research.

It is considerations such as these that have fostered the movement of *social constructionism* (Gergen, 1985). Heavily influenced by Wittgenstein, it sees social psychology not as an undertaking that accompanies many others but as subsuming all the social sciences, ruled as they are by social factors. Concepts beyond number—motivation, the self, gender, mind itself—depend less on external factors than on the cultural and historical context in which they are discussed; their very meaning changes with it, especially by the way they are used in language: "From the constructionist position the process of understanding is not automatically driven by the forces of nature, but is the result of an active, cooperative enterprise of persons in relationships and cannot be determined by direct observation of that world" (p. 267). Thus the study of such phenomena should not focus on their attributes per se but on their usage within a social context. This approach has elicited considerable commentary (*American Psychologist,* May, 1995), especially about its inherent relativism. Is there no absolute knowledge about concepts such as gender that is independent of its context? What comprises a context? Are there not conceivably as many as there are individuals who have ever lived? Might this not lead us to ask with Pilate, "What is truth?" Furthermore, Gergen (1994), while not excluding the gathering of "facts" or formulating laws (so long as they are presented not as ultimate truths but as relative to their contexts), cheerfully allows virtually any methodology that enables one to strengthen one's case. It should be evident that I would sympathize in principle to such a liberal view of what constitutes acceptable practice, but to play devil's advocate, it is only fair to point out that objectivist approaches did provide the tactic, however flawed, of the critical experiment to choose among competing accounts. What criteria are to be used now to make such choices? A Pandora's box of subjectivity beckons, "Right you are if you think you are," beckons, because to borrow from Cole Porter, Anything Goes!

CONCLUSION: A SPECULATION

If advocates of generalization and logical positivists are not sufficiently nettled by now, what follows should finish the job. So be it! Evolution preaches that species are constantly changing, and nature is inherently creative. It is plausible, then, that this might also be true for nature's laws; those that now hold may eventually be replaced by others or that lawfulness itself, even if presently the case, may disappear. The concept of *entropy,* that the universe is moving inexorably toward an ever more random state and eventually complete stasis, suggests this very possibility. By my understanding, in such a situation prediction of collective averages would be flawless, but of individual events no better than chance, and this state of affairs seems especially likely regarding human beings because of our unique ability: creativity. While there are inklings of it in lower animals, in the last analysis these are but pale reflections of the genuine article (Abra, l988b). Pfeiffer (1982) and Jaynes (1976) have speculated about how and why this quantum leap came about, but the key point is that it did. I am convinced that the universe was created by a force, for lack of a better word, called God; the big bang theory to me seems a most reverent hypothesis. Furthermore, we are told on good authority that we were created in God's image and the fact that we alone are endowed with one of His/Her/Its most defining attributes, creativity, enhances this notion's credibility. This very similarity stimulated a speculative exercise (Abra, l988a,) that applied known properties of the creative person and process to the omnipotent version to shed light on some otherwise inexplicable events in Genesis.

This similarity is again exploited here but now for prediction. Among other things, the creative process is inherently directed (Gruber, 1988) toward some ultimate purpose, however vague, such as an image in an artist's minds eye (Arieti, 1976). The desire to externalize this vision provides a powerful motive for creative work (Abra, 1997) and, more to the point, guides revision. Trial and error there is, but not an indiscriminate generation of every conceivable possibility a la Skinner; instead it uses *heuristics* to produce only those that have some discernible relevance. The process may not know precisely where it is going, but it knows full well where it is not going. God's initial inspiration was supposedly manifest in that dramatic first six days (van Gogh [Stone, 1937] alleged that the universe was one of God's first drafts, and one that didn't turn out very well!), and, if so, evolution can be viewed as the means by which He/She/It revises it. It follows that far from flying blind as some (Dawkins, 1986) would claim, it too must be working toward something. The number of species that might be generated is infinite, but, while supply does far exceed demand—as it must for natural selection to operate—relatively few seem actually to appear whose chances of survival are nil.

Moreover this goal-directedness must apply most of all to ourselves. As arguably the Divine Creator's greatest creation, we too must be undergoing revision towards a more polished product. And on balance have we not made progress, albeit with many setbacks such as the Third Reich, toward a better state called civilization? Bestial we still too often are but surely more compassionate, enlightened and less bent on destruction than during, say, the Middle Ages, let alone imperial Rome. People still attend public events, such as car races, partly hoping to witness mayhem but not certain death, as in the days of the Coliseum. During the recent Cold War, the superpowers trod perilously close to disaster on occasion, but the bottom line is that they did manage to avoid outright hostilities, which, in previous epochs, would surely have broken out between such fundamentally antagonistic societies. Now when war is undertaken it is with reluctance rather than eagerness, with acute awareness of the horrors that lie in store. While we have not learned as much from history as we might wish and too often are bent on rediscovering the wheel, the lessons we have learned give us an immeasurable advantage over the other animals, who have no sense whatever of history. So, cockeyed optimist that I am, I firmly believe that we are "getting better all the time"; Nietzsche's fabled Overpeople will eventually become not mutations but standard issue. Moreover, our evolution should accelerate if our creativity can overcome, as I have faith it will, the next great challenge: to avoid irreversible damage to the environment.

What has all this to do with generalization's looming obsolescence? In one crucial respect we are not like other creations. Perhaps the greatest of 'God's inspirations, and also the source of all His/Her/Its later dissatisfactions (Abra, 1988a), was to give this creature that same capacity for creativity. It is as if paintings, once created, were able to revise themselves. Furthermore, to follow Nietzsche again, this capacity in the Overhumans of the future should be greater still. The most fundamental act of creation we perform is on ourselves. Authorities as diverse as Sartre (1969), Adler (Ansbacher & Ansbacher, 1956), and Bandura (1978) have all contended that each of us is in large part a product of our own devising. Unlike animals, we choose who we will be, and since creativity is invariably a force for innovation and therefore diversity, it follows that differences among us should become ever more pronounced. Notwithstanding Simonton's (1984, 1990) discoveries of general trends among groups of creators, in absolute numbers exceptions abound, so every sweeping statement about them must be hedged by an emphatic "as a rule."

5

Determinism in Science

To make their activities meaningful, scientists assume that nature is not chaotic but lawful, has order, and can be understood. Determinism historically has also implied *causality*, that every phenomenon is determined by factors that must occur first and potentially can be identified. Few scientists nowadays accept the causality connotation (H. Kaufmann, 1968) as a sine qua non, but until recently most psychologists have (Underwood, 1957b), so it is included here. Why do sciences require such assumptions? Before answering, we must first consider their aims. The first is to *describe* their main concern, the phenomena of experience, preferably quantitatively, to observe what happens and through observer agreement establish reliability. Thus a post-Watson psychologist should first and foremost be so fascinated by behavior as to be a veritable voyeur. In the face of dramatic happenings, such as accidents, stock market crashes, or attractive members of the opposite sex entering a room, she would find other people's responses more interesting than the event itself. It says here!

However, most scientists are not content with description but want to *understand* or *explain* those events. In the last analysis, I understand something when I feel that I do (Turner, 1968), when my curiosity rests (Bridgman, 1927), so it is a personal matter. Explanation may include attempts at theorizing, but for the archetypal scientist it involves knowing why an event occurs by specifying its causes. There may be several—for behaviors there almost always are—in which case it may be that the presence of any one is sufficient to initiate the event (aggressive behavior can come about for a number of reasons) or that all must be present. Regardless, scientists assume, as another article of faith, that the number of causes for an event is finite (Underwood, 1957b); otherwise complete understanding would be a hopeless quest.

Lastly, most scientists want to *predict* and/or *control* phenomena, and causal understanding can facilitate both (although they can come about without it).

Once its antecedents have been identified, a phenomenon's occurrences can be predicted beforehand. In weather forecasting, should conditions arise that invariably herald thunderstorms, it is reasonable to suspect that one may shortly follow. Weather forecasters are reasonably accurate but hardly infallible, which indicates that as yet not all influential variables are known. Understanding may also allow control of phenomena, to either permit or prevent them by introducing or eliminating antecedents. Thus the scientist who specifies the factors that elicit dinner-hour telephone calls promoting the cleaning of one's furnace deserves a Nobel Prize for advancing not only peace but quiet! Unfortunately, understanding does not always lead to control. Most causes are other events that themselves are caused—A causes B causes C ad infinitum—so we may know why something happens but be helpless to prevent its antecedents. Many causes of earthquakes have been identified and our ability to predict them has increased greatly, yet they still occur with tragic regularity.

Why then must the scientist hold to some version of determinism? If one sets out to discover nature's order and the causes for phenomena, should one not assume that it/they can be found, to prevent an exercise in futility, a chasing of will-o'-the-wisps? Yet determinism, when all is said and done, is another article of faith that cannot be validated by scientifically legitimate means, empirical investigation. Perhaps nature is chaotic, as some systems maintain, but the scientist counters with the usual gambit: adopt determinism as a working hypothesis and proceed. If it is invalid, then science should prove ineffective, but we seem to have learned more about nature during the last few decades than in all the rest put together. Today's average high-school graduate it is said is more knowledgeable than Newton or Galileo, which increases confidence in the assumption's validity. As Einstein (1956) observed, the most incomprehensible thing about the universe is that it is comprehensible.

How does one go about discovering causes? Through one of human ingenuity's most elegant inventions, the *controlled experiment.* Any experiment compares events that occur in different situations. Someone wondering whether playing music to plants affects their growth might expose some to repeated waterings of Mozart, others to the latest noise topping the pop charts, still others to nothing and compare them. The controlled experiment is simply a special version, but the only kind that conclusively establishes causality. It rests on a reasonable but crucial assumption; if the situations being compared are identical in every way, no differences should be observed in their phenomena. A single factor is then allowed to vary between those situations, the *independent variable,* while all others are equated or *controlled.* Any differences in the phenomena we care to observe, the *dependent variable,* we can then attribute to the change in the independent variable—what else could be responsible?—and the fact stated as a functional relationship. This conclusion, however, obviously requires that all other potential variables have been controlled; otherwise the situations compared differ in more than one way, resulting in an *experimental confound.* If our audiophilic plants experienced varying acoustic bombardment and differing temperatures, either or both factors could have affected growth. A controlled experiment can have more than one independent variable—many do—but comparing situations that differ in more than one cannot reveal causality.

This explains why many experiments are conducted in a laboratory. The name may suggest Bunsen burners, computers, or other belching apparati, and some scientists utter it with the hushed reverence usually reserved for the holy of holies. In reality, it can be an empty room. It is merely an environment, admittedly artificial, that allows control over potentially confounding variables and thus the essential, manipulating one variable at a time. Experiments in the haphazard "real world," wherein many factors fluctuate together, gain ecological validity but sacrifice control. Still, naturalistic experiments are a good place to start, especially for psychologists. People watching provides hypotheses about possible causes for behavior and so of independent variables to manipulate. Why is that occupant of the next bar stool staring blankly into space and imbibing heavily? Jilted by a lover? Lost his job? Got a job? The list of possibilities is limited only by ingenuity, but their influence can only be verified by a controlled experiment's unblinking scrutiny.

DETERMINISM IN PSYCHOLOGY

The Controlled Experiment in Psychology: Subject Variables

Seeking behaviors' causes experimentally faces special obstacles. Since everyone is different, several people in identical situations will not necessarily behave identically, which invalidates that crucial initial assumption, that those situations would yield comparable phenomena. One solution is to compare effects of different situations on the same person, but such *repeated measures.* types of experiments risk confounds of their own, notably that exposure to one situation may affect reactions to others. The usual tactic is to compare several groups of subjects and assume that, they should on average behave identically in comparable circumstances, within a margin of error. As always, individual differences will occur but now both within and across groups and so should balance out—if, that is, two requirements are met. Each group must have a number of subjects, the larger the better, because as this increases so does reliability of group performance measures. Second, each subject must be assigned to a group by a random system, such as flipping coins, so they have an equal chance of being in either group. I must immediately warn: *random assignment* differs from *random selection*, which comes into play while first choosing the subjects who are to actually serve from a designated population, for example, sampling from all eligible voters in a country for a Gallup poll. Random assignment involves the next step; once selected, how are subjects placed in groups?

If those two conditions are met, the groups should be quite comparable, allowing any differences in average behavior greater than chance to be attributed to the independent variable's effects. However, the random assignment requirement raises special difficulties, one being that it is very easy to violate.

Consider an instructor who teaches two sections of a course, at 8 A.M. and noon. Observing an understandable variation in alertness among her students, she suspects that they may have internalized her pearls of wisdom to different degrees and so administers the same exam to both. Lo and behold, the early risers on average perform more poorly. Unfortunately, no causal conclusion can be drawn. Rarely are students assigned to sections randomly—usually they choose their own timetables—so those who opt for early ones may be atypical, perhaps in a propensity for masochism. This, then, exemplifies an all too common error in psychological experimentation against which every student is warned ad nauseum but which is continually made, even by experienced investigators, concluding causality from *correlation*. Events are correlated when as one changes the other does also in some predictable way, be it directly, inversely, or whatever—poverty and crime; level of education and income; spring and thoughts of love. It may be that one event causes the other, and if this is so they are correlated as well, but not all correlations indicate causality, in that one changes if and only if the other does so first.

Still, a controlled study on the effects of class time is possible in theory, by seeking volunteers who would allow themselves to be randomly placed in a given time slot. However, consider a correlation currently in the news, between smoking and lung cancer. There is considerable evidence that they covary, but groups of smokers and nonsmokers are hardly comparable. They no doubt differ in a myriad of probably extraneous factors, such as education, and in nutritional habits and perhaps biologically—one group's choice to smoke in the first place hints at an inborn predisposition—and these, not smoking per se, may be the culprits. Once again volunteers, of necessity all nonsmokers, could be randomly assigned to either take up smoking or not, but in practice such a study is difficult to carry out since few people are so public spirited as to allow themselves to be assigned without choice to possibly fatal conditions. Hence the frequent use of animals. They don't object to such machinations, at least not so they can be understood.

But consider a large class of potential factors in psychology called *subject variables,* characteristics that people possess and on which they differ, such as intelligence, sex, and age. There is every reason to suspect that these powerfully affect behavior, but how to check? In a subject variable experiment, subjects are not randomly assigned but the characteristic both provides the independent variable and determines their group. Unfortunately, such experiments must be hopelessly confounded; people of various ages for example also differ in a myriad other ways—amount and type of education, health, prior learning, and hence susceptibility to proactive interference to name only a few. Although effects depend on several factors, as a general statement younger subjects outperform their elders on memory tests (Craik, 1977). Why? Who knows!

We should also note the mathematical tools, *statistics*, that are routinely used to interpret data from experiments, controlled or otherwise. At the outset, I must mention an irony. These techniques provide probabilistic statements containing some uncertainty. Group means, standard deviations, and so on, are only estimated within a margin of error, and a probability is always stated that a difference observed between groups is due not to the independent variable but to chance. So here we have a discipline that avoids postquantum statistical explanation and clings fervently to certainty in causal statements, yet can only verify them probabilistically! Nevertheless, few beginners realize how important these matters become in psychology careers, but courses in them dominate undergraduate and graduate curricula. To discuss specifics here would be superfluous, but it would be remiss not to observe how much the enduring devices of correlation and analysis of variance, as well as more sophisticated newcomers, have contributed to understanding. Also, that given these tools' ubiquity, the would-be psychologist lacking mathematical skills has a tough row to hoe, even if heading in applied directions such as clinical psychology. The prevailing *scientist–practitioner* or *Boulder model* (APA, 1947) holds that clinicians should be trained first and foremost as psychologists, that is, as scientists with demonstrated abilities in statistics, experimental design, and performing original research of sufficient quality to earn a Ph.D. They should therefore be able to comprehend, evaluate, and, if occasion warrants, conduct such research. Hence graduate training typically includes appreciable doses of content in these areas; indeed, it may be deemed more important than others, perhaps to weed out candidates who want to help people but cannot function on the scientific wavelength that professional competence supposedly demands. With all this in mind, let us examine some content matters.

Influential Versions of Psychological Determinism

What are the implications in psychology of a wholesale deterministic outlook? That every behavior, thought, or what have you is presumed to be due to forces beyond our own control. The opposing view, *free will*, holds that we choose our actions and properties, unencumbered. To consider the many nuances of this debate would demand a book in itself, but it is worth glancing briefly at the history of Christianity, where it has repeatedly surfaced, if only to show that psychological determinism is an assumption, not inviolate truth. One episode contributed greatly to the Protestant schism, no less. One of free will's corollaries is that I am responsible for my actions, so any that are illegal, immoral, or fattening are my fault, and I deserve whatever punishments follow. Prior to the Reformation, the Church vacillated. Augustine had seen us as inherently evil, condemned by Original Sin. Only God could bestow salvation and the whims that might lead Him to save one and not another were beyond our understanding. However, Aquinas so persuasively espoused free will that it eventually became entrenched dogma. Luther disagreed, vehemently. In bitter debates with Erasmus, Luther maintained that God irrevocably decides each person's virtue and thus salvation or damnation. According to this doctrine of *predestination*, we are not good because our actions are moral, rather, our actions are moral because God has made us good. Thus this doctrine, like determinism, indicts antecedent factors, but differs in that they are beyond our influence or understanding, so it fosters fatalism, as in "God's will be done."

Freud. A few eyebrows may rise at this inclusion in what purports to be a discussion of scientific psychology. Many Freudian concepts contravene the empirical rule and for Popper (1972) exemplify poor or pseudoscientific theorizing. Still, they epitomize other scientific characteristics, notably determinism, and Freud himself always claimed, however inaccurately, that psychoanalysis was a science. Finally, he deserves inclusion if for no other reason than sheer influence; to many laypeople, Freud *is* psychology. The nineteenth century, influenced by romanticism and unprecedented material and scientific progress, tended toward optimism. Through our reason and powers of individual expression, we could remake the world however we chose to reach a blissful Utopia. Several factors caused the pendulum to swing, notably the slaughter of World War I that decimated an entire generation over issues that were increasingly obscure. As the war dragged on, our ability to control our destiny seemed ever more dubious.

Around this time the revolutionary views of Darwin, Freud and Marx were being widely disseminated. Marx's version of determinism was optimistic. Happiness and attaining our potential depends on favorable social and economic conditions. People are inherently good; it is capitalism's inequalities that breed misery and evil. But, as Freud (1958a) himself pointed out, Darwin's outlook and that of psychoanalysis were both pessimistic, in his estimation the second and third blows to human pride. (The first had come from Copernicus; if the earth does not center the universe but orbits around a second rate star, in the general scheme of things human affairs become insignificant). Darwin's contention, that we are not unique but mere animals had the same humbling effect, as did psychoanalysis' assertion that we are ruled by unconscious factors that lie beyond our control and awareness. Since Freud is anathema to a thoroughgoing scientific psychology, it is ironic that he should have been so influential an advocate of one of its most cherished beliefs. Although he generalized his explanation of disturbed behaviors as due to unconscious events to a host of others ranging from dreams to creative achievements, perhaps his notion of the *Freudian slip* best captures his deterministic convictions. Even mispronounced or misused words, which most of us would dismiss as chance occurrences, reflected unconscious hang-ups. Similarly, a niggling error in Leonardo da Vinci's diary supposedly betrayed negative feelings toward the father, causing Freud (1947) to observe wryly, "It is only a triviality to which anyone but a psychoanalyst would pay no attention . . . to him nothing is too trifling as a manifestation of hidden psychic processes" (p. 91).

It is fitting to take stock of Freud's mammoth contributions, since so many (e.g., Salter, 1964; Wood, 1985) dismiss him out of hand. Certainly some concepts, the penis envies and castration complexes, strain credulity, but again, authorities should be judged on their good rather than bad ideas. Thus skeptics who have obtained their Freud from secondary sources have not experienced his ability to plunge within a few paragraphs from the sublime to the ridiculous and back again, with an astonishing range of knowledge that he could bring to bear to defend even the most questionable positions and even in translation with an enviable prose style. His first seminal contribution was the concept of the unconscious and its key consequence—the causes of behaviors are often unknown to the person themselves. Freud did not invent this notion, it had been around since Plato (R. Watson, 1963), but he promoted its broad dissemination and invented methods to explore it. Arguably his greatest work, *The Interpretation of Dreams* (Freud, 1953a), followed directly. However one views the specifics of those interpretations, the basic supposition, that these nocturnal scenarios carry hidden messages, revolutionized thinking about them. Another major legacy was to point out the preeminent influence of sex and thus provide a telling force in the overthrow of Victorian morality, which had rendered sex unmentionable in polite company. In addition, if Freud did not invent the notion that the child is the father of the man, his speculations about the influence of early events meant that we have him as much as anyone to thank, or blame, for the countless tomes on child-rearing practices, parent-child relationships, and the like that now flood our bookstores. Previously these matters had seemed of little consequence.

A final landmark was the supremely unflattering mirror he held up to human nature. The unconscious, that ultimate determinant, is in essence a psychic garbage dump of base, primitive desires, largely sexual and/or aggressive, that are inherently at odds with and only tenuously held in check by civilization. And events of his day, particularly World War I, substantiated this pessimistic portrait (see films such as *Gallipoli* and *All Quiet on the Western Front*). At first, many young men saw the war as a romantic adventure to which they must hurry with all speed before it was over. In late 1915, when the horrible reality had begun to sink in, Freud's (1958c) contention that people should be grieved but, given our nature, not surprised by the war gained credibility. Still, he advised, that we are not so wonderful as we had believed provides a consolation, because we have therefore not sunk so low as we might suppose. And those who still doubt Freud's capacity for profound insight might consider what was soon to come. Fascists and Nazis preached acting on our bestial tendencies—the SS storm trooper is little more than the Freudian unconscious brought to consciousness. To many, this came all too easily.

S–R Psychology. This preeminently scientific position espoused by Watson, Hull, early functionalists, and others also pervades an adamant determinism, in which every act depends on the stimuli to which it is associated.

Skinner. It is striking that someone so opposed to theorizing was in this respect his own worst enemy, because beneath Skinner's seeming arch-empiricism lurks if not a formal theory then certainly a philosophy of human nature. Let me first reemphasize: however one views his specifics, one must applaud his desire to help better our lot. Convinced he held the key, Skinner seemed as frustrated as any missionary whose messages are paid little heed, because he voiced his repeatedly. It is striking too, therefore, how this apostle supreme of methods to change behavior in this respect failed to practice what he preached, that is, that passively internalized discourse is an ineffective means to this end.

Skinner (1971) blamed our failure to solve our enduring problems on our clinging to a mistaken view of ourselves called *autonomous man*. As part of the problem, this presumed being is supposed to have a mind, or *world within the skin,* that elicits such things as thoughts and feelings which in turn determine what we do. The importance of these entities has been propounded because of our desire for answers of some kind and no better ones were available. As another barrier to accuracy, autonomous man has properties portrayed as necessary for happiness. One is *freedom,* of a psychological not political kind, to choose our own actions. In the past, people have been controlled by aversive forces of the nobility and clergy, so events such as the French Revolution and the Reformation implanted a suspicion of any form of control and a propaganda system, *the literature of freedom,* has maintained it. Another property is *dignity*. We acquire it when we are recognized for our achievements, but strangely this only happens if we seem responsible for them, not when they are due to conspicuous external factors. A soldier who overwhelms a machine-gun nest because of his "bravery" is honored at the White House or 24 Sussex Drive, but not if it comes out that he was too drunk to know what he was doing. Admiration for a Wayne Gretzky suffers if his skills are attributed to genetics or an unusually encouraging father. As for Shakespeare, there is no evidence of stimulating domesticity or education (Schoenbaum, 1991), of university attendance, creative writing courses, or fraternity membership. How could he possibly concoct such masterworks? Thus the recurring suspicion that someone more qualified must have done so, be it Marlowe, the Earl of Essex, or Indiana Jones. No doubt a heartless scholar will one day show that he suffered from that peculiar Elizabethan malady, brain softening due to the creeping pox!

But, Skinner continues, autonomous man is a misconception we can no longer afford. Most problems we face stem from human behavior. Our very survival demands that it change, and the first, crucial step is to view ourselves accurately. Skinner, unlike Watson, does not deny that the world within the skin exists—introspection suggests otherwise—only that it controls behavior. Thoughts, feelings, and the like are also behaviors controlled by contingencies. Thoughts accompany a behavior, but that does not mean that they caused it. Good point! To bring home these truths, Skinner (1974) asserts, we must modify common turns of phrase that, by attributing behaviors to mental states, both reflect and affect beliefs. We may say that tennis success depends on feeling confident. Actually, backhands improve because correct movements produce successful shots which reinforce those same movements. Confidence also increases because it too is present and reinforced, so we conclude that it led to the improvement, when in fact it is another, albeit more surreptitious behavior. Or suppose I am asked why I did something. I reply, "Because I wanted to." Once more autonomous man speaks. I actually mean that I expect that the behavior will lead to reinforcement because it has in the past. So Shakespeare had it wrong. Reinforcement, not the wish, is father to the act (Skinnerian language is admirably precise, but few would accuse it of being stylish).

The main remedy, however, is to recognize freedom and dignity as the fictions they are (hence the title that landed Skinner on *Time*'s cover: *BEYOND Freedom and Dignity*). We are deterministic beings, our every act controlled by heredity and/or experience working by way of the contingencies. That is the nature of things, so rather than wishing it otherwise we should exploit it by establishing contingencies that encourage desirable and eliminate maladaptive behaviors. And the requisite technology is already available, brought not down from Sinai but up from laboratories. However, its effective application demands as always that an environment, in this case an entire culture, be designed and experimenters designated who select the behaviors to be encouraged and deliver reinforcers when they occur. Several objections will be raised in due course, but one deserves immediate attention because Skinner has been at pains to answer it. If reinforcement so effectively controls behavior, could such an appointee not become a veritable tyrant? It has often been said that the ability to control behavior provides more potential for misuse than atomic energy. When all is said and done, is Skinner not resurrecting the concept of an enlightened despot like Louis XIV whose iron rule was rationalized on grounds that he supposedly knew and would foster what was in the best interests of everyone? As history verifies, power corrupts and absolute power corrupts absolutely; self-interest soon takes over.

Which is precisely what Skinner's rebuttal assumes. First, he would place reinforcement in not one hand but an oligarchy of the most enlightened, who could act as checks on one another—which nicely reflects an era that features, one wag observed, no great people, only great committees. But even elite groups can become exploitative—witness the nobility—so other checks are needed, and they result, Skinner claims, from reinforcement's very nature. Consider a cartoon wherein a rat in a Skinner box informs another, "Have I got this guy shaped. Whenever he gives me food, I press the bar." Reinforcing another is itself a behavior, so it can be encouraged, like any other, by its contingencies. Even formal experiments are not one-way streets in which omnipotent experimenters give and subjects receive; rather, both give and receive to/from their partners. Or to use Skinner's term, reinforcement is *reciprocal* and labeling either participant as experimenter or subject depends on one's perspective. The cartoon's implied psychologist sees the behavior encouraged as rat-pressing-bar and the giving of food as the reinforcer, but the rat sees the reverse.

All of which clarifies what self-interest means. The concept of reinforcement assumes selfishness in that no one does anything without a payoff. Seemingly altruistic behaviors, such as risking one's life to rescue someone from a fire, do occur, but even these must be reinforced in some way, perhaps by public adulation, because the complete absence of reinforcement results only in extinction. The truly selfish take reinforcement from interactions but give none back, causing others to learn to avoid them. There is nothing new in all this. It simply rephrases the enduring Golden Rule, "Do unto others as you would have others do unto you," and since this remains a fine foundation on which to build ethical systems, Skinner's designed culture has more going for it than first meets the eye. How does reciprocity prevent controllers from abusing power? For their actions to continue they must be reinforced, so if we disapprove of the culture they contrive, we withhold their food pellets, resulting in a contract of "You scratch my back, I'll scratch yours." Thus experimenters and subjects, rulers and ruled, march arm in arm toward utopia or Walden II, but not, let us hope, toward 1984.

THE NATURE-NURTURE ISSUE

According to a deterministic psychology, heredity and experience provide the two great forces that influence every act. Scientists may disagree about their priority but not about this more basic point, for adhering to free will suggests that behavior cannot be studied scientifically. This bias has had noteworthy effects. Modern attitudes toward criminals, for example, stress rehabilitation and correction over punishment because their actions, it is assumed, are not their fault; this was hardly the prevalent view before Freud, S–R psychology et al. appeared. But justice systems are still chastised for mollycoddling—"They did it," proclaim Letters To The Editor, "let them take the consequences"—free will still has its adherents. That said, for virtually every behavior it can and sooner or later almost certainly will be asked whether nature or nurture is the primary precursor. Nor does this eternal debate merely reveal the scholar's propensity for splitting hairs. The answer has important ramifications, for it decides whether attempts are made to encourage desirable or inhibit unwanted behavior.

North American psychology has had a decided bias to blame environment and downplay heredity; Watson himself flatly denied that we possess any *instincts,* inborn tendencies shared by all members of a species. The Albert studies convinced him, if he wasn't already, that even such seeming reflexes as emotions with few exceptions (specifically, rage, fear, and love), were acquired, so he could confidently claim, "Give me a dozen healthy infants, well-formed, and my own specified world to bring them up in and I'll guarantee to take any one at random and train him to become any type of specialist I might select—doctor, lawyer, artist, merchant-chief and, yes, even beggar-man and thief, regardless of his talents, penchants, tendencies, abilities, vocations and race of his ancestors" (Watson, 1930, p. 104). To ignore genetics now seems naive, but in Watson's day its importance was little appreciated, Mendel's work being largely unknown. Nonetheless, this bias has persisted, which explains why theories of learning advanced by Hull, Tolman, and others cast such large shadows over the next generation. If environment is the be all and end all, then explaining learning is tantamount to explaining any behavior in which one might be interested, whether it involves social processes, psychopathology, or some other. Thus those theorizing about learning were seen as engaged in the most crucial of endeavors.

Why this bias? The North American mystique has historically featured a sometimes naive optimism. Most of us are not far removed from our pioneering foreparents, who left familiar environs to emigrate to a new land about which they knew little. They chose to battle frontiers in the belief that they could thereby make a fresh start and succeed by their own effort and so bestowed many cherished values and myths: initiative, rugged individualism, can do, the American Dream. Environmental explanations of behavior are similarly optimistic. They hold out possibilities for manipulating behaviors, whereas hereditary factors when all is said and done must be accepted with shrug-of-the-shoulder fatalism, "that's human nature." Moreover, an environmental bias expresses what most people hereabouts believe anyway. Consider juvenile delinquency. Most of us would accept as plausible the claims that delinquency stems from factors such as parental divorce or alcoholism, economic privation, or undesirable peer groups, while reflexively rejecting assertions that delinquents are inherently bad and nothing can be done about them.

Still, increasing data suggest that heredity must be assigned a larger role. Just as evidence of constraints on learning forced a tempering of Skinnerian optimism, so have studies of identical twins raised apart (Bouchard, Lykken, McGue, Segal & Tellegen, 1990). As Galton (1876) pointed out, such twins offer a ploy for separating nature and nurture, and this fact has been exploited to study a raft of psychological phenomena (see Plomin & McCearn, 1993). Since identical twins come from one fertilized egg and so have the same heredity, any differences must be due to environment. Fraternal twins on the other hand reflect variations in both factors, so comparing the variation in a commodity such as intelligence between pairs of identical as opposed to fraternal twins, especially when pair members have been raised in different circumstances, should reveal the role of each. Despite sometimes extreme environmental changes, identical twins show remarkable similarities not only in such obviously natural traits as appearance and health, but in psychological matters such as attitudes, temperament, and propensity for psychosis. There are the usual complications. To mention a few, nature's importance may change over the life span; it apparently increases for example for intelligence (McGue, Bouchard, Iacono & Lykken, 1993), even though experiences and hence, one might expect, their impact should grow. Also, an inherited trait such as introversion no doubt influences the environment in which one immerses oneself (shy people prefer libraries to cocktail parties, as well as other introverts), so heredity determines environment's effects (Rowe, 1993). Finally, the genetic component in alcoholism is far more significant in males than in females (McGue, 1993). As a rule of thumb, for a variety of behaviors, heredity accounts for about 50 percent of the variance.

Intelligence, the Jensen Controversy, and Academic Freedom

One battle has raged around the presumed commodity of intelligence that common parlance refers to as mental ability. The fires have been further stoked by difficulties of measurement and increasing attacks (R. Sternberg, 1985) on IQ scores from standard tests (Terman & Merrill, 1973; Wechsler, 1958) as relating more to abilities relatively unimportant for ultimate success. Still, whatever intelligence means, it is generally agreed that everyone has some of it and amounts vary, so it is reasonable to ask about the relative role of nature and nurture. Galton, after finding that genius ran in families, stressed an inborn component, a possibility the prevailing environmental bias soon rejected, but while many twin studies performed over the years differ, the conclusion in principle was the comfortable one for which any beginning student would opt, that both are important. There matters rested until Jensen (1969) recast the issue in an explosive context: the small but reliable superiority in average IQ scores of white over black North Americans. Previously, the nurture bias had also decreed that this must reflect blacks' environmental disadvantages, their disproportionate representation in lower socioeconomic classes, less access to quality education, and the like. However, Jensen assessed some identical twin data and concluded that the *heritability* of intelligence, that is, the proportion of the variance due to genetics, was about 80 percent. One implication that he touched on only briefly, but which soon became the focus of attention, was that blacks' inferiority was in large part innate. The Aryan myth had been reborn!

Since many sources, for example, Loehlin, Lindzey and Spuhler (1975), discuss the pros and cons of Jensen's data and conclusions as well as the plethora of studies that continue to be conducted on this topic, there is no need to trudge along every byway here, especially since empirical, rational, and in this case emotional arguments can be summoned to support every conceivable position. For example, concerning the critical question of intelligence's heritability, no one disputes so far as I know that it lies somewhere between 0 percent and 100 percent, but within these boundaries, disagreement reigns. Likewise, avowed nurturists, Freudian and behaviorist alike, assume that the first six years of life are crucial, so if environmental deficiencies are not corrected before children begin school, irreversible damage results, hence programs such as Head Start, the Johnson administration's attempt to enrich environments of disadvantaged preschoolers. Early assessments of the effectiveness of such interventions were discouraging, a major stimulus for Jensen's article, and seemed to vindicate his pessimistic conclusion that the IQ difference would remain regardless. But later evidence (e.g., Palmer & Anderson, 1979, cited in Atkinson, Atkinson, Smith & Bem, 1993) suggested that their impact could be considerable.

Finally, others objected to IQ tests themselves as being designed by and so biased toward the white middle-class, emphasizing abilities that they had more opportunity to master. Thus sociologist Adrian Dove (1968), with tongue planted firmly in cheek, devised the Chitlings Test, which posed conundra whose solutions residents of black/ghetto environs would be more likely to encounter, to wit: a "handkerchief head" is (a) a cool cat, (b) a porter, (c) an Uncle Tom, (d) a hoddi, (e) a preacher. The present white middle-class writer who suffers the further disadvantage of being from western Canada admits to not having a clue, ergo, he must lack intelligence. Point well taken. Yet later evidence indicated that test bias was at best a minor contributor to the racial difference (Kaplan,

1985, cited in Weiten, 1995). So the argument rages on and once more calls into question data's supposed ability to resolve controversy. My own suspicion is that final answers may be long in coming, because statistical machinations, however sophisticated, cannot overcome a basic difficulty, that comparing blacks and whites involves a subject variable and is therefore confounded. As they invariably differ in both nature and nurture, the causal role of each must remain doubtful—unless one can find identical twin pairs with one white and one black member. A recent discussion by Neisser, Boodoo, et al. (1996) strengthens this suspicion. The many complexities, conflicting findings, and plausible rival hypotheses they survey leave one with the distinct impression that there are precious few precise conclusions on which one can hang one's hat, which once again calls into question the ability of empirical investigation to provide them.

I prefer to focus on the political aftermaths of Jensen's work, because they shed more light on the scientific attitude. It should come as no surprise that he stirred up a hornet's nest, especially since, however one regards his conclusions, one must wonder about his sense of timing. As any card-carrying baby boomer will gladly reveal, the late 1960s was a special time of growing opposition to the Viet Nam debacle, the civil rights movement, the beginning of the women's movement, and so on. For young people it was de rigueur to accept nothing from authority figures and, especially on college campuses, at the least provocation to demonstrate and sit in. (So strong was this propensity that it even spilled over from Our Great Neighbor to the South, with its traditions of revolution and Men Who Have to Do What Men Have to Do, to this normally more docile country, albeit in forms that again demonstrated Canadians' historic preference for moderation, compromise over confrontation and, some would say, lethargy). When coupled with Jensen's residence at the University of California at Berkeley from which the student dissent movement first emerged and with a position that would be controversial at any time, the grievous indignities that Jensen (1972) reports suffering, the demonstrations, raided classrooms and threatening phone calls, are not completely unpredictable.

Most notable was the university's refusal to capitulate to demands, including some from powerful political and social forces, that he be dismissed and/or forced to forego his research and publication (political correctness obsessions are nothing new), because this refusal demonstrates a principle on which effective inquiry rests: *academic freedom.* It insures scholars' right to pursue any topics and adopt any positions they choose and is protected by the system of *tenure* or appointment without term by which, after a probationary period during which young scholars must demonstrate their worth, their jobs are guaranteed. Censorship has no place in universities! Besides the many examples in history of its dangers (Joyce's *Ulysses,* now seen as a landmark literary achievement, was for some time banned from North America), it is always possible that reality may fly in the face of prevailing attitudes, that it may not be nice, and science is in the business of seeking out things as they are, not as we would like them to be.

Therefore any idea, no matter how silly or repugnant it seems, has the right to open evaluation; if deficient, it will eventually be found out, but denying evaluation out of hand may eliminate valid possibilities. Thus the Council for the Society for the Psychological Study of Social Issues (SPSSI, 1969), which called Jensen's work into question on every ground imaginable, far from calling for retribution reaffirmed its commitment to free inquiry, and Hebb (1970) went further to express the attitude of most academics. After first deploring the level of criticism practiced by SPSSI, which in his opinion was little more than blind invective, he argued that, while he disagreed with Jensen, the latter had done science a service by making his views available for consideration, so they should be welcomed. It is well to remember how according to Darwin nature operates: far more possibilities are generated than the traffic will bear, and this provides more possibilities for and thus improves the quality of ultimate selections (Gruber, 1974). In any event, these Jensen critics all evinced the tolerance value described in Chapter 2. Furthermore, Canadian academics similarly rallied around the flag during our version of the Jensen brouhaha that involved Philip Rushton (1985), who likewise holds that blacks are inherently inferior to whites, but also that orientals surpass both. Similar demands for muzzling and/or dismissal arose. Rushton's institution, the University of Western Ontario, again stood firm.

Tolerance may not be the only scientific value shown here. Being unacquainted with Jensen or Rushton, I prefer to give both the benefit of the doubt that rather than being racists posing as scientists, each practices a genuine commitment to the priority of data even when these are personally distressing. An anecdote about Kepler (Koestler, 1970) is apposite. Copernicus had assumed that planetary orbits around the sun were circular; they had been designed by God, Who, being perfect, would certainly use this most perfect of forms. Unfortunately for the deeply religious Kepler, his calculations proved that they must be elliptical, causing him to exclaim that he had left behind a carload of dung. Yet he was too much the scientist to dismiss what was. Did Jensen or Rushton have similar sentiments? Certainly their positions have provoked painful episodes and made them virtually persona non grata both professionally and probably personally, so if nothing else one must admire them for having the courage of their convictions. As well, Jensen (1972) displays a firmer commitment to data priorities than do some of his critics whose doctrinaire environmentalism, one suspects, no amount of data could shake. Whether his interpretations of those data are warranted is a separate issue.

One could nonetheless accuse him of naivety. It is the scientist's job, he claims, to provide knowledge, most of which can be used for either good or evil, which implies that others must decide on its use. Although Jensen himself may not be racist, his arguments have been exploited by others who are, proving yet again that no scientist in these times can sidestep the moral implications of his work. So to avoid being misunderstood on so sensitive a matter, let me make my own views clear. In principle, it is not impossible, much as we might wish it otherwise, that there are inherent racial IQ differences and that attempts to achieve equality are doomed. However, we should only adopt this outlook if conclusive data demand it, and they are unlikely to become available because of formidable methodological problems. In the meantime, let us proceed as if intervention can make a difference. Being wrong loses nothing except money, and success offers huge benefits.

I want now to pursue another matter touched on above, because it relates to science's effects on psychology. As devil's advocate, I propose the heresy that to safeguard academic freedom a better alternative to tenure must be found, because its costs outweigh its benefits. First, the Rushtons and Jensens are few; precious little scholarly work evokes much interest let alone protest from external forces. Should a system be retained to protect a minuscule minority that breeds other evils and may threaten scholarly life itself? I do not refer to the usual objection that tenure gives one carte blanche to goof off and fosters deadwood. Most scholars work very hard indeed. The evils lie elsewhere. Academics should be both scholars/researchers and teachers and each activity should carry equal weight, but in practice the publish-or-perish syndrome has rendered teaching a peripheral factor in matters of promotion, salaries, and that most powerful motivator, peer recognition. So it suffers because there are those who make no bones about viewing it as a necessary evil to be floundered through as painlessly as possible. The phrase, "teaching load," which refers to contacts per week, nicely captures this attitude, implying as it does that teaching is a burden.

It is quite understandable when young scholars adopt this view. While under grievous pressure to publish, they must demonstrate usually only minimal teaching competence, and once the safety net of tenure has been installed, the door is open to get away with as little competence as possible, because anything more earns so few rewards. It speaks well for the prevailing sense of professional responsibility and personal pride that so many still try to do their best. Yet inevitably, since everyone, scholars included, is ruled by reinforcers, there is ever more dereliction from what should be viewed as not only a primary duty but a privilege, a chance to stimulate and influence bright young people. (I should stress that these remarks relate mainly to the teaching of undergraduates; graduate student teaching is an entirely different matter, usually involving much smaller classes or seminars in one's special field, so preparation is far less onerous, and such an audience will routinely put forward fruitful ideas that can lead to yet more publications). As a result, the taxpayers are becoming restless and rightly so, because it is they who foot the bills to support universities directly, via the increasingly stratospheric fees they pay for their progeny to attend, and indirectly, through taxes. Then those progeny are too often inflicted with undermotivated and/or inexperienced instructors (or sometimes even graduate students) who have rarely been trained in the rudiments of effective teaching but left to cope as best they can after being advised only to make sure their flies are done up or bra straps hidden! Senior, tenured professors reserve for themselves the less time-and energy-consuming senior courses, and those of world reputation, whose presence their universities trumpet in publicity releases, rarely set foot in undergraduate classrooms as a rule.

How does all this relate to science's impact on psychology? I can summon no conclusive data, but I suspect that these twisted priorities are most pervasive in the sciences; indeed this might be expected, since an empirical outlook would encourage them. One major reason that teaching is underemphasized is that no one has found a way to measure it effectively, good teaching being inherently a judgment call about which consumers differ (there are students, sadly, who if they don't hate you, it's a dead giveaway that you aren't doing your job properly). This being the case, psychology has, my experience suggests, also internalized this less desirable scientific value, whereas were it still domiciled in philosophy it might not have done so, since the humanities seem to attach more importance to teaching.

I revere the university as an invaluable institution, and I fear that if we do not clean up our own shop the taxpayers will become disenchanted and dangerously cut back their largesse. Teaching is to them far and away our most important task, and, if we do not place more emphasis on doing it well, the chickens will come home to roost. There are already ominous signs: severe cutbacks in government funding with few voices raised in protest and declining enrollments everywhere. Could a suspicion be growing that the university is no longer the best place to become truly educated? The naivety shown by some academics, that the public has a duty to pay them well for doing their research, which is some kind of sacred cow, is astonishing. The public is coming to realize that even most applied let alone pure research has no tangible impact whatsoever, so contrary to what academic propaganda claims, life would be little affected if most of it were to cease tomorrow. Those of us who love doing it must realize how fortunate we are to be paid quite well for doing what is basically a hobby, and act accordingly.

How would eliminating tenure improve matters? Academics thus protected from accountability can pursue research and its rewards exclusively while exploiting academic freedom as somehow giving the right to downplay this other duty—although freedom should never equal licentiousness. No matter how one teaches, chances are some consumers will approve and others complain, so dismissal for purported inadequacy should not be undertaken lightly, but there are a few who constantly, year after year garner nothing but complaints yet make no attempt to improve even when resources are available for doing so (most universities, after long and inexcusable failure to do so, now provide them). Universities must be able to force such derelicts to shape up or ship out. Are there alternatives to tenure that would still protect a Jensen or Rushton? I believe it would suffice if all university members, administrators and professors alike, vowed an en masse commitment, perhaps written into employment contracts, that threats to anyone's freedom of speech would be treated as threats to all, with strikes resorted to if necessary. In the workplace, such willingness to stand together to confront powerful forces holding the purse strings has proven its effectiveness, and the Jensen/Rushton episodes indicate that academics would do the same.

Aggression

This tendency to commit violent acts is obviously important, since it subsumes so many evils. Ethologist Konrad Lorenz (1966), like many pessimists (including Freud), saw it as part of human nature, more specifically as an instinct that is part of our genetic makeup because of its evolutionary value. Although when directed against other members of the same species it might now seem maladaptive, it also may have benefits, such as insuring that dominant and therefore biologically superior males sire progeny and that species members spread out over the habitat, so as not to exhaust resources. However, since our environment differs markedly from that of our ancestors, this once beneficial trait now threatens our very survival, and unfortunately an instinct cannot be held in check by, say, moral beliefs that it is wrong; it must be released. Most species that have such a dangerous tendency evolve *habit rituals,* actings out, often remarkably predictable ones, that let off steam harmlessly, but these must evolve over many generations, and we have not had to develop them because, being physically quite weak, we could not do much damage. But all this has changed, evolutionarily speaking, in the twinkling of an eye, for we alone can contrive artificial means to aggression, that is, weapons, and share such knowledge with one another, and evolution has not had time to catch up, making us now far and away the most dangerous of species. Compounding the danger is an instinct for *militant enthusiasm,* to band together in groups. It too would be adaptive in primitive environments, "united we stand," but the pernicious result is that our aggressive acts may involve not only individuals but larger entities, as in mobs or nations.

So it is no less than a question of survival that we find releasers to purge these tendencies. Lorenz suggests several, one being sports. Most involve competition in some form, ritualized aggression, and when we cheer the home team as a group, we release militant enthusiasm, suggesting that such apparently useless events as the Olympic Games serve a real purpose. Science is another release, so involving many in it offers benefits besides advancing knowledge. Its search for truth transcends national boundaries, making those involved collaborators rather than antagonists, together wrestling secrets from the common adversary, nature—and scientists do display hefty aggressive and competitive streaks (Abra, 1993). Finally, that uniquely human propensity, humor, is often aggressive, directed against some butt of the joke (Koestler, 1970), and it releases militant enthusiasm through its shared, social aspects. Do we not laugh more loudly and enjoy it more when in the company of others?

Lorenz's key concern, however, is that we realize that aggression and militant enthusiasm are instincts and so cannot be denied; to believe otherwise invites disaster. His arguments are persuasive, especially when the abundant observational data he provides are taken in conjunction with history, but invite several rejoinders. Sports certainly release aggressive tendencies, but whether they reduce them is debatable; witness soccer crowds. Second, if aggression is an instinct that must be worked off periodically, it should increase with further denial, yet as someone succinctly put it, there is no evidence that it builds up like urine in the bladder. Then, too, even if inborn it may not be instinctive in the sense of universal. If it were, then aggressive episodes, while far more common than we would wish, heaven knows, would be even more pervasive, with mayhem on every corner. Moreover, the majority of such acts are committed by a relative few while most people remain relatively peaceful, so it may be that the highly aggressive are genetically deviant. The notion that *super males* who have an extra Y chromosome are far more aggressive (see Jarvik, Klodin & Matsuyama, 1973, for discussion) is no longer tenable (Lefrancois, 1983), but this does not rule out other such possibilities. In a similar vein, one of the few reliable sex differences that Maccoby and Jacklin's (1974) pioneering comparisons found was in aggression, which reduces any propensity in the human population generally by about 50 percent—a considerable number still but a rosier picture than Lorenz painted (although it may be that the sexes are equally prone to aggression but express it differently and for different reasons, Eagly & Steffen, 1986).

Finally, Lorenz cited mainly animal evidence, and, even if we share such an instinct, it is possible that nurture is for us more important; Fromm (1977) saw human aggression stemming from experiences, such as boredom or alienation. So let us turn to other nurture explanations, the evidence for which Lorenz either ignored or dismissed out of hand. Several invoke reinforcement mechanisms. Appropriate contingencies can unleash fighting in ordinarily docile rats and in people; witness the effects of medals in wartime or fat salaries paid to hockey goons such as the notorious, Dave "Hammer" Schultz (1981), whose skills are not for the game but for fisticuffs and intimidation. The most influential proposal (Dollard et al., 1939) ties aggression to *frustration*, which presumably results from circumstances such as denial of access to anticipated goals (Amsel, 1958). Frustration, being aversive, should induce trial-and-error behaviors, including aggression against either the source of frustration or, in *displaced aggression*, another more convenient target, as when parents take out stresses from work on their children. Regardless, aggression that lessens frustration is reinforced and tends to recur. It follows that if eliminating aggression is deemed desirable frustrating circumstances should be minimized, which would vindicate permissive child-rearing espoused by such as Dr. Spock. Whether this practice has had favorable results is of course debatable, but if not it could be due to the strategy itself being flawed. Frustration is unavoidable in human existence. Therefore might it not be better that children experience it, but learn to cope with it using other responses?

Aggression can also be learned, especially by children, by *vicarious conditioning* or imitation, as in "monkey see, monkey do." Thus when some first observed a model belabor a bolo doll (when knocked over, it springs back up) and were then allowed access to it, their tendency to imitate the aggression depended on its results, being greater when the model was seen to be rewarded rather than punished afterwards (Bandura, 1965). Still, even these caveats oversimplify matters. Whether observing violence increases propensities for it has been copiously studied since television and violence thereon became omnipresent, particularly on children's programs such as cartoons. To survey this mammoth literature here is unnecessary, especially since as usual a final verdict is unavailable, but Berkowitz's (1964) ingenious studies deserve mention. They typically involve three phases. First, the actual subject and another, an experimenter confederate, interact while each takes a purported test, with the confederate either insulting the subject by making disparaging remarks about the latter's performance or going neutrally about her business. The second phase presents a film of boxing in which one adversary is savagely beaten. Everyone sees the same clip, but the violence is portrayed as either "justified"—the belaboree is a villain getting his just desserts—or "unjustified"—he was once a scoundrel, but no more. Finally, to assess aggressive tendencies, subjects judge a drawing supposedly done by the confederate and deliver electric shocks to the latter based on that judgment. Insulted and presumably angered subjects delivered more, as did those who had seen justified violence. Does then observing violence induce aggression? The answer must be it depends—on one's emotional state, how it is portrayed and a host of other factors (see Johnson, 1972).

These results do nonetheless challenge the do-gooders who would eliminate any and all violence from TV. If this would truly lessen violence in everyday life, then notwithstanding the dangers of censorship the possibility would deserve serious consideration, but this seems unlikely. If TV violence had such dastardly effects, acts of aggression would be copious. However, most children seem able to watch *Roadrunner* and other violent cartoons without noticeable harm, and eliminating them would penalize those children while the problem remained, for countless other triggers could set off the atypical few who are affected because of previous experience and/or inherent proclivity. John Hinkley, President Reagan's would-be assassin, was reportedly influenced by the film *Taxi Driver*, which is extremely violent. It is also superb, and myriad others saw it without being driven to assassinate the president. Should they be denied an enriching experience on the remote chance that this might mollify one troubled individual?

Language

What are the origins of this distinctive human ability? Animals can acquire language of sorts (Gardner & Gardner, 1969; Premack & Premack, 1972), but our abilities in this regard and its role in our lives are infinitely greater. Skinner (1957) provided one conspicuous nurture account, but it needs but brief elucidation, since he saw verbal behaviors as being like any other, obeying the principles already discussed. Infants supposedly emit trial-and-error utterances that environmental forces, mainly parents, selectively reinforce and shape toward acceptable ends, perhaps via cries of joy when random words emerge from a crib such as "mama," "dada," or, from that of prodigious tot Orson Welles, "The desire to take medicine is one of the greatest features that distinguishes men from animals" (quoted in Leaming, 1985, p. 9).

However, in a famous book review, linguist Noam Chomsky (1959) chastised this account for its inability to handle some basic facts. First, language is acquired with remarkable speed, whereas Skinner's scenario would be laboriously inefficient. Also, language usage is characteristically creative; we paraphrase and concoct utterances never used before. How could experience bestow such novelties? Finally, by G. Miller's (1965) reckoning, 1000 times the age of the earth would be needed to experience every linguistically acceptable sentence once. How then can we understand sentences never heard before? Chomsky therefore argued that everyone inherits various *language universals,* properties that all known languages express, albeit in varying vocabularies and forms (Latin places verbs at the ends of sentences), so we have the potential to grasp and use them. That children deprived of human contact (R. Brown, 1958) are enormously deficient in language ability shows that usage is not inevitable; experience must provide a particular language by which these universals can be expressed. Yet evident *critical periods* in maturation during which language is acquired more readily (Lenneberg, 1967), indicate again that nurture's effects depend on a stage set by nature.

Talent/Genius

Do those responsible for the landmarks of human culture have special gifts, or did Jane Austen fulfill potentials that, given similar advantaged circumstances, anyone could realize? The latter, nurture position has been taken by such otherwise diverse authorities as Skinner (1968, 1974) and humanists (Maslow, 1962; Rogers, 1970). For Skinner, creative achievements reflected accidentally emitted behavioral mutations and so need no special abilities; purported geniuses merely reflect a fortunate history of reinforcement. The humanists saw creativity as a basic need that everyone possesses. A metaneed atop Maslow's famous hierarchy, it inevitably occurs as a result of self-actualization but only after needs of higher priority, such as for basic nutrition or belonging, are met. Thus this need is an inherent one that probably cannot be enhanced, but can certainly be discouraged. A favorable environment therefore will satisfy basic needs, encourage the spontaneous "doing your own thing" propensities that, for humanists, promote health and hence creativity, and then get out of the way so this natural tendency can emerge.

These two positions differ appreciably about a preferable environment's specifics, but agree that it is necessary and that anyone exposed to it can achieve great things. As has been made abundantly clear already, I disagree. An inborn quality, genius if you will, seems to me essential and those who possess it are a breed apart. Since we have no idea what it is or how one gets it, far from explaining achievement it itself needs to be explained, but denying its reality raises both empirical and rational difficulties. It is only a potential; actual accomplishments still wait upon suitable experiences, whether of the hothouse or dastardly variety, but without it their impact is minimal. Silk purses do not come from sows' ears!

The Sex Difference in Creative Achievement

Even fervent feminists must admit that men have produced most of the achievements that have come to be called great. While women have more than held their own in literature and dance and dominate fields such as crafts, great composers, mathematicians, and scientists have by and large been male. Why? Nowhere have knee-jerk environmental explanations invoking that catchall villain, socialization, been more evident than here (e.g., Chicago, 1982; Heintz, 1977). The hypothesis is undeniably credible. Historically, women have suffered severe disadvantages of denial of access to necessary experiences (Greer, 1979; Woolf, 1977) or same-sex role models (de Mille, 1958), but to lay the blame solely at nurture's door is premature since a subject variable is involved. The sexes differ in both experiential and, according to most biology books, inherent aspects. Unfortunately then, Wooley's (1910) erstwhile observation vis-à-vis sex differences still holds: "There is perhaps no field aspiring to be scientific where flagrant personal bias . . . and even sentimental rot and drivel, have run riot to such an extent as here" (pp. 340–341).

Abra and Valentine-French (1991), after surveying many possible explanations, therefore felt obliged to play devil's advocate and speculate about nature's role. For one thing, it too could influence the qualities of self-confidence and persistence that buttress achievement. However, there are indications that the sexes may as a rule (for there are always exceptions) be predisposed to excel at different pursuits. Maccoby and Jacklin's (1974) generalizations, that men prevail in quantitative and spatial, and women in verbal abilities are now called into question, since sex differences seem to be declining overall (Feingold, 1988; Hyde & Linn, 1988). However, on SAT scores, boys vastly outnumber girls among the highest achievers in mathematical tasks, disproportions that are if anything increasing despite profound changes in sex roles (Stanley & Benbow, 1982), and similar differences appear elsewhere, for instance, more high achievers are female in verbal tasks. As a generalization, gender differences increase in more select samples such as the highly gifted (Becker & Hedges, 1984)—the very population likely to produce the great achievers of the future.

Differences in brain functioning provide one enticing explanation for these findings. The masculine brain is more *lateralized*, its functions more precisely localized in one hemisphere (Goleman, 1980; Kimura, 1987). Juschka (1987) therefore followed Gardner's (1983) notion that talent is field specific and speculated that men will excel in *asymmetric* fields, those whose requisites are more specific to one hemisphere (for several reasons music and visual art seemed to her of this kind) and women will excel in those needing less localized abilities, (for example, dance and literature). Several provisos are in order. First, the purported male superiority of the past thereby comes down to the arbitrary designation of certain fields (usually those in which men have done the most work) as inherently more worthwhile. Why should oil painting be seen as a major art form, crafts a minor? Also, if literature is indeed a bailiwick for female excellence, it is also yet another in which most seminal achievements to date have come from men. How many great writers have we lost because of the special difficulties talented women have faced in realizing their potential? Finally, it is no more sexist to suggest that men and women might have different spheres of excellence than contrasting apples with oranges is fruitist.

6

Psychological Determinism:
Problems and Alternatives

There are two problems, one logical the other empirical, that trouble any strict determinism and have led the natural sciences to modify their versions. First, assuming that everything has a cause raises the possibility of an *infinite regress*, a chain of events with no discernible end—if dust storms produce dry hair, it follows that another factor must cause dust storms, perhaps strong winds, but then there must be a cause for the winds, ad infinitum. One escape from this impasse hypothesizes an initial event that causes others but is itself uncaused, such as Aristotle's Unmoved Mover, that might be taken for a Supreme Being (R. Watson, 1963), but this gambit is unsatisfying; allowing one exception to a law such as causality opens the door to other exceptions to it.

Another difficulty emerges from Heisenberg's demonstration that we cannot simultaneously measure both the position and velocity of an electron because the operations needed to assess position, such as illuminating it, inevitably affect its velocity, while measuring the latter renders its position at any one time indeterminate. The implication? That observing phenomena changes them. Thus a degree of uncertainty is introduced into empirical investigation, which, together with the innovative outlooks such as Bohr's quantum mechanics that followed, demanded that strict determinism be abandoned because relations between variables can only be described statistically and within a margin of error. In turn, nature came to seem rather more capricious, especially human behavior, where in some opinions that margin now approaches free will, and behavior may seem to just happen. As Barnett (1948) put it, "If physical events are indeterminate and the future is unpredictable, then perhaps the unknown quantity called 'mind' may yet guide man's destiny among the infinite uncertainties of a capricious universe" (p. 35).

PROBLEMS WITH PSYCHOLOGICAL DETERMINISM

Subject Variables

The first problem lurked beneath the discussion of experiments of this kind. Comparisons of subjects assigned to groups with a shared characteristic are inevitably confounded. Some correlations thereby revealed can be broken to establish causal priority, but consider the substantial one between sex and creative achievement. Any number of explanations are possible (Abra & Valentine-French, 1991) because in the last analysis conclusive answers are not. Animal studies are of little help since genuine creativity lies beyond their grasp (Abra, 1988b), and subjects cannot be randomly assigned to groups until change of sex operations become morally acceptable. In general, psychology encompasses a host of independent variables, including some that there is every reason to suspect have powerful effects, that defy controlled investigation. Subject variable experiments are not completely useless. Correlations allow more accurate prediction—it is useful to know that memory tends to decline with age—and sophisticated design and statistical techniques now available (that discussion would take us too far afield) have rendered this enterprise more precise. In addition, subject variables provide crucibles for a theory (Underwood, 1975). Should it predict correlations that are not fulfilled, the theory is called into question. Nonetheless, subject variable experiments can only reveal what has happened, not why, which to most scientists is insufficient. As well, they provide a tempting trap into which it is all too easy to fall and against which one must constantly be on guard. The most common mistake by far in interpreting psychological data, committed constantly not only in the media and by politicians but also, too often, by psychologists themselves, is to infer causality from a correlation.

Another Tail Wags the Dog

I am of two minds about statistics' dominance of curricula. The necessity of some expertise is evident. Besides being useful, it helps weed out the "touchy-feelies" who want to help people but are traumatized by any hint of graph or equation, for this suggests deficiencies in a scientific attitude, and the profession can do without those incapable of rigorous thought. Yet the case can be made that statistics is overemphasized. Most graduate programs require at least one advanced course, and it typically consumes more time and causes more anxiety than any other, while those in the presumed matter of interest, content, take second place. Thus Skinner (1963) deplored the flight to statistics by both students and professionals that results in more knowledge about calculators (nowadays, computers) than behaving organisms. One need not go along with his reasons (that any genuine behavioral law, being universal, is demonstrable on a single subject, rendering statistical analysis of group trends superfluous) to find his objection compelling. Why has this happened? One likely culprit is psychology's increasingly diverse content. With prospects for a shared paradigm becoming ever more remote, the only curriculum matter on which department members of wildly differing perspectives can agree is that they all need statistics. Even exposure to psychology's greatest figures and ideas is by no means unanimously accepted. For some arch-empiricists, knowing the literature as it is called, that is, what has been done in one's specialty over the last few years, is all the knowledge of the past one needs, and apart from that, Henry Ford had it right. History is bunk!

But this undue emphasis poses dangers. For one, statistics courses have become powerful gatekeepers to the profession, a foremost sign of competence. Yet one of H. Gardner's (1983) seven independent talents, for interpersonal relations, would seem crucial for effective performance in subfields such as counseling and clinical practice. Might the preoccupation with statistics eliminate some students with much to offer in this respect while favoring others with less? By informal impression, the stereotypic number-cruncher's people skills are not awesome, yet a primary factor in the success of therapy is the quality of the therapist–patient relationship (Strupp & Binder, 1984). In addition, those who have received accreditation in the form of the Ph.D. dominate the profession and in most cases are committed to statistics and experimental design as a sine qua non. As they hire (and sometimes fire), edit journals, and evaluate grant requests, they tend to favor work that fulfills these standards. Here lies one likely reason for the mediocrity of so much published research. It cannot be faulted by the standards of prevailing priorities; its failings reflect an underemphasis on imagination in underlying content. On the other hand, there is work of unquestioned worth (Piaget's comes to mind) which any competent undergraduate can tear apart on methodological grounds and features precious little in the way of statistics, graphs, and the like. As a final drawback, among the most powerful motivators for scholars is the respect of one's colleagues, and, to earn it, along with brownie points at promotion and salary time, one must show a commitment to methodological and statistical priorities or be constantly forced to defend what one does, especially if it leans toward the qualitative or speculative. It must be remembered that statistics is like science a means to certain ends and should be exploited only so far as it allows progress toward them.

Circularity of Reasoning

Several deterministic theories fall victim to a weakness most apparent in Freud. An explanation, such as an unresolved Oedipus complex for homosexuality, cannot be verified empirically because the supposed antecedent cannot be manipulated in a controlled experiment. Thus such a concept can become *circular,* as when an Oedipal problem is used to explain a phenomenon, homosexuality, when the sole evidence for it is that same phenomenon. Why is someone homosexual? Because of an unresolved Oedipal problem. How do we know of the problem? Because they are homosexual. In other words, Freud's constructs are routinely invoked post hoc or after the fact, which is akin to betting on races already run. The theory does not specify beforehand the conditions that produce such an Oedipus complex or the behavioral effects that should follow (Popper, 1972).

But no one has more fervently advocated the priority of data or opposed untestable theories than Skinner. Surely, he cannot be taken to task on similar grounds! Oh? Reinforcers, we are told, must be present in some form, but to avoid post hoc explanation these must be specified in advance and defined by independent procedures. In laboratory situations this is easily done because of the control over organism and conditions; depriving rats of food insures the reinforcer's effectiveness, and random occurrences can be eliminated so that it alone consistently follows the behavior studied (Kimble, 1961). However, naturalistic situations do not allow such precision. Consider *altruistic* or, in Skinnerian language, seemingly unreinforced behaviors such as risking one's life to rescue someone. What are the payoffs? Possibilities can be suggested—praise, medals, and so on (but not feeling good, since such internal events supposedly have no influence) but whether reinforcement of any kind is operating is by no means certain. Yet Skinner remains adamant. If behaviors recur, there must be a reinforcer, however subtle, because they have recurred. Thus his analyses are as resistant to disproof as Freud's. A conclusive test requires a situation that certifiably eliminates any and all possible reinforcers to determine how behavior is affected, but such a one is well nigh impossible to come by and if it were to give Skinner the lie, ingenious disciples could no doubt identify overlooked possibilities. His contention that the world within the skin plays no causal role also defies disproof. As Skinner rightly points out, its phenomena and external reinforcement are so intertwined that situations invariably confound them. Determining priority would require a controlled experiment that manipulated one while holding the other constant. Even if such an experiment is possible, to my knowledge it has not been performed, so to attribute causality to one is premature.

Still More Self-Fulfilling Prophecies

The psychology given away in the post-Watson era stresses our deterministic status, but Lefcourt (1973), obviously responding to Skinner's advice that we accept it, presents several lines of evidence that this view may be unhealthy. The first involves the learned helplessness studies discussed earlier, which showed that a belief that one cannot control one's destiny may have dire consequences. Glass, Singer, and Friedman's (1969) studies carry similar undertones. Noise pervades modern life—sirens blare, motorcycles race in the wee hours of the morning, grass grows, caterpillars mate—how does it affect us? Glass et al.'s subjects experienced noise of varying loudness that appeared at either regular or unpredictable intervals. Efficiency on various tasks performed during this auditory bombardment decreased surprisingly little; the noteworthy effects came later when subjects tried to solve a series of puzzles, some of which had no solution, to reveal persistence in the face of frustration. Perhaps unexpectedly, louder noises did not lessen this, but the unpredictable kind did (which may explain how people manage to live in close proximity to airports or elevated trains; deafening the din may be, but it is as regular as clockwork). However, unpredictable noise's effects could be counteracted by providing a button that subjects believed would turn it off. In fact the button didn't work and they rarely used it, but apparently its availability was enough. Why is unpredictable noise unsettling? Presumably, it too suggests an environment that we are unable to control, but the illusion that we can helps us cope. In a similar vein, postsurgical patients require less pain-killing medication and report less suffering when they themselves rather than staff decide how much of it to take, and when (White, 1986).

Lefcourt's third line of evidence, although anecdotal, is especially poignant. A woman had for some years been incarcerated on a psychiatric hospital's floor that both staff and inmates knew housed hopeless cases, but while her room was being painted she was moved to the floor on which everyone knew resided those about to be released. Her psychotic behavior patterns immediately lessened but, sadly, when her room was finished she was returned to it. Within a week she died although no physical cause could be found, so some suggested it was because of despair. Lefcourt concludes that both determinism and free will are illusions, invented to make sense of experience, but our behaviors differ greatly depending on the one we accept and free will has more desirable results. Therefore, "To submit to however wise a master planner is to surrender an illusion that may be the bedrock on which life flourishes" (Lefcourt, 1973, p. 424).

Nor does Skinner's supposed safeguard against external control, the reciprocity of reinforcement, offer much comfort, for most of us intuitively suspect that the experimenter–subject partnership is less egalitarian than he supposed, and with good reason. In a cultural context, different reinforcer delays are likely, with experimenters delivering theirs soon after subjects respond, whereas the former would undergo longer delays before, say, elections. Thus by Skinner's own reckoning, subject responses would be more ingrained and experimenters would have more control. Experimenters would be better able to manipulate factors that increase reinforcer effectiveness as well, such as environmental design and deprivation of needs, to enhance subjects' motivation.

Why might the illusion that we are controlled foster evils? Perhaps because it denies two attributes crucial to well being. One is *hope*. May (1972) has observed that ours is an age of personal powerlessness; we too often feel like insignificant cogs in large machines. Witness the faceless high rises in which so many reside, the government bureaucracies and huge corporations that employ us, modern universities with their megasized classes and multiple choice examinations. Witness too those defining symbols of our age: computerized ID cards and unmanned telephones that put us on eternal hold while playing Muzak that we didn't request. For May, as for Nietzsche and Maslow, to achieve our potential and psychological health we need a sense of power over our lives. Haney, Banks, and Zimbardo (1973) dramatically verified this point. Student volunteers were assigned to be either "prisoners" or "guards" and given the trappings of their roles—uniforms, handcuffs, and the like—but soon were playing their parts all too well. Behavior on both sides began to resemble that in real prisons, with guards becoming exemplary petty tyrants, brutal and callous, and prisoners becoming sullen and rebellious. This seemingly harmless simulation had to be discontinued lest participants suffer serious damage. The authors surmised that power–victim situations such as prisons promote feelings of *deindividuation*, that one's actions are unnoticed and don't matter, so even ordinarily healthy people adopt unhealthy roles in them. Thus the tensions in real prisons may be inevitable, and better training of personnel or treatment of inmates is unlikely to help.

The second property determinism threatens is *responsibility*. Because behaviors are attributed to sources other than ourselves, less admirable ones are not our fault. *West Side Story*'s juvenile delinquents wickedly satirize some popular excuses that they don't for a moment believe, that their fathers are bastards, their mothers SOBs, their sisters wear mustaches, their brothers wear dresses, etc., and golly gee, that's why they're all messes (Bernstein/Sondheim, 1965). Mowrer (1960) for one believes that neurotics themselves accept responsibility for their problems and feel *guilt*, and we cannot hope to free them from its iron grip or from their disturbances so long as we cling to deterministic explanations. In other words, an ancient concept, *sin*, needs to be revived. Since it implies that transgressors are at fault and deserve judgment, if not damnation, it has become politically incorrect, but neurotics want to reform and regain self-respect through *repentance* (to use another unfashionable word).

A moral is lurking here. Values and morality supposedly lie outside science's domain because no empirical test can evaluate them. Campbell (1975) disagrees. Certain *recipes for living*, statements about good conduct as well as concepts such as sin and temptation have been tested in that ultimate critical experiment, history, and over many generations have survived to become part of common sense for the same reason that biological traits survive: because they work. They may seem mere superstitions, but psychology's contempt for them is undeserved. The concept of autonomous man, I would add, with its properties of freedom, dignity and responsibility, might be similarly defended. If it is as far off base as Skinner claims, why has it endured so long? In fact, as Lefcourt shows, this illusion, if such it be, may serve a real purpose, so even if determinism is our actual condition (which is by no means certain), perhaps we should not admit it. It is well to remember that people with severe depression evaluate their own popularity, capabilities, personal attractiveness, and so on more accurately than do others (Taylor & Brown, 1988), who lean toward delusions of grandeur. Perhaps is it is precisely these that keep the rest of us sane. Ibsen's *The Wild Duck* portrays a family that by remaining ignorant of some ominous skeletons locked in the closet and living a *life-lie* manages to cope reasonably well. A would-be reformer insists on revealing reality to them at whatever cost, engineers their destruction, so another character, clearly speaking for Ibsen, contends that by taking the life-lie away from average people you take away their happiness. Life would be better if only those dangerous people who pass on their ideals to everyone else would leave them alone.

Ethics, Politics, and Nature-Nurture

Since morality has surfaced, let us revisit it in the specific context of this issue, because the position taken is affected by factors other than the empirical. Politics is one. Marxist dogma proclaimed that a revolutionary society would produce a new kind of person, causing problems such as alcoholism to disappear. Lysenko's extreme nurturist views thus became gospel to the point that scientists in the late Soviet Union could not so much as hint at possible genetic or biological precursors for certain problems (L. Graham, 1986). So to pretend that science operates in a we-only-provide-the-knowledge vacuum is naive if not irresponsible. As the Jensen controversy showed, nature–nurture positions have enormous moral implications. Indeed, fears of unpalatable findings may have discouraged the study of *behavior genetics,* of nature's influence over behaviors (Rowe & Waldman, 1993), because nurture is a more optimistic and more morally appealing position. A belief that an individual difference is inherent, even if adopted for empirical or rational reasons, is easily twisted to imply superiority, as Nietzsche's ideas were by the Nazis, especially when linked, however carefully, with an identifiable subgroup. It can then be used to justify questionable practices such as selective breeding to say nothing of "ethnic cleansing" and other horrors of recent memory.

Nowhere are ethical considerations more convoluted than regarding homosexuality. A genetic precursor is unlikely—two gay parents are unlikely to produce a gay child—but biological changes in brain areas such as the hypothalamus (LeVay, 1991) or corpus callosum (Witelson et al., cited in "Gay, straight," 1994), seem increasingly plausible. Such a discovery would nicely undercut reactionary doctrine that this lifestyle is a choice that can be overcome by sheer will power (which ignores the fact that, although tolerance for it has increased greatly, so many difficulties remain that few would opt for it voluntarily; D. Skinner, personal communication, April, 1992) and thus further its acceptance as unavoidable and deserving of legal safeguards, and so forth. Still, there are fears that such a discovery might make it possible to determine whether a fetus had the potential, and since many prospective parents would be less than overjoyed by prospects of a gay child, questionable decisions to abort might follow.

However, nurture raises another dilemma, of control, and I wish to return to it because a behavior used to exemplify the issue is relevant. If possible, should aggressive propensities be curtailed? At first glance the answer is obvious. Don't such tendencies subsume all manner of evils? Nonetheless, as *A Clockwork Orange* reveals, even extreme cases have desirable aspects, making elimination a mixed blessing not only from the perpetrator's but from society's point of view. Consider a related behavior, competition. Some (Kohn, 1986) lay every psychological and social malady at its door and would replace it forthwith with everybody-love-everybody cooperation. But this assumes not only that competition/aggression is learned but that it has little good to offer. Of the many possible arguments to the contrary (Abra, 1993), one will suffice. Many great achievements came about as reactions against alternatives perceived as distasteful: romanticism against Enlightenment priorities, Nietzsche and Kant against Darwin and Hume, respectively, and modern dance against ballet's seeming abominations. Psychology has seen the humanist revolt against psychoanalysis and behaviorism (Goble, 1974), Watson against Wundt, and Gestalt against both. Perhaps the most telling rebuttal occurs in a fictional society which has eliminated competition entirely. It is depicted in Huxley's *Brave New World* and who would want to live there?

Creativity

Another reason why scientific psychology has avoided this deserving topic is the problems it raises for deterministic outlooks, whether they stress nature or nurture. Admittedly, success demands both inborn talent and experiences to provide necessary skills; thus Igor Stravinsky (1936) asserted that beginners must accept a discipline imposed from without to obtain the freedom they need to find their own form of expression, and Martha Graham (1957) similarly enjoined dancers. Moreover, creative people themselves routinely report that the process seems beyond their control, as if in the manner of the purported mediums of spiritualism an independent force is expressing itself through them (which may explain why so many later find their products strangely unfamiliar; Abra, 1988a). Still and all, as Stravinsky intimates, determinism provides a necessary but not sufficient explanation for creativity, and archapostle Freud (1961) recognized as much when he admitted that in the face of creative artists analysis had to lay down its arms. For one thing, artists also feel a paradoxical but overwhelming sense of responsibility for their works. Negative criticism is devastating precisely because these seem expressions of oneself and egos are on the line (Kauffmann, 1976)—so much so that for Henry Miller (1952) to fail as a writer meant to fail as a man. If deterministic explanations had introspective validity, one could blame inadequacies on inferior genes or upbringings, but such excuses don't suffice, least of all for oneself. And if each creation is by definition unique, so must be some factors that give rise to it, which again suggests personal autonomy. As Rothenberg and Hausman (1976) note:

Creations . . . are in some ways recognizable and familiar to us and, therefore, they must have something in common with antecedent experiences. However (they) are also radically new and therefore, in some respects, unfamiliar. *Their specific nature cannot be predicted from a knowledge of their antecedents.* . . . [Thus] the irreducible paradox: *creativity is both determined and undetermined at the same time.* (p. 23, italics added)

Difficulties such as these have fostered less rigid versions of determinism that see us as comprehensible and predictable only up to a point.

DEPARTURES FROM STRICT DETERMINISM: THE ACTIVE SUBJECT

Behaviorist orthodoxy, whether S–R or Skinnerian, promotes *passive subjects* who labor at the mercy of events, mainly environmental, beyond their control. As such, they resemble those machines that stand forlornly in hallways doing nothing until stimulated by a thirsty or addicted external agent who inserts coins and pushes buttons, at which point they unthinkingly provide coffee with double sugar but no lightener (or, all too often, coffee but no cup to hold it; a more paranoid outlook might suspect that they do have minds of their own after all, and of a distinctly sadistic kind!). Thus by these views (to change the metaphor) repeated hammerings from the environmental chisel impose ever deeper gouges on a passive marble slab. Likewise, the classic verbal learning tasks such as paired-associate learning were symptomatically labeled rote ones because they supposedly required sheer repetitive rehearsal ad nauseum à la multiplication tables. A competing view, however, promotes more *active subjects* who interpret and change external events and whose reactions are determined less by their objective characteristics as given as by those interpretations. The next section discusses such views.

Historical Antecedents

Kant and Gestalt. Kant represents one fountainhead of this tradition. For British empiricists of the Enlightenment—Locke, Berkeley, Hume and others—mind was largely determined by experience provided by sensation; inborn abilities were few. Thus Locke's view of the mind as being at birth a tabula rasa on which experiences are inscribed, and which possesses little more than that which experience puts in. Likewise, the stream of consciousness that comprises mental life depends on associations formed, which in turn depend on environmental contiguities over which the recipient has no say. Verifying Nietzsche's opinion that opposition is a stimulus to action, it was Hume in particular that roused Kant from his dogmatic slumbers (R. Watson, 1963). Mind, he retorted, includes inborn, a priori abilities that allow it to shape, modify, and so determine the impact of experiences. For example, by definition experiences provide no precedents for the innovations of genius, so how could the latter come about if the mind of genius was no more than the sum total of experience? Mind must therefore rely on an inborn and rare imagination that gives the rule to experience, not the other way round (Kant, 1976).

It was the *Gestalt* movement that introduced this notion of an active subject into scientific psychology. Gestalt arose in Germany around the time of World War I as an avowed psychology of protest (Heidbredder, 1935) first against Wundt and later, after Hitler's coming prompted its founders to emigrate to

America, against behaviorism. The second conflict reiterated Kant's with the empiricists. Gestalt also held that what matters is not the attributes of external events per se but what is done with them, how one organizes or relates them one to another, activities in which inborn proclivities play a large role. Two basic concepts suggest an active subject. First, behaviors are motivated by a state of *disequilibrium* or tension that results when experience seems incomprehensible. One aims to restore a sense of balance and completeness in which the components of experience blend with one another to produce a more complex, integrated unit or gestalt. A jigsaw puzzle metaphor is helpful: so long as one cannot fathom how pieces fit together they seem separate, but once they become part of the overall picture, they lose their individual identities. Thus experiences from a gestalt are qualitatively distinct from those given by its component parts, which fostered the famous motto: the whole is greater (or more accurately, different) than the sum of its parts. Behaviors aim then to replace disequilibrium with a sense of gestalt and (the key point) both experiences are in the beholder's eye; they result not from an event's objective properties but from the subject's interpretations.

Finally, despite the emphasis on inborn tendencies, gestaltists by no means denied the importance of learning (Wertheimer, 1959), but held that behaviors are gradually strengthened by sheer repetition and blind trial and error. Learning, inherently goal directed, has a sense that it wants to achieve equilibrium, and only responses that offer promise of doing so are emitted. Consider the problems Köhler (1925) posed to primates, such as obtaining a banana that hovered out of reach. Did they respond randomly and indiscriminately until happening upon the correct alternative (in this case, to pile up several boxes that lay at hand)? Once that response occurred, did it become only slightly more probable? No and no! Instead, they first contemplated the situation thoughtfully, then as virtually the first overt attempt piled the boxes as required, and thereafter did so without hesitation. Thus learning apparently developed suddenly, through *insight*, that mysterious Aha! when one discovers the solution to problems. Insight is achieved by *recentering* or looking at problems in new ways and fathoming different relations between components. For gestaltists, most learning involves such mechanisms. It can occur via the arduous rote repetition behaviorists describe, but the results of this atypical and inefficient approach are poorly ingrained and do not generalize to other situations.

We might note in passing how reminiscent Piaget's concepts were of Gestalt's in the importance attached to maintaining equilibrium and on the qualitative change in outlook, akin to insight, that comes with movement between cognitive stages. Piaget recognized these similarities, but also some differences (Gruber, 1994). For example, regarding insight's nature, while a changed outlook might appear instantaneous, it is preceded by much cognitive trial and error. Indeed, as Gruber points out, too sudden movement to the next stage would be traumatic, because the child's sense of identity would be completely disrupted. Furthermore, Gruber (1974) himself, flying in the face of the romantic tradition, questioned inspiration's seminal role in creative thought, at least in Darwin's case. Legend has it that while reading Malthus on overpopulation the concept of natural selection came to Darwin in this manner, but his notebooks suggest that it had been present, albeit in germinal form, long before. For Gruber then, such thought evolves gradually; any inspirations involve smaller components of the work—perhaps how to express a certain idea—and far from producing instant enlightenment, may later be revised further or rejected outright.

A Rejoinder to Freud: Adler. A recurring event in the psychoanalytic movement was that a once close associate of the founding father would propose alternatives to prevailing dogma that the latter would find heretical and become persona non grata both professionally and personally. An early example revolved around the issue before us. For Adler (Ansbacher & Ansbacher, 1956) *feelings of inferiority* are inevitable for youngsters, due not so much to experience itself as to their interpretation of it. It is the method of *compensation* chosen to overcome these feelings that is crucial. *Social interest*, the healthy choice, seeks togetherness and cooperation with others, the neurotic alternative seeks superiority and power over them. Individuals also have considerable leeway in choosing both their *style of life*, the general method by which they go about things, as well as a cardinal determinant of that style, their *fictional goals*, ideal visions in the unconscious of future aims, and the person they wish to become. Thus to overcome a disturbed style of life those goals must be uncovered and modified, which, since these matters depend on personal choice, requires idiographic methods. What is notable is the suggestion of active decision makers rather than laborers at the mercy of factors imposed on them, people who are inherently *creative*, "both the picture and the artist . . . of [their] personality" (Ansbacher & Ansbacher, 1956, p. 177).

Learning and Memory

S-R Versions. The active subject has also invaded this terrain once dominated by the more passive kind. As regards classical conditioning, Rescorla's (1988) elegant experiments show that what matters is not contiguity of CS and UCS, which is neither necessary nor sufficient, but the information the first provides about the second. If it gives none and so serves no purpose, subjects evidently decide that the connection is not worth making. Thus if two groups receive equal numbers of CS–UCS contiguities, but in one group a number of UCS–only presentations are interspersed among them, this group shows no conditioning because the CS is an unreliable herald of the UCS. Kamin's (1969, described in Medin & Ross, 1992) demonstration of *blocking* makes a similar point. Consider two CSs, such as a tone and light. If presented either individually or together in contiguity with an aversive stimulus such as shock, each will then suppress another behavior in which the animal is engaged, such as bar pressing; presumably they have come to evoke fear via classical conditioning. However, if only the tone is first paired with the shock and the light is added later (so the CS is initially tone, then tone + light) the latter alone does not suppress bar pressing. Its association with shock was blocked, since it gave no information about the latter's occurrence over and above that from the tone.

By the 1960s, the archempirical functionalist tradition also saw more active-subject outlooks emerge, which prompted Slamecka's bon mot, "The tide is surely ebbing in the house of Ebbinghaus" (1965, p. 245). Since Watson, the concept of *attention*—that we might selectively respond to some stimuli and ignore others—had received little, well, attention. It implied subjective processes and that effects might depend more on these than on those stimuli's physical characteristics. In addition, its study was associated historically with discredited introspective methods (Broadbent, 1962). Nonetheless, it became evident that it was too important a fact of life to ignore, particularly regarding applied situations such as airplane cockpits, which feature advanced technology and complex stimulus displays. Therein, errors due to failures in attention are disastrous. In a similar vein, when a variety of stimuli are present, their physical qualities determine in part those noticed, but so do subjective qualities such as relevance; witness the reliable *cocktail party phenomenon* (Cherry, 1953, cited in Klatzky, 1980)—if one's name is mentioned in another conversation, even in hushed tones, one is likely to overhear it. However, the work by Broadbent (1958) and others showed skeptics that attention could be studied empirically.

Young's (1962) distinction between nominal and functional stimuli clearly hints at attentional mechanisms in verbal learning and at active subjects who choose among several possibilities. So does the phenomenon of *stimulus selection* (Underwood, 1963)—when faced with a complex stimulus such as a nonsense syllable, subjects use only a part, such as the first letter, for association and ignore the rest. As a result, those who still preferred S–R language, true to their pragmatic heritage, came to mean by "the stimulus" whatever caused a behavior to occur (Underwood, 1963, 1964b), and this could well include subject-chosen and inner cognitive events. When coupled with the different connotations that so-called S–R theory had acquired (Kendler, 1968), this made it increasingly difficult for would-be critics, notably those with linguistic interests (see Dixon & Horton, 1968), not to sound as if they were attacking straw men.

Be that as it may, Martin's (1968) *encoding variability hypothesis* illustrates such an S–R theory. It assumes that any stimulus can indeed be perceived in a variety of ways, limited only by its properties and the perceiver's ingenuity. For example, to associate a student's name to their physiognomy I might attend to their hair color, nose, or myriad other features. Martin suggests that various encodings are tried to discover the most effective possibility, that is, one that distinguishes that stimulus from others to prevent errors (if only one student has red hair, I would link their name to that feature, but a dozen redheads demands incorporating other encodings as well) and that consistently occurs in that stimulus (associating names with where students sit is risky since they move around). Martin then argues that a response is associated not to the physical stimulus itself but to the encoding, which acts as a *mediator* between the two, so the actual sequence of events (see Figure 6.1) is not S–R but S–(s_{enc})–R. It

Figure 6.1
Martin's Encoding Variability Hypothesis

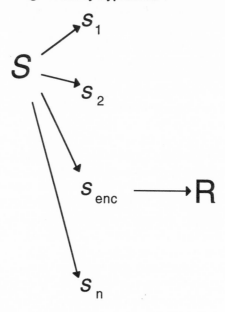

Each *s* represents a possible encoding of the physical stimulus *S*.

Source: Adapted from Martin (1968).

follows that accurate responding requires consistency of encoding; if s_{enc} changes between presentations of S—if I should notice red hair one day, a freckly complexion the next—errors result because the mediator, the functional stimulus, has changed. To verify this notion, Martin presented a list of paired-associates whose test trial list contained both these stimuli and some new distractors. As each item appeared, subjects had to indicate whether it had occurred on the study trial and also attempt to produce its response. Martin claimed that failure to recognize a list stimulus indicated an encoding change from study to test, and in these cases the probability of a correct response did indeed fall to chance.

S–S Learning: Tolman. Of the learning theories that collectively dominated the post-Watson decades, Tolman's (1932) at one time had relatively little influence, mainly because of his fondness for mentalistic hypothesized entities that the prevailing attitudes found suspect, but his light-hearted, jocular writing style (Hill, 1971) may also have hindered his being taken seriously. Nonetheless, his approach deserves attention because in retrospect it has considerable historical importance. Openly indebted to Gestalt outlooks (Hilgard, 1956), it provided a beachhead for introducing them into the mainstream and gaining attention they might not otherwise have had, for Tolman's behaviorist credentials were impeccable. He insisted that hypothesized entities be operationally defined, that observed behavior not introspections or subjectivities were the matter of concern, and he preferred animal to human research, being as fervent a rat runner as any.

His account of learning has been called an S–S one (Kimble, 1961) because associations acquired to, say, master a maze were formed not between stimuli and behavior but successive stimuli, with subjects supposedly learning *expectancies* of what leads to what, that given event A, B will follow. Hence his first unmistakable Gestalt theme is that responses to a stimulus depend less on its physical features than on interpretations of it, which depend in turn on inner events such as thoughts and expectancies. Another Gestalt theme is that subjects always have a goal or purpose in mind and can use a variety of behaviors to achieve it. Witness the ingenious studies of *place learning* (Tolman, Ritchie & Kalish, 1946). One group always had their maze goal box in the same location, but that of the start box varied over trials, so consistent success demanded employing a variety of behaviors—now turning left, now right, now running straight ahead. For a response-learning group, both start and goal box locations kept changing, but in such a way that reaching the latter always required the same response, for example, turning right. From an S–R angle the second situation should be easier—the same S–R association always applies—but Tolman's claim, that place learning should be easier since the different behaviors all serve the same ultimate purpose, was verified.

As still another Gestalt theme, he rejected analysis in favor of *molar behaviorism* that studied complex behaviors, not minuscule components. Finally, in the opinion of some (Kimble, 1961), he shared another less desirable attribute of being a more effective critic of other's ideas (his latent learning studies forced Hull to major theoretical revisions) than proponent of his own, some of which were so vague as to defy precise testing. Thus he was chided by Guthrie (1935) for failing to explain how presumed mental processes are translated into action, for leaving the rat, as it were, at the maze choice point, lost in thought. In light of later developments, it is unfortunate that Tolman's (1959) own assessment, made shortly before his death, seemed to agree with Hill's (1971) later one, that he had failed to achieve a wide and lasting following (although Hill also noted that he was widely respected, even loved). In the arts, those who earn fewer accolades than other contemporaries while alive often endure longer (witness the Mozart-Salieri reversal as depicted in *Amadeus*) and this seems to have been Tolman's fate as well. For while he is still far from a household name, as a bridge between Gestalt and behaviorist outlooks, his views stand up much better to modern eyes than once more influential adversaries such as Hull, so every cognitive revolutionary could be seen as of his lineage. Finally, we should mention his admirable involvement in another matter raised here earlier. In the heyday of McCarthyism in the 1950s, U.S. academics were required to either sign a loyalty oath or face dismissal. Tolman led the fight against this blatant threat to academic freedom and rather than sign, resigned from the University of California (Hill, 1971).

Levels of Processing. This laudably fruitful approach (Craik & Lockhart, 1972), like Martin's, assumes that stimuli can be encoded in many ways and that memory depends less on the stimulus itself than on what is done with it. It adds however that these responses differ in depth. Shallow processing focuses on physical or sensory features such as loudness of sounds or color of print, whereas deep processing stresses meaning or connotations, as when one thinks of a word's associates or whether it fits into a particular sentence. Deeper processing supposedly produces better memory. A related notion is Craik and Watkins' (1973) distinction between *maintenance rehearsal* of a stimulus itself, as in rote repetition, and *elaborative rehearsal,* enriching it by summoning its associations and connotations. Because these activities involve shallow and deep processing, respectively, the latter should and does improve memory. So demanding rote rehearsal to master, say, spelling may be inappropriate, since it is quality not quantity of rehearsal that matters. Countless studies have verified deeper processing's benefits. For example, Craik and Tulving (1975) presented a series of words and prior to each asked a question designed to encourage a certain level—shallow by asking perhaps "Is it in capital letters?"; medium, "Does it rhyme with ____ ?"; and deep, "Does the word fit into the sentence 'The dog lay under the ____ ?'." When the word appeared, subjects pushed one button to respond yes and another for no as quickly as possible. Across many procedural variations the results were remarkably consistent. Deeper processing and questions answered yes produced better memory. The second finding has, along with other anomalies, led to substantial revisions in the theory (Cermak & Craik, 1979), whose discussion here would be superfluous.

Organization. Conceptually, memory like a computer requires input or learning, storage, and retrieval. By every indication, long-term storage capacity far exceeds that of retrieval at one point in time. Recognition performance such as on multiple-choice tests routinely surpasses recall of the same material, presumably because retrieval is guided; one is looking to match presented with stored information. Furthermore, without further input, hypnosis and reminders can restore seemingly lost memories, and, as another of life's delightful little ironies, information unavailable when we need it most, such as a name or answer for a Trivial Pursuit question, blithely appears later on. Both happenings show that those memories were in storage all along. To demonstrate retrieval's limited capacity, Tulving (1968) gave subjects a *free recall* test, to produce as many words from a presented list as they could in any order they wished. Without the list being presented again, they then received several more such tests. Although the amount recalled on each remained constant, the particular items produced kept changing, with only about 50 percent being recalled on every occasion. For the rest, one came at the expense of another, suggesting that with enough tests every word would have been recalled at least once and in turn that the entire list was stored but only a fixed amount could be retrieved at one time.

Which suggests the role of organization. Supposedly, during input bits of information are not stored randomly. Instead, a subject notes possible connections among them and groups those that in his estimation belong together even if they were not presented in contiguity. Thus in *clustering* (Bousfield, 1953), several members of a category such as flowers, even if interspersed throughout the list, are recalled together, which suggests that they were grouped in storage. Even from a list of purportedly unrelated words, over a series of trials, the same words will be recalled together consistently (Tulving, 1962), although groupings are now idiosyncratic to each subject. Memory organization like many classification systems features *hierarchies*, with ever more specific groupings residing within more general ones. A library is a useful analogy. A general category may occupy an entire floor, each more specific category within it, a few cabinets, and finally specific volumes within these, a few inches. Memories are organized for the same reason: to help locate and retrieve items. Specifically, it is believed that organization counteracts retrieval's limited capacity; hence the considerable correlation found between amount of organization and recall. G. Miller (1956), in a seminal paper, proposed that the average person can only retrieve about seven units of information, or *chunks*, at one point in time. This cannot be changed, but by grouping one can place more items into each chunk and so retrieve more. For example, a subject who treats each letter in the string RCMPIBMCIANBA as separate should recall about seven, but someone who divides the sequence into the familiar acronyms therein—RCMP, IBM, CIA, NBA—would retrieve many more (presumably seven acronyms).

We can now ask why memory improves with repetition. Why does practice make memory if not perfect, at least better? For advocates of a passive subject, each repetition automatically strengthens it so it must always improve. However, if more efficient organization is the key, repetition merely provides more opportunities to fit more information into each chunk. Thus another of those predictions that contradict common sense: situations might be concocted in which repetition does not improve memory, for this should be the result if organization does not increase. Enter the *part-to-whole experiment* (Tulving, 1966). Task 2 in this transfer study involved a lengthy list that was presented to both an experimental and control group and recalled repeatedly until mastered. Only the experimental group, however, performed Task 1, in which they received some items from this list beforehand, and these were likewise presented repeatedly until recalled perfectly. Views that emphasize repetition per se must predict superior experimental group performance on Task 2; they have already learned 50 percent of the material and as Figure 6.2 shows, early trials verified this prediction. But they did not improve because, further analyses showed, while they recalled the familiar Task 1 items, they persistently omitted the new ones. The upshot was that the control group, like the proverbial tortoise who eventually passed the hare, mastered Task 2 more quickly. Advocates of organization have it that a subject learning Task 1 would seek groupings most compatible with that material. However, a scheme that was effective here might not be so for the entire set, yet she would be reluctant to give it up for this would temporarily impede recall of familiar items, whereas control subjects, since Task

Figure 6.2
Transfer from Part-to-Whole Learning

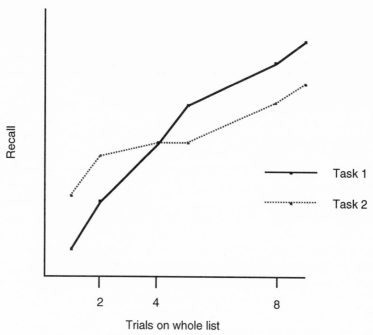

Recall

Task 1

Task 2

2   4   8

Trials on whole list

Task 1, prior learning of part of Task 2; *Task 2,* whole list.

Source: Tulving, E. (1966), p. 196. Used with permission of Academic Press, Inc., and the
author.

2 material is all new, from the outset seek schemes that work best for it. Thus
by stressing groupings and insight as opposed to relentless incremental learning,
organization views fall firmly within the Gestalt tradition (Postman, 1972).

Coding. The notion here is that subjects change presented material, so storage contains a translated version (organization is one example) that for accurate
retention must usually be decoded back to its original form. Bartlett (1932) had
subjects memorize a story, *The War of the Ghosts.* That they omitted or changed
details is in keeping with passive subjects, but their many *errors of commission,*
such as paraphrasing and remembering things that were not presented, are not;
sponges or tape recorders should never do such things. Bartlett concluded that
memory involves *reconstruction.* Like Sherlock Holmes or Perry Mason, who
use a few clues to reconstruct an entire crime, so too do rememberers exploit
those in storage to recreate an event as they suppose it to have been. As further
support, Bransford and Franks (1971), composed sets of sentences based on four
single propositions, such as (1) the ants were in the kitchen, (2) the jelly was on
the table, (3) the jelly was sweet, (4) the ants ate the jelly. Combining any two

provides a two-proposition sentence, for example, "the jelly on the table was sweet," any three, a three-proposition sentence—2 + 3 + 4 becomes "the ants ate the sweet jelly that was on the table"—and one four-proposition sentence combines all—"the ants in the kitchen ate the sweet jelly that was on the table." Some sentences from a set were presented interspersed with others, including all the one-proposition entries, some twos and threes, but never the four. The entire set was then shown and subjects were asked which ones they believed had been presented and then to rate their confidence. They were most confident of having seen the four-proposition sentence and of not having seen the one-proposition ones, so whether a sentence was actually presented had no bearing on whether they "remembered" it. Presumably they had converted the set into the concise, four-proposition form and so were conned into recognizing it.

Loftus's (1975, 1980) justifiably renowned studies of testimony by eyewitnesses to crimes make the same point. Such persons are undergoing a test of memory whose accuracy seems to be taken for granted because their testimony carries enormous weight. In one study, two groups serving as jurors in a mock trial heard the same evidence, except one group also heard a single eyewitness testify having seen the accused commit the crime. They voted 71 percent for conviction, the other group only 18 percent. This credibility is unsettling if one believes that a wrongful conviction is the most serious error a justice system can make, because Loftus has shown that what eyewitnesses "remember" depends greatly on a host of factors, for example, how lawyers word questions—factors that would not affect tape recorders one iota. In another study, subjects first saw a film of a car crash and were then asked questions about it that suggested certain erroneous possibilities. "Did another car pass the red Datsun while it was stopped at the yield sign?" assumes a red Datsun and yield sign that in fact were not present. On a subsequent recognition test most subjects chose these alternatives over the correct ones—a blue Datsun and stop sign—as having been in the film. Loftus therefore denies that memory is a passive recording that fades. Rather, it is enriched and amplified.

Of Mnemonics and Mnemonists. Mnemosyne, the Greek goddess of memory, was a daughter of Zeus, one whom he perhaps preferred to forget. Regardless, a *mnemonic device* is a strategy to improve memory, while *mnemonists* are people with memories for which the rest of us would kill, and indications of how it/they work again suggest a coding scenario. One device, the *method of loci* or "places" (Yates, 1966) was taught in ancient times to would-be Demosthenes or Ciceros who practiced the art of rhetoric, public speaking, because an accurate memory was a necessity when speeches might last several hours and using notes was unthinkable. A speaker first imagined a familiar place, such as their residence, then visualized each speech item along with one component of the place; thus the first point might be imaged with the front door, the second with the entrance hall, and so on. During delivery, speakers simply walked through the place in their mind's eye to recall both the points and their sequence. With practice, this stratagem can also dramatically improve modern memories (Bower, 1970). So can jingles or rhymes. We have seen the effectiveness of the peg-word system, "one is a bun, two is a shoe," and so forth (Bugelski, 1968). In a similar vein, the first letters of the words in "Kids play catch over Farmer Green's stable" suggest the hierarchy of biological classification (kingdom, phylum, class, order, family, genus, species) and generations of medical students, to recall the first letters of the twelve human cranial nerves, have memorized "On Old Olympus Towering Tops, a . . ." and I forget the rest of the jingle.

As for mnemonists, Soviet psychologist Luria's (1968) subject, known in good cloak-and-dagger manner befitting the Cold War era only as S, could perform such feats as recalling perfectly after one hearing a lengthy poem in an unfamiliar language, or even several years later a list of seventy unrelated words. Did he have a photographic memory that accurately stored information as given? In part he did seem able to see information in his mind's eye, but in other respects he changed it out of all recognition. His key ability that allowed this, Luria surmised, was for *synesthesia*, a tendency most noticeable during altered states of consciousness in which stimuli are experienced on other sensory modalities besides the usual one. Thus S not only heard sounds but also felt, touched, and smelled them, as in his description of a certain tone: "It looks something like fireworks tinged with a pink red hue. The strip of color feels rough and unpleasant and it has an ugly taste—rather like a briny pickle. . . . You could hurt your hand on it" (quoted in Luria, 1968, p. 23). How would such a propensity help memory? Perhaps, since forgetting stems from interference which depends in turn on similarity, converting experiences into unique, bizarre events prevents their confusion. Someone who falls off the roof and breaks a leg at age nine probably remembers it very well, it being a once in a lifetime occurrence. In any event, S's abilities were not overly helpful. Being unable to experience anything without bizarre associations arising must be an unsettling way to go through life, almost as if one were on a permanent mescalin trip—S had difficulty reading for example, and ended up with a menial job because although an effective memory was once mandatory to be enlightened, this is no longer the case, given the many artificial means available for storing information. To remember a shopping list, who would bother to visualize celery hanging from doorknobs or potatoes swimming in toilet bowls? We write it down. At any rate, the effectiveness of both mnemonics and mnemonists further implicate coding's role in memory in that it suggests that we are predisposed to remember in this way. For at first glance coding seems inefficient; it adds superfluous material to memory and risks errors while decoding. Wouldn't we be better advised to remember material as given? Nonetheless, the pudding again provides the proof. Coding works.

Imagery. This phenomenon follows directly, since mnemonics and mnemonists both rely on it. Imagery defies definition, but implies a mental representation of events not present in sensation. While visual images in the mind's eye are not the only kind conceivable, the present discussion focuses on them. During psychology's drive to sciencehood, Galton pioneered, and Wundt, Titchener and followers continued, the study of imagery, but it then languished for reasons that are not difficult to fathom: it connotes the mentalistic. Indeed the *imageless thought controversy*, about whether we can think at all without forming an image, did much to provoke Watson's insistence that psychology should ignore all such topics, because it soon degenerated into psychology's version of medieval debates about the number of angels that could sit on the head of a pin. To Watson, psychology could not hope to progress until it rid itself of such unresolvable rubbish. Still, imagery proves that a little ingenuity can bring many seemingly inviolate topics to empirical heel, for discussions are now routine in impeccably scientific sources.

One hurdle was operational definition, so Paivio, Yuille, and Madigan (1968) had subjects rate each of 925 words of varying frequency for its ability to evoke a visual image and the mean rating constituted its *imagery value*. High imagery items such as concrete nouns also facilitate learning, particularly on the stimulus side of paired-associate lists, and actual pictures are more effective still, presumably because they provide images directly so subjects need not form their own (Paivio, 1965). Paivio's (1969, 1971) *dual-coding hypothesis* suggests one explanation for imagery's benefits. It postulates two long-term memory stores that are independent but connected. A verbal store represents knowledge in words and in sequences, whereas the second stores material in visual form (the similarities to linear and nonlinear thought are apparent). Storing stimuli in both systems rather than one, which higher imagery value would facilitate, supposedly improves memory.

Much of the debate has concerned whether the second, visual system is necessary. Some favorable evidence comes from indications, from split-brain studies and such, that there are brain areas specialized for visual imagery, making the hypothesis plausible on reductionistic grounds. Second, Shepard and Metzler's (1971) inventive *rotation studies* assessed the time needed to decide whether pairs of three-dimensional shapes (see Figure 6.3) were identical or not. However, when they were, one had been rotated through a varying number of degrees in space, so a decision required rotating one of them in the mind's eye, that is, using a visual image. That subjects could make accurate decisions at all strongly suggests that images can be formed, but, of particular note, an increased angle of rotation, which presumably increased the mental rotation needed for a decision, lengthened reaction time. Were other stratagems used such as logical or verbal deduction, this relationship should not be so systematic. As further support, Kosslyn, Ball, and Reisser's (1978) subjects saw a picture of an object such as a boat and were asked to image it. It was then taken away and they were told to start at, for instance, the stern and when another element was mentioned, such as anchor, to visualize a dot moving from there to that element and to press a yes button when it reached it. Reaction times increased with distance between starting point and destination, suggesting that subjects could use their minds' eyes—again, nonvisual tactics should not yield so systematic a relationship. Also, elements not present in the picture (for which a no button was to be pressed) produced the longest reaction times of all, presumably because such a decision required scanning the entire picture.

Figure 6.3
Shepard and Metzler's Rotation Figures

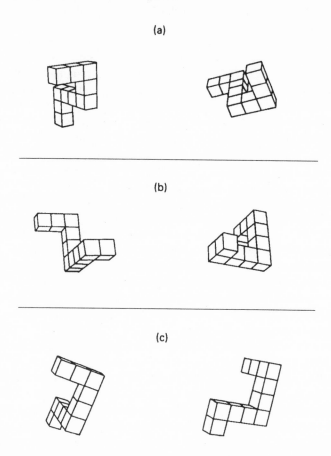

(a)

(b)

(c)

The concept of a visual store provoked strong objections, notably from Paivio's colleague at Western Ontario, Pylyshyn (1973) (most department meetings of my experience are stormy enough without scholarly disagreements to fan the flames). One reason no doubt is the suspicions the empirically inclined have for this vestige of psychology's mentalistic past, and parsimony is another, producing skepticism that such a second system is needed to explain the data. A final credible reason is psychology's unrivaled intimacy, because people may differ in their ability to visualize. The romantics believed as much, and, while most people queried by Galton (1883) reported that they often had images, many scientists denied it, leading Galton to claim that the typical man of science had feeble powers of visualization. More recently, however, Roe (1951) found this to be an overgeneralization. Biologists reported considerable imagery but, indicatively, few scientific psychologists did. Are they skeptical about images because these do not jibe with their own experience? Furthermore, do these rejections perhaps become more emotional with the realization that others find the notion introspectively acceptable, which suggests that one is somehow deficient? As usual, experiments and arguments, however convincing and numerous, do not sway those who fervently do or do not believe in the concept. Again we see that the ideal of the skeptical but open-minded scientist whose opinions are decided by empirical evidence is just that: an ideal.

Rejoinders to Skinner: Bandura and Chein

Here again an active subject is implied. Were we restricted to trial and error, learning to, say, cross freeways would endanger life and limb. Fortunately, as Bandura's pioneering studies of vicarious conditioning demonstrate, while observing others we can imagine ourselves in their situation and conceive possible responses and likely results. Moreover, Skinner sees reinforcers working retroactively to strengthen previous events, but for Bandura (1977) they act as *future incentives*, fostering expectancies that a behavior will achieve them, as witness that immortal line in the film *Field of Dreams*: "If you build it, he will come." Bandura's main departure, however, is that reinforcers need not be administered by external sources. We can set *internal standards* of the perform-ance we expect of ourselves in a situation and by reaching that standard reinforce ourselves with pride and self-satisfaction, or, if we fall short, deliver punishers such as discontentment. By the same token, certain activities seem intrinsically reinforcing, indulged in for sheer pleasure rather than as a means to receive external reinforcers; indeed, delivering them for such a task, rather than increas-ing participation as expected, actually lessens it (Lepper & Greene, 1975). Furthermore, the effects of reinforcers such as paychecks depend less on their objective properties than on how they compare to one's standards, so the same result may satisfy one person, disappoint another. To the self-perceived jour-neyman in *Bull Durham*, merely having a cup of coffee in the major leagues would provide the thrill of a lifetime, but not to someone of Ken Griffey Jr.'s talents. Thus that rampant disease, procrastination, is often due to unrealistically high internal standards because failure in one's own eyes, if no one else's, is guaranteed from the outset (Burka & Yuen, 1983).

Several personal observations support these contentions. First, there is a puzzling inconsistency in Skinner. If reinforcement is reciprocal, if A can reinforce B's behaviors and B reinforce A's, why is it unthinkable that they might do the same for their own behaviors and monitor themselves as well as others? As well, Skinner provides compelling answers to many aspects of creative work (Abra, 1988a). Creators indulge in trial and error while seeking elusive perfection and do work for extrinsic reinforcers; Dr. Sam Johnson opined that no sane person wrote except for money (Bate, 1979), and peer recognition is a powerful motivator for scholars and scientists (Merton, 1973; Roe, 1965). Furthermore, this perspective helps explain the sex difference, since women of the past faced all manner of environmental deterrents. But intrinsic motives must operate as well (Abra, 1997), for such work borders on the masochistic. Few poets, for example, realize the rewards mentioned by Freud (1963)—honor, power, wealth, fame, and the love of women—and they suffer constant frustration, sleepless nights, and the tortures of the damned to produce something of which almost no one will take notice. Yet contra Skinner, creative behaviors, far from diminishing, border on the compulsive, and dedication is the common denominator in productive lives. Therefore the moments of euphoric ecstasy experienced during the process itself, whether called peak experiences, flow (Csikszentimihalyi, 1990), or some other, must provide the rewards and most creative people, when asked, say so.

To return to Bandura, what factors determine internal standards? Modeling is one. By observing others controlling their own behaviors, children come to realize that they need such standards and internalize those that models display. Thus parents of high achievers not only preach but practice doing your best (Bloom, 1985), which presumably leads their children to do the same. Another source is one's previous actions and their results. As another instance of self-fulfilling prophecies at work, success in a situation such as the classroom breeds self-confidence and hence still higher expectancies, whereas failure suggests incompetence and encourages tendencies to give up. All of which makes people less predictable than trait portraits would have them. The same person may be now a perfectionist, now an underachiever, especially since their standards may differ for different pursuits. Yet another explanation for the male preponderance among great achievers is that women have historically stressed excellence in perhaps the greatest of all creative acts, raising children, while settling for less elsewhere. As Norman Mailer (1967) observed, the most important factor in becoming a great writer may be to believe that it is important to be a great writer. Also, in deciding which task to undertake, women emphasize its perceived value, men their past success in it (J. S. Eccles, 1985).

Underlying all this is Bandura's (1978) philosophical view of *reciprocal determinism*. Freud or Skinner, by attributing behaviors to factors beyond control, recall push-pull machinery (see Figure 6.4's left panel). Bandura claims however that we interact in a reciprocal relationship with rather than respond to our environment. Since nowadays it is largely of our own making, clearly we act upon as well as being acted upon by it. Moreover, Bandura adds a third factor, *intermediate cognitive processes* such as thought, attention, and internal standards, which interact with both the others. The environment affects these processes, yet they in turn influence our impressions of it, as when attention determines the aspects we notice. Likewise, thoughts and standards affect overt behaviors and evaluations of them, and behaviors influence self-concepts such as confidence and thus standards set for future activities. As Figure 6.4's right panel shows, the three factors are in constant interplay, with priority being a chicken-

Figure 6.4
Two Types of Determinism

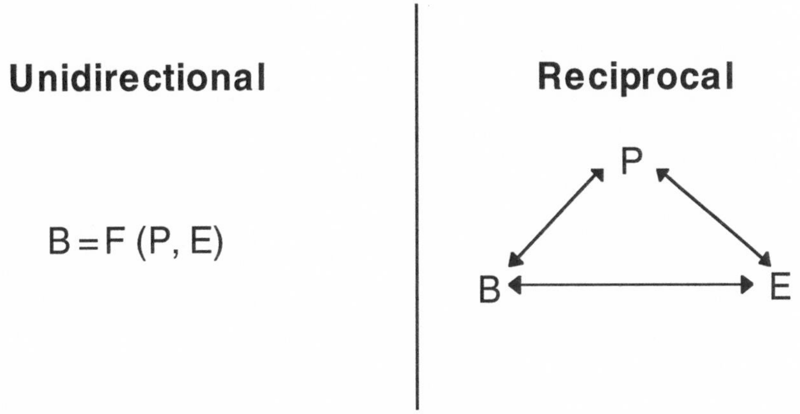

Unidirectional | # Reciprocal

$$B = F (P, E)$$

Note: B = behavior; *P* = cognition; *E* = environment.

Source: Bandura, A. (1978). The Self system in reciprocal determinism. *American Psychologist, 33,* 344–358. Copyright © 1978 by the American Psychological Association. Reprinted with permission. Used with permission of A. Bandura.

and-egg matter. Therefore, "Individuals are neither powerless objects controlled by environmental forces, nor entirely free agents who can do whatever they choose" (Bandura, 1978, pp. 356–357).

Chein's (1972) position is similar. If it is admitted that our motives are an important influence and are not completely bestowed by the environment but are in part internal, then we have allowed that we have freedom. This does not imply free will in the traditional sense, but only that behavior is not completely determined by heredity and environment, that it is chosen from a range of alternatives based partly on these inner factors. However, the portrait that emerges is of an active, responsible agent, because to say that we are responsible within a deterministic framework is simply to say that our acts have conse- quences and that their major influences are within us.

Clinical Psychology and Therapy

Cognitive Behavior Therapy. These approaches (e.g., Beck, 1976; Ellis, 1973) clearly share the preceding outlooks, since problems such as depression are attributed to the way people think about their experiences rather than the experiences themselves; thus Ellis's *rational emotive therapy* challenges mistaken or distorted beliefs in a confrontational, sometimes abrasive manner. These approaches resemble standard behavior therapies in that behavior defines disturbance and it is its change that is sought, and Ellis also dismisses case histories and long-winded chit-chat as only making patients feel better, not get better. However, cognitive systems part company in the importance they attach to subjective events as determinants of behavior and targets for alleviation, and they have had marked success in treating depression, anxiety, headache, and bulimia (Nietzel, Bernstein & Milich, 1994). In addition, most therapists of this persuasion share another attribute with the Kant tradition (K. Dobson, B. McElheran, personal communications, March, 1996)—they assign appreciable responsibility for final decisions about therapy's procedures and goals to the patient, while the therapist clarifies options and advises rather than dictates as to the preferable ones. Thus by implication the hierarchical patient-therapist relationship bequeathed by the medical model, with its tacit assumption that the therapist knows best, is replaced by a collaborative partnership.

Wood's (1985) *moral therapy* is typical. First, he would eliminate neurosis as a misleading concept; it has caused many to be classified as disturbed who merely lack adequate approaches to life's inevitable difficulties. He then attacks two groups of purported experts: talk-therapists such as analysts who encourage such people to chatter on about but never surmount their problems, and medico-biologists who prescribe chemical panaceas such as Valium at the drop of a symptom. However, these leftovers from the medical model have vested interests in the status quo. Besides providing them with a livelihood, it maintains that ego boosting hierarchical relationship and gives patients little responsibility for improvement. But Wood asserts that no one, least of all the scientifically and/or medically trained, is especially expert at healthy living. His approach, he admits, offers nothing to genuine psychotics or the clinically depressed; they need other treatments. But these aside, happiness demands that we come to respect and like ourselves or (recalling Mowrer) suffer guilt, which actually serves as a valuable warning of psychological problems just as pain does for physical ones. Therefore moral therapy places the onus on individuals to discover and work toward becoming the person they would like to be, given their 'druthers. For we must realize that we have no inalienable right to happiness; that crucial self-respect comes from seeking out and striving to overcome difficulties, not from moaning about them. Thus moral therapy offers not panaceas but challenges.

Happiness and its attainment is also Csikszentmihalyi's (1990) concern and his solutions have a similar ring. In his view, it comes about not through relaxing or doing nothing but by being deeply involved in challenging and meaningful pursuits that provide an almost mystical experience called *flow*. It resembles Maslow's peak experience and so need not be described, but the relevant point is that flow is not given to us; we are responsible for obtaining it and thus happiness. By exercising imagination, self-discipline, and will power we can, and many have, obtain it even in such unpromising activities as working on assembly lines. Finally, Frankl's (1984) terrible experiences in a concentration camp and the conclusions he drew from them, add a poignant note. Those who managed to survive the horrors, he felt, were set apart by having something, whether a project or another person, that provided an answer to those unavoidable questions, especially in a desperate situation, "What is the meaning of life? Why should I continue?" and gave the person a reason not to give up. Frankl concluded that people have an inherent need to make sense of their worlds and if they cannot they become neurotic. His *logotherapy* therefore aims to help them accomplish this, but here again it is assumed that each must discover for themselves what will provide that meaning; therapists can only suggest possibilities.

Clinical Training: The Doctor of Psychology (Psy.D.). Here is another indication that in clinical spheres science in the narrow sense no longer reigns supreme. For this alternative to the scientist-practitioner model is becoming so popular that practicing psychologists with the Psy.D. degree now outnumber those with the Ph.D.—a prime reason for the APA's aforementioned change of direction and for some states now having more qualified psychologists than the traffic will bear (K. Dobson, personal communication, March, 1996). (For a variety of reasons Psy.D. programs, despite several attempts, have yet to get off the ground in Canada, and training is still linked to the Ph.D., although Psy.D.s can be licensed). Psy.D. programs first appeared in the 1960s in response to increasing discontent with the Boulder model's perceived overemphasis on statistics and research competence, which are rarely used in practice, at the expense of more relevant skills. Some programs are housed in universities, others in independent institutions, but in either case while there remains a commitment in principle to science as the desirable way to go and while most graduates would probably call themselves scientists, the terms have clearly taken on new meanings. The emphasis is placed on competence to keep abreast of and evaluate new research rather than provide it, so dissertations are replaced by more course work, clerkships, and the like, thus increasing the relative weighting in the scientist-practitioner equation toward the latter end. Furthermore, less rigorous and more qualitative as opposed to quantitative research is now accepted. Which approach produces better clinicians it is difficult to say. Psy.D.s may be less proficient at such things as program evaluation, but perhaps the type of training matters less than personal qualities. Perhaps when all is said and done there are only two kinds of clinicians, good and bad. Certainly that label that some hold in awe, the Ph.D., doesn't guarantee anything.

Social Psychology

The Gestalt Influence: Kurt Lewin. After Gestalt's pioneers migrated to the United States, the social psychologists who came under their influence comprise a veritable who's who of the next generation (Ash, 1985), and its imprint on many seminal contributions, cognitive dissonance to name but one, is unmistakable. One such pioneer, Lewin, also contributed elsewhere (see Deutsch, 1954), notably in describing various types of conflict (Lewin, 1935), and in his pupil Zeigarnik's (1927, cited in Deutsch, 1954) classic demonstration of better memory for interrupted than completed tasks (presumably because the feeling of unfinished business produced disequilibrium, which induced more attention).

Overall, however, Lewin's (1935) key concept is the *life space*, made up of the entirety of psychological facts that influence someone at one point in time. They arise from a variety of sources—the environment, inner events, and past experience—and are constantly changing, so in contrast to trait theories, which see us as static, Lewin's system is thoroughly dynamic, meaning that interpretations and hence effects of the same environment can differ for, say, a child and an adult. This so-called *field theory* (Lewin, 1951) does owe something to the field theory in physics, which stressed events in the here and now as determinants of phenomena over action at a distance. For in the life space Lewin attaches more importance to factors of this kind than did Skinner or Freud, who were preoccupied with histories of reinforcement or childhood traumas.

Despite this debt to physics, Lewin was adamant that influential psychological phenomena such as hopes and desires cannot be reduced entirely to nor equated with physical or physiological events, because as always the former depend on how the latter are interpreted. Thus in a system replete with mathematical symbolization, one characteristic formula, $B = f \, (p, \, e)$, asserts that person and environment are interdependent and behavior is a function of both. How is someone's life space determined? Until better options come along, Lewin favored a *make-do methodology* featuring introspective reports. Despite their problems, he found controlled experimentation still more unsatisfactory. The effects of a variable in isolation differ greatly from those in life spaces wherein many other variables are present; since they affect one another, the entire situation must be taken into account. And because one pivotal constituent of any life space is other people, Lewin's involvement in social psychology is understandable to the extent that he virtually founded its experimental study (Deutsch, 1954). For several reasons, behaviorists had ignored groups as possible causal stimuli. A group is a group because it is perceived as such and so becomes an inherently subjective concept. As well, because it is a definitive gestalt whose members influence one another, its effects differ beyond measure from when members' effects are studied individually. Then too, those effects depend less on a group's objective qualities than as perceived by the subject and since the group and its individual members, including that subject, are interdependent, their relationship is not amenable to one-way, cause–effect description.

Perhaps Lewin's major contribution was to legitimize discussion of groups and show how they could be studied scientifically, albeit preferably in realistic rather than contrived laboratory situations, via *action research* (and those who collaborate in creative work often fulfill the Gestalt tenet of the whole being greater than sum of its parts, Abra, 1994; Gilbert & Sullivan when working separately produced nothing but mediocrities but together forged masterpieces, Pearson, 1950). Lewin also impelled other now standard topics. Given his experiences in Germany, it is understandable that prejudice and its alleviation, especially in the workplace, would be a primary concern (Lewin, 1948). Likewise, his notion of *level of aspiration*, the standard of achievement one sets for oneself in a situation, fostered a voluminous literature and as a motive it carries unmistakable Gestalt undertones, since it depends as much on personal decisions and future aims as on external factors and past events. So too with studies of how our responses to someone else are affected by his status and prestige, which also depend more on personal judgments than on his objective properties.

Social Interaction as Drama. Concerning recent contributions with evident Gestalt ancestry, Harré and Secord (1972) focus on but hardly limit themselves to social activity. They first deny that only mechanistic models of people as passive automatons satisfy science's requirements. They admit that behavior is sometimes controlled by external events in the traditional S–R sense, but far more common are *formal episodes* wherein behavior depends on the rules and meanings we give a situation and on *reasons*, or explanations we generate to justify our actions. Thus situations allow considerable leeway for interpretation. As well, as in Gestalt, most behaviors have *plans* aiming at specific outcomes, to which end we can choose among several courses of action, leading the authors to chastise behaviorists for ignoring the role of purpose (somewhat unfairly: it was central to Tolman's theory and the later Hull's, in the hypothesized entity of *incentive motivation*).

In any event, while computers and animals are useful metaphors for human activity to a point, we differ in our capacity for *self-monitoring*. We are aware of how we act, why, and to what end, and moreover are aware that we are aware and this combined with our greater language capacity allows us to observe, comment upon, and explain our conduct. But various social situations—marriages, say, as opposed to sports events—imply different rules and conventions that influence our choices among alternatives. So do the meanings and interpretations we attach to a situation, and behaviors may vary appreciably if these differ. By the same token, similar behavior reflects similarities in meanings, conventions, and rules more than in external stimuli. Passive subjects cannot ignore stimuli, but rules are made to be broken. So since people have many social selves depending on the situation as interpreted, they resemble actors playing roles and follow scripts of their own devising, which they constantly revise as they monitor their own behaviors and reactions of others. Truly "all the world's a stage" whose audience is the social psychologist trying to make sense of events thereon.

Harré and Secord then renew Lewin's attack on orthodox experiments on grounds of what amounts to ecological validity. These, they contend, are *social interactions* between the experimenter and the subject, so the latter as always will impose rules and interpretations, as demand characteristics bear witness. And since such a situation is contrived, those invoked and hence the subject's behavior may have little relevance to reality. First, she has less information than usual about what's going on. Second, she is interacting with a stranger, and only briefly, and so will act differently than with intimates of longer acquaintance; thus experimenters who disclose more about themselves affect the E-S interaction and in turn the phenomena observed (Jourard and Kormann, 1968). Attitude surveys are perhaps the reductio ad absurdum of artificiality. One must rate one's reactions to a hypothetical stranger as described about whom one is given little information and none of those intangible but influential factors regarding appearance or personal warmth are described. How then are formal as opposed to causal episodes to be studied? Again, ask the subjects! The things people say about themselves, their actions and reasons for them, and about other people should be taken seriously. Such introspective data reveal the rules and interpretations invoked, provide relevant explanations, and also, contra Wittgenstein, indicate phenomena that really exist. It follows that more qualitative descriptions of what people say about why they did what they did should take priority over measurements of what they did. Finally, since differences in interpreting a situation underlie individual differences, to understand them, idiographic methods are mandatory.

Determinism and Autonomy as Cohabitants

For completeness, I also consider another line taken at times on the determinism–free will issue. It sees the alternatives as not mutually exclusive but as applicable in different circumstances. Thus Easterbrook (1978) contends that those deprived of basic needs such as food or an addicting substance are undeniably controlled by independent factors and will do whatever it takes to obtain satisfaction, but this does not mean that all behaviors are so controlled. As intelligence, competence in a situation, and (another self-fulfilling prophecy) beliefs in one's autonomy increase, one becomes ever more the master of one's fate and the captain of one's soul. On the other hand, even the most autonomous behaviors, while they do involve choice and a sense of purpose, are still affected by nature and nurture. In short, determinism and autonomy represent extremes on a continuum along which the degree of responsibility varies. Legal circles tacitly admit as much. Premeditated murders are seen to involve more responsibility and therefore to warrant more severe retribution than do those committed on impulse or while under emotional duress, although the act and results are identical.

Maslow's (1954) familiar *hierarchy of needs* (see Figure 6.5) has similar implications. The various needs supposedly vary in priority, with the first being those such as for nutrition that must be met to survive. After this, however, others arise, such as needs for security and belonging. At the top of the hierarchy lie the *growth* or *metaneeds* such as for self-actualization and creativity that only come to the fore once deficiency needs are satisfied. The presence of growth needs distinguishes people from animals, health from neurosis (those preoccupied with deficits miss the best of what life has to offer), and therefore existing from genuine living. Here again it is implied that as one ascends the hierarchy, autonomy and responsibility increase.

Finally, Jaynes (1976) presents another perspective by claiming that autonomy has changed over the ages. Our distant ancestors supposedly had a *bicameral mind* within which lurked a representative of collective society, a sort of internalized god that dictated prevailing attitudes, beliefs, and therefore behaviors to the occupied—creative inspirations, for example, presumably came from such external sources. However, a series of cataclysms that brought about increasing social fragmentation caused the defining human psychic trait, consciousness, to evolve. The result was a different homo sapien, able for the first time to think

Figure 6.5
Maslow's Hierarchy

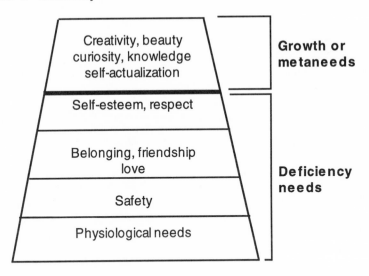

Creativity, beauty
curiosity, knowledge
self-actualization

**Growth or
metaneeds**

Self-esteem, respect

Belonging, friendship
love

**Deficiency
needs**

Safety

Physiological needs

Source: Adapted from Maslow (1954).

for itself, plan ahead, and choose and therefore was endowed with that decidedly mixed blessing, a sense of personal responsibility for its acts. While these suppositions may seem arbitrary, Jaynes's arguments are compelling, and in any event, since the new outlook was first manifest in ancient Greece (in a few passages in *The Iliad*) it is fitting that one statement of it should come from those supreme imitators of Greek culture, the Romans: "The fault, dear Brutus, lies not in our stars, but in ourselves" (*Julius Caesar*, 1.2). We now move beyond moderates that soften determinism to those who deny it entirely, along with every other scientific assumption.

THE ROMANTIC REJOINDER: EXISTENTIALISM

This outlook, it is generally agreed, formally came into being when Kierkegaard set out to demolish Hegel, but gained special prominence in Europe after World War II when its bleak messages struck responsive chords. Despair and anxiety did seem inherent to our condition. Once inviolate religious, political, or psychological systems that claimed to provide final answers to life's great questions had only compounded the problems of people trying to cope, because two cataclysmic wars and countless lesser skirmishes and crises had shown where these isms led.

To discuss existentialism in general is almost contradictory since like its great ancestor romanticism it is first and foremost a philosophy of the individual, with truth being subjective rather than universal and what is valid for one being perhaps not so for another. Thus existentialism wears many guises. Still, according to Sartre (1947b), one defining belief is that *existence precedes essence*. "Essence" refers to a human nature or a set of presumed properties found in everyone that makes each existing person an exemplar of a general concept, the human being (Stern, 1967). But to existentialists we are thrown into the world given only existence, free to respond to and interpret it however we will, and it is these choices and the acts that follow from them that determine our individual properties or essence. So what we do decides who we are, not vice versa as determinism would have it. It follows that, since any subsequent act can revise one's previous essence, it is constantly changing and unpredictable. George may be a depressed auto mechanic now but could choose to give the lie to these descriptions at any moment. Furthermore, freedom to choose means people will have little in common; indeed, everybody's different! In spades! Thus grandiose systems such as Hegel's with their sweeping statements about existence in general provoked Kierkegaard's wrath as pie in the sky, professorial games having no relevance for individuals facing down-to-earth reality. (This insistence on dealing with the here and now, incidentally, is one significant departure from romanticism, which favors a retreat into the world of imagination and fantasy; W. Kaufmann, l956).

By the same token, the existentialist routinely despises academics and scientists; when told he resembled an engineer, Sartre was grievously insulted (Grene, 1948). Such people assume the ridiculous, that existence is deterministic, coherent, and lawful. In fact, if we can interpret it however we like, then it defies understanding and becomes *absurd* (Camus 1956, 1969), even pathetically funny, as are some plays that adopt this perspective, such as Stoppard's *Rosencrantz and Guildenstern Are Dead* and Beckett's *Waiting for Godot*, although the humor is of a decided gallows kind. Nonetheless, our freedom induces not the euphoria one might expect, but anxiety, dread, and anguish. These reactions follow directly from our condition and indicate not that one is neurotic but that one is human. Hence a Sartrian (1947a) character observes that man is *condemned* forever to be free. Why in these circles does paranoia run rampant? First, because there are no comforting, certified answers to that cosmic Rorschach test, existence; responsibility falls on us to interpret it alone. As well, one's freely chosen statement of existence as one thinks it should be also indicates what it should be in general, so we become responsible to all humanity. To avoid these burdens, some cowardly liars do pretend that existence has meaning but for Sartre such *salauds* (a discrete translation is "filthy stinkers") are guilty of *bad faith*.

Another source of anxiety is the one unalterable exception to our freedom. We cannot become that which we most want to be: immortal. From the moment of birth, death permeates existence and the trauma is increased because we realize as much. Finally, Sartre (1969) stressed our uncertainty about who we are, that self-concepts must be fleeting and hazy. More specifically, we might distinguish a *subjective self* possessed by each individual—free, unpredictable, and always under construction—from an *objective self*—impersonal, static, comprehensible, and captured in the generalizations and neat pigeon-holings that psychologists fling around. Sartre claims that real people desperately want but do not have such objectivity. It is a fictional ideal, so existence is a *lack*, as our feelings of *desire* indicate. We therefore spend our lives seeking objectivity and it is toward this end that we constantly recreate our subjective selves. In short, our *fundamental project* is to unify the two, to coincide with ourselves. Need it be said that this can never be, that existentialism being what it is, that which we most want we cannot have? Were the subjective to become objective or the free deterministic, it would no longer be human. Like mules harnessed to carts with a carrot tied to the end of a stick that is affixed to the shafts, each of us in trying to reach the carrot pulls our cart forward, but the carrot always dangles hypnotically just beyond our reach. So too with objectivity.

Still, at the moment of death, when I have no more possibilities, my essence is fixed, and all my pasts coincide with my future, so like a Pompeian corpse, death petrifies me in the midst of an activity. Also, when I interact with another person, when that Other contemplates me, and I come under his *gaze*, I experience a kind of death by becoming in his eyes a thing rather than a free, unpredictable subjectivity. When I contemplate most objects in my environment I am free to make of them whatever I wish, but now I experience one that gazes back, doing to me what I do when I gaze at others and categorize them as well dressed perhaps or attractive. Now I get a taste of my own medicine, which threatens my freedom because the Other also has subjectivity and a universe that he centers from which he perceives objects, including me, in a way I can never know. His gaze therefore takes over my subjectivity and I experience *shame*. Sartre provides a telling example of this different perspective. Suppose I peek through a keyhole and watch those within; since they cannot see me, I am master of all I survey. Suddenly I hear footsteps. Someone is watching me. No longer the all-powerful *perceiver*, the center of my own experiential universe, but an *object of perception*, I am *seen*.

Supposedly then, whenever two freedoms interact, a struggle for psychological supremacy ensues, causing Sartre to assert that hell is other people. Both cannot retain freedom any more than the earth and sun can both center the solar system. Thus (to switch the metaphor) two solitary Gary Coopers confront one another at High Noon. This town isn't big enough for both of them. Neither will physically die, since they are armed with retinas rather than revolvers, but psychologically one surely will. There are two possible resolutions. First, like the children's game in which one tries to outstare the other and the one who looks away first is the loser, gazal antagonists may try to convince the Other to submit to objectivity. But there is an alternative. One may voluntarily surrender freedom while allowing the Other to keep hers and reduce himself to a pure object who exists only in her gaze, a psychological parasite. For power is a subtle commodity, and giving it up may actually enhance it, a gambit that according to Sartre (1971), writer Jean Genet played to perfection. The Other possesses that objective self I have spent my life seeking. She sees me as I desperately want to see myself but cannot, so seeing myself through her eyes may provide the missing piece in my psychic puzzle. And does not everyone at times wonder what they look like to others? Sadists and masochists exemplify the two reactions—sadists try to debase their adversaries/lovers into dependent objects, masochists to debase themselves and be manipulated. Predictably, both attempts, as Sartre shows at some length, are doomed to fail.

This provocative (and too little noted by psychologists) description of human interaction has intriguing implications. First, all such interactions including those of love and/or sexuality involve power struggles. Reciprocity and equality are impossible; relationships can be no more symmetrical than can sex itself. There must be a dominant donor and submissive receiver. Each needs the Other but their needs, and roles, differ. Thus Sartre's long-time companion, Simone de Beauvoir's (1962) description of the psychology of women. Evaluated by their physical attractiveness, conscious of being gazed at, they have by and large accepted object, dependent status and become obsessed with their appearance, to wonder not Who am I?, but What do they think of me?

This same masochistic reaction may also subsume creative people's most characteristic trait: persistence *cum* obsession. As Sartre (1981) intimates regarding himself, if others label you as creative or talented, and you adopt these labels as part of your self-concept, you must then produce constantly or suffer that most powerful of motivators, guilt. Furthermore, the gaze concept gave Laing (1965) an explanation for schizophrenia. The self-consciousness that everyone feels under a gaze is here unusually intense so to protect their sensitive subjectivity victims hide it behind an artificial public alternative and become "split" (the literal meaning of "schizophrenia"). Finally, ballet dancers can be hereby explained (Abra, 1987). Since the appearance of their bodies to others, to audiences, and especially to choreographers determines their success, they allow those Others to determine their self-concepts—the masochist's defining reaction. Which may explain why they are masochists in the physical sense as well (Gruen, 1976), as they must be. Dancing hurts!

7

Analysis and Reductionism

These related strategies both seek understanding through explanations that are more fundamental than the phenomena of concern. Neither is obligatory, but their popularity among psychologists especially in North America has greatly affected the discipline. To deal first with analysis, it involves breaking complex phenomena down into constituent parts, and for Underwood (1957b) the history of science involves its relentless practice. Chemistry provides a familiar example. Physical matter is routinely analyzed into various compounds and these into elements once taken as final, irreducible parts but now thought to consist of electrons, positrons, and such. Similarly, descriptions of human anatomy delineate complex functional systems such as the respiratory and circulatory, the organs that make them up (the circulatory system includes heart, large arteries, capillaries, and so on), and then components of these components until the single cell level is reached. In short, new entities in nature come about not only when previously unrelated entities combine but when complex units separate into several novel offspring; thus Darwin's proposals for the origins of species rest on a branching tree of nature (Gruber, 1974), with a common ancestor giving rise to ever more diverse varieties. Generalization and analysis respectively recapitulate these mechanisms and underlying both is the notion of hierarchies—ascending organizations of increasingly complex items that at one level have certain defining similarities and join together to form a unit at the next level, some of which combine to form a yet more complex unit at a third level, and so on. Koestler (1970) claims that most of the phenomena in our experience form hierarchies, and many scientists seem to agree because generalization and analysis, which move respectively upwards and downwards through them, are so popular.

Other assumptions specific to analysis should also be noted. First, understanding of something like a radio is enhanced by taking it apart and examining the bits and pieces strewn about. But there is a potentially troublesome fly in the ointment: how to reassemble this auditory Humpty Dumpty? Second, analysis manifests a *corpuscularian view* of nature (Harré, 1985) that while not necessarily accurate has endured for so long that we are hard put to conceive alternatives. With atomic theory providing the classic example, this view assumes that phenomena are composed of smaller, discrete units or *corpuscles* that are separate and independent but (usually) indistinguishable and therefore interchangeable (if you've seen one electron, one might say, you've seen them all). A complex phenomenon's properties then, such as its mass or motility, depend on the arrangement of its corpuscles; when this changes, so do those properties, so understanding them demands that the operations of and events that influence its corpuscles be identified. One of this view's attractions is that corpuscles can be counted, which opens the way to quantification.

Several corollaries follow. One is a preference in assessing properties such as temperature or speed to count presumed units that supposedly make them up, such as degrees or seconds. But doing so requires assumptions that the property lends itself to corpuscularian analysis and that either nature or science has provided an absolute *standard of reference*, an ideal indicant of this entity's attributes, because other versions can only be validated by comparing them to it. Obviously then, if such an ultimate standard should fluctuate, chaos looms, for all its imitations along with measures that have used them become obsolete and unreliable. To deny this unseemly possibility, another scientific article of faith becomes necessary, that clocks and other repetitive processes are steady, so that "unless a thing, material or process is interfered with, it will continue to run unchanged. . . . Things and processes do not change of themselves" (Harré, 1985, p. 149).

Regarding reductionism, in practice it attempts to account for the phenomena of more complicated disciplines such as psychology by referring to the phenomena or concepts of presumably more fundamental disciplines such as physiology. Examples of its usefulness abound. A biological concept, survival of the fittest, helps understand competitive free enterprise economies. A key step for astronomy came with the realization that principles of physics could account for the behavior of heavenly bodies. Biochemical studies of DNA and RNA have helped biologists fathom genetic inheritance. As for psychology, it is evident that much of our functioning is controlled by the nervous system. Evidence from physiology, biochemistry, and even physics about brain mechanisms offers enormous benefits, for example, in trying to understand and perhaps treat people who, say, commit unspeakable crimes but show little remorse or ability to distinguish right from wrong.

What is clearly implied here is an *ascending tree of the sciences* (Jessor, 1963). In most opinions physics and mathematics are the most fundamental and form the base, followed by chemistry, physiology, and psychology, and then social sciences. Designating some disciplines as more basic may seem arbitrary, but there is wide agreement about the ordering. At any rate, phenomena from higher disciplines are routinely explained by recourse to the lower but the reverse, while less common, does occur, as when a psychological concept such as stress is invoked to account for tumors. Since psychology lies in the middle of the pack, it is both reduced to more basic disciplines and borrowed from by those above, as when its concepts explain economic or political developments. Reductionism is probably popular for the same reason as is generalization, because it provides a simpler, more unified view of nature (Jessor, 1963). Putting it differently, a position that psychological phenomena are not merely complex variations of principles from other sciences is unparsimonious, only to be taken if necessary.

ANALYSIS IN PSYCHOLOGY

Long before the scientific era, Locke (Watson, 1963) defined the units of mental life as simple ideas mainly stemming from sensory experience. They comprised more complex ones while retaining their separate properties and since psychic experience consisted of a sequence of ideas, understanding them was tantamount to understanding it. Locke's empiricist successors came to see associations between ideas as the basic elements, but otherwise this propensity for analysis, for what came to be called *mental chemistry*, remained strong, and in this respect the pioneers of psychology's move to science were of similar mind. Indicatively, Freud labeled his purported science as psycho*analysis*, presumably because it sought the unconscious's components, and Wundt's more legitimate attempt was known as *structuralism* because it aimed to uncover the psychic elements of consciousness. Wundt thereby implanted a bias for an *analytical* experimental psychology—although he himself suspected that the tactic could not tackle things such as cognitive processes (Boring, 1957).

Reaction Time (RT) and Information Processing

Donders (1862, cited in D. Taylor, 1976) provided the first example of analysis when he measured the RT to stimulus situations to reveal the mental operations that different ones demanded. If stimulus A required T seconds and A with B required additional time U, the T–U difference presumably revealed the time needed for a subprocess, stimulus discrimination, that the first case did not require. Thus this *subtraction method* parceled RT into the component operations needed in a given situation. Donders's elegant work is important historically. It predated even Wundt and his followers' pioneering attempt to assess inner processes empirically and influenced Galton and the testing movement by demonstrating the importance of individual differences. Unfortunately, the RT measure was later adopted, unsuccessfully, by Wundt to assess more subjective phenomena quite at odds with Donders's intent, which soiled its reputation and condemned it to a lengthy spell of disuse (D. Taylor, 1976). Luckily its possibilities were eventually recognized and *chronometry*, the study of the time course of information processing in the human nervous system (Posner, 1978), has become a growth industry for assessing apparently unempirical phenomena.

Since much of this literature is more relevant to Chapter 1, I limit this discussion to a seminal example that used RT for analytic purposes and so lies directly in Donders's tradition.

S. Sternberg (1969) presented a set of items such as single digits (1, 4, 6, 8) followed by a single probe item and assessed the RT to decide yes or no whether the probe was a member of the set. Since set sizes were less than the immediate memory span, subjects could perform without error, but total RT presumably included the substages of storing the set and probe, comparing the latter to the former, making the decision, and initiating the response. However, Sternberg questioned the subtraction method's assumption that subprocesses are independent and that adding one did not affect time needed for the others, so that any increase in RT must reflect the addendum. He therefore devised a *method of additive factors* to reveal whether two variables are independent. If so, and they affect different stages, their effects on RT should be additive à la Donders, but if both influence the same stage and hence one another, the effect of one should depend on the value of the other, that is, they should interact statistically. Criticisms of this method (D. Taylor, 1976) are beyond our scope, but we might note Sternberg's conclusion that the comparison stage involves a *serial-exhaustive search* in which the probe is compared with each set member, and with all of them, before making the decision. Alternative possibilities such as *parallel search* (comparing the probe with the entire set simultaneously) or *self-terminating–serial search* (successively comparing each member, but ending when a match occurs) were not supported by the data; for example, under the second scenario, positive instances in which the probe is a set member should take less time than negative, since only then would every set member have to be compared, but this was not the case. The serial-exhaustive tactic might seem less efficient—why continue searching once a match is made?—but self-termination requires a decision after each comparison, the exhaustive only one, after all have been made, so RT might actually be shorter.

Serial Learning

Regarding this second example of analysis, behaviorists may have parted company with Wundt on other matters but here they followed suit. A complex behavior such as hitting a tennis ball, they assumed, consisted of many independent units occurring in sequence, which Skinner (1938) referred to as *response chaining*. Those that compose a well-learned sequence may appear unified but are in fact independent in that some are affected by, say, removing reinforcement, while others are not. True to form, Skinner expressed no opinion about how or why responses form chains, but for the more theoretically inclined the analytic assumption means that the question of how serial learning is accomplished becomes crucial, the key to understanding virtually all behavior. Ebbinghaus's studies of learning lists of nonsense syllables have much broader implications than has sometimes been realized!

Most S–R theorists, Hull being exemplary, saw serial learning as involving *stimulus feedback*, or *response produced cues*. Muscles and glands contain sensory receptors, so whenever a response is emitted, this information is picked up for relay to the central nervous system. Therefore these automatic, unique consequences of a response are stimuli just as are external events that affect receptors in the eye or ear. Which means that another response can perforce be associated to such a one and it is by such mechanisms that a chain of S–R units results, with each response cueing the next. Furthermore, the environmental bias decreed that these units must be learned, and the mechanisms governing acquisition of ever more microscopic S–R habits consequently became the main concern. Thus K. Spence (1956), to study learning in the ubiquitous rat, preferred a straight runway over the mazes usually employed because it requires fewer component behaviors, is less subject to competing error tendencies, and so more closely resembles the ideal, a task to reveal how variables affect a single, isolated habit. Understand that and the riddle of any behavior is solved!

Young's (1962) evidence that chaining may not occur, at least for serial verbal lists, cast a shadow over these analyses and led to the controversy about the functional stimulus therein. However, in retrospect it is indicative that whether the preferred candidate was thought to be a preceding event, serial position, or some combination thereof, apart from a few heretics (Lashley, 1951 and Arthur Jensen, 1962, who again showed his readiness to fly in the face of prevailing opinion), the more basic supposition that sequences consist of separate component behaviors and that each must be associated to something, emerged unscathed, along with the presumption that it was legitimate to treat sequences analytically.

The Scientific Attitude Revisited

So far this attitude's advantages have been played up, but developments vis-à-vis serial learning reveal a less desirable aspect. The learning of sequence is a seminally important albeit unanswered question, but my overriding impression is that since the cognitive revolution it has been swept under the rug. I therefore randomly surveyed examples of those indicants par excellence of current interests, textbooks. That those entered in the introductory psychology course sweepstakes contained not one discussion of either the topic or classic contributions to it is forgivable, given the plethora of deserving topics competing for inclusion. Whether this state of affairs held a generation ago could not be determined—libraries tend to jettison outdated texts. However, it was also omitted from most sources purportedly concerned with cognition, learning, and/or memory, which if *my* memory serves *is* a change. Furthermore, in both types of textbooks most treatments of interference phenomena, which notwithstanding their limitations possess considerable explanatory potential, were cursory if not misinforming, for example, discussions of PI's importance and changes over time were rare and no doubt for the same reason: the association with now unfashionable S–R and functionalist approaches. The few exceptions (apart from Baddeley, 1990, whose evident sympathies for tradition may reflect his British background) usually had several editions, suggesting authors old enough to recall when these matters were deemed deserving.

The differing fates of two estimable discussions of serial learning are especially instructive. An unmistakable cognitive aura pervades Lashley's (1951) classic and hence, being ahead of its time, it at first attracted little notice. However, it now provides an exception to the preceding conclusions because, since the mid-1960s when the cognitive revolution took hold, it was increasingly cited to the point that on this score it now far outdistances Lashley's seminal contributions to neuropsychology (Bruce, 1994). On the other hand, the methodological complexities of Slamecka's (1977) studies prevent my giving them the treatment they deserve, so let it simply be said that he provides persuasive arguments both rational and empirical for a chaining explanation based on that venerable notion, response-produced cues. Nonetheless, I found only one, casual reference to this work, so it seems to have sunk without a trace. (Incidentally, it is ironic in view of developments that, according to Bruce, another factor that stimulated interest in Lashley's article was its inclusion in a book of readings edited by that same Slamecka, 1967).

These events support Boring's (1957) contention that an idea's impact depends in good part on the *zeitgeist*, the prevailing spirit and attitudes of the time, which must be ready to receive it. I see more chicken and egg here than Boring seems to allow (do not notable ideas determine the *zeitgeist* as well?) but he does indicate that in science as in most things, timing is everything! However, the main point for us lies elsewhere. Although serial learning is eminently deserving of attack, the few discussions put before tomorrow's scholars manage to hide this fact effectively or, by focusing exclusively on Lashley, to give the impression that it has been solved. Neither situation is likely to encourage those scholars to take it on. It has not been solved, and Lashley, as he no doubt realized, raised as many questions as he answered, and bringing modern perspectives to bear on them could prove productive. Sadly, this seems unlikely to happen.

Which reveals a general drawback: scientists' excessive preoccupation with the topical while consigning predecessors to the dustbin. It is commonly supposed that the history of science interests only elder statespersons whose best research years are behind them! Science certainly does not demand these priorities, but from a Kuhnian angle they are understandable. If scientific revolutions produce wholesale changes, then that which has gone before is irrelevant if not discomforting, especially if it cannot be easily reconciled with the new outlook. But there is a considerable difference between being genuinely knowledgeable about a topic and merely knowing the literature, and according to that overused but accurate cliché, those who don't know history are condemned to repeat it. Does eternally rediscovering the wheel provide the best equipment for traveling down the road of progress?

The danger may be less acute in the natural sciences wherein some innovations do render predecessors truly obsolete, but psychology's basic concerns are the same enduring riddles with which our forebears, whether empirically or philosophically inclined, grappled; it sometimes seems that only the jargon changes. Thus Postman (1971, 1972) showed that once differences of this kind are surmounted, some supposedly new cognitive concepts recall those of classical associationism and the debates that have arisen recall the earlier ones between Gestalt and S–R psychology. These supposedly new bottles contain some well-aged wine! Be that as it may, today's investigators might do worse than give those forebears heed, for they too had inspired moments. If, as Whitehead alleged, all philosophy is but a footnote to Plato, could the same be said of empirical psychology and Aristotle? So I share Baddeley's (1990) distaste for psychology's fixation on the here and now—a mark, perhaps, of its youth, for who is more prone to bandwagon jumping than adolescents? Indeed, one aim here has been to show the virtues of and reawaken interest in earlier work, because among those enamored of science, Watson has not been the only one guilty of tossing promising babies out with the bathwater!

The Two-Stage Analysis of Paired-Associate Learning (PAL)

It is fitting that the functionalist verbal learning tradition should also provide another example of analysis, for as Underwood (1957b) intimated, it was therein a favored tactic. *Interference theory* attributed forgetting to several component factors (Postman, 1961b; Keppel, 1968). This version of analysis was later abandoned (Postman, Stark & Henschel, 1969), but another contribution stands up well. In many fields it has been common to hypothesize various stages for a complex process. Examples include Freud, Piaget, several discussions of creativity (Wallas, 1970; Stein, 1974), and PAL provides another. The initiating puzzle concerned the effects of item meaningfulness (M), the number of responses elicited in free association. If PAL demanded only that each response be associated to its stimulus, each should play an equivalent role and a variable should have comparable effects on either. Yet increased stimulus M while holding response M constant produced a much smaller improvement in learning speed than did higher response M.

Underwood and Schulz (1960) therefore proposed that PAL requires two stages. In Stage 1, list responses are learned to availability so one can produce them in their entirety; presumably stimuli do not have to be learned because one need not produce them (the authors said little about what is learned about them, but presumably they must only be recognized and discriminated from one another to prevent misplacing responses). Depending on the responses in the list, then, time for this stage may vary enormously. High M responses such as table are already familiar and available, but integrating a novelty such as ZVQ is an arduous task. Once responses are learned (conceptually this stage occurs first, but this need not be so), Stage 2, S–R association, follows to link up the two members. Underwood and Schulz presumed that high M of either stimuli or responses also assists this stage, although they recognized that it might in fact prove detrimental in that more associations might interfere but regardless, from their standpoint high response M should be more beneficial overall than stimulus M because it facilitates both stages, the latter only the second.

Although others had suggested this analysis before, Underwood and Schulz felt that its possibilities had not been exploited. It is ironic then that they did not extend it beyond PAL's restricted horizons because it has yet broader implications. Do not many other tasks, for example, athletic skills such as stick handling in hockey, when all is said and done also require learning both what to do and when to do it—essentially what the proposed stages involve? Classical conditioning is an exception—responses are automatically elicited by the UCS, making Stage 1 unnecessary—but in operant tasks, shaping provides a means to facilitate this stage when the response required is not in the subject's repertoire. Similarly, the stages nicely explain two types of errors children routinely make while learning a language. One features utterances not part of the legitimate vocabulary (although they usually approximate same, such as "psketti" for "spaghetti") which suggest Stage 1 deficiencies. Another type sees legitimate responses emitted to inappropriate stimuli, as when a porcupine is called a doggie, indicating that Stage 1 is virtually complete but Stage 2 still has a way to go. However, analysis of PAL did not end here. Underwood and Schulz themselves referred in passing to several other probably necessary components such as discriminating among stimuli, and Battig (1968) claimed that at times as many as ten could come into play. A seemingly simple business, linking two verbal units, was becoming complicated!

Structure of Intellect: Guilford

Unlike the foregoing, the final example involves analysis not of a dynamic process but of a presumed trait, so it resembles breaking down radios or other static commodities. Does "intelligence" refer to a general entity that affects ability in every sphere or are there several field-specific intelligences, as Piaget and Gardner respectively assumed? Spearman (1927), coming down firmly on top of the fence, hypothesized both a widely applicable g (general) and various s (specific) factors, with performance in an activity dependent on both the amounts of g and of the various ss relevant to it. Later, Wechsler (1958) aimed to overcome a weakness in Binet-inspired IQ tests, their excessive emphasis on verbal ability, by developing two groups of subtests, the *verbal* and *performance*. The latter depend less on verbal ability and the separate IQ determined for them might better indicate some people's actual intelligence, notably those whose first language is not English.

It was Guilford (1967) who took this analytic approach to the extreme. However one views his specifics, he deserves kudos for having pioneered the study of creativity as a legitimate concern for a psychology with scientific aspirations, since his commitment to empiricism, analysis, and the like was apparent. His APA presidential address (Guilford, 1950), which lambasted the profession for ignoring creativity despite its importance (he reckoned that during the preceding twenty-five years only .2 percent of psychological studies had focused on it) or equating it with intelligence, was a watershed factor in correcting this state of affairs (although there are indications that this commitment may again be flagging, Simonton, 1990). Furthermore his model was unquestionably fruitful; it stimulated much research and his tests have often served as criterion measures to decide the effects of variables on creativity, or the amount of creativity that individuals allegedly possess (Stein, 1974).

Guilford stressed traits, those enduring characteristics that distinguish one person from another. He felt they result from both nature and nurture and form continuous dimensions, and so can be measured and scaled. To this end he employed *factor analysis*, which parcels up the variance in test scores into independent components and then, using semirigorous criteria, hypothesizes what each might be. From these machinations his *structure of intellect model* (see Figure 7.1) evolved. It proposes that the intellect trait varies along three independent dimensions, each with several categories. *Content* involves the

Figure 7.1
Guilford's Structure of Intellect Model

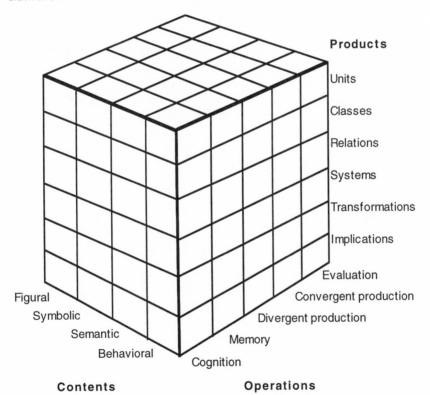

Source: Guilford, J. P. (1967). *The nature of human intelligence* (p. 63). Copyright © 1967. Reproduced with permission of The McGraw-Hill Companies.

various types of information that a person might prefer, such as visual, semantic, or symbolic, *products* includes the various means through which one might express oneself, such as in units, classes, or relations (their descriptions are extremely vague, but they are distinguished operationally), while *operations* concerns the types of thought one might prefer, such as memory (which presumably identifies someone prone to nostalgia), evaluation (judging), and divergent thinking. The last named is particularly relevant to creative thinking since it surveys a broad range of ideas, none certifiably correct. Each cell in Figure 7.1's matrix designates a psychological factor, of which there are no less than 120 in all (6 products x 5 operations x 4 contents). The final step is to name and identify each factor and concoct a test to operationally define it. Thus divergent production of semantic units is called *ideational fluency* and *plot titles*, its measure, requires devising as many titles as one can for a presented story.

   In short, a commodity such as creativity comes in many guises, since divergent thinking encompasses twenty-four cells so Guilford, like Gardner, rejects a nonspecific *g* for both creativity and intellect. Rather, a variety of specific abilities each affect some endeavors, so to predict various creativities, different tests are needed for each; a test that purported to measure a general such trait was for Guilford a contradiction in terms. Thus his rejoinder to evidence (Amabile, 1983) that his tests do not predict ultimate achievement. Many "tests of the tests" evaluate their prediction of a nonspecific creativity, which assumes the very thing he denied, that there is such a thing. However, another problem may also contribute to the tests' failings. Although Guilford claimed to have faced the problem of quality, his commitment to scientific priorities rarely allowed it. For example, counting the number of white and edible objects a subject can name may assess flexible thinking, but apart from the questionable relation of such a task to, say, devising dances, it does not verify that one can produce or recognize worthwhile ideas, a negative note that provides a fitting introduction to a more critical perspective.

CRITIQUES OF ANALYSIS

The Whole is Different than the Sum of Its Parts

   Those who seek a "mental chemistry" might be led to avoid rather than practice analysis in that most compounds differ markedly from their constituent elements; little can be learned about water by studying hydrogen and oxygen. Consider the dispute within the Mills family of philosophers (Boring, 1957). Father James ardently supported the strategy on grounds that ideas and associations retained their character while forming the larger unit called mind, but son John Stuart retorted that a qualitatively different entity results. Lack of respect for parental authority, it seems, is nothing new! The rise of science saw similar objections to Wundt's structuralism. To James (1890), mental life is experienced as a *stream of consciousness*, one thought leading to the next in an unbroken continuity. Therefore its analysis into bits and pieces must be as misinforming as individual drops of water are about a waterfall. To switch the metaphor, those preoccupied with individual trees are likely to miss the forest.

The most influential objection however came from the Gestaltists (Heidbredder, 1935). An elegant demonstration by Wertheimer (one of the pioneering triumvirate, along with Koffka and Köhler) captured its essence. Two slightly separated lights, if flashed in alternation at an appropriate rate are perceived as moving and joined. This *phi phenomenon* is exploited in neon signs, as when a flashing arrow shoots into a restaurant to stylishly exhort one to EAT! JAKE'S! However, its theoretical significance lies in its proof that many an experience does not mirror and cannot be understood by the component stimuli that give rise to it (the two lights) or the sensations each produces. Wertheimer's conclusion, forthwith inscribed as it were on the movement's regimental banners, was the famous slogan (in the version I prefer) that heads this section. That movement, whose German title roughly translates as a "whole" or "unit," did not oppose all analyses, only those taken too far. The genuine units of experience should be the focus of attention or their essence is lost, because essence depends on how constituents are organized and relate to one another. The effects of a melody or the meaning of a sentence differ qualitatively from those of their individual notes or words and can no more be understood from their parts than can the metaphorical blind men, by each feeling part of an elephant, grasp the essence of elephantness. Polanyi (1968) directed similar criticisms against orthodox science. As we know, a fact can interpreted in many ways depending on one's outlook and a prime determinant of this are other available facts and the manner of their integration, so it may be interpreted differently when taken by itself. Often a scholarly work's significance is overlooked until one reexperiences it within the context of others that bear on the same topic and it falls into place in the overall scheme of things. And for Polanyi, recognizing relations depends as much on tacit as logical processes.

When Gestalt's pioneers emigrated to the United States they encountered other examples of analysis in behaviorism's several versions. The specific units these proposed differed from Wundt's, but Gestalt objections remained the same. Witness Lashley's (1951) rejoinders to analytic discussions of serial learning. Component behaviors in sequences like typing or musical arpeggios, he claimed, could not each be elicited by a separate event such as a feedback stimulus because they can be reeled off far more rapidly than the time the nervous system needs to process and conduct information. Those components must form an integrated unit with the sole functional stimulus being the beginning of the sequence. As well, the sequence must be governed by a central plan of action that senses its overall meaning and the end to which the components lead (Bruce, 1994). Otherwise, since no item in a sentence, such as The cow jumped over the moon, is the dominant association to its predecessor, and since in different sequences a component such as "the" can adjoin myriad others, the potential for interference from extraneous interlopers would be overwhelming.

But this raises the question about what is meant by "a response," and it is more than academic. In measuring memory for a sequence such as the example sentence above, does correct reproduction equal one response (the sentence), six (the number of words), twenty-three (the number of letters), or some other? What level of analysis is appropriate? From a Gestalt standpoint this should be decided by what is experienced as one response, and certainly it is tenuous in the extreme to claim à la Skinner that emitting an entity such as "table" constitutes five responses. Still, it may be that this changes with the degree of learning, that separate components are at first each linked to an antecedent (whatever it might be), and that with practice this drops out and the sequence attains unity (Mandler, 1962)—a change in quality as well as quantity.

Some disclaimers to Lashley should also be mentioned. There are now indications that feedback cues can occur quickly enough to mediate rapid sequences such as typing (Bruce, 1994; Slamecka, 1977). As well, Gestaltists were frequently chided for being better critics than originators; their ingenious arguments and demonstrations effectively embarrassed other accounts but many of their own were so vague as to defy testing. Thus Lashley tells us little about how components become integrated—they "just do"—nor about the empirical implications. Could one reason for the current disinterest in serial learning be that the one "explanation" young investigators encounter discourages involvement because it lacks that crucial attribute, falsifiability? As unappealing as S–R accounts of serial learning are to me on introspective grounds, they did generate clear predictions and critical experiments. Harré (1985) hints at another reason for disinterest. Physics, he claims, no longer sees the corpusclarean view that subsumes analysis as viable, so true to form, psychology is clinging to an outlook its revered model has abandoned. More to the point, this view is attractive to the scientifically inclined because it justifies quantification. It follows that phenomena which cannot be so subdivided will tend to be avoided, and as described by Lashley, serial learning is one.

Does Analysis Increase Understanding?

The strategy's popularity implies as much, but that its opposite, generalization, supposedly increased simplicity and parsimony suggests the reverse. For one thing, infinite regress beckons, that is, components can be analyzed and analyzed again. Disciplines wherein the strategy has proved helpful set clear if arbitrary limits to indicate where to stop (R. Sainsbury, personal communication, 1980). Historically, chemistry and physics dealt with units, atoms or elements, that by definition were irreducible parts, but psychology never established set limits, freeing analysis to descend to reductio ad absurda. The examples provided here all intimate that even moderately analyzing heretofore unitary phenomena may open a Pandora's box, so a picture that is initially clarified becomes increasingly opaque. The two-stage analysis in my view helped understand PAL, but Battig's ten components, to say nothing of Guilford's mammoth model of intellect, force one to ask whether things can really be that complicated. The question is one of parsimony and even so ardent a proponent of

analysis as Underwood (1972) expressed doubts on this score, with tongue
planted firmly in cheek.

Ten years ago it might have been said that most conceptualizations of memory were
impoverished or simplistic in that they did not at all reflect the variety of phenomena. . . . If an increase in the size of . . . vocabulary signals escape from conceptual
poverty, we have become liberated. Memories now have attributes, organization, and
structure . . . storage systems, retrieval systems, and control systems . . . iconic,
echoic, primary, secondary, and short-, medium- and long-term memories . . .
addresses, readout rules, and holding mechanisms . . . T-stacks, implicit associational
responses, natural-language mediators, images, multiple traces, tags, kernel
sentences, markers, relational rules, verbal loops, and one-buns. Surely it is only
fitting that the workers in the field of memory should have available such an
enormously rich and flexible vocabulary to provide the topic the awe it so rightfully
deserves. (1972, p. 1)

Some historical notes are relevant. Gestalt, like its ancestor Kant, shared
many of the romantics' biases, and they too, perhaps reacting against Descartes
splitting the mind from the body, espoused a sense of unity over diversity. For
example, they preferred subjective over empirical knowledge because knowing
the world reveals many things but when we know ourselves we know but one.
Their search for unity also provided a criterion for beauty. For Coleridge beauty
was that in which the many, still seen as many, becomes one, and he valued
imagination in good part because its *modifying power* allowed it to unify
sensation's components into integrated images (Furst, 1969). Finally, this search
subsumed the famous preoccupation with love as the ultimate bliss; such intense
interpersonal feeling could unite all things to achieve greater truth. The humanists have been another force for promoting romantic attitudes in psychology
(Abra, 1988a) and they too have objected to analysis as a hallmark of narrow,
cautious science, a defense against that clear and present danger, subjectivity. By
focusing on an entity's components, we can ignore its discomforting uniqueness
and value-laden attributes—in Maslow's (1966) words, "[Through] the general-
atomistic technique of dissection, one can avoid feeling stunned, unworthy or
ignorant before, let us say, a beautiful flower, or insect, or poem simply by
taking it apart and feeling masterful again" (p. 143). But if the aim is knowledge
of an entire person, analysis can be a hindrance. I would add that it can also
protect narrow science by maintaining the viability of beliefs its practitioners
wish to adopt anyway; for example, determinism may prove valid for an entity's
components such as eye blinks or muscle twitches, but not for the entity itself,
the person.

All of which suggests why, according to Pirsig (1974), analysis dominates
Western thought. Supposedly we can interpret the world in two ways. *Classical
understanding* prefers analysis because it sees phenomena in terms of their form,
which is made up of components; mechanics confront motorcycles in this
manner. *Romantic understanding* stresses appearances, is primarily imaginative
and intuitive, and so sees motorcycles as objects for riding on. (The similarities

to Ornstein's, 1972, linear and nonlinear thought, respectively, are evident.) The West, Pirsig contends, is addicted to the classical alternative as not *one* but *the* road to travel, apparently because in ancient Greece a battle was waged and won. One camp, led by Plato and Socrates, held Truth to be objective, independent of any one mind and so potentially discoverable, but for the Sophists, it was subjective. Because the first group won the day their successors, even those who have never attended university and wouldn't know Plato from Pluto, have inherited their bias. Unfortunately, Pirsig notes, something is never gained without something else being lost. The advances provided by classical understanding and its offshoot science are beyond dispute, but they have come at the expense of our ability to see ourselves as part of the world rather than separate from it, for scientists are ideally objective and detached. Above all, they opt for analysis to avoid the attribute that is Pirsig's main concern: quality.

Specialization

This tendency that prevails in all sciences nowadays, like analysis favors narrower horizons and increasingly specific forms by confining interest and expertise to ever more restricted subfields. Hence the truism: today's scholars know more and more about less and less. There are defenses for specialization, if only that with the torrent of publication induced by publish or perish, keeping up would otherwise be impossible, but Bohm and Peat (1987) argue persuasively that on balance the practice has been harmful. Why, they ask, since the number of talented people now doing science is greater than ever, and their working conditions comparatively speaking are far more encouraging, is genuinely creative science so rare? Where are the Newtons, Darwins, and Einsteins? One of several villains they indict is specialization. By consensus, (Poincaré, 1952; Mednick, 1962; Koestler, 1970), creative insights come about by that process of bisociation that forges several ideas, perhaps each familiar in themselves, into a previously unrealized combination. Specialization seems less likely to foster new combinations than that breadth of knowledge that the giants of yesteryear almost all possessed (Root-Bernstein, 1989). Freud's was astonishing, and Newton was at various times deeply involved not only in mathematics and physics, but alchemy, religious history, politics, and of all things the civil service (Westfall, 1980). Bohm and Peat therefore argue that scientists should seek breadth but unfortunately are stronger on diagnosis than treatment and have little to say about how to encourage them to do so.

I have practiced such eclecticism toward a few of creativity's conundra, its decline with age (Abra, 1989), sex difference (Abra & Valentine-French, 1991), and motivation (Abra, 1997). The position concerning the phenomenon in question is determined for the various branches of psychoanalysis, behaviorism, cognitive psychology, existentialism, and so on. Despite their sometimes wildly contradictory philosophical underpinnings, each is then taken as part of the answer, so the various contributions are seen as not mutually exclusive but complementary pieces in a complex puzzle. The down side is that the practice may invite schizophrenic overinclusiveness, but even this, in my view, is preferable to and certainly more interesting than the other extreme because if any discipline demands breadth, it is psychology. The range of topics is unrivaled—indeed, it is partly to bring this home that contributions discussed here have been taken from many subfields. Majors who wonder which other courses to take should stop worrying. Anything from classics to nuclear physics is relevant! Yet sadly, fragmentation reigns even here. The formation of APS, that rival organization to APA, by some eminent, mainly academic psychologists reflected their belief that its priorities no longer reflected theirs, and some universities reportedly now see the discipline as so heterogeneous that some subfields should become separate departments. Certainly many of my colleagues have less in common with one another than with others housed elsewhere! Yeats's heartfelt cry, that things fall apart and the center cannot hold, suits modern psychology to a T. More's the pity!

REDUCTIONISM IN PSYCHOLOGY

The most noteworthy attempts in this regard stem from physiological psychology, which investigates relationships between behavior and various anatomical structures, notably those in the central nervous system.

Memory and Localization of Function

How the brain stores experiences is a fascinating and significant puzzle. Presumably some enduring, tangible record must remain if they are to be available for later retrieval, as is the case with devices such as audio recordings and photographs. It is possible of course that memory involves no such physical events, but most scientific psychologists assume otherwise (Hebb, 1949), because the alternative, that unempirical factors are involved, does not bear thinking about. Moreover, many studies vindicate this faith. For example, Penfield and Perot (1963, cited in Loftus & Loftus, 1980) exposed the cerebral cortex of neurosurgery patients who remained conscious to report their experiences, and then stimulated various locations with an electric probe. Those patients often claimed to have had remarkably detailed and dramatic memories of past events, almost as if these were being relived, suggesting that every experience of a lifetime may be inscribed "up there" somewhere. Why then do we forget? An item may be unavailable from any system that stores vast amounts of information, such as a computer, not because it is lost but because it cannot be located and retrieved.

Pavlov provided an early proposal about the nature of this *memory trace* or *engram* to account for classical conditioning (Kimble, 1961), and Gestaltists also dabbled in this exercise, but I focus here on Lashley's (1950) search. In myriad studies, he in essence trained animals in a task, damaged part of their brains, and then tested retention, and concluded that the loss depended not on the area but on the sheer amount of tissue damage. His *principle of mass action* therefore asserted that in storing a memory, the brain acts as a whole. Yet intuitively, must there not be some *localization of function*, with different areas controlling specific and differing activities? Were one piece of paper used repeatedly to write an entire novel, wouldn't various passages become indecipherable? The reasoning seems faultless. Lashley's data said otherwise.

Later work tempered this bleak scenario. The brain shows considerable specialization, albeit not of the simplistic one-area-does-one-thing-and-different-areas-do-different-things variety. For example, the visual area in the occipital lobe services other functions as well and several visual abilities are controlled elsewhere (Kolb & Whishaw, 1996). As another twist, the brain is remarkably plastic; should one area be damaged, the functions it controls may suffer only temporarily and gradually return as other areas take over. Still, Hubel and Wiesel's (1979) landmark studies vindicate specialization claims in principle. Electrodes were inserted into single cells of the visual system at various levels from the retina up to the brain to record their activity and identify stimuli to which they responded. Not only did cells differ in their *receptive fields*, that is, the group of retinal receptors that caused them to fire, but some responded only to specific stimulus orientations, others to certain shapes, to diffuse but not specific light, or to movement. Similarly, H. Gardner (1983) held the seven cognitions to be independent in part because damage to a given area has markedly different effects on each, which suggests localization. For example, language ability suffers from both left and right hemisphere damage, visual artistry only from the right. And the distinction between left and right hemisphere functioning has become a veritable cliché (albeit one that vastly oversimplifies matters; B. Bland, personal communication, 1996). Witness apparent differences in emotions. Left hemisphere damage results in an overridingly gloomy outlook filled with anger and despair, suggesting that negative feelings are the right's domain, whereas left overactivity causes uncontrollable laughter (Kinsbourne, 1981).

Nonetheless, between Watson's revolution and the 1950s attempts to relate brain and behavior were few. Whether Lashley's findings contributed to this state of affairs is difficult to say but they surely discouraged investigation because without localization, relating brain and behavior seemed most unpromising— Lashley himself sardonically noted that he sometimes wondered whether memory was possible at all! Hull did hypothesize entities that had a vague physiological ring, but they took little note of the brain's known properties and hardly anyone suspected they might actually exist. Also, the firmly peripheralist orientation of most behaviorists, notably Skinner and his followers, led them to ignore any events, physical or other, that might intervene between environmental antecedents and behavior.

Enter Hebb's (1949) watershed account of how the brain might store memories and perform its other duties. Although based on a few known facts, it involved, he admitted, a lot of speculation, conveying a distinct impression (Hebb, 1959) that in true Popperian fashion he aimed less at being correct than awakening interest in physiological approaches. Any experience, he proposed, causes a group of adjacent brain cells to fire in sequence. This *cell assembly* forms a closed circuit, so members can continue to stimulate one another after the initiating event's removal and when one cell repeatedly causes a neighbor to fire, some physical change occurs to increase this ability henceforth. But for a cell assembly to become an event's permanent engram, two distinct phases must be completed. The first, later called *short-term memory* (STM), lasts while the event is present and for a brief interlude thereafter and is a dynamic stage of *reverberation* wherein the component cells fire repeatedly in sequence. This phase can fail if reverberation is interrupted or loses intensity, in which case the status quo returns, but if carried to completion a second, *long-term memory* (LTM) develops, featuring an enduring structural change in the relevant cells or what came to be called *consolidation* (Glickman, 1961). Forgetting by and large now reflects interference.

Several lines of evidence are supportive. That traumas to the brain such as blows or electroconvulsive shock cause forgetting is hardly surprising, but of greater note is a reliable time effect (Glickman, 1961), that they obliterate events just prior to them but leave others more remote intact; someone who suffers a head injury in an accident may have no memory of the event itself but those of childhood remain. Supposedly, traumas inhibit reverberating but not consolidated cell assemblies. As well, Milner's (1964) studies of a patient whose temporal lobe was surgically removed found that his presurgical LTMs remained available, as did postsurgical STMs; he retained presented information, such as names, as long as he was allowed to focus on them. However, even a brief distraction destroyed any memory whatsoever, suggesting that the temporal lobe is needed for consolidation; moreover, similar effects appear in *Korsakoff's syndrome*, which is caused by chronic alcohol abuse (Eccles & Robinson, 1984). Such abrupt, either-or effects are more easily reconciled with a two-phase than unitary view, indicating as they do that permanent memory requires transfer from one store to another.

Several other developments are also noteworthy. The implied possibility that STM differs qualitatively from LTM, coupled with the development of an attractive technique for studying STM (J. Brown, 1958; Peterson & Peterson, 1959), made it for a time a lively topic of investigation. Hebb was often credited (e.g., Melton, 1963; Postman, 1964) with introducing the notion that the operation of decay as opposed to interference is STM's key difference. Although this is certainly a plausible extension of his thinking, I have come across no direct statements of his to this effect, but regardless, others soon provided them (Brown, 1958; Murdock, 1961) and the battle was joined. The prevailing conclusion now seems to be that STM does indeed differ, but apart from very brief interludes (Sperling, 1960), interference rather than decay still operates (Keppel & Underwood, 1962), but of a different kind that obeys different rules (Kintsch & Bushke, 1969; Waugh & Norman, 1965). Hebb also intimated that the facilitation of cells forming assemblies reflected events at the *synapse*, a slight space between adjacent neurons across which nerve impulses travel. *Neurotransmitter substances* such as acetylcholine, like chemical ferry boats, carry impulses across (J. C. Eccles, 1964). Therefore Rosenzweig (1984) and his colleagues (Rosenzweig, Bennett & Diamond, 1972) pursued the possibility that experience might affect these substances. The results were of the good news–bad news variety. Animals raised in enriched environments showed unimpressive gains in chemical neurotransmitters, but concentration of glial cells and weight of the cortex did increase, so experiences did have a physical impact of a sort.

Another possibility later mooted about was that memory storage involves changes in the structure of brain molecules. The nucleic acids DNA and RNA provided two intriguing candidates (Gaito, 1963). Given that DNA's structure carries the genetic code (J. D. Watson, 1968) might this not be viewed as a kind of memory, for an ancestor's characteristics? Still, most speculations along these lines ruled out DNA as "the memory molecule" since its structure is extremely resistant to modification, but RNA's case received a boost from McConnell's (1976) tantalizing studies of cannibalism in planaria that purported to show that (1) this worm (for such it is) can be classically conditioned, (2) it will ingest other planaria presented in a suitably delectable manner, that is, chopped up, and (3) untrained gorgers thereupon show "retention" of habits previously learned by gorgees. Did training perchance modify some RNA molecule(s) deep in the slithering anatomy's reaches, so ingestion of same allowed transfer? This possibility gained credibility when RNA extracted from trainees and injected into hosts had similar effects. In addition, experiences have been found to affect certain varieties of RNA in both their concentration (Gaito & Bonnet, 1971) and molecular structures (Hydèn & Lange, 1968).

Unfortunately, the bloom soon came off the rose. Apart from the moral quandaries (would superior students have to avoid solitary evening walks, lest less successful colleagues should try to imbibe their enlightened corpuscles using the dental techniques introduced by Dracula?), the approach later foundered on the usual reefs, methodological complications and failures to replicate findings involving cannibalism and injection (Gaito & Bonnet, 1971) and sometimes initial conditioning of the planaria (Lefrancois, 1983). These difficulties had the usual effect, to redirect research attention to seemingly greener pastures, but one delightful residue remained. *The Worm Runner's Digest*, founded by McConnell and named after his preferred subjects, provides a wonderfully irreverent spoof of the dry, pedantic sources through which we scholars must constantly slog.

However, interest increasingly turned to proteins as a possible memory constituent (Dunn, 1980). Agranoff's (1967) work is exemplary. Since protein synthesis precedes many long-term changes in organisms, and LTM represents such a change, he injected the antibiotic *puromycin*, which blocks protein synthesis, into the skulls of goldfish that had learned a simple task. The effects resembled those of brain traumas; injections immediately after training eliminated memory entirely, whereas those administered beyond one hour had no effect. Injections prior to learning allowed it to proceed unencumbered but severely hampered later retention. In short, puromycin seemed to inhibit consolidation. Sadly, after surveying this literature Dunn (1980) felt compelled to write, "Can one then conclude that protein synthesis is necessary for . . .

LTM? Alas, not with certainty" (p. 375). The last sentence might serve as a leitmotif for the ability of empirical investigations in general to provide final answers.

The main point is that Hebb's aim to resuscitate physiological psychology was a resounding success. Overnight this previously moribund subfield acquired an aura of being where the action was, and many first-rate students made the pilgrimage to McGill University to study at the foot of the master. Still, Hebb's work was not the sole impetus. Soon after, Olds and Milner (1954) discovered that brief shocks delivered via implanted electrodes to certain areas below the cortex encouraged recently emitted behaviors such as bar pressing; in other words, the stimulation was reinforcing. There was initial euphoria about the possibility that a physiological explanation for one of psychology's most important phenomena might lie within reach, but this proved premature, as complications began to appear (Kimble, 1961). Brain stimulation reinforcement had some singular effects, notably that some areas of the brain produced incomparably more intense responding and very rapid extinction, which suggests that far from subsuming any and all reinforcement it may be atypical. Nonetheless, Olds and Milner spawned another lively area of investigation.

Psychopathology

Many psychological afflictions have a physical basis and so might be called diseases in the medical sense. As a few examples, some forms of mental retardation reflect oxygen deprivation during birth that results in irreversible brain damage, and in the genetic disorder *phenylketonuria*, the chemical phenylalanine is not adequately broken down (so diets that avoid this chemical counteract the condition; Barlow & Durand, 1995). Also suggestive are correlated physical abnormalities. Most schizophrenics have enlarged brain ventricles that contain cerebrospinal fluid (Cannon & Marco, 1994, cited in Comer, 1995) and Alzheimer's disease, the tragic, ultimately fatal condition that afflicts many older people is associated with a variety of cellular changes as well as reductions in cortical size and neurotransmitter substances such as acetylcholine (Kolb & Whishaw, 1996). However, the adamant reductionist assumes that a physical basis also exists for conditions without a known pathology, a faith buttressed when physical interventions such as drugs curtail them. Reserpine, although no longer used because of its dangerous side effects, effectively counteracts schizophrenia, (Pinel, 1997), and lithium moderates the extreme mood swings from acute mania to severe depression that define bipolar disorder (Comer, 1995). Likewise, suspicions that depression might reflect deficiencies of the neurotransmitters serotonin and norepinephrine are supported by the effectiveness of the monoamine oxidase inhibitors, which block the action of an enzyme that can destroy those transmitters (Atkinson, Atkinson, Smith & Bem, 1993).

Furthermore, such findings encourage one to speculate about other conditions. I know of no direct supporting evidence, but it seems reasonable to suspect that since lesions to the medial and lateral areas of the hypothalamus produce overeating and a refusal to eat respectively (Anand & Brobeck, 1951; Hetherington & Ranson, 1942), similar aberrations might subsume eating afflictions such as anorexia nervosa and bulimia. Indeed, notwithstanding that reductionists supposedly have their feet planted firmly in concrete events, they too have indulged in speculations, notably about schizophrenia. One of these that focused on serotonin (Abood, 1960) especially tickled my fancy, based as it was on the intriguing observations that (1) psychedelic drugs such as LSD produce the same array of symptoms—extreme mood changes, hallucinations, delusions and feelings of depersonalization—that appear in psychotic episodes and (2) these drugs closely resemble serotonin in molecular structure. Could it be that the latter is somehow converted into an LSD clone, so schizophrenics are on an acid trip that never ends? They were once rumored to show serotonin deficiencies, however, a possible increase is now being bandied about (Kane & Freeman, 1994), and in general the foregoing notion seems to have gone by the boards, since it is not mentioned in recent sources. Pity!

Another transmitter, dopamine, is currently receiving the lion's share of the attention. Drugs such as reserpine that counteract schizophrenia are known to reduce levels of dopamine, while amphetamine (Pinel, 1997) and L-dopa (Comer, 1995) which can trigger schizophrenic episodes, raise its levels. One suggestion, then, is that dopamine synapses may be overactive because the presynaptic neurons produce too much of it (Carlsson, 1978). There are also recent, informal reports (Siegfried, 1996) of another promising suggestion involving the opposing action of glutamate and GABA (gamma-aminobutyric acid). These substances respectively stimulate and calm nerve cells, so lack of the first named means less of the second and thus an overaroused brain. Whichever hypothesis one prefers, the current *zeitgeist* favors a reductionistic explanation of some kind so it might be said that rather than one being schizophrenic, one these days has schizophrenia.

The Mind-Body Problem Revisited

Reductionism assumes that psychological phenomena can be explained by physical events. A corollary for many advocates is that no mystical entity, be it spirit, mind, or soul, need be postulated because these ghosts in the machine explain nothing. Thus these versions of mind-body debates pit *mechanism* against *vitalism*, which respectively deny and affirm the nonphysical aspect. Neither reductionism nor science demand complete materialism (Brain, 1966). The neurophysiologist Sherrington saw a mystical side as a real possibility, although one not amenable to scientific investigation, and science's purported founder, Aristotle, was a fervent vitalist (R. Watson, 1963). But those for whom mind equals brain are many. Hebb (1974) himself asserted, "Biological science long ago got rid of vitalism. The idea of an immaterial mind controlling the body . . . has no place in science. . . . Mind then is the capacity for thought, and thought is the integrative activity of the brain" (p. 75).

The idea that people might be explained entirely by chemical and physical laws and resemble machines is not new. Descartes held that our crucial difference from animals is that we alone have souls. Yet in dualism, soul borders on the irrelevant; for explaining natural events at least, scrapping it entirely would change little. Descartes' faith prevented him from taking this audacious step, but to his successor la Mettrie we were indeed nothing more than machines. More recently, Langer (1951) also championed the qualitative differences between ourselves and animals, notably in our propensities for using symbols and for activities such as religion and language which are laden with them. Yet she too could state, "That man is an animal I certainly believe. . . . He has no supernatural essence . . . enclosed in his skin. . . . His substance is chemical, and what he does, suffers, or knows is just what this sort of chemical structure may do, suffer, or know" (1951, p. 44). Finally, few have objected more strongly to equating living with nonliving entities or elemental components than von Bertalanffy (1952), "The individual chemical reactions that take place in a living organism [cannot] indicate any basic differences between them and those that go on in inanimate things, or in a decaying corpse" (p. 13). Nonetheless, he too refused to attribute this difference to soul and thus admit that the problem of life cannot be explained by natural law and therefore referred to a unique organization of components. Our physical and chemical parts do resemble those of machines, but combine differently, so that properties of units at higher levels of a hierarchy such as the body change qualitatively and become alive (Gestaltists, as well as Koestler, 1970, have presented similar proposals). Although von Bertalanffy sought out laws of this organization, it remains unclear how and why this qualitative shift occurs, making the device seem as arbitrary as any ghost in the machine.

CRITIQUES OF REDUCTIONISM

Von Bertalanffy also observed that the mechanism–vitalism issue resembles a game of chess played out over the ages, with the same arguments eternally reappearing. To reopen it then might seem pointless, except that its implications are too important for it to be dismissed as a pseudoissue. Ultimately of course one's position is a matter of faith and, romantic that I am, I admit to being an unapologetic vitalist who refuses to believe that we are no more than a collection of stuff. It is not that I find reductionism absurd—there is too much evidence to the contrary—but only that to see us devoid of spirit is unacceptable. If the arguments to come then seem mere rationalizations, so be it.

Psychology and Physiology: A Seamless Equation?

That zealous mechanist Hebb (1974) admitted that from this perspective such experiences as consciousness should always correlate with antecedent physical processes and in support he cited the split-brain studies wherein hemisphere separation produced the experience of two minds in one body

(Sperry, 1964). Furthermore, to Brain's (1966) rejoinder, that the sense of time passed does not reflect time taken by events in the nervous system, one might answer that drugs like the psychedelics severely alter that sense, which suggests a physical locus. Nonetheless, difficulties arise. Natsoulas (1978) agrees with Hebb that science cannot encompass subjective matters, but maintains that their prominence in experience demands that they be included in psychology. Following Nagel (1965, cited in Natsoulas), he denies that mind equals brain because unlike other physical entities, I am aware (mentally) of owning my physical attributes, which provides a strong sense of detachment. How could a brain, if that is all there is, be aware of being a brain? Natsoulas parts company with the view taken here in that rejecting materialism does not lead him to accept a spiritual aspect as doing the experiencing. The important point, however, is that awareness of being aware is so reliable that it cannot be ignored merely because it embarrasses a purely physical account. Thus once again that cardinal factor, intimacy, changes things from natural science. An ardent reductionist might retort that these subjectivities may be described physically, perhaps by bio-chemical reactions, but these do not go far enough. To anticipate a point, they do not reveal why a psychological experience has the attributes it does.

As well, much of the evidence that the psychological equals the physical is correlational. Reflecting medical model biases, antecedent status is invariably assigned to the latter when questions of chicken and egg remain or when there may be reason to follow the mystics' belief of mind over matter! As evidence, stress induces physical afflictions such as ulcers, and some "drugs" alleviate physical symptoms not because of their chemical effects, which are minimal, but through the power of suggestion or *placebo effect*, due to expectations from having taken a drug. In fact Wilkins (1986) suggests that such effects, usually dismissed by reductionists as a mere nuisance in evaluating a drug's physical effects, could be put to therapeutic use. In this regard, Peele (1981) refers to the prevailing tendency to prefer physical explanations and treatment programs for pathologies such as surgery or drugs over psychological alternatives that invoke such factors as attitudes or personality characteristics. This rush onto the reductionistic bandwagon may lead therapists down dangerous garden paths. At the least, the two factors may interact; for example, a pain relief program using morphine may or may not lead to addiction (Alexander, Coambs & Hardaway, 1978) depending on the circumstances of administration, so to explain addiction solely by the drug's physical effects oversimplifies matters. Indeed, physical programs that ignore psychological influences may actually prove detrimental. The depressed may become psychologically addicted to Valium to relieve their suffering if those influences are not attacked.

Sperry (1968, 1969, 1970) too raises the chicken-egg question. The reality of phenomena such as consciousness is introspectively self-evident and for him they determine physical processes as much as vice versa, so they can no longer be ignored or dismissed as epiphenomena, byproducts of those processes. In describing the relationship, Sperry like others invokes qualitative changes at higher levels of a hierarchy, in this case the brain. Component physical structures and processes interact in such a way that a mentalistic entity, consciousness, emerges, which then becomes a Gestalt-like higher control center that governs those components. Curiously, it is those same split-brain studies that Hebb cited to dismiss mind that, one gathers, have led Sperry, their author, to the opposite opinion, that mind not only exists but determines the physical. I confess that I am unable to fathom how those studies suggested this view, other than by inducing him to think deeply about the entire matter. Split-brain surgery results in several separate streams of consciousness, whereas that which Sperry then advocates is an integrated unity (and Sperry, 1977, admits that no empirical proof exists to verify either matter over mind or the reverse; it is a question of preference). Sperry (1977) was thereby led to debate the relationship between science and values, since the latter are one of consciousness's main manifestations. They too powerfully affect behavior, for among alternatives we choose those we most value; therefore a science that truly has nothing to say about them becomes trivial. In fact for Sperry, as for others discussed earlier, modern science, as our primary source of information about what is (and what is not), can also help us decide what ought to be. Value judgments based on facts rather than vague impressions, biases, and emotion as is currently the case are more likely to prove effective.

As another variation on this theme, few have surpassed Freud's (1947) materialist convictions; even the most psychological phenomena such as the unconscious had organic bases. Early on, therefore, he sought these out but eventually gave up (Parisi, 1987), in good part because of a perplexing problem he recognized (Freud, 1887–1902/1954). How do physical processes become psychological experiences? Furthermore, Parisi maintains, too many reductionists who lack Freud's insight continue to ignore this problem. Having pinpointed physical underpinnings, they allow their curiosity to rest prematurely, and leave explanations that are insufficient as complete accounts of phenomena. I can do no better than borrow an example from Polanyi (1981). Those observing an object such as a cat have a different experience than a physiologist observing the neural mechanisms by which they do so. They see the cat, but not the mechanisms they use, whereas the physiologist sees these but not their experiences. Now the physiologist can up to a point imagine those experiences, since as a fellow human being she too may have had them; likewise a subject can understand a description of his own mechanisms although unable to observe them. Still and all, the experience of seeing differs substantially from a knowledge of the mechanism of seeing.

For similar reasons Eccles and Robinson (1984) reject the popular analogy between human cognition and computers. The similarities are many, but we alone somehow convert input received into psychological experiences such as perception, whereas a computer is oblivious to its own existence. So for these authors, brain corresponds to a computer, mind to its programmer. However, their main concern is our era's moral deficiencies. Let it first be noted that they hardly qualify as touchy-feely science bashers; J. C. Eccles's (1964) studies of synaptic mechanisms won him a Nobel Prize. Yet they hold modern science, especially as applied to the human realm, as a major reason for our seeming determination to go to hell in a handbasket, since our views of ourselves so affect what we become. Their purpose then is to show that we are not what a completely materialistic science would have us be.

They first, like Sperry, discuss consciousness, and in much the same manner, but also include another unique human commodity, language. Although primates simulate it to a point, our version differs qualitatively. Animals employ only two functions, the *expressive*, to symptomatize and release emotions à la Langer, and the *signaling*, to induce reactions in others, but we also seek to *describe* our experiences to others and to *argue*. As well, no primate approaches the creativity of our usage, as when we try out possibilities until we hit upon the best way to say it. So for Eccles and Robinson also, human mentation arises from but not does not slavishly depend on physical events. Rather, it supersedes and controls them. Witness studies involving the brain's supplementary motor area. An intention to do something not yet done results in activity therein, followed by activity in other areas that it stimulates, but activity in this area is never preceded by any in other areas (at least none that has been discovered). Thus a thought without a physical correlate induces physical events that foster others. The wish, it seems, is father not only to the act but brain activity! The implications? We thereby regain that which materialistic science would remove, freedom of choice, along with moral responsibility and duty, which are desirable because we can no longer blame our iniquities on factors beyond our control.

Memory poses more problems for wholesale materialism. Loftus and Loftus (1980) found Penfield and Perot's cortical stimulation evidence unimpressive. The memories actually reported were not nearly as detailed as legend supposes and their accuracy was not verified. Then too, many memories lost to amnesia later return (Kolb & Wishaw, 1996), whereas information erased from recordings is gone for the duration, as the celebrated twenty-three minutes missing from President Nixon's tapes which were uncovered during the Watergate scandal demonstrated. Beneath these objections lurks Loftus's (1980) belief that memory involves not the passive internalizing that reductionism implies, but active reconstruction, another phenomenon that poses difficulties for materialism. Even assuming that physical changes are the basis for remembering, findings such as errors of commission suggest that more psychological processes affect their use.

Of Evicted Babies and Procrustean Beds

When reductionistic explanations are preferred, legitimate topics not amenable to them may suffer. Creativity, for example, may well have physical underpinnings—the notion that an inborn ingredient called talent or genius is necessary certainly suggests as much—but its reductionistic study faces a formidable obstacle. In the last analysis it is a uniquely human endeavor (Abra, 1988b). Animals do solve problems but this, while similar, is by no means an identical behavior (a poem, unlike a crossword, offers no certifiably correct answers, which introduces a plethora of complicating factors such as anxiety about how others will evaluate a solution), and animal displays of the genuine article (Skinner, 1980) are country miles removed from *Hamlet* or the theory of relativity! Controlled reductionist studies usually involve intervening with physical structures via lesions, implanted electrodes or the like, and these cannot be performed on human beings, objecting as they do to tampering with their brains, however helpful this may be to science. In short, only correlational studies are possible, such as of the effects of brain damage due to accident or illness (H. Gardner, 1982). Besides their interpretive problems, such studies allow no control over the location, type, or extent of damage—putting it bluntly, investigators must take what they get—and creative people who suffer such damage, thankfully, are few in number. In the face of obstacles such as this, therefore, ardent reductionists may ignore a topic and cause more desirable babies to be jettisoned or worse, dismissed as imaginary. Too many reductionists concoct restricted universes wherein one need account for only those phenomena with which one feels comfortable, so the strategy determines not only what is studied but what is admitted to exist. Another gambit is to imitate Procrustes and reshape the phenomenon to fit the preferred approach. Thus to facilitate reductionistic study, creativity may be equated with problem solving.

Of Life Lies, and Recipes for Living

Another point that deserves revisiting concerned common beliefs about our-selves that, inaccurate or not, provide security needed for well being and whose endurance testifies to their utility (D. Campbell, 1975). The concept of soul, I submit, is one. Consider Hebb's reason for advocating mechanism—we should not accept spiritual concepts unless data appears that cannot be explained in physical terms. Thus he stands on parsimony's hallowed ground to place the burden of proof on vitalism. However, he invokes it not to reject a new concept but rather an ancient, remarkably pervasive one. Most religions espouse an afterlife and/or reincarnation, beliefs that must assume something that survives our physical demise. Moreover, it may well be, as Rank (1961) claimed, that such a belief, by providing comfort against the otherwise overwhelming terror of death, is so crucial that it has become a kind of inherited race memory. That so many people regardless of culture or upbringing believe fervently in a soul verifies not that it exists, but that we need to believe it exists. That being so, it should not be too casually dismissed.

Indeed, Rank contends that it is because of modern psychology's adamant materialism that many laypeople reject it out of hand, especially when it offers no proof to the contrary yet derides vitalistic concepts as superstition. Pirsig (1974) observed, "A philosophical school called *realism* [holds that] a thing exists . . . if a world without it can't function normally. If we can show [this], then we have shown that [it] exists, whether it's defined or not" (p. 210). Might not soul be such an "it"? For these reasons, I suggest, tradition takes precedence over parsimony and the burden falls instead on mechanists to prove there is no soul. Which is of course unfair, as such a negative can never be proven; because something has not yet been found does not guarantee it won't be found in the future. This injustice bothers me not a whit, for in demanding that vitalists defend themselves, the mechanist is equally unfair. He requires evidence that soul is necessary, but the only kind he will accept as a scientist is empirical, and soul by its very nature does not qualify.

8

Conceptual Devices

To explain phenomena, scientists exploit several tools of varying rigor. Marx (1963b) draws some helpful distinctions among them. A *hypothesis* is a least-confirmed proposition, an educated guess, whereas a *theory* has more empirical support but is still somewhat speculative, and a *law* has survived the tests of time and empirical investigation to establish not its validity, which unlike the others is not in doubt, but limits. Also, a theory typically has broader scope than a law, as it routinely pulls several of them together (Turner, 1968). These distinctions seem clear enough, but the term "theory" in practice carries such a welter of connotations as to cause considerable confusion (Underwood, 1957b). Boring (1953) found no less than fourteen types in psychology ranging from simple lawful statements to others so vague as to border on the hypothetical. I focus therefore on points about which there is general agreement. However, another device, the *model*, should first be introduced. In a scientific context, this refers to an analogy or metaphor that resembles and so may help understand a phenomenon. Thus discovering effective models displays that hallmark of creativity, perceiving similarities among previously unconnected events. To Bohr, the hydrogen atom's structure resembled a solar system, with electrons circulating around a nucleus like planets around a sun (Tweney, Doherty & Mynatt, 1981). Einstein enthusiastically exploited metaphors both to fathom and communicate relativity's intricacies (Barnett, 1948) and to these ends imagined passengers on trains that passed one another in opposite directions, or scientists trapped in freely falling elevators letting objects fall. People too have been modeled. Aristotle compared memory to a stamp leaving its mark on an impressionable material, in this case the soul (Chapanis, 1963), and on other occasions we have been likened to machines (by LaMettrie) and Watt's steam engine.

The empirically obsessed such as Skinner (1950) and the early functionalists would deny that theories serve any useful purposes, but such people are in the minority. The first use (Hill, 1971) is to *summarize*. Merely collecting myriad lawful relationships would yield a chaotic catalogue beyond comprehension, so if lawful statements unite many observations, effective theories form a hierarchy's next level and do the same for a plethora of laws (K. Spence, 1963a, 1963b). Thus they also aid simplicity and parsimony by summarizing a number of facts and laws in a few principles (Underwood, 1957b). A related function is *organization*. By providing precise, preferably quantitative statements about relationships among laws, an effective theory ties them together, although the increased removal from the data makes it more likely to prove invalid. Hill (1971) provides a helpful example of this function. Suppose we investigate the effects of five variables: (1) depriving animals of water, (2) reducing food intake (3) restricting time to drink, (4) providing only dry food, and (5) injecting a salt solution into their stomachs. Each variable affects several behaviors for a water reinforcer such as running speed down an alley or lever pressing, as well as time spent drinking water when allowed. We might express each of the fifteen functional relationships separately, but is it not more economical to hypothesize that each variable affects one construct, thirst, that influences each behavior (see Figure 8.1), especially if based on the data we can state how that construct's amount varies with each variable and in turn how each behavior is affected by it? Still, because thirst is measured only indirectly by these observables, it is a theoretical rather than empirical concept.

In most opinions theories should have a future as well as past orientation, assisting speculation and the search for as yet undiscovered laws, that is, they should have *fertility* (Underwood, 1957b). Good models are especially useful in this regard; by encouraging one to examine familiar phenomena from different

Figure 8.1
A Theoretical Construct's Organizing Function

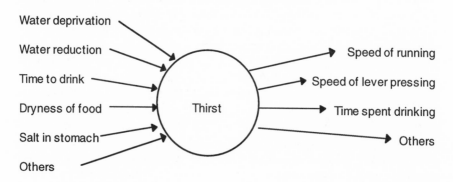

Source: Adapted from Hill (1971).

perspectives, they reveal otherwise overlooked possibilities. For example, the currently popular exercise of simulating human cognition with the computer may cause humanists to jib, but finding how to increase its problem-solving capacities may increase understanding of how we do these things—although it must always be kept in mind that it does not necessarily go about things exactly as we do. Thus as regards the phenomena it purports to explain, a model unlike a theory may have too much rather than too little content, with some being irrelevant (Simon & Newell, 1963).

Most important, science's devices should make precise *predictions* that allow empirical test, although here again models part company. Chosen strictly for their ability to assist understanding and fertility, they are therefore never dismissed for being "wrong" (Marx, 1963b) because this is accepted from the outset; no one pretends that the model actually is the phenomenon any more than a youngster playing shinny who shouts "I'll be Gretzky" believes that he actually is the hallowed #99. As Boring (1953, p. 179) put it, "You do not think that [models] may eventually acquire thinghood." That being the case, the only reason to reject one is because of infertility. A final purpose may surprise those whose sole acquaintance with science is through overly serious tomes called textbooks, but it is not to be underestimated, for models especially: to have fun. Playing this game of let's pretend shows that scientists like most creative people have something of the child in them, so they can view the world with freshness and wonder (Abra, 1988a); having fun in the sense of enjoyment and stimulation is a major motive for creative work (Abra, 1997).

KARL POPPER

The Characteristics of Scientific Theories

What sets scientific theories apart from other attempts to make sense of existence such as religion and art? The answer once favored was that since science alone relies on induction, only its theories have a firm empirical base. Popper (1981) denied this distinction because of Hume's conclusive demonstration that induction is neither possible nor desirable. Instead, he concluded, they alone have *falsifiability*. Wonderfully unambiguous, they generate precise predictions that can be proven wrong. In contrast, *pseudosciences* such as psychoanalysis and astrology have the veneer of science but are so vague that their seeming predictions can be twisted to make them fit any and all facts once the latter are in (Popper, 1972), rather like betting on horse races already run. Thus according to psychoanalysis, one might say, if you love your mother, or hate your mother, or have no mother you'll be neurotic. Maybe. Or maybe not. Depending. On what? We're not sure! Similarly, astrologers, may blame a poor barley crop on Jupiter's alignment with Mars, but confronted with the latter event beforehand, won't bet the rent on there being a barley shortage. And since hindsight is always 20/20, such "theories," by explaining almost everything, may seem extraordinarily convincing.

However, Popper retorts, we should not be too impressed by the number of phenomena a theory can explain; the more vague it is, the more there will be. I defer to no one in my admiration for Freud, but Popper provides another reason to suggest that his greatness was not as a scientist but as an artist. We don't ask works of art to be measurable or testable but imaginative and stimulating and by these criteria Freud stands tall. His study of Leonardo da Vinci (Freud, 1947) resembles a first-rate detective story (Abra, 1988a) in which the villain turns out to be, needless to say, the mother. Marxist socialism for Popper was another pseudoscience (Magee, 1973), although it sinned not by being vague but because its disciples clung to it with the fervor of Hoffer's (1951) true believers, ignoring evidence that falsified it beyond redemption.

On the other hand, genuine scientific theories epitomized by relativity venture out on limbs, placing precise bets in advance including some that may fly in the face of "common sense." For example, against all belief Einstein held that when light passed large heavenly bodies their gravitational pull should cause shifts in frequency of vibration and therefore color. Hence that famous expedition to Africa to test this prediction during a total eclipse, when the sun would not obscure light from other celestial sources (Clark, 1973), with the result that the inconceivable was verified. Moreover, a scientific theory not only can be proven wrong but sooner or later no doubt will be, and probably sooner. Theories of the man who came to dinner type that hang around too long likely defy disproof and are therefore of little use to science. For, Popper contends, science progresses by falsifying incorrect ideas, by *criticism*, which in his opinion is one of our greatest inventions. Therefore, in contrast to the optimism of earlier times, he saw science as not moving ever closer to some Final Truth wherein all question have been answered, but merely away from error. It becomes less wrong.

Several corollaries follow. First, Popper stresses that fundamental, that a scientific theory alone is answerable to the data. It must generate testable predictions and if it does not, it is sent packing. As well, if critical experiments are to resolve disputes, all competing theories must yield such predictions. Second, no real scientist calls a theory correct or true (Turner, 1968); at best she might label one better because it accounts for known facts more adequately or stumbles over fewer disconfirming instances. For one thing, history repeatedly shows that seemingly inviolate entries such as Aristotle's and Newton's will eventually be brought crashing to earth by those lascivious termites, raw data. But mainly, from a Popperian angle, a theory can never be proven true. No matter the number of confirmations, it is always possible that contradictory ones will one day emerge, for we can never have performed every conceivable observation or critical experiment.

Popper's Additives to the Scientific Attitude

The remaining corollaries require revisiting this topic. The first attribute a Popperian scientist needs is *courage*, not only to risk failure but to accept it. If theories are doomed to disproof, their authors are sure to be left one day with egg on their faces and some have had to face not only psychological but physical danger. Columbus's voyage to the New World was in essence an empirical test of a theory; it bet the participants' very lives that the earth was round so they would not fall off its edge. Second, if Final Truth is nonexistent and disproof of every belief inevitable, scientists should manifest *humility*. Arrogance is excusable in a nineteenth-century Mr. Gradgrind but not today. But isn't this trait more commonly associated with the scientist's antithesis, the dogmatically religious, especially Christians? Didn't Christ Himself both preach and practice it (although the film *The Passover Plot* presents a very different, to me more plausible portrait of Him than do the Gospels)? Yet those true believers who claim to know God's thoughts and therefore to speak for Him/Her/It seem far more guilty of pride than scientists who are never quite sure. Jerry Falwell or Jimmy Swaggert (the latter name itself is suggestive) humble? It is to laugh!

Still, dogmatists celebrate when God's ways defy our puny attempts to understand Nature's incomprehensibility, attempts that betray unseemly arrogance akin to building the Tower of Babel to reach unto the heavens (11 Genesis). Camus (1956) agreed. Creative work is *metaphysical rebellion* against God, because it not only features God's most defining activity but subtly expresses dissatisfaction with His Creation by indicating alternatives; Camus, however, advocated rather than deplored such hubris. A related objection to these attempts is that successes reduce the wonderful to the commonplace. Consider psychology. Won't learning too much about ourselves compromise our mystery? Beneath all these variations lurks our most enduring problem, first posed in Eden. Should we eat of the fruit of knowledge and risk expulsion? Scientists agree with their adversaries that Nature resists understanding (Popper implies as much) but not about what to do about it. Whereas the dogmatist deplores the Fall as symptomatic of unseemly pride, they like Camus are all in favor of biting apples. Understanding a phenomenon can only increase one's appreciation of it. Who loves cars more than knowledgeable mechanics? Most of us understand how and why birth occurs. Do we therefore maintain cool detachment as we watch our offspring come into the world? No way! Explaining the miracles around us enhances our feelings of humility in relation to God's achievements— another reason why for Einstein science was a supremely reverent activity.

Popper also advises that scientists deal with their inevitable failures with what might be called *masochism*. Camus (1969) imagined Sisyphus, condemned by the gods to push a rock up a mountain over and over again for eternity, to be happy. Scientists, similarly facing a seemingly futile and hopeless situation, should likewise perversely enjoy it and, far from being affronted when a pet theory is disproved, after having done their part for progress they may bow out honorably. Whether this advice is psychologically realistic for human beings as opposed to saints is a moot point. Most scientists have considerable labor and ego invested in their theories, so admitting that it was all in vain could invite cognitive dissonance. Popper's advice that they should seek out disproofs may also be unrealistic, for as Francis Bacon (1620/1981) long ago observed, "The human understanding, when once it has adopted an opinion . . . draws all things else to support and agree with it. And though there be a greater number and weight of instances to be found on the other side, yet these it either neglects [or] despises . . . It is [its] peculiar and perpetual error *to be more moved and excited by affirmatives than by negatives*" (p. 33, italics added). Still, J. C. Eccles (1981) found Popper's advice liberating because about being wrong, it preaches "be not afraid," for this should earn you wreathes of olives, not thorns. To err is not only human, it is scientific.

CONCEPTUAL DEVICES IN PSYCHOLOGY

Theories of Learning

The nurture bias of earlier days intimated that ascertaining how and why learning occurs would open the way to understanding virtually every behavior. For several decades following Watson's revolution such theories dominated scientifically oriented circles, their self-evident importance decreeing among other things that familiarity with them was de rigueur for every student regardless of ultimate goals. Their powerful influence on psychology's development should alone justify exposing them to today's students, who typically hear little about them, but there is another defense as well. One theory in particular openly aimed to fulfill the criteria of what a scientific theory should be like and thus exemplifies several principles discussed.

Hull's Theory. At the outset, an admission. What follows is far from all encompassing and somewhat simplified (although hopefully not misleading), because Hull (1943, 1952) in the original parades a mass of postulates in mathematical, technical jargon that for our purposes are superfluous (for a fuller account, see Hilgard, 1956). The equation $sEr = sHr \times D \times K$ captures his essence. sEr, *reaction potential*, expresses the tendency to produce a certain response R to a stimulus S to which it has become associated, such as a rat's to turn left at a choice point in a maze. The factors on which this depends are (1) sHr, *habit strength*, which states the strength of that S–R association, (2) D, *drive*, the organism's overall level of motivation at that point in time, which increases with deprivation of needs such as for water or food, (3) K, *incentive*, which also affects motivation but depends on other factors, notably the amount of reward offered.

Several implications are noteworthy. First, Hull aimed at a general theory of learning whose principles would apply not only to rats learning mazes (although much of the relevant evidence came from such sources) but to every circumstance. Thus he followed the scientific credo, thou shalt generalize, but at a more abstract level involving hypothesized entities such as habit strength than at the direct empirical one espoused by Skinner. And since these principles supposedly operated in any and all situations they were extended by either Hull himself or sympathizers, albeit at times in modified form, to diverse phenomena such as personality (Dollard & Miller, 1950), verbal learning (Gibson, 1940), thinking

(Maltzman, 1955), creativity (Mednick, 1962) and emotions such as frustration (Amsel, 1958) and anxiety (J. Taylor, 1953).

The view of motivation has several intriguing aspects. It supposedly depends on several factors. Drive, D, arises from deficiencies in basic needs, but rather than separate drives such as thirst or hunger, Hull postulated one nonspecific state to which these various *sources of drive* each contribute. Not only is this view more parsimonious, it has reductionistic credibility. Destruction of the *reticular formation* in the brain produces a comatose state—information still arrives from the senses but is not acted upon—and stimulation via electrodes implanted therein induces high arousal in even sleeping animals (French, 1957). Thus this area apparently maintains a general state of alertness and arousal and as such resembles Hull's drive. The other motivational construct, K, refers to an anticipatory factor, "if I do this, this will happen," that increases with the magnitude of the reinforcer foreseen. In short, motivation depends on two operationally distinct factors, with behavior being both pushed by a desire to overcome need deficiencies and pulled by the anticipation of events that will do so.

Another postulate that follows directly concerns a seminally important question. Are there properties that reliably distinguish effective reinforcers from other events that are not? If so, what a boon in practical contexts, to be able to predict effectiveness beforehand, whereas for Skinnerians this can only be determined empirically. Hull proposed that all reinforcers reduce drive; the corollary, that behaviors are acquired that serve this purpose, reveals his Darwinian streak, since for him learning served first and foremost to satisfy basic needs and assist survival. One provocative implication of this postulate is that since drive for Hull is nonspecific, one is not motivated for something particular such as food, but simply motivated. Thus an event might be reinforcing that does not satisfy the momentary source of deprivation, for example, water for a starving but not thirsty rat. The evidence on this possibility is mixed (Kimble, 1961).

It should be pointed out that Hull too saw learning in S–R terms, since sHr, which expresses its amount, refers to the strength of the S–R association. Two extensions are notable. Unlike Gestalt views that featured one-trial insight, sHr increases gradually with each S–R contiguity, but only if this is followed by reinforcement. The notion that learning requires reinforcement provided an example of the *hypothetico-deductive* approach to theorizing Hull preferred. As the name suggests, it incorporates both induction and deduction. The first step is to gather enough preliminary facts to indicate the likely course of events and from these work out various postulates and axioms, so unlike pure deduction these are not plucked from thin air. Finally, precise predictions are deduced and if found wanting empirically, modified accordingly. Latent learning (see Chapter 2) provided the exemplary episode when it showed conclusively that reinforcement increases performance not learning and therefore apparently affects motivation. First of all, Hull like Tolman distinguished learning from performance in that sHr was not the sole determinant of sEr, the measure of the latter. In his terms then, varying reinforcement affects not sHr but D and/or K. He therefore revised his theory so that only a little was necessary for *sHr* to develop (and again, that a situation is certifiably devoid of reinforcement is impossible to prove). Further increases affected not *sHr* but *K*, through the machinations of r_g, an unobservable but presumed response known as little argee to the generations of students it mystified and over which we need not dally, it being now of interest only to historians. What is notable is that this gambit allowed Hull to predict latent learning, albeit some years after it had been demonstrated.

The theory's claims for scientific status are substantial. It strongly adhered to the empirical rule; each hypothesized entity was tied to specific measurables, be they stimulus conditions or behaviors. It stressed quantification to a point that to the mathematically uninclined might seem oppressive. Equations specify the precise relation between each entity and its observables, so it was stated, for example, not only that *K* increases with reinforcer magnitude but that the curve was a negatively accelerated one whose exact form depended on stated considerations. Finally, on the face of it the theory generated precise, falsifiable predictions, although those concerned with semantic niceties might debate whether explaining a phenomenon such as latent learning after the fact should be dignified as prediction. In any event, we can now consider the evidence concerning two key Hullian proposals. One of these even he eventually had to admit had been disproved, but the other stands up well to those two great evaluators, time and data.

The first involves the notion that reinforcers reduce drive. At first glance it can be falsified by discovering events that do not, but are effective nonetheless, but as with many of Hull's postulates this disproof turned out to be difficult to achieve, inducing suspicions that their falsifiability was more apparent than real. Consider findings that saccharine, a sweet tasting but nonnutritive and so presumably not drive-reducing substance, is reinforcing (Sheffield and Roby, 1950). Hullians' rejoinders were sufficiently plausible to result in a hung jury (see Kimble, 1961); indeed, food reinforcers generally provided inconclusive tests, it being unclear whether drive reduction came about when they enter the mouth, the stomach, or the blood stream where they lessen taste sensations, hunger pangs, or cell deficiencies, respectively. Sex however avoids this complication since the drive-reducing event, in males at least, is abundantly clear: ejaculation. Hence one of those experiments (Sheffield, Wulff & Backer, 1951) that deserves notice if only for its sheer outlandishness. Male rats learned a maze wherein a correct response produced a mixed blessing. They were allowed to mount and penetrate a female in heat but not ejaculate because they were separated from their partners before this happened (how the investigators accomplished this formidable task is not clear, since their paper is a model of discretion). In case the bizarre machinations should sidetrack the reader, it should be pointed out that they provide an ideal test of Hull's postulate. Such experiences, far from reducing drive should push it to stratospheric heights. Yet the rats learned.[1] But it was

---

1. Lest it be thought that professors are too involved in ethereal pursuits to fall victim to such crass human failings as Freudian slips, I once described this study to a

brain stimulation (Olds & Milner, 1954) that delivered the coup de grace. Most reinforcers are only effective if the organism has been deprived of them; food presupposes hunger. Thus with repeated usage their influence wanes, in Hull's view because they have temporarily reduced drive. With brain stimulation satiation is never reached. Animals bar press for it continually, to exhaustion, suggesting that drive is not being reduced. Some findings can be dismissed as unimportant exceptions to a rule, but since brain stimulation is by far the most powerful reinforcer known and in some views subsumes the effects of all others, the inability to handle its effects proved fatal.

We might note in passing another view of reinforcement's essential properties, because it spawned another ingenious study and also anticipated Bandura's concept of intrinsic reinforcement. Premack (1965) proposed that reinforcement is provided not by the event delivered per se but by the behaviors it induces, *consummatory responses*. Thus food and a receptive female rat are effective because they respectively allow eating and . . . whatever. What distinguishes a reinforcing from reinforced behavior? Why does eating normally increase, say, running in an exercise wheel but not vice versa? For Premack, behaviors of greater probability, those more likely to occur given a choice between them, reinforce those less likely and this probability increases with time since one last emitted the behavior. Ordinarily eating has been longer deprived than running but a counterintuitive possibility therefore becomes conceivable, that if exercising but not eating were to be curtailed, the usual contingency should be reversible and subjects would learn to eat in order to exercise. And they will.

Another Hullian prediction fares better and indicates that his wholesale demise has been unfortunate. Hull's notion of the *habit–family hierarchy* assumes that stimuli can have several responses associated to them. "Table" for most people first elicits "chair" but also "furniture," "food," and others, although these responses differ in priority and thus in sHr to that stimulus. A habit–family hierarchy arranges these competitors in order of their sHrs. On occasion a weaker one may occur, but the strongest or dominant response is most probable and becomes more so as the absolute difference in sEr between it and the others increases. Since sEr depends not only on sHr but on D and K, and since these combine in a multiplicative way, it can be easily shown that as D or K increases so must that difference. Thus the hierarchy diverges and the dominant response becomes increasingly likely.

The significant question concerns the effect on performance efficiency. Folk wisdom and enduring values such as the puritan work ethic preach that those who try harder, that is, are more motivated, invariably perform better and the belief persists, although one of psychology's most pervasive laws, the Yerkes–Dodson (1908) function shown in Figure 8.2, suggests otherwise. Specifically, with complex, difficult tasks especially, too much arousal/drive, as panic shows,

---

class as follows: "Hull would predict that the rats shouldn't keep going through the maze, but in fact they kept coming and coming and coming," a turn of phrase that needless to say did not exactly enhance the spirit of serious intellectual inquiry.

can prove as detrimental as too little. Hull too predicts a more complicated possibility. Increased motivation should only increase efficiency when a dominant response is correct; if not, then it should actually be harmful, as it will intensify an erroneous tendency. Glucksberg (1962) performed an exemplary test. One standard problem-solving task presents several objects including a candle, matchbox, and tacks and subjects must discover how to mount the candle on a wall. The solution (to tack the matchbox to the wall and place the candle inside) is made more difficult if the matchbox is shown filled with the tacks, presumably because it is incorrectly perceived as a container for tacks, whereas if the tacks are separate, the appropriate perception, as a potential container for the candle, is dominant. Glucksberg varied task difficulty in this manner and varied motivation by manipulating the financial reward for solution. The results, shown in Figure 8.3, substantiated Hull's predictions; moreover, they have been verified in eyelid conditioning and paired-associate tasks (K. Spence, 1956) and J. S. Brown (1961) found the evidence for them generally strong (Kimble, 1961, was more skeptical). If theories gain credibility by generating counterintuitive but valid predictions, Hull's certainly qualifies.

Figure 8.2
The Yerkes-Dodson Function

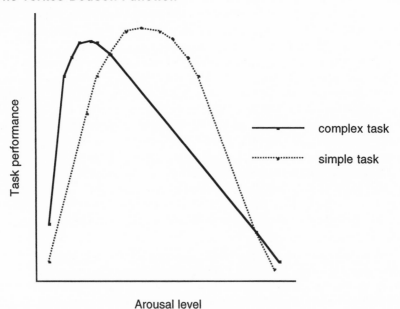

Arousal level

Source: Adapted from Yerkes and Dodson (1908).

Figure 8.3
The Effect of Increased Motivation on Problem-Solving Efficiency

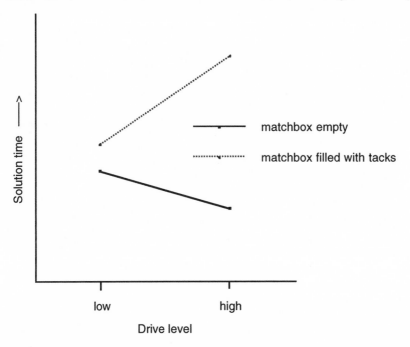

Source: Adapted from Glucksberg (1962).

His analysis also clarifies aspects of creativity. Since in most opinions creative responses must be unusual, recessive items in a hierarchy are more likely candidates, as dominant ones tend to be common. Mednick's (1962) test of creativity therefore assumes that creative people are distinguished by their less steeply sloped hierarchies, that is, smaller strength differences between competing responses, which enhances availability of those weaker alternatives. As well, by anecdotal evidence, many creative insights arrive not when being desperately sought but at times of low arousal, such as while lying in bed or performing mundane tasks such as shaving. Again, lower motivation can be beneficial.

The Demise of Learning Theories and an Evaluation

Avoidance learning led to the first compromise of Hull's monolithic attempt to explain all learning. He himself realized the difficulties. An aversive event such as shock presumably provides both drive (when it appears) and reinforcement (when a response succeeds in removing it and thus reduces drive). However, successful evasive actions to a preceding warning stimulus prevent that event entirely. How then is responding motivated in the first place and how is it reinforced? On the face of it such behaviors, even if emitted, should soon extinguish, but in fact they are remarkably durable (Solomon & Wynne, 1954). Mowrer (1947) took it upon himself to solve the puzzle in Hullian terms. In essence, he proposed that avoidance learning had both classical and instrumental conditioning components and that only the latter required reinforcement in the form of drive reduction, whereas the first named needed only CS-UCS contiguity. Interestingly, another Hull sympathizer, Spence (1956), soon attacked other difficulties by proposing the reverse, that only classical conditioning needs reinforcement, but what matters is that both victories were pyrrhic, achieved at the price of a tacit admission that not all learning tasks obey the same principles. As such, they were in retrospect among the first nails in the coffin of Hull's and indeed all the grandiose theories of learning, for soon after the latter's influence began to wane, and theorizing increasingly focused on more specific situations such as classical conditioning.

Maslow's (1954) compelling hierarchy of needs hints at another nail, albeit a more tender-headed one. He admitted that basic survival needs have first priority and until they are satisfied nothing else matters. But whereas Hull's views ended here, Maslow, less blinded by Darwinian priorities, proposed that once this happens other psychological needs arise that culminate in uniquely human metaneeds such as self-actualization. In a real sense they cannot be reduced, yet in healthy people they dominate the motivational picture. Thus contrary to Hull's sweeping principles, reducing biological needs is far from behavior's sole purpose.

With hindsight, what did the theoretical era leave psychology? At the time Skinner (1950) objected to the entire business on grounds that valuable resources were being wasted; data gathered to test theories have no lasting value if those theories ultimately prove worthless, as they no doubt will. Thus one could question Popper's presumption that disproving incorrect theories represents progress; an infinitude of these can be generated, making any disproof a drop in the bucket at best. The theories' hegemony may also have discouraged theorizing about topics such as personality and social psychology, since learning supposedly subsumed all. Hilgard (1956) prognosticated that Hull's main contribution might lie less in specific principles than in pointing the way for a quantitative system to unite the disparate schools that had plagued the discipline, but if anything the opposite has transpired, with more outlooks and methods evident than ever and an integrating paradigm a remote prospect (a diversity that unlike Hilgard I see as all to the good). Was this era then psychology's version of the Dark Ages that saw little progress prior to the Renaissance of the cognitive revolution?

While I am no historian, this is certainly not my opinion. An all-encompassing account of learning would have been a major step forward, so if nothing else the attempts were surely worth making. Even if the results were wholesale failures, they were honorable ones, and in my view they were nothing of the kind. Much of what resulted has little lasting interest but this is true of most movements in science and the best of the empirical studies that resulted deserve plaudits for sheer ingenuity if nothing else. Like all classics, they set a standard of excellence and also introduced some theoretical possibilities and issues worth resurrecting. Finally, dominant perspectives are often important for the opposition they provoke. Just as we might not have gained Kant, Nietzsche, or romanticism but for Hume, Darwin and the Enlightenment, respectively, movements such as humanistic psychology, the cognitive revolution, and the quest for ecological validity were in large part inspired by the failings of the learning theories. Nonetheless, other blessings were more mixed. The era instilled enduring beliefs whose pros and cons we have been debating, about how research should be done, theories tested, and experiments performed, as well as that preoccupation with statistics and experimental design as the be all and end all of curricula. It also strengthened biases that already existed for nature over nurture, Darwinism, and animal research that took some time to moderate.

Models in Psychology

Creative people have been likened to children (Kris, 1952), the disturbed/schizophrenic (Arieti, 1976; Becker, 1973; Rank, 1932), athletes and religious innovators (Abra, 1997), and the creative process to play (Freud, 1958b), humor (Koestler, 1970) and even alchemy (J. Briggs, 1988). Although strictly speaking none of these analogies qualifies as a scientific model, they clarify both the virtues and pitfalls of the practice. In particular, model and prototype always have important differences as well as similarities, which simulators of creativity have been laudably conscientious about pointing out and exploiting. Would that those employing the two examples to follow that are concerned with learning and cognition had been similarly vigilant!

The first features the mathematical models that flourished for a time (e.g., Bush & Mosteller, 1955; Estes, 1960). However, the early optimism some expressed about this approach (Hilgard, 1956) has faded (Hulse, Deese & Egeth, 1975), so that apart from a few loyalists it is now ignored, receiving at best only cursory mention in texts. I for one do not mourn their demise, since I confess to being underwhelmed from the outset. Curves and equations splashed hither and yon without evident need or benefit suggest not only the usual obsession with appearing scientific, but a greater interest in the analogy itself than in it as a means to the supposed end, clarifying psychological phenomena. Too often assumptions that bordered on the ludicrous were made about the phenomena to facilitate the mathematics. This was not always the case. For example, many models assumed that associations are formed on one trial (Estes, 1960), although common-sense, incrementalists such as Hull and learning curves themselves suggest otherwise. Nonetheless, the one-trial–incremental issue has periodically flared up regarding several subtopics such as discrimination learning, and while the usual hung jury tends to result, suggestive empirical evidence certainly exists. Indeed, at a microscopic level of analysis, something unknown on one trial must be known on the next for progress to be made at all. If nothing else, the desire to buttress this notion stimulated several studies (Rock, 1957; Estes,

1960) whose inventive methodologies forgive their seemingly supportive findings being probably artifactual (Postman, 1963).

Other assumptions, however, had neither empirical nor introspective backing, for example, that subjects do not remember and so learn nothing from their errors (Restle, 1962), and despite individual differences being a fact of life, parameters in equations having approximately the same value for all subjects (Bush & Mosteller, 1955). As well, models must above all be fruitful, but the situations to which these were applied were so artificial as to conceal any overlap with standard laboratory let alone real world ones—in comparison, even paired-associate learning was a paragon of ecological validity—which called the entire enterprise into question as mere game playing. Finally, I have personal doubts about another popular practice, wherein preliminary data indicates the parameters for a curve that best fits them and from it predictions about further findings in the situation are generated. Lo and behold, these predictions are invariably fulfilled and if somehow they are not, the parameters are blithely changed. To my mathematically unsophisticated eye, the emperor has no clothes. How can what seems to be a blatantly circular exercise provide conceptual gains? How far removed this is from risking falsification, which Popper so admired. Curve fitters never end up with egg on their faces!

In a second, currently voguish modeling enterprise, *artificial intelligence* (AI), computer mechanisms simulate various cognitive activities. Acceptance was slow in coming. Pioneering attempts (Miller, Galanter & Pribram, 1960; Newell and Simon, 1972) had little impact until enough workaday psychologists became computer literate to appreciate the outlook (Gigerenzer and Goldstein, 1996), but recent effort has more than made up for lost time, so an adequate survey would be both lengthy and frankly undesirable, for once more, I cannot summon much enthusiasm. Here again are questionable assumptions about phenomena, for example, when AI models of creativity (see Boden's, 1992 survey) portray it, inaccurately (Abra, 1988a), as achieving novelties and as equivalent to problem solving. Such Procrustean distortions to make something more tractable (Schrank, 1988) recall the inebriated gentleman who looked for his glasses not in the dark location where he had lost them but under the street lamp, because the light was better. Similarities between computer and human processes are unmistakable, but so are crucial differences. To add others to those mentioned earlier, Kendler (1964), an early skeptic, stated that he would take the metaphor seriously when computers begin to worry about their parts wearing out. Likewise, one wonders, do they have heroes among other computers that they try to imitate? Can they paraphrase input information into their own version, or evince unique senses of value or humor, factors that color our dealings with information? Can that love of learning that critic Northrop Frye says somewhere is the first aim of higher education be instilled, so they want to learn more about what they know? (As an aside, might this metaphor's popularity be one reason why modern education equates information acquisition, or "knowing stuff," with enlightenment, since in computers it is?) Nickles (1994) also points out that computer function is unaffected by the social context or the presence of other computers, and can be fully described by precise, logically specifiable processes, whereas tacit, romantic factors such as emotions immensely influence ours. Thus he suggests, as do Sternberg & Lubart (1996), that even when computers accomplish certifiably creative work, they probably go about it differently, for instance, problem finding (Getzels & Csikszentmihalyi, 1976), that crucial ability to sense potentially fruitful problems or solutions, is not involved.

None of these differences by themselves would be fatal, since no simulation can be perfect, but with enough major ones suspicions begin to grow that the entire enterprise is providing not simplification but outright error. Nor is this point merely academic. As Giggerenzer and Goldstein (1996) argue, popular models have a way of becoming theories cum paradigms that determine prevailing conceptions of the prototype. Just as the Darwinian, materialistic model of the behaviorist era distorted views of human attributes (Koch, 1981), so too may its computer replacement, especially since it is now so familiar a weapon in most psychologists' arsenals. Ironically then, while most areas of psychology have embraced an active subject, devotees of AI have adopted a species whose passivity far exceeds even the most rigid of S–R accounts. As that ubiquitous phrase, "garbage in, garbage out" reveals, computers are definitive tabula rasa, at the mercy of their input. As well, morsels of computerese such as input, retrieval, and encoding are now routinely used to discuss learning and cognition and if language does influence thought (Whorff, 1956), another dangerous self-fulfilling prophecy looms. By seeing ourselves uncritically as kin, might we find ourselves becoming more like computers than is desirable? Let it never be forgotten: they are machines. It has been said that several centuries ago psychology lost its soul and later, with Watson's coming, lost its mind. With the growing popularity of this metaphor, is it now in danger of losing its very life?

9

Conclusion and Epilogue

Contributions prior to the 1970s such as from Watson, Freud and Skinner have received the bulk of attention, but there have been enormous changes in the interim as well, summarized in the phrase the cognitive revolution (see H. Gardner, 1985 or Kessel & Bevan, 1985 for full accounts). Actually, to refer to these changes as revolutionary is, in comparison to Watson's movement at least, somewhat misinforming, because they have come about so quietly and gradually that only by comparing psychology then and now does one realize their magnitude. Likewise, it has been much more of a bottom-up movement, keyed not by a few highly visible personalities but many relatively anonymous grass roots workers who, independently and without fanfare but sharing a disenchantment with prevailing practices (the zeitgeist of that time made it de rigueur to reject any and all tradition), turned in new directions. Nonetheless, the overall effect has equaled Watson's. Although history delivers its verdicts about significant people and events slowly, I would guess that few recent figures will be seen as having had the influence of the giants of yesteryear, but if Kuhnian revolutions are defined by results more than time span or identifiable leaders and by replacing feelings of stasis with those of excitement and new beginnings, then the cognitive revolution undoubtedly qualifies. The last twenty-five years has been as exhilarating a time as any in which to be involved in psychology!

What has brought all this about? My nominee would be maturity. Psychology's attempts to imitate and impress the natural sciences even at the expense of what should have been some major concerns was a tad childish, but science's once overlooked limits and realities and the unique problems the subject matter raises have gradually been taken to heart—not unanimously by any means, for naiveté and rigid scientism still run rampant—and those once dismissed as misfits are now grudgingly allowed their place. With the adaptations that have resulted, the discipline has gained its own brand of science, not one borrowed, inaccurately, from elsewhere.

The major attributes of this new version have been intimated already. First, there is a broadening of topics deemed legitimate for study. "Cognition" literally refers to "thought," but it has acquired a plethora of connotations so that beginning with the work that according to Kessel and Bevan (1985) first focused the new directions, Neisser's (1967) *Cognitive Psychology*, it has come to connote entities such as perception, imagery, problem solving, and creativity once derided as mentalistic. A generation ago their discussion in reputable sources was rare. Now they are freely bandied about and some have journals devoted to them. This does not indicate a retreat to pre-Watson priorities. The empirical rule has been bent, not broken, so it is still desired that phenomena be given objective, preferably operational definition, but nowadays a topic's importance is stressed more than the means by which it is investigated, that is, what constitutes data has on the whole been considerably broadened to include more qualitative and introspective phenomena, but the key consideration is still reliability, that there be agreement about their authenticity. Maslow's (1966) call not to eliminate but to broaden science has evidently been heard.

Second, subjects are generally viewed as active rather than passive, their reactions depending less on an external event's objective characteristics than their interpretations of it. Evident too is a softening of behaviorism's environmental bias in favor of inborn antecedents. For both empirical and rational reasons, youth's optimism has been tempered by the reluctant realism of maturity. Third, the concern for processes that are uniquely human, notably higher mental ones such as abstract thought and creativity, has led to a noticeable decline in knee-jerk Darwinism. As a result, apart from investigators pursuing reductionistic approaches, animal studies are less common and the rat runner of yore has become an endangered species! Yet in another sense subject populations have become more diverse. Whereas the college sophomore was once seen as Everyperson, the indicator supreme of universal behavioral laws, children, the elderly, and others now receive their fair share of attention as the realization has dawned that to understand phenomena manifest by a given group such as great achievers (Gruber, 1980), one must focus on those who are members.

Fourth, generalization from lab to real world is less cavalier. As the limits of controlled experiments came to be recognized and concerns for ecological validity grew, researchers became ever more willing to sacrifice control and rigor and venture into natural settings. Fifth, applied fields such as clinical, industrial, and organizational psychology have increasingly dominated the once inviolate pure research tradition and the APA. At one time that ultimate indicant of professional eminence, its presidency, fell on a steady stream of people who represented pure science. No more! But people with applied interests tend to be less doctrinaire about being scientific at all costs, ready to adopt whatever approach best serves the immediate problem at hand. Finally, the cognitive revolution has affected some content areas more than others—neuropsychology has been one noticeable holdout—which has further enhanced psychology's increasing fragmentation and diversity, for cognitive outlooks have so far achieved nothing like the hegemony behaviorism once enjoyed. In short, it is apparent that once ignored messages have become mainstream—notably from Gestalt, Piaget, and Tolman, from proponents of constraints on learning and Chomskian linguistics, from psychoanalysts and others concerned with unmeasurables, even those from the sworn opposition, romanticism and existentialism, albeit in moderated form, courtesy of their humanist sympathizers.

Yet in my view these developments do not go far enough, so my answer to the question posed at the outset, should psychology be a science, is a firm yes and no. The cognitive version is a distinct improvement on that bequeathed by logical positivism but retains many of the weaknesses. The shotgun wedding couple's changes have been considerable from their honeymoon days, but more substantive ones are needed. One valid response to criticisms of the scientific approach is that with all its shortcomings, no one has yet come up with a good alternative. However, I do not propose that science be discarded—both history pre-Watson and the evident progress made in the interim verify that this would be foolish—but that the discipline be broadened still more to incorporate other contributions not usually placed under its rubric. Science is not the only means by which we gain knowledge about ourselves, indeed it is a relative newcomer, and we have denied ourselves other tools of proven worth, notably the arts and humanities. Novelists and playwrights, for example, concern themselves with what makes people tick. Shakespeare was surely, among other things, one of the greatest psychologists, and writers such as Dickens, George Eliot, and Chekhov were no slouches either. I would therefore advocate that most topics be studied as creativity already is, by a thoroughgoing eclecticism that uses any and all approaches, scientific and other, that offer promise, with the tacit assumption that each provides part of the story. The husband is going to have to accept some wifely dalliances elsewhere, if not outright polygamy, but since he has long been free to so indulge, this should be seen by this age of sexual equality as no more than a fitting reversal of a double standard. And who knows, it might enhance marital satisfaction, if turnabout should turn out to be not only fair play but foreplay!

Feyerabend (1993) also suggests that the natural sciences can learn much from other sources, especially since it is impossible to decide what is and what is not science anyway. This must be even more the case for the social/human sciences and a few examples already exist. Stone and Stone (1966) selected excerpts from literary works to exemplify different personality disturbances, and I have used films such as *Five Easy Pieces*, *Providence*, and *My Brilliant Career*, to convey to the uninitiated some realities about the creative personality and process. Landman (1993) furnishes a particularly promising model. To study the pervasive emotion of *regret*, she exploited among other things decision, economic, and psychological theory, philosophical analysis and empirical observation, and also literary sources that portray it such as Woolf's *Mrs. Dalloway* and Dostoevsky's *The Lower Depths*. Her *dialectical process* subjected each contribution to criticism and refutation to separate wheat from chaff and what remained was then integrated into a higher level, a hopefully more informative synthesis. Perhaps her approach is more promising for what it holds for future work than for immediate dividends received regarding this topic over and above those provided by the various sources—a whole is not always *greater* than the sum of its parts—but as a test of uncharted waters it deserves nothing but praise.

One implication of the present proposal is that education should be broadened. For majors and graduate students a background in the arts and humanities becomes as desirable as one in science or engineering once was thought to be, and courses in seminal works that have a psychological aspect as de rigueur as those in statistics and experimental design are now. Similarly, S. Jones (1994) has called for exposure to another heretofore underexploited source of enlightenment, religion. The recent rapprochement with it largely reflects psychological content being used to study its concerns, whereas psychologists show little interest in the reverse possibility—in good part, Jones suggests, because of their unusually low levels of religious involvement: only 33 percent of clinicians report it to be the most important influence in their lives, as against 72 percent in the general population, which hampers their appreciation of its possibilities or importance to others. Jones advocates an equal partnership, with each field helping the other. Given the subjectivity of data interpretation and the central role faith plays in science, Jones shows that it is more compatible with religion than is often supposed. They have many similarities, notably in the attempt to make sense of experience. Clinical practitioners, however, are Jones's main interest. Their clients constantly raise issues with which religions have always been concerned, such as morality, faith, and the meaning of life, and clinicians must often try to provide comfort for life's traumas and insecurities, historically one of religion's essential purposes. Therefore clinical training should pay more attention to its contributions vis-à-vis these matters; not to equip prospective professionals with this weaponry is derelict. Moreover such exposure, I would add, might also prove fruitful for the more purely scholarly inclined.

A much discussed analysis by Snow (1959) suggests that realizing the partnership proposed here may not be easy. A writer by trade but scientist by training, Snow straddled both the arts/humanities and science traditions, but asserted that this is rarely done; intellectual life in the West is increasingly split into two groups that not only have little contact but share a mutual incomprehension that borders on hostility. Most scientists see the products of so-called traditional culture as irrelevant to their interests and are unfamiliar with them, but culture's representatives are as unappreciative of science, and as unjustifiably, "[a]s though the scientific edifice of the physical world was not, in its intellectual depth, complexity and articulation, the most beautiful and wonderful collective work of the mind of man" (Snow, 1959, p. 15), so twentieth-century art has assimilated little of science. While one can certainly dispute this last statement—what of computer-generated music, op art, and sculpture that demands an expertise in materials that would put an engineer to shame?—the claim that the two cultures remain poles apart is difficult to gainsay.

Furthermore, several objections to this proposal can be raised and need to be answered. First, would some prospective psychologists not find such content offputting? Certainly courses must be carefully designed, probably by psychologists themselves. Most literature professors, I suspect, can no more meet our unique needs here than can math professors, experience has shown, as regards statistics, and mere exercises in "lit crit" or the like would indeed by superfluous. But the student who remains resistant even when such courses achieve the purpose probably has no business being a psychologist in the first place, since this suggests an insufficient interest in people. William James, depending on his aims, could function both within and outside a scientific approach. Although as admired a figure in psychology as any, he has thus far been one praised more in the breach than the observance, but students of the future could do worse than take him as a model. It may be objected that you can lead horses to water but you can't make them drink. Perhaps, but it is equally likely that if they aren't led to water they certainly won't drink. This exposure will add beneficial perspectives to students' interests and ultimately attract some who, because they were more interested in people than statistics, have in the past too often taken themselves elsewhere.

Another possible objection comes from adamant dogmatists, that psychology is a science and that's the end of it. In the extreme, they personify the *scientism* that Smith (1976) shellacked. Whereas genuine science studies that which it can and realizes its limits, scientism, to which too many psychologists have succumbed, dismisses other approaches as invalid, which is inherently contradictory since the assertion that there are no truths other than scientific truths cannot be verified by the sort of evidence science itself demands. Thus one behaviorist nonpareil, K. Spence (1963a), deplored the number of persons with unscientific interests becoming psychologists under the mistaken impression that psychology is one of the arts, and Marx (1963a) saw the literary biases of some psychologists as having no more place in a strictly scientific endeavor than objective points of view have in artistic ones. Attitudes such as these are easily dismissed, assuming as they do that the commitment to science is chiseled in stone and needs no defense. Hebb (1974) however offered one, that for understanding people, history supposedly shows that science works better than the arts and humanities. What, he asked, have the latter contributed that compares to such giant exemplars of the scientific approach as Piaget, Lashley, or Harlow? Well, one might answer, a long list of names springs to mind that was introduced a moment ago and began with Shakespeare! Fortunately, Hebb redeemed himself from this gaff by admitting that one turns not to psychological science but to literature to find out what grief and jealousy do to people or how power does or does not corrupt, so I detect some latent sympathy for the present approach. Certainly, it is unclear why someone of these persuasions would be unwilling to admit that *Othello*, say, is psychology. Surely "psychologists" should be identified by what they study, not how they study it. Thus Underwood (1957b) welcomed the efforts of artists to record their interpretations of behavior so long as they were clearly distinguished from those based on scientific alternatives, so the latter provide one road along which to travel to see where it goes and those who prefer others are not berated as threats to the entire enterprise.

Another objection is essentially the reverse, that since the scope of acceptable topics is now far broader, much material has already been incorporated. To some degree this is true, but topics such as creativity, religion, and death have only their small circles of devotees and are rarely discussed in mainstream courses or textbooks, and those who specialize in these areas are not exactly hot prospects for employment. Ads for their services are few and far between. A final possible objection is that contributions from these areas lack that crucial ingredient, reliability. Wouldn't we end up with a hodgepodge of idiosyncratic observations having no general utility? As Chapter 4 intimated, complete answers must include some of these observations, but more to the point, supposedly individual depictions in literary works of one person at one time can attain a wider truth. Jung (1966) voiced the common belief that one hallmark of great artistic work is that it transcends the individual to communicate to all people everywhere; for Alexander Pope, (1951, p. 393) greatness arose from "what oft was thought, but ne'er so well expressed." We may be unable to state precisely why we perceive a work as valid but when it hits so many on a gut level it shows the reliability of its content. Thus intimacy has its advantages because we can thereby verify nonscientific contributions as we do any data, empirical or other, against our experience.

In conclusion, this approach obviously demands a new definition of psychology. Why not simply *the study of human beings*? Nothing need be said about acceptable methods or sources, making everything grist for the mill. Whatever works! Even animal studies are allowed as long as the ultimate aim is to understand ourselves.

EPILOGUE

It seems appropriate to finish by dispelling another myth about psychology, one that brings us full circle in that it is routinely put forward to explain a phenomenon discussed early on: the discipline's huge popularity among students. The myth is that courses in psychology are Mickey Mouse credits, so it attracts those who want to get a degree painlessly. It won't wash! First, it rests on an inaccurate generalization about today's students, who as a group seem more serious about their studies than any others I know of. For many students of the past, university was a license for frivolity that involved regularly ingesting intoxicating vapors both liquid and gaseous (at one time, even goldfish) or, for women in prefeminist times, getting your Mrs. degree by finding a suitable spouse who could support you in the manner to which you would like to be accustomed. The concept of *the gentleman's C* conveys the commitment to mediocrity—do enough to avoid flunking out but never, God forbid, so much as to earn labels such as grind or keener that derided the overly zealous. Such attitudes, praise be, have gone the way of panty raids and pep rallies. If anything, most students nowadays are so worried, and rightly, about careers and thus so obsessed with grades that it interferes with enjoying the pursuit of knowledge for its own sake, which should have first priority.

More to the point, the myth misrepresents psychology. As our discussion has verified, its body of knowledge is in sheer amount enormous, in diversity unmatched, and in difficulty the equal of any; it deserves the label discipline in every sense of the word. Those who undertake it as an easy road to the hallowed diploma are soon rid of their illusions and either knuckle down or take themselves elsewhere, and those who do make it through have accomplished a truly formidable task. As for scholars, the riddle of the human being is a Gordian knot of ideas that in comparison reduces figuring out how to build bridges, solve equations, or track high-energy particles to child's play—one reason why methods that worked so well for these matters have sometimes come up short for psychology. Agreed, progress to improve life has been slow, but that is the challenge, to improve this state of affairs, because the storied "last frontier" lies not under the seas or up in the heavens but within our own heads and hearts, the biggest reason of all why psychology is so exciting a calling. Moreover, any discipline that counts among its disciples such as Freud and Jung; Watson, Skinner, Harlow, and Hull; the Gestaltists, Festinger and Tolman; William James and Piaget; Lashley and Hebb; Camus and Sartre, ad infinitum needs to make no apologies for the quality of its greatest achievements. Of course they were wrong in part, sometimes wildly so, but so were Descartes, Newton, Darwin, and Einstein. As Popper reminds us, it is the scientist's (and for that matter everyone's) fate to be wrong; what matters is to be stimulating and provocative. Furthermore, psychology's giants have sometimes been absolutely bang on. By the same token, most of its content is unquestionably trivial, but so too is most of physics, chemistry, and mathematics. It is the sublimities at the top that establish a discipline's worth and here again psychology takes a back seat to none.

All this needs to be said because psychology's devotees, students and professionals alike, still seem afflicted with massive inferiority complexes that make them feel they must apologize, especially to "real scientists," for what they do. Furthermore, many scientists remain unconvinced (not entirely without reason) about psychology's ability to play by the rules and are in extreme cases openly contemptuous about its inherent worth. Among students and academics both, putting down psychology is a popular pastime. However, these attitudes are most strongly held by those who know precious little about either its difficulties or accomplishments and base their opinions on no more than introductory courses once taken and/or a perusal of the local book store's pop psychology offerings (which is about as reasonable as ridiculing astronomy because of the quality of the astrology writings displayed at supermarket checkouts). Unfortunately, psychologists have played along instead of dismissing such attitudes as the ignorance they are. This probably reflects the enduring belief that intelligence is a unitary entity, which scientists and mathematicians have more of than do psychologists. Thus I have heard it said that the best of the latter, a Freud or

Skinner, need less than does an Einstein or Newton. Let psychologists remind themselves: this belief is no longer sacrosanct. From a Gardner/Guilford perspective, ability in science indicates not more but merely different intelligence. The comparison pits apples against oranges. Some first-rate scientists and mathematicians do not, to put it diplomatically, bowl me over with their brilliance in other domains. Perhaps waxing derogatory is unseemly, but I for one am sick unto death of my best students and some of my heroes being patronized by mediocrities from other disciplines, whom no one has ever heard of and never will. So, psychologists, it's time to fight back! No more apologies! Walk tall!

References

Abercrombie, L. (1926). *Romanticism*. New York: Barnes and Noble.

Abood, L. G. (1960). A chemical approach to the problem of mental illness. In D. D. Jackson (Ed.), *The etiology of schizophrenia* (pp. 91–119). New York: Basic Books.

Abra, J. C. (1987). The dancer as masochist. *Dance Research Journal, 19*, 33–40.

Abra, J. C. (1988a). *Assaulting Parnassus: Theoretical views of creativity*. Lanham, MD: University Press of America.

Abra, J. C. (1988b). Is creative ability widespread? *Canadian Review of Art Education, 15*, 69–89.

Abra, J. C. (1988c). Should we be studying "creativity"? *Creative Child and Adult Quarterly, 13*, 168–175.

Abra, J. C. (1989). Changes in creativity with age: Data, explanations and further predictions. *International Journal of Aging and Human Development, 28*, 105–126.

Abra, J. C. (1993). Competition: Creativity's vilified motive. *Genetic, Social and General Psychology Monographs, 119*, 291–342.

Abra, J. C. (1994). Collaboration in creative work: An initiative for investigation. *Creativity Research Journal, 7*, 1–20.

Abra, J. C. (1995). What you see isn't always what you get. *Creativity Research Journal, 8*, 431–438.

Abra, J. C. (1997). *The motives for creative work: An inquiry*. Creskill, NJ: Hampton.

Abra, J. C. (in press). Motives for criticism: Some theoretical speculations and introspective data. In M. Runco (Ed.), *Critical creative processes*. Cresskill, NJ: Hampton.

Abra, J. C., & Valentine-French, S. (1991). Gender differences in creative achievement: A survey of explanations. *Genetic, Social and General Psychology Monographs, 117*, 233–284.

Adams, H. E., & Sturgis, E. T. (1977). Status of behavioral reorientation techniques in the modification of homosexuality: A review. *Psychological Bulletin, 84*, 1171–1188.

Agnew, N. M., & Pyke, S. W. (1969). *The science game.* Englewood Cliffs, NJ: Prentice-Hall.

Agranoff, B. W. (1967). Memory and protein synthesis. *Scientific American, 216,* 115–122.

Alexander, B. K., Coambs, R. B., & Hadaway, P. F. (1978). The effect of housing and gender on morphine self-administration in rats. *Psychopharmacology, 58,* 175–179.

Allport, G. W. (1940). The psychologist's frame of reference. *Psychological Bulletin, 37,* 1–28.

Allport, G. W. (1961). *Pattern and growth in personality.* New York: Holt, Rinehart & Winston.

Allport, G. W. (1969). *The person in psychology: Selected essays.* Boston: Beacon.

Amabile, T. M. (1983). *The social psychology of creativity.* New York: Springer-Verlag.

American Psychological Association. (1947). Recommended graduate training programs in clinical psychology. *American Psychologist, 2,* 539–558.

American Psychological Association. (1990). Ethical principles of psychologists. *American Psychologist, 45,* 390–395.

American Psychologist. (May, 1995). Commentaries on Gergen (1994).

Amsel, A. (1958). The role of frustrative nonreward in noncontinuous reward situations. *Psychological Bulletin, 52,* 102–119.

Anand, B. K., & Brobeck, J. R. (1951). Hypothalamic control of food intake in rats and cats. *Yale Journal of Biological Medicine,* 123–140.

Anastasi, A. (1988). *Psychological testing* (6th ed.). New York: Macmillan.

Ansbacher, H. L., & Ansbacher, R. R. (1956) (Eds.). *The individual psychology of Alfred Adler.* New York: Basic Books.

Arieti, S. (1976). *Creativity: The magic synthesis.* New York: Basic Books.

Arnheim, R. (1966). *Toward a psychology of art.* Berkeley, CA: University of California Press.

Aronson, E., Ellsworth, P. C., Carlsmith, J. M., & Gonzales, M. H. (1990). *Methods of research in social psychology* (2nd ed.). New York: McGraw Hill.

Asch, S. E. (1955). Opinions and social pressure. *Scientific American,* offprint #450. San Francisco: Freeman.

Ash, M. G. (1985). Gestalt psychology: Origins in Germany and reception in the United States. In C. E. Buxton (Ed.), *Points of view in the modern history of psychology* (pp. 295–344). New York: Academic Press.

Ashcroft, M. H. (1994). *Human memory and cognition* (2nd ed.). New York: Harper & Collins.

Atkinson, R. L., Atkinson, R. C., Smith, E. E., & Bem, D. J. (1993). *Introduction to psychology* (11th ed.). New York: Harcourt Brace Jovanovich.

Ayllon, T., & Azrin, N. H. (1965). The measurement and reinforcement of behavior of psychotics. *Journal of the Experimental Analysis of Behavior, 8,* 357–383.

Bacon, F. (1620/1981). The idols of human understanding (excerpt from *Novum organum*). In R. D. Tweney, M. D. Doherty & C. R. Mynatt (Eds.), *On scientific thinking* (pp. 31–32). New York: Columbia University Press.

Baddeley, A. (1990). *Human memory: Theory and practice.* Toronto: Allyn & Bacon.

Bahrich, H. P., Bahrich, P. O., & Wittlinger, R. P. (1975). Fifty years of memory for names and faces: A cross-sectional approach. *Journal of Experimental Psychology: General, 104*, 54–75.

Bandura, A. (1965). Influence of models' reinforcement contingencies on the acquisition of imitative responses. *Journal of Personality and Social Psychology, 1*, 589–595.

Bandura, A. (1977). *Social learning theory*. Englewood-Cliffs, NJ: Prentice-Hall.

Bandura, A. (1978). The self system in reciprocal determinism. *American Psychologist, 33*, 344–358.

Barlow, D. H., & Durand, V. M. (1995). *Abnormal psychology: An integrated approach*. Pacific Grove, CA: Brooks/Cole.

Barnett, L. (1948). *The universe and Dr. Einstein*. New York: Bantam.

Barron, F. (1965). The psychology of creativity. In *New directions in psychology II* (pp. 1–134). New York: Holt Rinehart & Winston.

Bartlett, F. C. (1932). *Remembering*. London: Cambridge University Press.

Bate, W. J. (1979). *Samuel Johnson*. New York: Harcourt Brace Jovanovich.

Battig, W. F. (1968). Paired-associate learning. In T. R. Dixon & D. L. Horton (Eds.), *Verbal behavior and general behavior theory* (pp. 146–171). Englewood Cliffs, NJ: Prentice-Hall.

Beamon, A. L., Cole, C. M., Preston, M., Klentz, B., & Stebloy, N. M. (1983). Fifteen years of foot-in-the-door research: A meta-analysis. *Personality and Social Psychology Bulletin, 9*, 181–196.

Beauvoir, S. de. (1962). *The second sex*. New York: Alfred A. Knopf.

Beck, A. T. (1976). *Cognitive therapy and the emotional disorders*. New York: International Universities Press.

Becker, E. (1973). *The denial of death*. New York: The Free Press.

Becker, B. J., & Hedges, L. N. (1984). Meta-analysis of cognitive gender differences: A comment on an analysis by Rosenthal and Rubin. *Journal of Educational Psychology, 76*, 583–587.

Beit-Hallahmi, B. (1984). Psychology and religion. In M. Bornstein (Ed.), *Psychology and its allied disciplines, Vol 1: The humanities* (pp. 241–282). Hillsdale, NJ: Erlbaum.

Bem, D. J., & Allen, A. (1974). On predicting some of the people some of the time: The search for cross-situational consistencies in behavior. *Psychological Review, 81*, 506–520.

Berkowitz, L. (1964). The effects of observing violence. *Scientific American, 210*, 430–436.

Berlyne, D. E. (1959). Motivational problems raised by exploratory and epistemic behavior. In S. Koch (Ed.), *Psychology: A study of a science* (Vol 5, pp. 284–364). New York: McGraw-Hill.

Bertalanffy, L. von. (1952). *Problems of life: An evaluation of modern biological thought*. London: Watts & Co.

Bevan, W. (1980). On getting in bed with a lion. *American Psychologist, 35*, 779–789.

Bevan, W. (1982). A sermon of sorts in three parts. *American Psychologist, 37*, 1303–1322.

Bieber, I. (1962). *Homosexuality: A psychoanalytic study*. New York: Basic Books.

Birren, J. E., & Schroots, J. J. F. (1996). History, concepts, and theory in the psychology of aging. In J. E. Birren & K. W. Schaie (Eds.), *The handbook of the psychology of aging* (4th ed., pp. 3–23). San Diego: Academic Press.

Bliss, M. (1982). *The discovery of insulin.* Toronto: McClelland & Stewart.

Bloom, B. S. (1985). *Developing talent in young people.* New York: Ballantine.

Boden, M. (1992). *The creative mind: Myths and mechanisms.* New York: Basic Books.

Bohm, D., & Peat, F. D. (1987). *Science, order and creativity.* Toronto: Bantam.

Bolles, R. C. (1970). Species-specific defense reactions and avoidance learning. *Psychological Review, 77,* 32–48.

Boring, E. G. (1953). The role of theory in experimental psychology. *The American Journal of Psychology, 66,* 169–184.

Boring, E. G. (1957). *A history of experimental psychology* (2nd ed.). New York: Appleton-Century-Crofts.

Bouchard, T. J., Lykken, D. J., McGue, M., Segal, N. L., & Tellegen, A. (1990). Sources of human psychological differences: The Minnesota study of twins reared apart. *Science, 250,* 223–228.

Bousfield, W. A. (1953). The occurrence of clustering in the recall of randomly generated associates. *Journal of General Psychology, 49,* 229–240.

Bower, G. (1970). Analysis of a mnemonic device. *American Scientist, 58,* 496–510.

Brady, J. P. (1971). Brevital-aided systematic desensitization. In R. D. Rubin, A. A. Lazarus, H. Fensterhein, & C. M. Franks (Eds.), *Advances in behavior therapy* (pp. 77–83). New York: Academic Press.

Brain, Lord. (1966). *Science and man.* London: Faber & Faber.

Bransford, J. D., & Franks, J. J. (1971). The abstraction of linguistic ideas. *Cognitive Psychology, 2,* 331–350.

Breland, K., & Breland, M. (1961). The misbehavior of organisms. *American Psychologist, 16,* 681–684.

Bridgman, P. W. (1927). *The logic of modern physics.* New York: MacMillan.

Briggs, G. E. (1954). Acquisition, extinction and recovery functions in retroactive inhibition. *Journal of Experimental Psychology, 53,* 60–67.

Briggs, J. (1988). *Fire in the crucible.* New York: St. Martin's Press.

Broadbent, D. E. (1958). *Perception and communication.* New York: Pergamon.

Broadbent, D. E. (1962). Attention and the perception of speech. *Scientific American,* offprint #467. San Francisco: Freeman.

Bronowski, J. (1965). *Science and human values.* New York: Harper & Row.

Brown, A. S. (1991). A review of the tip-of-the-tongue phenomenon. *Psychological Bulletin, 109,* 204–223.

Brown, J. (1958). Some tests of the decay theory of immediate memory. *Quarterly Journal of Experimental Psychology, 10,* 12–21.

Brown, J. S. (1961). *The motivation of behavior.* New York: McGraw-Hill.

Brown, R. (1958). *Words and things.* New York: Free Press.

Brown, R., & Kulik, J. (1982). Flashbulb memories. In U. Neisser (Ed.), *Memory observed* (pp. 23–40). San Francisco: Freeman.

Brown, R. W., & McNeill, D. (1966). The "tip of the tongue" phenomenon. *Journal of Verbal Learning and Verbal Behavior, 5,* 325–337.

Bruce, D. (1994). Lashley and the problem of serial order. *American Psychologist, 49,* 93–103.

Bugelski, B. R. (1968). Images as mediators in one-trial paired-associate learning. II: Self-timing in successive lists. *Journal of Experimental Psychology, 77,* 328–334.

Burka, J. B., & Yuen, L. M. (1983). *Procrastination.* Menlo Park, CA: Addison-Wesley.

Bush, R. R., & Mosteller, F. (1955). *Stochastic models for learning.* New York: Wiley.

Buss, A. (1966). *Psychopathology.* New York: Wiley.

Campbell, D. T. (1960). Blind variation and selective retention in creative thought as in other knowledge processes. *Psychological Review, 67,* 380–400.

Campbell, D. T. (1975). On the conflicts between biological and social evolution and between psychology and moral tradition. *American Psychologist, 30,* 1103–1126.

Campbell, J. (1988). *The power of myth.* New York: Doubleday.

Camus, A. (1956). *The rebel.* New York: Vintage.

Camus, A. (1969). *The myth of Sisyphus and other essays.* New York: Alfred A. Knopf.

Carlsson, A (1978). Does dopamine have a role in schizophrenia? *Bio Psychiatry, 13,* 3–21.

Cattell, R. B. (1986). *The handbook for the personality factor questionnaire.* Champagne, IL: Institute for Personality and Ability Testing.

Cermak, L. S., & Craik, F. I. M. (Eds.) (1979). *Levels of processing in human memory.* Hillsdale, NJ: Erlbaum.

Chapanis, A. (1963). Men, machines and models. In M. Marx (Ed.), *Theories in contemporary psychology,* (pp. 104–129). New York: Macmillan.

Charness, N. (1976). Memory for chess positions: Resistance to interference. *Journal of Experimental Psychology: Human Learning and Memory, 2,* 641–653.

Chein, I. (1972). *The science of behavior and the image of man.* London: Tavistock.

Chicago, J. (1982). *Through the flower.* New York: Anchor.

Chomsky, N. (1959). Review of Skinner's *Verbal Behavior. Language, 35,* 26–58.

Clark, R. W. (1972). *Einstein: The life and times.* New York: Avon.

Comer, R. J. (1995). *Fundamentals of abnormal psychology.* New York: Freeman.

Cooper, R. M. (1982). Comment: The passing of psychology. *Canadian Psychology, 23,* 264–267.

Costello, C. G. (1970). Classification and psychopathology. In C. G. Costello (Ed.) *Symptoms of psychopathology: A handbook* (pp. 1–26). New York: John Wiley.

Costello, C. G., Belton, G., Abra, J. C., & Dunn, B. (1970). The amnesic and therapeutic effects of bilateral and unilateral ECT. *British Journal of Psychiatry, 116,* 69–78.

Council for the Society for the Psychological Study of Social Issues. (1969). Statement by SPSSI on current IQ controversy: Heredity versus environment. *American Psychologist, 24,* 1039–1040.

Craik, F. I. M. (1977). Age differences in human memory. In J. E. Birren & K. W. Schaie (Eds.), *Handbook of the psychology of aging* (pp. 384–420). New York: van Nostrand Reinhold.

Craik, F. I. M. (1996). Aging and memory. Colloquium, Dept. of Psychology, University of Calgary.

Craik, F. I. M., & Lockhart, R. S. (1972). Levels of processing: A framework for memory research. *Journal of Verbal Learning and Verbal Behavior, 11,* 671–684.

Craik, F. I. M., & Tulving, E. (1975). Depth of processing and retention of words in episodic memory. *Journal of Experimental Psychology, General, 104,* 268–294.

Craik, F. I. M., & Watkins, M. J. (1973). The role of rehearsal in short-term memory. *Journal of Verbal Learning and Verbal Behavior, 12,* 599–607.

Cronbach, L. J. (1975). Beyond the two disciplines of scientific psychology. *American Psychologist, 30,* 116–127.

Csikszentmihalyi, M. (1990). *Flow: The psychology of optimal experience.* New York: Harper Collins.

Darley, J., & Latané, B. (1968). Bystander intervention in emergencies. Diffusion of responsibility. *Journal of Personality and Social Psychology, 10,* 202–214.

Dawkins, R. (1986). *The blind watchmaker.* London: Penguin.

Deese, J. (1969). Behavior and fact. *American Psychologist, 24,* 515–522.

Deffenbacher, J. L., & Suinn, R. W. (1988). Systematic desensitization and the reduction of anxiety. *Couselling Psychologist, 16,* 9–30.

Dellas M., & Gaier, E. L. (1970). Identification of creativity: The individual. *Psychological Bulletin, 73,* 55–73.

Dess, N. K., & Overmier, J. B. (1989). General learned irrelevance: Proactive effects on Pavlovian conditioning in dogs. *Learning and Motivation, 20,* 1–14.

Deutsch, M. (1954). Field theory in social psychology. In G. Lindzey (Ed.), *Handbook of social psychology* (Vol. 1, pp. 181–222). Reading, MA: Addison-Wesley.

Digman, J. M., & Inouye, J. (1986). Further specification of the five robust factors of personality. *Journal of Personality and Social Psychology, 50,* 116–123.

Dixon, T. R., & Horton, D. L. (Eds.). (1968). *Verbal behavior and general behavior theory.* Englewood Cliffs, NJ: Prentice-Hall.

Dobson, K. S., & Pusch, D. (1994). Psychopathology. In *Encylopaedia of human behavior* (Vol. 3, pp. 631–640). New York: Academic Press.

Dollard, J., Doob, L. W., Miller, N. E., Mowrer, O. H., Sears, R. R., Ford, C. S., Hovland, C. I., & Sollenberger, R. T. (1939). *Frustration and aggression.* New Haven: Yale University Press.

Dollard, J., & Miller, N. E. (1950). *Personality and psychotherapy.* New York: McGraw-Hill.

Dove, A. (1968). *Dove counterbalance general intelligence test.* New York: Newsweek.

Dunn, A. J. (1980). Neurochemistry of learning and memory: An evaluation of recent data. *Annual Review of Psychology, 31,* 343–390.

Eagly, A. H., & Steffen, V. J. (1986). Gender and helping behavior: A meta-analytic review of the social psychology literature. *Psychological Bulletin, 100,* 283–308.

Easterbrook, J. A. (1978). *The determinants of free will.* New York: Academic Press.

Ebbinghaus, H. (1885). *Memory.* New York: Teachers College, Columbia University (1913).

Eccles, J. C. (1964). The synapse. *Scientific American,* offprint #1001. San Francisco: Freeman.

Eccles, J. C. (1981). In praise of falsification. In R. T. Tweney, M. E. Doherty, & C. R. Mynatt (Eds.), *On scientific thinking* (pp. 109–111). New York: Columbia University Press.

Eccles, J. C., & Robinson, D. N. (1984). *The wonder of being human: Our brain and our mind.* New York: Free Press.

Eccles, J. S. (1985). Why doesn't Jane run? Sex differences in educational and occupational patterns. In F. D. Horowitz & M. O'Brien (Eds.), *The gifted and talented: Developmental perspectives* (pp. 251–300). Washington, DC: American Psychological Association.

Einstein, A. (1952). Letter to Jacques Hadamard. In B. Ghiselin (Ed.), *The creative process* (pp. 43–44). New York: New American Library.

Einstein, A. (1956). *Out of my later years.* New York: Citadel.

Einstein, A., & Infeld, L. (1938). *The evolution of physics.* New York: Simon & Schuster.

Eisenberg, L. (1966). Discussion of Dr. Szasz' paper. In L. D. Eron (Ed.), *The classification of behavior disorders* (pp. 171–177). Chicago: Aldine.

Ellis, A. (1973). Rational-emotive therapy. In R. Corsini (Ed.), *Current psychotherapies* (pp. 167–206). Itasca, Il: F. E. Peacock.

Ellman, R. (1988). *Oscar Wilde.* New York: Penguin.

Engell, J. (1981). *The creative imagination.* Cambridge, MA: Harvard University Press.

Erikson, E. (1950). *Childhood and society.* New York: Norton.

Estes, W. K. (1960). Learning theory and the new "mental chemistry." *Psychological Review, 67,* 207–223.

Evans, R. I. (1969). *Psychology and Arthur Miller.* New York: Dutton.

Eysenck, H. J. (1952). *The scientific study of personality.* New York: MacMillan.

Eysenck, H. J. (1960). *Handbook of abnormal psychology: An experimental approach.* London: Pitman Medical

Eysenck, H. J. (1965). *Fact and fiction in psychology.* Harmondsworth, England: Penguin.

Eysenck, H. J. (1967). *The biological basis of personality.* Springfield, IL: Thomas.

Eysenck, H. J., & Rachman, S. (1965). *The causes and cures of neurosis: An introduction to modern behavior theory based on learning theory and the principles of conditioning.* San Diego: Knapp.

Feingold, A. (1988). Cognitive gender differences are disappearing. *American Psychologist, 43,* 95–103.

Feldman, D. (1980). *Beyond universals in cognitive development.* Norwood, NJ: Ablex.

Feldman, D. (1982). A developmental framework for research with gifted children. In D. H. Feldman (Ed.), *Developmental approaches to giftedness and creativity* (pp. 31–45). San Francisco: Jossey-Bass.

Feldman, M. (1966). Aversion therapy for sexual deviation: A critical review. *Psychological Bulletin, 65,* 65–79.

Feldman, M., & MacCullough, M. J. (1965). The application of anticipatory avoidance learning to the treatment of homosexuality: I. Theory, technique and preliminary results. *Behavior Research & Therapy, 2,* 165–183.

Ferster, C. B., & Skinner, B. F. (1957). *Schedules of reinforcement.* New York: Appleton-Century-Crofts.

Festinger, L. (1957). *A theory of cognitive dissonance*. Palo Alto, CA: Stanford University Press.

Feyerabend, P. (1993). *Against method* (3rd ed.). New York: Verso.

Flynn, J. R. (1987). Massive IQ gains in 14 nations: What IQ tests really measure. *Psychological Bulletin, 101,* 171–191.

Frankl, V. (1984). *Man's search for meaning*. New York: Washington Square Press.

French, J. (1957). The reticular formation. *Scientific American*, offprint # 66. San Francisco: Freeman.

Freud, S. (1887–1902/1954). *The origins of psychoanalysis, letters to Wilhelm Fliess, drafts and notes: 1887–1902*. New York: Basic Books.

Freud, S. (1947). *Leonardo da Vinci*. New York: Vintage.

Freud, S. (1953a). *The interpretation of dreams*. London: Hogarth.

Freud, S. (1953b). Three essays on the theory of sexuality. In J. Strachey (Ed.), *The complete psychological works of Sigmund Freud* (Vol. 7, pp. 125–245). London: Hogarth.

Freud, S. (1958a). One of the difficulties of psychoanalysis. In B. Nelson (Ed.), *On creativity and the unconscious* (pp. 1–10). New York: Harper & Row.

Freud, S. (1958b). The relation of the poet to daydreaming. In B. Nelson (Ed.), *On creativity and the unconscious* (pp. 44–54). New York: Harper & Row.

Freud, S. (1958c). Thoughts for the time on war and death. In B. Nelson (Ed.), *On creativity and the unconscious* (pp. 206–235). New York: Harper & Row.

Freud, S. (1961). Dostoevsky and parricide. In J. Strachey (Ed.), *The complete psychological works of Sigmund Freud* (Vol. 21, pp. 175–198). London: Hogarth.

Freud, S. (1963). Introductory lectures on psychoanalysis (Part III). In J. Strachey (Ed.), *The complete psychological works of Sigmund Freud* (Vol. 16). London: Hogarth.

Fromm, E. (1960). *The fear of freedom*. London: Routledge & Kegan Paul.

Fromm, E. (1977). *The anatomy of human destructiveness*. Middlesex: Penguin.

Furst, L. R. (1969). *Romanticism in perspective*. Toronto: MacMillan.

Gagne, R. M. (Ed.). (1967) *Learning and individual differences*. Columbus, Ohio: Charles E. Merrill.

Gaito, J. (1963). DNA and RNA as memory molecules. *Psychological Review, 70,* 471–480.

Gaito, J., & Bonnet, K. (1971). Quantitative versus qualitative RNA and protein changes in the brain during behavior. *Psychological Bulletin, 75,* 109–127.

Galin, D. (1974). Implications for psychiatry of left and right cerebral specialization. *Archives of General Psychiatry, 31,* 572–583.

Galton, F. (1869). *Hereditary genius: An inquiry into its laws and consequences*. London: Macmillan.

Galton, F. (1876). The history of twins as a criterion of the relative powers of nature and nurture. *Royal Anthropological Institute of Great Britain and Ireland Journal, 6,* 391–406.

Galton, F. (1883). *Inquiries into human facility and its development*. New York: Macmillan.

Garcia, J., Ervin, F. R., & Koelling, R. A. (1966). Relation of cue to consequence in avoidance learning. *Psychonomic Science, 5,* 121–122.

Gardner, H. (1982). *Art, mind and brain: A cognitive approach to creativity*. New York: Basic Books.

Gardner, H. (1983). *Frames of mind.* New York: Basic Books.

Gardner, H. (1985) *The mind's new science.* New York: Basic Books.

Gardner, H. (1993a). *Creating minds.* New York: Basic Books.

Gardner, H. (1993b). *Multiple intelligences: The theory in practice.* New York: Basic Books.

Gardner, M. (Ed.) (1984). *The sacred beetle and other great essays in science.* New York: New American Library.

Gardner, R. A., & Gardner, B. T. (1969). Teaching sign language to the chimpanzee. *Science, 165,* 664–672.

Garfield, S. L. (1993). Methodological problems in clinical diagnosis. Cited in Weten, W. (1995). *Psychology: Themes and variations* (3rd ed.). New York: Brooks/Cole.

Gay, straight brains differ. (Nov. 19, 1994). *Calgary Herald.*

Gazzaniga, M. S. (1967). The split brain in man. *Scientific American, 217,* 24–29.

Geison, G. (1995). *The private life of Louis Pasteur.* Princeton, NJ: Princeton University Press.

Gergen, K. J. (1976). Social psychology as history. In L. H. Strickland, F. E. Aboud & K. J. Gergen (Eds.), *Social psychology in transition* (pp. 15–32). New York: Plenum.

Gergen, K. J. (1985). The social constructionist movement in psychology. *American Psychologist, 40,* 266–275.

Gergen, K. J. (1994). Exploring the postmodern: Perils or potentials. *American Psychologist, 49,* 412–416.

Getzels, J. W., & Csikszentmihalyi, M. (1976). *The creative vision.* Toronto: John Wiley.

Gibson, E. J. (1940). A systematic application of the concepts of generalization and discrimination to verbal learning. *Psychological Review, 47,* 196–229.

Gigerenzer, G., & Goldstein, D. G. (1996). Mind as computer: Birth of a metaphor. *Creativity Research Journal, 9,* 131–144.

Gilligan, G. (1982). *In a different voice.* Cambridge, MA: Harvard University Press.

Ginsberg, H., & Opper, S. (1969). *Piaget's theory of intellectual development: An introduction.* Englewood Cliffs, NJ: Prentice-Hall.

Glass, D. C., Singer, J. E., & Friedman, L. M. (1969). Psychic cost of adaptation to an environmental stressor. *Journal of Personality and Social Psychology, 12,* 200–210.

Glickman, S. E. (1961). Perseverative neural processes and consolidation of the memory trace. *Psychological Bulletin, 58,* 218–233.

Glucksberg, S. (1962). The influence of strength of drive on functional fixedness and perceptual recognition. *Journal of Experimental Psychology, 63,* 36–51.

Glynn, S. M. (1990). Token economy approaches for psychiatric patients: Progress and pitfalls over 25 years. *Behavior Modification, 14,* 383–407.

Goble, F. (1974). *The third force.* New York: Simon & Schuster.

Goldberg, P. (1968). Are women prejudiced against women? *Trans-action, 5,* 28–30.

Goldstein, J. (1980). *Social psychology.* New York: Academic Press.

Goleman, D. (1980). Special abilities of the sexes: Do they begin in the brain? In *Annual editions in psychology* (pp. 43–49). Sluice Dock, Guilford, CT: Dushkin.

Graham, L. (1986). Heredity debate crucial to Soviets. *Calgary Herald*, Feb. 4, A5.

Graham, M. (1957). *A dancer's world.* (Film). New York: Rembrandt Films.

Graham, M. (1991). *Blood memory.* Toronto: Washington Square.

Greenacre, P. (1971). The childhood of the artist: Libidinal phase development and giftedness. In P. Greenacre (Ed.), *Emotional growth* (Vol. 2, pp. 479–504). New York: International Universities Press.

Greer, G. (1979). *The obstacle race.* London: Secker & Warburg.

Grene, M. (1948). *Introduction to existentialism.* Chicago: University of Chicago Press.

Grice, G. R. (1948). The relation of secondary reinforcement to delayed reward in visual discrimination learning. *Journal of Experimental Psychology, 38,* 1–16.

Gruber, H. (1974). *Darwin on man: A psychological study of scientific creativity.* New York: E. P. Dutton.

Gruber, H. (1980). "And the bush was not consumed." The evolving systems approach to creativity. In S. Modgil & C. Modgil (Eds.), *Toward a theory of psychological development* (pp. 269–299). Windsor, England: NFER Publishers.

Gruber, H. (1988). The evolving systems approach to creative work. *Creativity Research Journal, 1,* 27–51.

Gruber, H. (1994). Insight and affect in the history of science. In R. J. Sternberg & J. E. Davidson (Eds.), *The nature of insight* (pp. 397–431). Cambridge, MA: MIT Press.

Gruen, J. (1976). *The private world of ballet.* Toronto: Penguin.

Gruneberg, M., Morris, P. E., & Sykes, R. N. (Eds.). (1978). *Practical aspects of memory.* New York: Academic Press.

Guilford, J. P. (1950). Creativity. *American Psychologist, 5,* 444–454.

Guilford, J. P. (1967). *The nature of human intelligence.* New York: McGraw-Hill.

Guilford, J. P. (1970). Traits of creativity. In P. E. Vernon (Ed.), *Creativity* (pp. 167–188). New York: Penguin.

Guthrie, E. R. (1935). *The psychology of learning.* New York: Harper.

Haney, C., Banks, C., & Zimbardo, P. (1973). Interpersonal dynamics in a simulated prison. *International Journal of Criminology and Penology, 1,* 69–97.

Harlow, H. F. (1949). The formation of learning sets. *Psychological Review, 56,* 51–65.

Harré, R. (1985) *The philosophies of science.* New York: Oxford University Press.

Harré, R., & Secord, P. F. (1972). *The explanation of social behavior.* Oxford: Basil Blackwell.

Hebb, D. O. (1949). *The organization of behavior.* New York: Wiley.

Hebb, D. O. (1959). A neuropsychological theory. In S. Koch (Ed.), *Psychology: A study of a science* (Vol. 1, pp. 92–157). New York: McGraw-Hill.

Hebb, D. O. (1970). A return to Jensen and his social science critics. *American Psychologist, 25,* 568.

Hebb, D. O. (1974). What psychology is about. *American Psychologist, 29,* 71–79.

Heidbredder, E. (1935). *Seven psychologies.* New York: Appleton-Century.

Heintz, D. L. (1977). *An integration of the literature on creativity and sex roles.* Ann Arbor, MI: University Microfilms International.

Hess, E. H. (1959). Imprinting. *Science, 130,* 133–141.

Hetherington, A. N., & Ranson, S. W. (1942). The spontaneous activity and food intake of rats with hypothalamic lesions. *American Journal of Physiology, 136,* 609–617.

Hilgard, E. L. (1956). *Theories of learning.* New York: Appleton-Century-Crofts.

Hilgard, E. L. (1980). Consciousness in contemporary psychology. *Annual review of psychology, 31,* 1–26.

Hill, W. F. (1971). *Learning: A survey of psychological interpretations* (rev. ed.). Toronto: Chandler.

Hirst, W. (1982). The amnesic syndrome: Descriptions and explanations. *Psychological Bulletin, 91,* 435–460.

Hoffer, E. (1951). *The true believer.* New York: Harper Row.

Holton, G. (1988). *Thematic origins of scientific thought* (rev. ed.). Cambridge MA: Harvard University Press.

Honorton, C. (1985). Metanalysis of psi ganzfeld research: A response to Hyman. *Journal of Parapsychology, 49,* 51–91.

Housman, A. E. (1952). The name and nature of poetry. In B. Ghiselin (Ed.), *The creative process* (pp. 86–91). New York: New American Library.

Houston, J. P. (1991). *Fundamentals of learning and memory* (4th ed.). Toronto: Harcourt Brace Jovanovich.

Howard, G. S. (1985). The role of values in the science of psychology. *American Psychologist, 40,* 255–265.

Hubel, D. H., & Wiesel, T. N. (1979). Brain mechanisms of vision. *Scientific American, 249,* 150–162.

Hudson, L. (1976). *The cult of the fact.* London: Jonathon Cape.

Hudson, L. (1996). *Night life: The interpretation of dreams.* London: St. Martin's Press.

Hull, C. L. (1943). *Principles of behavior.* New York: Appleton-Century-Crofts.

Hull, C. L. (1952). *A behavior system.* New Haven: Yale University Press.

Hulse, S. H., Deese, J., & Egeth, H. (1975). *The psychology of learning* (4th ed.). New York: McGraw-Hill.

Hultsch, D. E., & Dixon, R. A. (1990). Learning and memory in aging. In J. E. Birren & K. W. Schaie (Eds.), *Handbook of the psychology of aging* (3rd ed., pp. 258–274). New York: Academic Press.

Hwang, K. (1986). Behavior of Swedish primary and secondary caretaking fathers in relation to mother's presence. *Developmental Psychology, 22,* 739–751.

Hyde, J. S., & Linn, M. C. (1988). Gender differences in verbal ability: A meta-analysis. *Psychological Bulletin, 104,* 53–69.

Hydèn, H., & Lange, P. W. (1968). Protein synthesis in the hippocampal pyramidal cells of rats during a behavioral task. *Science, 159,* 1370–1373.

James, W. (1890). *The principles of psychology.* New York: Holt.

James, W. (1902). *The varieties of religious experience: A study in human nature.* New York: Longmans, Green.

James, W. (1907). *Pragmatism: A new name for some old ways of thinking.* New York: Longmans, Green.

Janis, I. L., & Mann, L. (1965). Effectiveness of emotional role-playing in modifying smoking habits and attitudes. *Journal of Experimental Research in Personality, 1,* 84–90.

Jarvik, L. F., Klodin, V., & Matsuyama, S. S. (1973). Human aggression and the extra Y chromosome. *American Psychologist, 28,* 674–682.

Jaynes, J. (1976). *The origin of consciousness in the breakdown of the bicameral mind*. Boston: Houghton Mifflin.

Jenkins, J. B., & Dallenbach, K. M. (1924). Oblivescence during sleep and waking. *American Journal of Psychology, 35,* 605–612.

Jensen, A. R. (1962). Transfer betwen paired-associate and serial learning. *Journal of Verbal Learning and Verbal Behavior, 1,* 269–280.

Jensen, A. R. (1969). How much can we boost IQ and scholastic achievement? *Harvard Educational Review, 39,* 1–123.

Jensen, A. R. (1972). *Genetics and education*. London: Methuen.

Jessor, R. (1963). The problem of reductionism in psychology. In M. H. Marx (Ed.), *Theories in contemporary psychology* (pp. 245–256). New York: Macmillan.

Johnson, R. N. (1972). *Aggression in man and animals*. Toronto: Saunders.

Jones, E. E. (1985) Major developments in Social Psychology during the past five decades. In G. Lindzey & E. Aronson (Eds.), *The handbook of social psychology* (Vol. 1, 3rd ed., pp. 47–107). New York: Random House.

Jones, S. L. (1994). A constructive relationship for religion with the science and profession of psychology. *American Psychologist, 49,* 184–199.

Jourard, M., & Kormann, L. A. (1968). Getting to know the experimenter. *Journal of Humanistic Psychology, 8,* 155–159.

Judson, H. F. (1979). *The eighth day of creation: Masters of the revolution in Biology*. New York: Simon & Schuster.

Jung, C. G. (1923). *Psychology of types*. London: Routledge & Kegan Paul.

Jung, C. G. (1956). Symbols of transformation. In H. Read, M. Fordham & G. Adler (Eds.), *The collected works of C. G. Jung* (Vol. 5). Princeton, NJ: Princeton University Press.

Jung. C. G. (1959). The archetypes and the collective unconscious. In H. Read, M. Fordham & G. Adler (Eds.), *The collected works of C. G. Jung* (Vol. 9, Whole Part 1). Princeton, NJ: Princeton University Press.

Jung, C. G. (1966). Psychology and literature. In H. Read, M. Fordham & G. Adler (Eds.), *The collected works of C. G. Jung* (Vol. 15, pp. 84–105). Princeton, NJ: Princeton University Press.

Juschka, B. (1987). *Neuropsychology of artistic abilities*. Unpublished manuscript, University of Calgary, Dept. of Psychology.

Kamin, L. J. (1974). *The science and politics of IQ*. Potomac, MD: Erlbaum.

Kane, J. M., & Freeman, H. L. (1994). Towards more effective antipsychotic treatment. *British Journal of Psychiatry, 165* (suppl. 25), 22–31.

Kant, I. (1976). Genius gives the rules. In A. Rothenberg & C. R. Hausman (Eds.), *The creativity question* (pp. 37–42). Durham, NC: Duke University Press.

Kasof, J. (1995). Social determinants of creativity: Status expectations and the evaluation of original products. In *Advances in group processes* (Vol. 12, pp. 167–220). JAI Press.

Kauffmann, S. (1976). Interview. In S. Rosner & L. E. Abt (Eds.), *The creative expression* (pp. 201–220). Croton-on-Hudson, NY: North River.

Kaufmann, H. (1968). *Introduction to the study of human behavior*. Toronto: Saunders.

Kaufmann, W. (1956). *Existentialism from Dostoevsky to Sartre*. New York: World Publishing.

Kaufmann, W. H. (1974). *Nietzsche: Philosopher, psychologist, antichrist*. Princeton, NJ: Princeton University Press.

Kausler, D. H. (1974). *Psychology of verbal learning and memory*. New York: Academic Press.

Kazdin, A. E. (1988). The token economy: A decade later. In G. Davey & C. Cullen (Eds.), *Human operant conditioning and behavior modification*. New York: John Wiley.

Kendall, P. C., & Hammen, C. (1995). *Abnormal psychology*. Boston: Houghton Mifflin.

Kendler, H. H. (1964). The concept of the concept. In A. W. Melton (Ed.), *Categories of human learning* (pp. 211–236). New York: Academic Press.

Kendler, H. H. (1968). Some specific reactions to S–R theory. In T. R. Dixon & D. L. Horton (Eds.), *Verbal behavior and general behavior theory* (pp. 388–403). Englewood Cliffs, NJ: Prentice-Hall.

Keppel, G. (1968). Retroactive and proactive inhibition. In T. R. Dixon & D. L. Horton (Eds.), *Verbal behavior and general behavior theory* (pp. 172–213). Englewood Cliffs, NJ: Prentice-Hall.

Keppel, G., & Underwood, B. J. (1962). Proactive inhibition in short-term retention of single items. *Journal of Verbal Learning and Verbal Behavior, 1*, 153–161.

Kessel, F. S., & Bevan, W. (1985). Notes toward a history of cognitive psychology. In C. E. Buxton (Ed.), *Points of view in the modern history of psychology* (pp. 259–294). New York: Academic Press.

Kimble, G. A. (1961). *Hilgard and Marquis' conditioning and learning* (2nd ed.). New York: Appleton-Century-Crofts.

Kimura, D. (1987). Are men's and women's brains really different? *Canadian Psychology, 28*, 135–147.

Kinsbourne, M. (1981). Sad hemisphere, happy hemisphere. *Psychology Today, 15*, 92.

Kintsch, W., & Buschke, H. (1969). Homophones and synonyms in short-term memory. *Journal of Experimental Psychology, 80*, 403–407.

Klatzky, R. (1980). *Human memory: Structures and processes* (2nd ed.). San Francisco: Freeman.

Koch, S. (1964). Psychology and emerging concepts of knowledge as unitary. In T. W. Wann (Ed.), *Behaviorism and phenomenology* (pp. 1–41). Chicago: University of Chicago Press.

Koch, S. (1981). Psychology and its human clientele: Beneficiaries or victims? In R. A. Kasschau & F. S. Kessel (Eds.), *Psychology and society: In search of symbiosis* (pp. 24–47). New York: Holt, Rinehart & Winston.

Koestler, A. (1970). *The act of creation*. London: Pan.

Kohlberg, L. (1984). *Essays on moral development: Vol. 2. The psychology of moral development*. San Francisco: Harper & Row.

Köhler, W. (1925). *The mentality of apes*. New York: Harcourt Brace.

Kohn, A. (1986). *No contest: The case against competition*. Boston: Houghton Mifflin.

Kolb, B., & Wishaw, I. Q. (1996). *Fundamentals of Human Neuropsychology* (4th ed.). New York: Freeman.

Kosslyn, S. M., Ball, T. M., & Reisser, B. J. (1978). Visual images preserve metric spatial information: Evidence from studies of image scanning. *Journal of Experimental Psychology: Human Perception and Performance, 4,* 47–60.

Kreitler, H., & Kreitler, S. (1972). *Psychology of the arts.* Durham, NC: Duke University Press.

Kris, E. (1952). *Psychoanalytic explorations in art.* New York: International Universities Press.

Kuhn, T. (1962). *The structure of scientific revolutions.* Chicago: University of Chicago Press.

Laing, R. D. (1965). *The divided self.* Harmondsworth, England: Penguin.

Lambert, W.W., & Lambert, W. E. (1973). *Social psychology* (2nd ed.). Englewood Cliffs, NJ: Prentice-Hall.

Landman, J. (1993). *Regret.* New York: Oxford University Press.

Langer, S. K. (1951). *Philosophy in a new key.* New York: Mentor.

Langer, S. K. (1953). *Feeling and form.* New York: Charles Scribner's.

Lashley, K. W. (1950). In search of the engram. *Symposia of the Society for Experimental Biology, 4,* 454–482.

Lashley, K. W. (1951). The problem of serial order in behavior. In L. A. Jeffries (Ed.), *Cerebral mechanisms in behavior: The Hixon Symposium* (pp. 112–146). New York: Wiley.

Leaming, B. (1986). *Orson Welles.* Harmondsworth, England: Penguin.

Leeper, R. W. (1963). Theoretical methodology in the psychology of personality. In M. H. Marx (Ed.), *Theories in contemporary psychology* (pp. 389–413). New York: Macmillan.

Lefcourt, H. M. (1973). The functions of the illusions of control and freedom. *American Psychologist, 28,* 417–425.

Lefrancois, G. (1983). *Psychology* (2nd ed.). New York: Wadsworth.

Lenneberg, F. H. (1967). *Biological foundations of language.* New York: Wiley.

Lepper, M. R., & Greene, D. (1975). Turning play into work: Effects of adult surveillance and extrinsic rewards on children's intrinsic motivation. *Journal of Personality and Social Psychology, 31,* 479–486.

LeVay, S. (1991). A difference in hypothalamic structure between heterosexual and homosexual men. *Science, 253,* 1034–1037.

Leventhal, H., & Cleary, P. D. (1980). The smoking problem: A review of the research and theory in behavioral risk modification. *Psychological Bulletin, 88,* 370–405.

Lewin, K. (1935). *A dynamic theory of personality.* New York: McGraw-Hill.

Lewin, K. (1948). *Resolving social conflicts.* New York: Harper.

Lewin, K. (1951). *Field theory in social science.* New York: Harper.

Linton, M. (1975). Memory for real-world events. In D. A. Norman & D. E. Rumelhart (Eds.), *Explorations in cognition* (pp. 376–404). San Francisco: Freeman.

Lips, H. M. (1988). *Sex and gender: An introduction.* Mountain View, CA: Mayfield.

Loehlin, J., Lindzey, G., & Spuhler, J. (1975). *Race differences in intelligence.* San Francisco: Freeman.

Loftus, E. (1975). Leading questions and the eyewitness report. *Cognitive Psychology, 7,* 560–572.

Loftus, E. (1980). *Memory.* New York: Addison-Wesley.

Loftus, E. (1993). The reality of repressed memories. *American Psychologist, 48,* 518–537.

Loftus, E., & Loftus, G. R. (1980). On the permanence of stored information in the human brain. *American Psychologist, 35,* 409–420.

Lorenz, K. (1962). *King Solomon's ring.* New York: Time.

Lorenz, K. (1966). *On aggression.* New York: Harcourt, Brace and World.

Lubinski, D., & Benbow, C. P. (1995). An opportunity for empiricism. *Contemporary Psychology, 40,* 935–938.

Luria, A. R. (1968). *The mind of a mnemonist.* New York: Basic Books.

Maccoby, E. E., & Jacklin, C. N. (1974). *The psychology of sex differences.* Stanford, CA: Stanford University Press.

MacCorquodale, K., & Meehl, P. E. (1948). On a distinction between hypothetical constructs and intervening variables. *Psychological Review, 55,* 95–107.

Mackintosh, N. J. (1974). *The psychology of animal learning.* New York: Academic Press.

Maddi, S. (1975). The strenuousness of the creative life. In I. A. Taylor & J. W. Getzels (Eds.), *Perspectives in creativity* (pp. 173–190). Chicago: Aldine.

Maddi, S. R., & Costa, P. T. (1972). *Humanism in personology. Allport, Maslow and Murray.* Chicago: Aldine-Atherton.

Magee, B. (1973). *Popper.* Glascow: Fontana/Collins.

Mailer, N. (1967). Interview. In G. Plimpton Ed.), *Writers at work: The Paris Review Interviews* (pp. 251–278). New York: Viking.

Maltzman, I. (1955). Thinking: From a behavioristic point of view. *Psychological Review, 66,* 367–386.

Mandler, G. (1962). From association to structure. *Psychological Review, 69,* 415–427.

Martin, E. (1968). Stimulus meaningfulness and paired-associate transfer: An encoding variability hypothesis. *Psychological Review, 75,* 421–441.

Marx, M. H. (1963a). Confusion in attitudes towards clinical theory. In M. H. Marx (Ed.), *Theories in contemporary psychology* (pp. 311–323). New York: Macmillan.

Marx, M. H. (1963b). The general nature of theory construction. In M. H. Marx (Ed.), *Theories in contemporary psychology* (pp. 4–46). New York: Macmillan.

Maslow, A. H. (1954). *Motivation and personality.* New York: Harper and Brothers.

Maslow, A. H. (1962). *Toward a psychology of being.* Toronto: D. van Nostrand (Canada).

Maslow, A. H. (1966). *The psychology of science: A reconnaissance.* Chicago: Henry Regnery.

Maslow, A. H. (1970). *Religions, values and peak-experiences.* New York: Viking.

Maslow, A. H. (1976). *The farther reaches of human nature.* Markham, Ont.: Penguin.

Masson, J. M. (1984). *The assault on truth: Freud's suppression of the seduction theory.* New York: Farrar, Strauss, Giroux.

Matsumoto, D. (1994). *People: Psychology from a cultural pespective.* Pacific Grove, CA: Brooks Cole.

May, R. (1969). *Love and will.* New York: Dell.

May, R. (1972). *Power and innocence.* New York: W. W. Norton.

Mazur, J. E. (1994). *Learning and behavior* (3rd ed.). Englewood Cliffs, NJ: Prentice-Hall.

McConnell, J. V. (1976). Worm-breeding with tongue in cheek and the confessions of a scientist hoist by his own petard. *UNESCO Courier,* April, 12–15.

McGeogh, J. A. (1942). *The psychology of learning.* New York: Longmans, Green.

McGeogh, J. A., & Irion, A. L. (1952). *The psychology of human learning* (2nd ed.). New York: David McKay.

McGovern, J. B. (1964). Extinction of associations in four transfer paradigms. *Psychological Monographs, 78* (16, Whole No. 593).

McGue, M. (1993). From proteins to cognitions: The behavioral genetics of alcoholism. In R. Plomin & G. E. McClearn (Eds.) *Nature, nurture and psychology* (pp. 245–268). Washington, DC: American Psychological Association.

McGue, M., Bouchard, T. J., Jr., Iacono, W. G., & Lykken, D. T. (1993). Behavioral genetics of cognitive ability: A life-span perspective. In R. Plomin & G. E. McClearn (Eds.), *Nature, nurture and psychology* (pp. 59–76). Washington, DC: American Psychological Association.

Medin, D. L., & Ross, B. H. (1992). *Cognitive psychology.* New York: Harcourt Brace Jovanovich.

Mednick, S. A. (1962). The associative basis of the creative process. *Psychological Review, 69,* 220–227.

Melton, A. W. (1963). Implications of short-term memory for a general theory of memory. *Journal of Verbal Learning and Verbal Behavior, 2,* 1–21.

Merton, R. K. (1973). *The sociology of science.* Chicago: University of Chicago Press.

Merton, R. K. (1983). Behavior patterns of scientists. In R. S. Albert (Ed.), *Genius and eminence* (pp. 253–261). Toronto: Pergamon.

Milgram, S. (1974). *Obedience and authority.* New York: Harper & Row.

Mille, A. de. (1958). *And promenade home.* Boston: Little, Brown.

Miller, G. A. (1956). The magical number seven, plus or minus two: Some limits on our capacity for processing information. *Psychological Review, 63,* 81–97.

Miller, G. A. (1965). Some preliminaries to psycholinguistics. *American Psychologist, 20,* 15–20.

Miller, G. A. (1969). Psychology as a means of promoting human welfare. *American Psychologist, 24,* 1063–1075.

Miller, G. A., Galanter, E., & Pribram, K. H. (1960). *Plans and the structure of behavior.* New York: Holt, Rinehart & Winston.

Miller, H. (1952). Reflections on writing. In B. Ghiselin (Ed.), *The creative process* (pp. 178–185). New York: New American Library.

Miller, L. K. (1976). The design of better communities through the application of behavioral principles. In W. E. Craighead, A. E. Kazdin, & M. J. Mahone (Eds), *Behavior modification: Principles, issues and applications.* Boston: Houghton-Mifflin.

Miller, N. E. (1985). The value of behavioral research on animals. *American Psychologist, 40,* 430–440.

Milner, B. (1965). Brain mechanisms suggested by studies of temporal lobes. In F. L. Darley & C. H. Millekan (Eds.), *Brain mechanisms underlying speech and language.* New York: Grune & Stratton.

Mischel, W. (1968). *Personality and assessment.* New York: John Wiley.

Mischel, W. (1984). Convergences and challenges in the search for consistency. *American Psychologist, 39,* 351–364.

Mitroff, I. (1974). *The subjective side of science*. Amsterdam: Elsevier.

Morison, R. S. (1963). The principle of gradualness. In M. H. Marx (Ed.), *Theories in contemporary psychology* (pp. 286–303). New York: Macmillan.

Mowrer, O. H. (1947). On the dual nature of learning. A re-interpretation of "conditioning" and "problem solving." *Harvard Educational Review, 17,* 102–148.

Mowrer, O. H. (1960). "Sin," the lesser of two evils. *American Psychologist, 15,* 301–304.

Murdock, B. M. (1961). Short-term retention of individual verbal items. *Journal of Experimental Psychology, 58,* 193–198.

Natsoulas, N. (1978). Residual subjectivity. *American Psychologist, 33,* 269–283.

Neisser, U. (1967). *Cognitive psychology*. New York: Appleton-Century-Crofts.

Neisser, U. (1982). *Memory observed: Remembering in natural contexts*. San Francisco: Freeman.

Neisser, U., Boodoo, G., Bouchard, T. J., Jr., Boykin, A. W., Brody, N., Ceci, S. J., Halpern, D. F., Loehlin, J. C., Perloff, R., Sternberg, R. J., & Urbina, S. (1996). Intelligence: Knowns and unknowns. *American Psychologist, 51,* 77–101.

Neisser, U., & Winograd, E. (1988). *Remembering reconsidered: Ecological and traditional approaches to the study of memory*. New York: Cambridge University Press.

Newell, A., & Simon, H. A. (1972). *Human problem solving*. Englewood Cliffs, NJ: Prentice-Hall.

Nickles, T. (1994). Enlightenment versus romantic models of creativity in science—and beyond. *Creativity Research Journal, 7,* 277–314.

Nietzel, M. T., Bernstein, D. A., & Milich, R. (1994). *Introduction to clinical psychology* (4th ed.). Englewood Cliffs, NJ: Prentice-Hall.

Nietzsche, F. (1952). Composition of "Thus Spake Zarathustra." In B. Ghiselin (Ed.), *The creative process* (pp. 201–203). New York: New American Library.

Nijinsky, R. (1954). *Nijinsky*. New York: Penguin.

Nisbett, R. E., & Wilson, T. D. (1977). Telling more than we can know: Verbal reports on mental processes. *Psychological Review, 4,* 231–259.

Ochse, R. (1990). *Before the gates of excellence: The determinants of creative genius*. New York: Cambridge University Press.

Oden, M. H. (1968). The fulfillment of promise: 40-year follow-up of the Terman gifted group. *Genetic Psychology Monographs, 77,* 3–93.

Ohman, A., Dimberg, U., & Ost, L. G. (1985). Animal and social phobias: Biological constraints on learned fear responses. In S. Reiss & R. R. Bootzin (Eds.), *Theoretical issues in behavior therapy*. New York: Academic Press.

Olds, J., & Milner, P. (1954). Positive reinforcement produced by electrical stimulation of septal area and other regions of rat brain. *Journal of Comparative and Physiological Psychology, 47,* 419–427.

Ornstein, R. (1972). *The psychology of consciousness*. San Francisco: Freeman.

Osborn, A. F. (1963). *Applied imagination*. New York: Scribner's.

Overmier, J. B., & Seligman, M. E. P. (1967). Effects of inescapable shock upon subsequent escape and avoidance learning. *Journal of Comparative and Physiological Psychology, 63,* 23–33.

Paivio, A. (1965). Abstractness, imagery and meaningfulness in paired-associate learning. *Journal of Verbal Learning and Verbal Behavior, 4,* 32–38.

Paivio, A. (1969). Mental imagery in associative learning and memory. *Psychological Review, 76*, 241–263.

Paivio, A. (1971). *Imagery and verbal processes.* New York: Holt, Rinehart & Winston.

Paivio, A., Yuille, J. C., & Madigan, S. (1968). Concreteness, imagery and meaningfulness values for 925 nouns. *Journal of Experimental Psychology, 76* (1, Pt. 2).

Parisi, T. (1987). Why Freud failed: Some implications for neuropsychology and sociobiology. *American Psychologist, 42*, 235–245.

Pearson, H. (1950). *Gilbert and Sullivan.* Toronto: Penguin.

Peele, S. (1981). Reductionism in the psychology of the eighties: Can biochemistry eliminate addiction, mental illness, and pain? *American Psychologist, 36*, 807–818.

Perkins, D. N. (1981). *The mind's best work.* Cambridge, MA: Harvard University Press.

Peterson, L. R., & Peterson, M. J. (1959). Short-term retention of individual verbal items. *Journal of Experimental Psychology, 58*, 193–198.

Peterson, S. B., & Potts, G. R. (1982). Global and specific components of information integration. *Journal of Verbal Learning and Verbal Behavior, 21*, 403–420.

Pfeiffer, J. E. (1982). *The creative explosion: An inquiry into the origins of art and religion.* New York: Harper & Row.

Pinel, J. P. (1997). *Biopsychology* (3rd ed.). Needham Heights, MA: Allyn & Bacon.

Pirsig, R. M. (1974). *Zen and the art of motorcycle maintenance.* New York: Bantam.

Plomin, R., & McClearn, G. E. (Eds.) (1993). *Nature and nurture and psychology.* Washington, DC: American Psychological Association.

Poincaré, H. (1952). Mathematical creation. In B. Ghiselin (Ed.), *The creative process* (pp. 33–42). New York: New American Library.

Polanyi, M. (1959). *The study of man.* Chicago: University of Chicago Press.

Polanyi, M. (1968). Logic and psychology. *American Psychologist, 23*, 27–43.

Polanyi, M. (1981). The creative imagination. In D. Dutton & M. Krausz (Eds.), *The concept of creativity in science and art* (pp. 91–108). London: Martinus Nijhoff.

Pope, A. (1951). An essay on criticism. In J. M. Smith & E. W. Parks (Eds.), *The great critics* (3rd ed., pp. 386–404). New York: Norton.

Popper, K. (1972). *The logic of scientific discovery.* London: Hutchinson.

Popper, K. (1981). The myth of inductive hypothesis generation. In R. T. Tweney, M. E. Doherty, & C. R. Mynatt (Eds.), *On scientific thinking* (pp. 109–111). New York: Columbia University Press.

Posner, M. (1978). *Chronometric explorations of mind.* Hillsdale, NJ: Erlbaum.

Postman, L. (1961a). Extra-experimental interference and the retention of words. *Journal of Experimental Psychology, 61*, 97–110.

Postman, L. (1961b). The present status of interference theory. In C. N. Cofer (Ed.), *Verbal learning and verbal behavior* (pp. 152–179). New York: McGraw-Hill.

Postman, L. (1963). One-trial learning. In C. N. Cofer & B. S. Musgrave (Eds.), *Verbal behavior and learning: Problems and processes* (pp. 295–321). New York: McGraw-Hill.

Postman, L. (1964). Short term memory and incidental learning. In A. W. Melton (Ed.), *Categories of human learning* (pp. 146–201). New York: Academic Press.

Postman, L. (1971). Organization and interference. *Psychological Review, 78,* 290–302.

Postman, L. (1972). A pragmatic view of organization theory. In E. Tulving & W. Donaldson (Eds.), *Organization of memory* (pp. 3–48). New York: Academic Press.

Postman, L., Stark, K., & Henschel, D. (1969). Conditions of recovery after unlearning. *Journal of Experimental Psychology Monographs, 82,* (1, Pt. 1).

Premack, A. J., & Premack, D. (1972). Teaching language to an ape. *Scientific American, 227,* 92–99.

Premack, D. (1965). Reinforcement theory. In D. Levine (Ed.), *Nebraska symposium on motivation.* Lincoln, NE: University of Nebraska Press.

Pylyshyn, Z. W. (1973). What the mind's eye tells the mind's brain. A critique of mental imagery. *Psychological Bulletin, 80,* 1–24.

Rachman, S. J., & Wilson, G. T. (1980). *The effects of psychological therapy* (2nd ed.). New York: Pergamon.

Randi, J. (1980). *Flim-flam!* New York: Lippincott & Crowell.

Rank, O. (1932). *Art and artist.* New York: Knopf.

Rank, O. (1961). *Psychology and the soul.* New York: A. S. Barnes.

Rescorla, R. (1988). Pavlovian conditioning: It's not what you think it is. *American Psychologist, 43,* 151–160.

Restle, F. A. (1962). The selection of strategies in cue learning. *Psychological Review, 69,* 320–343.

Reynolds, B. S. (1981). Erectile dysfunction: A review of behavioral treatment approaches. In R. J. Doitzman (Ed.), *Clinical behavior therapy and behavior modification* (Vol. 2, pp. 121–166). New York: Garland Press.

Rhine, J. B. (1953). *New world of the mind.* New York: Sloane.

Riegel, K. F. (1978). *Psychology, mon amour.* Boston: Houghton Mifflin.

Ring, K. (1967) Experimental social psychology: Some sober questions about some frivolous values. *Journal of Experimental Social Psychology, 3,* 113–123.

Rock, I. (1957). The role of repetition in associative learning. *American Journal of Psychology, 70,* 186–193.

Roe, A. (1951). A study of imagery in research scientists. *Journal of Personality, 19,* 459–470.

Roe, A. (1965). Changes in scientific activities with age. *Science, 150,* 313–318.

Roediger, H. L. III (1990). Implicit memory. *American Psychologist, 45,* 1043–1056.

Rogers, C. R. (1970). Towards a theory of creativity. In P. E. Vernon (Ed.), *Creativity* (pp. 137–151). New York: Penguin.

Rogers, C. R. (1973). Toward a modern approach to values: The valuing process in the mature person. In M. Bloomberg (Ed.), *Creativity: Theory and research* (pp. 115–128). New Haven CN: College & University Press.

Rogers, C. R. (1977). *Carl Rogers on personal power.* New York: Delacorte.

Rokeach, M., & Mezei, L. (1966). Race and shared belief as factors in social choice. *Science, 151,* 167–172.

Root-Bernstein, R. S. (1989). *Discovering.* Cambridge, MA: Harvard University Press.

Rosenhan, D. L. (1973). On being sane in insane places. *Science, 179,* 250–258.

Rosenthal, R., & Jacobson, L. F. (1968). Teacher expectations for the disadvantaged. *Scientific American, 218,* 19–23.

Rosenzweig, M. R. (1984). Experience and the brain. *American Psychologist, 39,* 365–376.

Rosenzweig, M. R., Bennett, E. L., & Diamond, M. C. (1972). Brain changes in response to experience. *Scientific American, 226,* 22–29.

Rothenberg, A. (1979). *The emerging goddess.* Chicago: The University of Chicago Press.

Rothenberg, A., & Hausman, C. R. (1976). Introduction. In A. Rothenberg & C. R. Hausman (Eds.), *The creativity question* (pp. 3–26). Durham, NC: Duke University Press.

Rowe, D. C. (1993). Genetic perspectives on personality. In R. Plomin & G. E. McClearn (Eds.), *Nature, nurture and psychology* (pp. 179–195). Washington, DC: American Psychological Association.

Rowe, D. C., & Waldman, I. D. (1993). The question "How?" reconsidered. In R. Plomin & G. E. McClearn (Eds.) *Nature, nurture and psychology* (pp. 355–373). Washington, DC: American Psychological Association.

Runco, M. A. (1988). Implicit theories and ideational creativity. Paper presented at the Creativity Conference, Pitzer College, Claremont, CA, Nov. 11–12.

Rushton, J. P. (1985). Differential K theory and race differences in E and N. *Personality and Individual Differences, 6,* 769–770.

Russell, B. (1969). *The autobiography of Bertrand Russell. The middle years: 1914–1944.* New York: Bantam.

Sage, W. (1974). Crime and the clockwork lemon. *Human Behavior, 3,* 16–25.

Salter, A. (1964). *The case against psychoanalysis.* New York: Citadel.

Sartre, J. P. (1947a). *The age of reason.* New York: Alfred A. Knopf.

Sartre, J. P. (1947b). *Existentialism.* New York: Philosophical Library.

Sartre, J. P. (1969). *Being and nothingness.* New York: Citadel.

Sartre, J. P. (1971). *Saint Genet: Actor and martyr.* New York: New American Library.

Sartre, J. P. (1981). *The words.* New York: Vintage.

Schab, F. R. (1991). Odor memory: Taking stock. *Psychological Bulletin, 109,* 242–251.

Schoenbaum, S. (1991). *Shakespeare's lives.* Oxford: Clarendon.

Schonfield, D., & Robertson, B. A. (1966). Memory storage and aging. *Canadian Journal of Psychology, 20,* 228–236.

Schrank, R. C. (1988). Creativity as a mechanical process. In R. Sternberg (Ed.), *The nature of creativity* (pp. 220–238). New York: Cambridge University Press.

Schultz, D. (1981). *The Hammer.* Toronto: Collins.

Sears, R. S. (1977). Sources of life satisfactions of the Terman gifted men. *American Psychologist, 32,* 119–128.

Segraves, R. J. (1981). Female sexual inhibition. In R. J. Doitzman (Ed.), *Clinical behavior therapy and behavior modification* (Vol. 2, pp. 33–71). New York: Garland.

Seligman, M. E. P. (1968). Chronic fear produced by unpredictable shock. *Journal of Comparative and Physiological Psychology, 66,* 402–411.

Sheffield, F. D., & Roby, T. B. (1950). Reward value of a nonnutrative sweet taste. *Journal of Comparative and Physiological Psychology, 43,* 471–481.

Sheffield, F. D., Wulff, J. J., & Backer, R. (1951). Reward value of copulation without sex drive reduction. *Journal of Comparative and Physiological Psychology, 44*, 3–8.

Sheldon, W. H. (1940). *The varieties of human physique.* New York: Harper.

Sheldon, W. H. (1942). *The varieties of temperament.* New York: Harper.

Shepard, R. N., & Metzler, J. (1971). Mental rotation of three-dimensional objects. *Science, 171*, 701–703.

Siegfried, T. (1996). Chemical glitches in the brain cell galaxy result in illness. *The Calgary Herald,* June 29.

Simon, H. A., & Newell, A. (1963). The uses and limitations of models. In M. H. Marx (Ed.), *Theories in contemporary psychology* (pp. 89–104). New York: Macmillan.

Simonton, D. K. (1984). *Genius, creativity and leadership.* Cambridge, MA: Harvard University Press.

Simonton, D. K. (1990). *Scientific genius: A psychology of science.* New York: Cambridge University Press.

Singer, B. F. (1971). Toward a psychology of science. *American Psychologist, 26,* 1010–1015.

Skinner, B. F. (1938). *The behavior of organisms.* New York: Appleton-Century-Crofts.

Skinner, B. F. (1948). *Walden II.* New York: Macmillan.

Skinner, B. F. (1950). Are theories of learning necessary? *Psychological Review, 57,* 193–216.

Skinner, B. F. (1951). How to teach animals. *Scientific American,* offprint # 423. San Francisco: Freeman.

Skinner, B. F. (1957). *Verbal behavior.* Englewood Cliffs, NJ: Prentice-Hall.

Skinner, B. F. (1963). The flight from the laboratory. In M. H. Marx (Ed.), *Theories in contemporary psychology* (pp. 323–338). New York: Macmillan.

Skinner, B. F. (1968). *The technology of teaching.* New York: Appleton-Century-Crofts.

Skinner, B. F. (1971). *Beyond freedom and dignity.* New York: Knopf.

Skinner, B. F. (1974). *About behaviorism.* New York: Knopf.

Skinner, B. F. (1976). A behavioral model of creation. In A. Rothenberg & C. R. Hausman (Eds.), *The creativity question* (pp. 267–273). Durham, NC: Duke University Press.

Skinner, B. F. (1980). *Cognition, creativity and behavior* (film). Colwell Systems.

Slamecka, N. J. (1960). Retroactive inhibition of connected discourse as a function of practice level. *Journal of Experimental Psychology, 59,* 104–108.

Slamecka, N. J. (1965). In defence of a new approach to old phenomena. *Psychological Review, 72,* 242–246.

Slamecka, N. J. (1966). Differentiation versus unlearning of verbal associations. *Journal of Experimental Psychology, 71,* 822–828.

Slamecka, N. J. (1967). *Human memory: Selected readings.* New York: Oxford University Press.

Slamecka, N. J. (1977). A case for response produced cues in serial learning. *Journal of Experimental Psychology: Human Learning and Memory, 3,* 222–232.

Smith, H. (1976). *Forgotten truth.* New York: Harper & Row.

Snow, C. P. (1959). *The two cultures and the scientific revolution.* New York: Cambridge University Press.

Solomon, R. L., & Wynne, L. C. (1953). Traumatic avoidance learning: Acquisition in normal dogs. *Psychological Monographs, 67,* (No. 354).

Solomon, R. L., & Wynne, L. C. (1954). Traumatic avoidance learning: The principles of anxiety conservation and partial irreversibility. *Psychological Review, 61,* 353–385.

Spearman, C. (1927). *The abilities of man.* New York: Macmillan.

Spence, J. T. (1985). Achievement American style: The rewards and costs of individualism. *American Psychologist, 40,* 1285–1295.

Spence, K. W. (1956). *Behavior theory and conditioning.* New Haven, CT: Yale University Press.

Spence, K. W. (1963a). The emphasis on basic functions. In M. H. Marx (Ed.), *Theories in contemporary psychology* (pp. 272–286). New York: Macmillan.

Spence, K. W. (1963b). Types of constructs in psychology. In M. H. Marx (Ed.), *Theories in contemporary psychology* (pp. 162–178). New York: Macmillan.

Sperling, G. (1960). The information available in brief visual presentations. *Psychological Monographs, 74* (Whole No. 498).

Sperry, R. W. (1964). The great cerebral commissure. *Scientific American, 210,* 42–52.

Sperry, R. W. (1968). Hemisphere deconnection and unity in conscious awareness. *American Psychologist, 23,* 723–733.

Sperry, R. W. (1969). A modified concept of consciousness. *Psychological Review, 76,* 532–536.

Sperry, R. W. (1970). An objective approach to subjective experience: Further explanation of a hypothesis. *Psychological Review, 77,* 585–590.

Sperry, R. W. (1977). Bridging science and values: A unifying view of mind and brain. *American Psychologist, 32,* 237–245.

Spitzer, R. L., Forman, J. B. W., & Nee, J. (1979). DSM-III field trials: 1. Initial inter-rater diagnostic reliability. *American Journal of Psychiatry, 136,* 815–817.

Spoto, D. (1992). *Laurence Olivier: A biography.* New York: Harper Collins.

Stanley, J. C., & Benbow, C. P. (1982). Huge sex ratios at upper ends. *American Psychologist, 37,* 972.

Stein, M. I. (1974). *Stimulating creativity, Vol. 1: Individual Procedures.* New York: Academic Press.

Stein, M. I., & Heinze, S. J. (1960). *Creativity and the individual: Summaries of selected literature in psychology and psychiatry.* Glencoe, IL: The Free Press.

Stendhal (1953). *Scarlet and black.* Harmondsworth, England: Penguin.

Stern, A. (1967). *Sartre: His philosophy and existential psychoanalysis.* New York: Dell.

Sternberg, R. J. (1985). *Beyond IQ: A triarchic theory of human intelligence.* New York: Cambridge University Press.

Sternberg, R. J., & Lubart, T. I. (1996). Investing in creativity. *American Psychologist, 51,* 677–688.

Sternberg, S. (1969). Memory scanning: Mental processes revealed by reaction-time experiments. *American Scientist, 57,* 421–457.

Stevens, S. S. (1961). To honor Fechner and repeal his law. *Science, 113,* 80–86.

Stevens, S. S. (1963). Operationism and logical positivism. In M. H. Marx (Ed.), *Theories in contemporary psychology* (pp. 47–76). New York: Macmillan.

Stone, A. A., & Stone, S. S. (1966). *The abnormal personality through literature.* Englewood Cliffs, NJ: Prentice-Hall.

Stone, I. (Ed.) (1937). *Dear Theo: The autobiography of Vincent van Gogh.* New York: New American Library.

Stoppard, T. (1967). *Rosencrantz and Guildenstern are dead.* New York: Grove.

Stravinsky, I. (1936). *An autobiography.* New York: Norton.

Strupp, H. H., & Binder, J. L. (1984). *Psychotherapy in a new key.* New York: Basic Books.

Szasz, T. S. (1966). The psychiatric classification of behavior: A strategy of personal constraints. In L. D. Eron (Ed.), *The classification of behavior disorders* (pp. 126–170). Chicago: Aldine.

Tannenbaum, A. J. (1986). Giftedness: A psychosocial approach. In R. M. Sternberg & J. E. Davidson (Eds.), *Conceptions of giftedness* (pp. 21–52). New York: Cambridge University Press.

Tart, C. T. (Ed.) (1969). *Altered states of consciousness.* New York: John Wiley.

Taylor, D. A. (1976). Stage analysis of reaction time. *Psychological Bulletin, 83,* 161–191.

Taylor, J. T. (1953). A personality scale of manifest anxiety. *Journal of Abnormal and Social Psychology, 48,* 285–290.

Taylor, R. (1979). *Richard Wagner: His life, art and thought.* London: Paul Elek.

Taylor, S. E., & Brown, J. D. (1988). Illusions and well being: A social psychological perspective on mental health. *Psychological Bulletin, 103,* 193–210.

Terman, L. M., & Merrill, M. A. (1973). *Stanford-Binet intelligence scale: 1972 norms edition.* Boston: Houghton-Mifflin.

Terman, L. M., & Oden, M. H. (1947). *Genetic studies of genius: IV. The gifted child grows up.* Stanford, CA: Stanford University Press.

Terman, L. M., & Oden, M. H. (1959). *Genetic studies of genius : V. The gifted group at mid-life.* Stanford, CA: Stanford University Press.

Thorndike, E. L. (1903). *Educational psychology.* New York: Lemcke and Buechner.

Tinbergen, N. (1951). *The study of instinct.* Oxford: Oxford University Press.

Tolman, E. C. (1932). *Purposive behavior in animals and men.* New York: Appleton-Century.

Tolman, E. C. (1959). Principles of purposive behavior. In S. Koch (Ed.), *Psychology: A study of a science* (Vol. 2, pp. 92–157). New York: McGraw-Hill.

Tolman, E. C., & Honzik, C. H. (1930). Introduction and removal of reward, and maze performance in rats. *University of California Publications in Psychology, 4,* 257–275.

Tolman, E. C., Ritchie, B. F., & Kalish, D. (1946). Studies in spatial learning: II. Place learning vs. response learning. *Journal of Experimental Psychology, 36,* 221–229.

Torrance, E. P. (1962). *Guiding creative talent.* Englewood Cliffs, NJ: Prentice-Hall.

Tulving, E. (1962). Subjective organization in free recall of "unrelated" words. *Psychological Review, 69,* 344–354.

Tulving, E. (1966). Subjective organization and the effects of repetition in multi-trial free-recall learning. *Journal of Verbal Learning and Verbal Behavior, 5,* 193–197.

Tulving, E. (1968). Theoretical issues in free recall. In T. R. Dixon & D. L. Horton (Eds.), *Verbal behavior and general behavior theory* (pp. 2–36). Englewood Cliffs, NJ: Prentice-Hall.

Tulving, E. (1972). Episodic and semantic memory. In E. Tulving & W. Donaldson (Eds.), *Organization and memory* (pp. 381–403). New York: Academic Press.

Tulving, E. (1985). How many memory systems are there? *American Psychologist, 40,* 385–398.

Turner, M. B. (1968). *Psychology and the philosophy of science.* New York: Appleton-Century-Crofts.

Turner, R. M., DiTomasso, R. A., & Delaty, M. (1985). Systematic desensitization. In R. M. Turner & L. M. Ascher (Eds.), *Evaluating behavior therapy outcomes* (pp. 15–55). New York: Springer.

Tweney, R. T., Doherty, M. E., & Mynatt, C. R. (Eds.). (1981). *On scientific thinking.* New York: Columbia University Press.

Underwood, B. J. (1948). Proactive and retroactive inhibition after five and forty-eight hours. *Journal of Experimental Psychology, 38,* 29–38.

Underwood, B. J. (1957a). Interference and forgetting. *Psychological Review, 64,* 49–60.

Underwood, B. J. (1957b). *Psychological research.* New York: Appleton-Century-Crofts.

Underwood, B. J. (1963). Stimulus selection in verbal learning. In C. N. Cofer & B. S. Musgrave (Eds.), *Verbal behavior and learning: Problems and processes* (pp. 33–48). New York: McGraw-Hill.

Underwood, B. J. (1964a). Degree of learning and the measurement of forgetting. *Journal of Verbal Learning and Verbal Behavior, 3,* 112–129.

Underwood, B. J. (1964b). The representativeness of rote verbal learning. In A. W. Melton (Ed.), *Categories of human learning* (pp. 47–78). New York: Academic Press.

Underwood, B. J. (1966). *Experimental psychology.* New York: Appleton-Century-Crofts.

Underwood, B. J. (1972). Are we overloading memory? In A. W. Melton & E. Martin (Eds.), *Coding processes in human memory* (pp. 1–23). Washington, DC: Winston.

Underwood, B. J. (1975). Individual differences as a crucible in theory construction. *American Psychologist, 30,* 128–134.

Underwood, B. J., Boruch, R. F., & Malmi, R. A. (1978). Composition of episodic memory. *Journal of Experimental Psychology: General, 107,* 393–419.

Underwood, B. J., & Ekstrand, B. R. (1966). An analysis of some shortcomings in the interference theory of forgetting. *Psychological Review, 73,* 540–549.

Underwood, B. J., & Schulz, R. (1960). *Meaningfulness and verbal learning.* Philadelphia: Lippincott.

Vasudev, J., & Hummel, R. C. (1987). Moral stage sequence and principled reasoning in an Indian sample. *Human Development, 30,* 105–118.

Viney, W. (1993). *A history of psychology: Ideas and context.* Boston: Allyn & Bacon.

Wagner, M. W., & Monnet, M. (1979). Attitudes of college professors toward extrasensory perception. *Zeletic Scholar, 5,* 7–17.

Wallace, D. B., & Gruber, H. (Eds.) (1988). *Creative people at work.* New York: Oxford University Press.

Wallach, M. A. (1985). Creativity testing and giftedness. In F. D. Horowitz & M. O'Brien (Eds.), *The gifted and talented: Developmental perspectives* (pp. 99–123). Washington: American Psychological Association.

Wallas, G. (1970). The art of thought. In P. E. Vernon (Ed.), *Creativity* (pp. 91–97). New York: Penguin.

Watson, J. B. (1913). Psychology as the behaviorist views it. *Psychological Review, 20,* 158–177.

Watson, J. B. (1929). *Psychology from the standpoint of a behaviorist* (3rd ed.). Philadelphia: Lippincott.

Watson, J. B. (1930). *Behaviorism* (2nd ed.). New York: Norton.

Watson, J. B., & Rayner, R. (1920). Conditioned emotional reactions. *Journal of Experimental Psychology, 3,* 1–14.

Watson, J. D. (1968). *The double helix.* New York: New American Library.

Watson, J. D. ((1977). Competition in science. *Dialogue, 10,* 18–24.

Watson, R. I. (1963). *The great psychologists.* Philadelphia: Lippincott.

Waugh, N. C., & Norman, D. A. (1965). Primary memory. *Psychological Review, 72,* 89–104.

Wechsler, D. (1958). *The measurement and appraisal of adult intelligence* (4th ed.). Baltimore: Williams & Wilkins.

Weisberg, R. (1986). *Genius and other myths.* San Francisco: Freeman.

Weisberg, R. (1993). *Creativity: Beyond the myth of genius.* New York: Freeman.

Weiten, W. (1995). *Psychology: Theme and variations* (3rd ed.). New York: Brooks/Cole.

Wertheimer, M. (1959). *Productive thinking.* New York: Harper and Brothers.

Westfall, R. S. (1980). *Never at rest: A biography of Isaac Newton.* New York: Cambridge University Press.

White, P. F. (1986). Patient-controlled analgesia: A new approach to the management of postoperative pain. *Seminars in Anaesthesia, 4,* 255–266.

Whorff, B. (1956). *Language, thought and reality.* New York: MIT Press-Wiley.

Wilkins, W. (1986). Placebo problems in psychotherapy research. *American Psychologist, 41,* 551–556.

Williams, M. (1985). Wittgenstein's rejection of scientific psychology. *Journal for the Theory of Social Behavior, 15,* 203–223.

Williams, R. (1983). *Keywords.* London: Fontana.

Wittgenstein, L. (1958). *Philosphical investigations* (3rd ed.). New York: Macmillan.

Wolpe, J. (1958). *Psychotherapy by reciprocal inhibition.* Palo Alto, CA: Stanford University Press.

Wolpe, J. (1974). *The practice of behavior therapy* (2nd ed.). New York: Pergamon.

Wood, G. (1985). *The myth of neurosis.* New York: Harper & Row.

Wooley, H. T. (1910). A review of the recent literature on the psychology of sex. *Psychological Bulletin, 7,* 335–342.

Woolf, V. (1977). *A room of one's own.* New York: Granada.

Woolfolk, R. L., & Richardson, F. C. (1984). Behavior therapy and the ideology of modernity. *American Psychologist, 39,* 777–786.

Wordsworth, W. (1952). Preface to second edition of lyrical ballads. In B. Ghiselin (Ed.), *The creative process* (pp. 83–84). New York: New American Library.

Wortman, C. B., Abbey, A., Holland, A. E., Silver, R. L., & Janoff-Bulman, R. (1980). Transitions from the laboratory to the field: Problems and progress. In L. Bickman (Ed.), *Applied social psychology annual* (Vol. 1, pp. 197–233). London: Sage.

Yates, F. A. (1966). *The art of memory*. London: Routledge & Kegan Paul.

Yerkes, R. M., & Dodson, J. D. (1908). The relation of strength of stimulus to rapidity of habit formation. *Journal of Comparative Neurology, 18*, 459–482.

Young, R. L. (1962). Tests of three hypotheses about the effective stimulus in serial learning. *Journal of Experimental Psychology, 63*, 307–313.

Young, R. L. (1968). Serial learning. In T. R. Dixon & D. L. Horton (Eds.), *Verbal behavior and general behavior theory* (pp. 122–145). Englewood Cliffs, NJ: Prentice-Hall.

Young, R. L., Hakes, D. T., & Hicks, R. Y. (1965). Effects of list length in the Ebbinghaus derived-list paradigm. *Journal of Experimental Psychology, 70*, 338–341.

Name Index

Abbey, A., 79
Adam, 88
Adams, H. E., 82
Adler, A., 41, 97, 130
Agranoff, B. W., 170
Allport, G., 71, 72, 74
Amabile, T., 40, 76
Amsel, A., 20
Angell, James, 21
Aquinas, St. Thomas, 102
Aristotle, x, 17, 120, 172, 182
Arnheim, R., 32
Asch, S., 49
Ashcroft, M. H., 89
Augustine, St., 102
Austen, Jane, 117

Baby Albert, 19, 62, 107
Bach, J. S., 25
Bacon, Francis, 51, 183
Baddeley, A., 157, 159
Ball, T. M., 139
Bandura, A., 97, 141-43
Banks, C., 124
Barnett, L., 120
Barron, F., 4
Bartlett, F. C., 136
Basie, Count, 39
Battig, W., 160, 164
Beamon, A. L., 80

Beauvoir, Simone de, 152
Becker, E., 46
Beckett, Samuel, 150
Beethoven, L. van, 70, 75, 76, 88
Benbow, C. P., 92
Berkeley, G., 17, 128
Berkowitz, L., 116
Bertalanffy, L. von, 173
Bevan, W., 48-49, 195
Bieber, I., 63
Binet, A., 25, 28, 160
Bloom, B. S., 28, 93
Bohm, D., 166
Bohr, N., 45, 120, 179
Boodoo, G., 110
Boring, E., 33, 158, 179, 181
Brain, Lord, 174
Bransford, J. D., 136-37
Breland, K., 79
Breland, M., 79
Bridgman, P. W., 1, 13
Broadbent, D., 131
Bronowski, J., 44, 47, 51
Brown, J. S., 188
Brown, R., 78
Brown, R. W., 78
Bruce, D., 158
Brutus, 36, 149
Bugelski, B. R., 89
Burgess, A., 87

Burtt, Cyril, 31, 31 n.1
Buss, A., 80

Caesar, Julius, 88
Campbell, D., 75, 125
Campbell, Joseph, 44
Camus, A., 183, 200
Cattell, R., 26
Charness, N., 89
Chein, I., 141, 143
Chekhov, Anton, 196
Chomsky, N., 117, 196
Chopin, F., 70
Christ, Jesus, 5, 45, 183
Cicero, 137
Cole, C. M., 80
Coleridge, Samuel, 51, 70, 165
Columbus, Christopher, 183
Comte, A., 1
Cooper, Gary, 151
Cooper, R., 35
Copernicus, N., 3, 6, 7, 103, 111
Craik, F. I. M., 134
Crick, F., 15, 46, 79
Cronbach, L. J., 93
Csikszentmihalyi, M., 4, 28, 144

Dallenbach, K. M., 66
Darley, J., 49
Darwin, Charles, 7, 15, 21, 25, 45, 51,
    54, 72-73, 75, 85, 103, 111, 127,
    129-30, 153, 166, 185, 190, 191,
    193, 195, 200
Davis, Bette, 91
Deese, J., 37
Delacroix, Eugene, 70
Demosthenes, 137
Descartes, R., x, 19, 36, 52, 165, 173,
    200
Dess, N. K., 89
Dewey, John, 21
Dickens, Charles, 13, 196
Dimberg, U., 80
Donders, F. C., 155, 156
Dostoevsky, Fyodor, 196
Dove, Adrian, 109
Dracula, Count, 170
Dunn, A. J., 170

Easterbrook, J. A., 148
Eastwood, Clint, 26
Ebbinghaus, H., 20-21, 78, 156
Eccles, J. C., 175-76, 184
Einstein, Albert, xiii, 3, 9, 10, 12, 13,
    28, 31, 40, 45, 99, 166, 179, 182,
    183, 201
Eisenberg, L., 86
Ekstrand, B., 77
Eliot, George, 39, 75, 196
Elizabeth I, 105
Ellis, A., 143-44
Erasmus, Desiderius, 102
Erikson, E., 68, 69
Essex, Earl of, 105
Eysenck, H., 26, 27, 80, 84, 87

Falwell, J., 5, 183
Fechner, G. T., 56
Feldman, D., 91
Feldman, M., 64, 82
Festinger, L., 81, 200
Feyerabend, P., xi, 196
Fischer, Bobby, 91
Ford, Henry, 122
Frankl, V., 82, 144-45
Franks, J. J., 136-37
Freud, S., xiii, xiv, 16, 22, 41-42, 45,
    46, 62, 64, 66, 68, 75, 76, 81, 94,
    103-4, 107, 109, 114, 122-23, 127,
    130, 142, 146, 155, 159, 166, 175,
    182, 186-187 n.1, 194, 200
Friday, Joe, 21
Friedman, L. M., 123
Fromm, E., 4, 82, 115
Frye, Northrop, 192

Galileo, G., 6, 7, 44, 99
Galton, F., 25, 28, 108, 109, 138, 140-
    41, 155
Gardner, H., 91-92, 94, 118, 122, 160,
    162, 168, 201
Gauss, K. F., 12
Geller, Uri, 11
Genet, Jean, 151
Genovese, Kitty, 49
Gergen, K. J., 94-95
Getzels, J., 4, 28

Gigerenzer, G., 193
Gilbert, W. S., 79, 146
Gilligan, G., 92
Glass, D. C., 123
Glucksberg, S., 188
Gogh, Vincent van, 39
Goldberg, P., 35
Goldstein, D. G., 193
Gordon, Charlie, 88
Goya, Francisco, 70
Gradgrind, Mr., 13-14, 183
Graham, Martha, 75, 92, 127
Grand Inquisitor, The, 45
Gray, Dorian, 47
Gretzkey, Wayne, 105, 181
Griffey, Ken, Jr., 141
Gruber, Howard, 72-73, 76, 92, 129-30
Gruneberg, M., 78
Guilford, J. P., 28, 75, 160-62, 164,
    201
Guthrie, E. R., 133

Hakes, D. T., 23
Hamlet, 33, 34, 81
Haney, C., 124
Harlow, H., 22, 198, 200
Harré, R., 12, 92-93, 147-48, 164
Harvey, William, 2
Hausman, C. R., 127
Haydn, J., 71
Hebb, D. O., iii, 168-69, 171, 172,
    173, 174, 175, 177, 198, 200
Hegel, Georg W. F., 149, 150
Heisenberg, Werner, 120
Henderson, Paul, 78
Hicks, R. Y., 23
Hilgard, E. L., 190
Hill, W., 133, 180
Hinkley, John, 116
Hippocrates, 26
Hitler, A., 6, 48, 128
Hoffer, E., 182
Holland, A. E., 79
Holmes, Sherlock, 136
Horatio, 34
Housman, A. E., 43
Houston, J. P., 88, 89
Howard, G. S., 48, 49
Hubel, D. H., 168

Hudson, L., 94
Hull, C. L., xiii-xiv, 21, 104, 107, 133,
    147, 157, 168, 184-90, 191, 200
Hume, David, 10, 17, 54, 127, 128,
    181, 191
Huxley, A., 87, 127

Ibsen, Henrik, 125
Irion, A. L., 89

Jacklin, C. N., 115, 118
Jacobsen, L. F., 14, 86
James, William, 5, 12, 16, 17, 162,
    198, 200
Janoff-Bulman, R., 79
Jaynes, J., 96, 148-49
Jenkins, J. B., 66
Jensen, A., 109-13, 126, 157
Johnson, Samuel, 15, 141-42
Jones, Indiana, 105
Jones, S., 197
Joyce, James, 110
Jung, C. G., 26, 41, 42, 76, 199, 200
Juschka, B., 118

Kamin, L. J., 31, 130
Kant, I., x, 127, 128, 144, 165, 191
Karamazov, Alyosha, 46
Karamazov, Ivan, 45
Keats, John, 39, 70
Kendler, H. H., 192
Kennedy, President John F., 78
Kepler, J., 7, 111
Kesey, K., 88
Kessel, F. S., 195
Keyes, D., 88
Keynes, John Maynard, 73
Khomeni, Ayatollah, 6
Kierkegaard, S., 149, 150
Kimble, G., xi, 188
Klentz, B., 80
Koch, S., 8, 43
Koestler, Arthur, 51, 153
Koffka, K., 163
Kohlberg, L., 68, 69, 92
Köhler, W., 129, 163
Kosslyn, S. M., 139
Kraepelin, E., 64
Kris, E., 83

Kuhn, T., 9-10, 11, 18, 35, 43, 46,
   158, 194
Kulik, J., 78

Laing, R. D., 152
Landman, J., 196-97
Langer, S., 34, 43, 173, 176
Lashley, K., 158, 163, 164, 167-68,
   198, 200
Latané, B., 49
Lefcourt, H. M., 123-24
Leibniz, G., 15
Lenin, V., 18
Lewin, K., 145-46, 147
Lindzey, G., 109
Linnaeus, Carl, 52, 83
Linton, M., 77-78
Locke, John, x, 17, 128, 155
Loehlin, J., 109
Loftus, E., 137, 176
Loftus, G. R., 176
Loman, Willy, 85
Lorenz, Konrad, 114-15
Louis XIV, 106
Lubart, T. I., 40, 193
Lubinski, D., 92
Luria, A. R., 138
Luther, Martin, 102
Lysenko, T., 126

Maccoby, E. E., 115, 118
MacCullough, M. J., 64
Madigan, S., 139
Mailer, Norman, 142
Malagrida, R. P., 16
Malpighi, M., 2
Malthus, T., 51, 130
Marlowe, Christopher, 105
Marshall, Donald, 4
Martin, E., 131-32, 134
Marx, Karl, 103, 126, 182
Marx, M. H., 179, 198
Maslow, A., 34, 45-46, 47, 75, 87,
   117, 124, 144, 148, 149, 165, 190,
   195
Mason, Perry, 136
May, R., 44, 46, 82, 88, 124
Mazur, J. E., 79
McCarthy, Senator Joseph, 133

McConnell, J. V., 170
McGeogh, J., 21, 89
McNeill, D., 78
Mednick, S. A., 189
Mendel, G., 107
Mendeleev, Dmitri, 52, 83
Mettrie, J. de la, 173
Metzler, J., 139-40
Milgram, S., 49-50
Miller, Arthur, 85
Miller, G., 49, 117, 135
Miller, Henry, 127
Mills, James, 162
Mills, John Stuart, 162
Milner, Brenda, 169
Milner, P., 171
Milquetoast, Casper, 28
Mnemosyne, 137
Molière, 33
Monnet, M., 11
Morison, R. S., 52
Morris, P. E., 78
Mowrer, O. H., 125, 144, 190
Mozart, W. A., 58, 71, 91, 99, 133

Natsoulas, N., 174
Neisser, U., 78, 110, 195
Newton, Isaac, 9, 15, 44, 45, 52, 99,
   166, 182, 201
Nickles, T., 192
Nietzsche, F., 75, 97, 124, 126, 127,
   128, 191
Nijinsky, V., 40
Nisbett, R. E., 16
Nixon, President Richard, 176

Oedipus, 62
Ohman, A., 80
Olds, J., 171
Olivier, Laurence, 26
O'Neill, Eugene, 76
Ornstein, R., 37-38, 166
Orwell, George, 85, 87, 88
Osborn, A. F., 79
Ost, L. G., 80
Overmier, J. B., 63, 89

Paivio, A., 90, 139, 140
Parisi, T., 175

Pasteur, Louis, 10
Pavlov, I., 18, 19, 20, 46, 52, 87
Peat, F. D., 166
Peele, S., 174
Penfield, W., 167, 176
Perot, P., 167, 176
Pfeiffer, J. E., 96
Piaget, J., xiv, 26, 68-69, 72, 74, 91-
    92, 93, 122, 129, 159, 160, 196,
    198, 200
Picasso, Pablo, 72
Pilate, Pontius, 95
Pinter, Harold, 44
Pirsig, R. M., 39, 40, 165-66, 177
Plato, x, 104, 159, 166
Poincaré, H., 13, 40, 42
Polanyi, M., 11-12, 38, 163, 175
Polonius, 5
Pope, Alexander, 199
Popper, K., 10, 48, 103, 168, 181-82,
    183-84, 190, 192, 200
Porter, Cole, 95
Postman, L., 78, 159
Premack, D., 187
Preston, M., 80
Procrustes, 40, 177, 192
Proxmire, Senator W., 3
Pylyshyn, Z. W., 140

Rand, Ayn, 87
Rank, O., 177
Rayner, R., 18, 19
Reagan, President Ronald, 116
Reisser, B. J., 139
Rescorla, R., 130
Richardson, F. C., 82
Ring, K., 50
Roberts, Oral, 5
Robinson, D. N., 175-76
Roe, A., 141
Rosenhan, D. L., 86
Rosenthal, R., 14, 86
Rosenzweig, M., 169
Rothenberg, A., 127
Rushton, P., 111-13
Russell, Bertrand, 13, 54

Salieri, Antonio, 133
Sartre, J. P., 86, 97, 150-52, 200

Schab, F. R., 89
Schultz, Dave, 115
Schulz, R., 159, 160
Schumann, Robert, 70
Secord, P. F., 147-48
Seligman, M. E. P., 63
Sellers, Peter, 26
Shakespeare, William, 105, 196, 198
Sheldon, W. H., 27
Shepard, R. N., 139-40
Sherrington, C., 172
Silver, R. L., 79
Simon, T., 25
Simonton, D. K., 72, 73, 97
Singer, J. E., 123
Sisyphus, 183
Skinner, B. F., ix, xiv, 19, 46, 49, 54,
    57-61, 69, 75, 76-77, 79, 80, 81, 82,
    96, 104-7, 108, 116, 117, 121, 123,
    124, 125, 128, 141, 142, 146, 156,
    164, 168, 180, 184, 185, 190, 194,
    201
Slamecka, N. J., 77, 131, 158
Smith, H., 198
Snow, C. P., 197
Socrates, 16, 46, 51, 166
Spearman, C., 160
Spence, J. T., 31
Spence, K., 157, 190, 198
Sperry, R. W., 174-75, 176
Spinoza, Baruch, 45
Spock, Dr., 115
Spuhler, J., 109
Stebloy, N. M., 80
Stein, Gertrude, 11
Sternberg, R., 40, 193
Sternberg, S., 156
Stevens, S. S., 5, 57
Stone, A. A., 196
Stone, S. S., 196
Stoppard, Tom, 150
Stravinsky, Igor, 40, 92, 127
Sturgis, E. T., 82
Sullivan, Arthur, 79, 146
Swaggert, Jimmy, 183
Sykes, R. N., 78
Szasz, T. S., 83, 86

Terman, L. M., 25

Thomas, Doubting, 5
Thorndike, E. L., 22
Titchener, E., 138
Tolman, E. C., 4, 21, 107, 132-33,
    147, 185, 196, 200
Tulving, E., 90, 134, 136
Turner, J. M. W., 70

Underwood, B. J., x, 67, 77, 78, 153,
    159, 160, 165, 198

Valentine-French, S., 118
Vinci, Leonardo da, 41, 103, 182

Wagner, M., 11
Wagner, Richard, 70
Wallace, A. L., 15
Watkins, M. J., 134
Watson, James, 10, 15, 46, 79
Watson, John B., 17-19, 20, 21, 25,
    33, 36-37, 44, 46, 59, 71, 98, 104,
    105, 107, 123, 127, 131, 139, 168,
    184, 193, 194, 195, 196, 200
Wayne, John, 26
Weber, E. H., 56
Wechsler, D., 160

Weisberg, R., 75
Welles, Orson, 86, 116
Wertheimer, M., 163
Whitehead, Alfred North, 159
Wiesel, T. N., 168
Wilde, Oscar, 63
Wilkins, W., 174
Wilson, T. D., 16
Winograd, E., 78
Wittgenstein, L., 95, 148
Wood, G., 144
Wooley, H. T., 118
Woolf, Virginia, 76, 196
Woolfolk, R. L., 82
Wordsworth, William, 34, 70, 71
Wortman, C. B., 78
Wundt, W., 16, 18, 20, 21, 24, 127,
    138, 155, 156, 162, 163

Yeats, William Butler, 167
Young, R., 22-23, 131, 157
Yuille, J. C., 139

Zeigarnik, B., 145
Zeus, 137
Zimbardo, P., 124

Subject Index

Abortion, 47, 60, 126
Absurd, the, 150
Academic freedom, 110-13
Accommodation, 69
Acetylcholine, 169, 171
Acronyms, 21, 135
Action research, 146
Active subject, 128-52, 193, 195
Actors, 26
Actuaries, 72
Addictions, 56, 62, 82, 148
Adjustment, 87
Advertising, 18, 60
Africa, 182
Afterlife, 177
Aggression, 83, 114-16, 126-27, 151-52
Aging, 47, 56; in computers, 192; and intelligence, 93; and memory, 68, 90-91, 121; as a subject for study, 74, 195; as a subject variable, 101
AIDS, 5, 7, 47
Alchemy, 166, 191
Alcoholism, 108, 126, 169
Alienation, 115, 124
All Quiet on the Western Front, 104
Altruism, 106-7, 123
Alzheimer's disease, 171
Amadeus (Shaffer), 133

American Dream, the, 108
America's Funniest Videos, ix
Amnesia, 90, 176
Analysis, criticisms of; 162-67; definition of, xiv; in psychology, 155-62, 191; in science, 153-54
Analysis of variance, 102
Anatomy, 153, 167
Anectine, 88
Animals, 19, 22, 33, 37, 43, 52, 55-56, 58, 72, 73-74, 76, 79, 86, 106, 133, 167-68, 199; creativity in, 96, 121; differences to people, 97, 115, 116, 121, 147, 148, 173, 176-77, 195; ethical treatment of, 85; sense of history in, 97
Anomalies, 9, 10, 69
Anorexia nervosa, 55, 172
Anthropomorphism, 74
Antivivisection, 85
Anxiety, 82, 144, 149-52, 185
APA (American Psychological Association), xv, 50, 73, 145, 160, 167, 195
A priori abilities, 128
APS (American Psychological Society), 73, 167
Archaeology, 62
Archetypes, 41, 42

Architecture, 74

Art, 9, 13, 28-29, 32, 34, 38, 39, 41, 43-44, 72, 74, 79, 84, 93, 133, 196, 197; child prodigies in, 91; contrasted to science, 181, 182; romanticism in, 70-71; similarities to science, 51; as source of knowledge, 196-98; visual, 118, 168

Artificial intelligence. See Intelligence, artificial (AI)

Artists, xi, 70-71, 75, 197; Freud as, 182; sense of responsibility in, 127

Aryan myth, 53, 75, 109. See also Fascism

Asia, 92

Assimilation, 69

Association, the, 17-18, 80; bizarre, 138; dominant, 163; in levels of processing, 134; one-trial learning of, 191; R-S, 59, 128; S-R, 18, 20-24, 59, 133; verbal, 66-67, 77, 88-91. See also Contiguity; Learning, paired-associate; Learning, serial

Astrology, 181, 200

Astronomy, 4, 7, 15, 24, 43, 103, 111, 154, 182, 200

Atheism, 45

Athletes, 191

Atomic structure, 179

Attention, 131, 142, 145

Attitudes, 60, 108, 148, 174, 199; change of, 60-61, 80; surveys of, 147-48

Auschwitz, ix

Autonomic nervous system, 26

Autonomous man, 105-7, 125

Awareness. See Consciousness; Self-monitoring

Bad faith, 150

Ballet. See Dance

Baseball, 91, 141

Beauty, 165

Behavior genetics, 126

Behaviorism, xi, 18-20, 21, 25, 36-37, 41, 43, 46, 47, 94; analytic bias of, 156, 163; applications to creativity, 166; and attitudes, 61; determinism in, 104-7; evolutionary bias of, 55,

73-74, 75, 85, 191, 193; Gestalt reaction against, 129, 163-64; hegemony of, 196; humanists' reaction against, 75, 127; ignoring of brain's role, 168; ignoring of groups, 146; and imagery, 139; nurture bias of, 107, 109, 111, 157, 184, 191, 195; passive view of subjects, 128, 135, 136, 147, 195; radical, 57-59; Tolman's version of, 132-33

Behavior therapies, 62-64, 81-82, 88

Belief congruence, 60

Beyond Freedom and Dignity (Skinner), 106

Bible, 6, 183

Big bang theory, 96

Bingo. See Gambling

Biographies, 54

Biology, 83, 138

Bipolar mood disorder, 83, 171

Birth, 183

Bisociation, 51, 166, 179

Blocking, 130-131

Boredom, 115

Botany, 18, 52, 99

Boulder model. See Scientist-practitioner model

Boyle-Charles law, xiv, 53

Brain, 37-38, 55, 174; effects of damage to, 167-69, 171-72, 177; localization of function in, 118, 167-71; plasticity of, 168; sex differences in, 118; stimulation of as reinforcing, 187. See also Cerebral cortex; Hypothalamus

Brainstorming, 79

Brainwashing, 61, 80, 81

Brave New World (Huxley), 87, 127

Brooklyn, 81

Brooklyn Bridge, 31

Buddhism, 38

Bulimia, 55, 144, 172

Bull Durham, 141

Bystander apathy, 49-50, 94

Calgary Herald, 56

Canada, 1, 4, 12, 61, 78, 84, 111

Cancer, 3, 5, 7, 61, 79, 83, 87, 101

Cannibalism, in planaria, 170
Capillaries, 2, 153
Capital punishment, 47, 60
Caretaker, The (Pinter), 44
Cartoons, 106, 116
Castration complex, 103
Causality, xiv, 98. *See also*
  Determinism; Indeterminism
Ceiling effect, 77
Cell assembly, 168-69
Censorship, 6, 110, 116
Cerebral cortex, 37, 167. *See also* Brain
Chaining hypothesis, 22-24, 157, 158
Chemistry, 43, 52-53, 83, 153, 154,
  164, 200; mental, 155, 162
Chess, 89, 91, 173
Child prodigies, 86, 91-92
Children, 26, 37, 41, 52, 53, 56, 73,
  74, 86, 107, 109, 195; Freud's view
  of, 104; games played by, 151;
  language learning in, 116-17, 160; as
  models of creators, 191; permissive
  rearing of, 115; raising of, 142;
  stages of development of, 68-69, 93
China, 81
Chitlings Test, 109
Christianity, 45, 102-3, 183
Christmas, 56
Chronometry. *See* Information
  processing
Chunk, 135
Circularity of reasoning, 122-23, 192
Citizen Kane, 86
Civil rights movement, 110
Civil service, 166
Classical understanding, 165-66
Classic experiments. *See* Experiments,
  classic
Classics, 167
Classification, 37, 52-53, 138; in
  psychology, 64-65, 82-85. *See also*
  Generalization
Clockwork Orange, A (Burgess), 87,
  126
Close-binding mother, 63
Clustering, 135. *See also* Organization
Cocktail party phenomenon, 131
Coding, 136-37. *See also* Memory
Coffee dispensers, 128

Cognition, 37, 59; Bandura's view of,
  142-43; computer models of, 175,
  181; development of, 68-69, 91-92;
  textbooks of, 157. *See also* Therapy,
  cognitive behavior
Cognitive dissonance, 81, 145, 183
Cognitive Psychology (Neisser), 195
Cognitive revolution, xi, xiii, 128-52,
  157-59, 190, 191, 194-96. *See also*
  Active subject
Cold War, 96, 138
Coliseum, 96
Collaboration, 114, 144
Collective unconscious, 41
Communism, 48, 61, 81, 103, 126, 182
Compensation, 130
Competition. *See* Aggression
Computers, 60, 94, 121, 134, 167;
  differences to people, 147, 175, 192-
  93; as models for cognition, 181,
  192-93
Concentration camps, 49, 50, 87, 144-
  45
Conceptual devices, 179-93; in
  psychology, 179, 184-93, 196; in
  science, 179-81. *See also*
  Hypotheses; Laws; Models; Theories
Conditioning: classical, 18-20, 57, 58,
  73, 80, 88, 89, 130-131, 160, 167,
  170, 188, 190; counter, 63, 64;
  differences between types, 59;
  operant, 57-64, 160, 190; vicarious,
  20, 115-16, 118, 141, 142, 192
Confidence, 105
Conflict, 145
Conformity, 49-50, 87, 94
Confound, 99, 101
Consciousness, x, 16-18, 37, 38, 62;
  altered states of, 38, 138; analysis of,
  155; origins of, 148-49; relation to
  brain processes of, 173-76; stream
  of, 17, 128, 162, 175
Conservation problem, 68
Consolidation, 169, 170
Constant probability of success model,
  72-73
Contiguity, 18, 19, 22, 57, 80, 128,
  135, 190. *See also* Association
Contingencies. *See* Reinforcement

Controlled experiments. *See*
Experiments, controlled
Conversation, 44
Cooperation, 127
Corpus callosum, 126
Corpuscularean view of nature, 154, 164
Correlation, 101, 102, 121, 177
Crafts, 118
Creationism, 10-11
Creativity, xi, 4, 9, 25, 28-29, 32, 33,
50, 97, 195, 199; Adler's view of,
130; age and, 166; appropriate
populations for studying, 75-76;
Camus' view of, 183; collaboration
in, 79, 146; confluence approach to,
40; consensus definition of, 40; as
deterministic, 127; differences to
problem solving, 176-77; eclectic
approach to, 40, 73, 166-67, 196;
elitist views of, 76, 117;
environments for fostering, 76, 105,
117, 127; in experimenters, 76; as
field specific, 91, 118, 122; Freud's
explanation of, 103, 127, 142; God
and, 45, 96; Guilford's studies of,
160-62; Hullian explanation of, 185,
189; humanist views of, 117;
inspiration in, 51, 129-30, 148, 189;
in language usage, 117, 176;
measures of, 161-62, 189;
mechanism behind, 166, 179; as a
metaneed, 148-49; methods for
improving, 79; methods for studying,
72-73, 196; models of, 191, 192;
motivation of, 40, 46, 73, 76, 96,
127, 152, 166, 181; in nature, 95;
neglect of, 39-40, 160; peak
experiences in, 45; pre-romantic
views of, 70; reductionistic
approaches to, 176-77; romantic
views of, 71; scarcity in modern
science of, 166; in self-actualized
people, 75; sex difference in, 40,
118-19, 121, 142, 166; Skinner's
account of, 58, 117, 141-42; stages
of, 159; as unique to humans, 96, 97,
176-77
Crime, 136, 137, 148, 154

Criminals, 26, 62, 73, 88, 101;
rehabilitation of, 107
Critical experiments. *See* Experiments,
critical
Critical periods, 68, 117
Critics/criticism, 32, 44, 76, 127, 177,
182, 196
Crusades, 6
Cultural relativism, 94-95
Curve fitting, 192

Dance, xiii, 40, 92, 118, 127, 152, 162
Dancer's World, A, 75
Dark Ages, 190
Data, 2, 6-7, 9; changes over time in,
94; as means to resolve controversy,
2-3; 10-14, 110
Death, 46-47, 73, 74, 96, 150-51, 177,
199
Death of a Salesman (Miller), 85
Deduction, method of, 52, 185
Deindividuation, 125
Delinquency, 52, 108, 125
Demand characteristics, 14, 79, 147
Denmark, 34
Dentistry, 170
Dependent variable, 99
Depression, 62-63, 83, 84, 125, 143,
144, 171. *See also* Neurosis
Desensitization, 63
Detective stories, 182
Determinism: definition of, xiv;
existential view of, 150-52; as
limited to simple entities, 165;
problems with, 120-28; in
psychology, 57, 98, 100-8, 121-52;
reciprocal, 142-43; religion and, 45;
in science, 98-100, 120. *See also*
Causality
Diabetes, ix, 65
Dialectical process, 196-97
Dignity, 105-8, 125
Disequilibrium, 69, 129, 145
Distributed practice, 77
Divergent thinking, 28
Divorce, 108
DNA (Deoxyribonucleic acid), 10, 15,
46, 154, 170

Doctrine of formal discipline, 21-22
Dogma, 6, 9, 10, 102, 183, 198
Dopamine, 172
Double blind experiments. *See*
   Experiments, double blind
Dragnet, 21
Drama, 147, 196
Dreams, 41-42, 62, 94, 104
Drive. *See* Motivation
Drugs, in therapy, 82-83, 84, 87-88,
   171-72, 174
DSMs (*Diagnostic and Statistical
   Manuals of Mental Disorders*), 64-65,
   82-85
Dual-coding hypothesis, 139

Earthquakes, 99
Eclipse, solar, 3
Ecological validity. *See* Validity,
   ecological
Economics, 46, 154, 155, 196
ECS (Electroconvulsive shock), 83, 169
Ectomorph, 27-28
Education, 22, 25, 30-31, 59-60, 68,
   80; Gardner's influence on, 92; and
   income, 101; of psychologists, 102,
   121, 197; purpose of, 192. *See also*
   Learning
EEG (Electroencephalograph), 38
Electrons, 153, 154
Elephants, 163
Emotion, 19-20, 26-27, 33-34, 82; in
   artistic expression, 71; and attitudes,
   61; brain localization of, 168;
   control over behavior of, 105, 193;
   as inborn, 107; and vicarious
   conditioning, 20
Empiricism: drawbacks of, 30-50; Dust
   Bowl, 21; Hull's emphasis of, 186; in
   psychology, 15-29; rule of, 1-5, 7-8,
   11-14, 111, 195. *See also*
   Operational definitions
Encoding variability hypothesis, 131-
   32, 134
Endocepts, 38, 96
Endomorph, 27
Engineering, 197, 200
England. *See* Great Britain
Engram, 167-71

Enlightened despot, 106
Enlightenment, 6, 70, 71, 127, 128,
   191
Entropy, 95
Environment. *See* Learning
Epilepsy, 38
Equilibrium, 69, 129
Errors of commission, 136-37, 176
ESP (Extrasensory perception), 11, 14
Essence, 150
Ethics. *See* Morals
Ethology, 68, 76, 114-15
Europe, 70, 149
Evolution, 20, 55-56, 58, 95, 96, 114,
   125; theory of, 10, 15, 21, 25, 51-
   52, 54, 55-56, 57, 72-73, 75, 85,
   103, 111, 129-30, 153, 154
Evolving systems approach, 72-73
Existential philosophy, xi, 41, 149-52,
   166, 196
Expectancies, 133, 141
Experimental aesthetics, 32-33, 39
Experimental confound. *See* Confound
Experimenter bias, 14, 80
Experiments: classic, xiii, 13, 190-91;
   controlled, 99, 146, 147, 195;
   critical, 3, 14, 22-24, 95, 182;
   double blind, 14; part-to-whole, 135-
   36; repeated measures, 100; subject
   variable, 100-101, 110, 118, 121
Extinction, 171
Extraversion, 26, 80, 84
Eyewitness testimony, 137

Factor analysis, 26, 161
Falsifiability, 181-82, 186
Fascism, 4, 53, 75, 96, 104, 126
Fechner's Law, 57
Feminism, 74, 110, 199
Fictional goals, 41, 42, 130
Field of Dreams, 141
Field theory, 146
Film, 36, 79
Five Easy Pieces, 196
Flow. *See* Peak experiences
Flowers for Algernon (Keyes), 88
Foot-in-the-door technique, 61, 80
Forgetting. *See* Memory
Formal episodes, 147

Frames of mind. *See* Mind, frames of
Fraternal twins, 108
Free association, 41, 62. *See also*
    Psychoanalysis
Free will, 102, 107, 120, 124; Chein's
    view of, 143; as compatible with
    determinism, 148-49; existential
    view of, 150-52. Skinner's view of,
    105-7. *See also* Responsibility
French Revolution, 4, 105
Freudian slip, 103, 186-187 n.1
Frustration, 20; and aggression, 115;
    Hullian explanation of, 185; and
    persistence, 123-24
Functionalism, 20-24, 66, 78, 131,
    157, 159, 180
Functional relationship, 21, 99, 180
Fundamental project, 151

GABA (Gamma-aminobutyric acid), 172
Galápagos islands, 51
Gallipoli, 104
Gallup poll, 100
Gambling, 55, 93
Ganzfeld, 11
Garden of Eden, 183
Gaze, the, 151-52
Generalization, 5; definition of, xiv;
    existentialist attitude towards, 150;
    Hull's practice of, 184; as opposite to
    analysis, 153, 155, 164; problems
    with, 70-97; in psychology, 54-69,
    195; in science, 51-54, 153, 155
Generative ideas, 43. *See also*
    Paradigms
Genesis, Book of, 6
Genetic engineering, 40, 47
Genius, 25, 76, 109, 117, 128, 195
Gentleman's *C*, 199
Geology, 8-9
Germans/Germany, 20, 128-29, 146
Gerontology. *See* Aging
Giftedness. *See* Creativity
Glial cells, 170
Glutamate, 172
God, 7, 45, 49, 52, 96, 97, 102, 103,
    111, 120, 183
God Save the Queen, 58
Golden Rule, 106-7

Gordian knot, 200
Gradient of deepening coherence, 38
Great Britain, 18, 58, 70, 158
Greece/Greeks, 10, 84, 149, 166
Grief, 198
Groups, 60, 146. *See also* Psychology,
    social
Guilt, 86, 125, 141, 144, 152

Habit, 18; rituals of, 114
Habit-family hierarchy, 187-89
Habit strength, 184-89
Hamlet (Shakespeare), 34, 177
Happiness, 144
Hard Times (Dickens), 13
Headaches, 144
Head Start, 109
Heisenberg principle, 14, 16, 120
Heredity, 57, 76, 79-80, 101, 105, 106,
    154, 170. *See also* Nature-nurture
    issue
Heritability, 109
Heuristics, 96
Hierarchies, 52, 64-65, 135, 138, 153,
    173, 174-75, 180
Hierarchy of needs, 117, 148-49, 190
Hiroshima, 15, 47, 88
History, 6, 45, 97, 106, 114, 118, 122,
    125, 158, 182, 194
HMS *Beagle*, 54
Hobbies, 4, 113
Hockey, 78, 105, 115, 160, 181
Home on the Range, 12
Homosexuality, 63-64, 82, 83, 84,
    122, 126
Hope, 74, 124-25, 146
Horse racing, 40, 123, 181
Human engineering, 48
Humanities, the, 113, 196, 197, 198
Human nature. *See* Essence
Humor, 74, 114, 150, 191, 192
Humpty Dumpty, 154
Hunger drive, 55, 58, 80, 148, 171-72,
    185, 186, 187
Hypnosis, 63, 134
Hypothalamus, 55, 126, 171-72
Hypotheses. *See* Theories
Hypothesized entities, 2, 12, 24-29,
    33, 41, 132-33, 168, 184, 186

Hypothetical constructs, 2

Identical elements, 22
Identical twins, 31 n.1, 108-10
Idiographic methods, 54, 71-73, 92, 130, 148
Iliad, The (Homer), 149
Imageless thought controversy, 139
Imagery, 25, 89, 137-41
Imagination, 70; Coleridge's view of, 165; Kant's view of, 128; in research, 122
Imitation. *See* Conditioning, vicarious
Incest, 41
Independent variable, 99-100, 102
Indeterminism, 45. *See also* Causality
Individual differences, 24-29, 54-55, 59, 71, 100, 126, 150, 155, 192
Induction, method of, 9, 47, 51-52, 54, 181, 185
Industrial Revolution, 3
Inferiority complex, 130
Infinite regress, 120, 164
Information processing, 155-56
Inhibition, retroactive and proactive. *See* Interference
Inquisition, ix, 6
Insight, 129
Instincts, 107, 114-15
Intelligence, 2, 88; age changes in, 93; analysis of, 160-62; artificial (AI), 192-93; changes over time in, 94; effect on personal control of, 148; as field specific, 91, 92, 200-201; nature-nurture issue and, 108-12; racial differences in, 109-10; as a subject variable, 101; twin studies of, 108. *See also* Psychological tests of intelligence
Intention, 176
Interference, 66-68, 101; ecological validity in studies of, 77; and imagery, 138; limits on laws of, 88-91, 93; textbooks' ignoring of, 157-58; theory of, 159; versus decay, 169. *See also* Memory
Internal standards, 141-42
Interpretation of Dreams, The (Freud), 104

Intervening variables, 2
Intimacy, problem of, 8-9, 37, 74, 140, 174, 199
Introspection, 16-17, 21, 37, 42, 105, 131, 141, 146, 148, 192, 195
Introversion, 26-27, 80, 84, 108

Jazz, 39
Jealousy, 198
Jigsaw puzzles, 129
Jnd (just noticeable difference), 56
Johns Hopkins University, 18
Journal of Experimental Psychology, 35
Julius Caesar (Shakespeare), 149
Jupiter, 6, 181
Jupiter Symphony (Mozart), ix

Korean War, 61
Korsakoff's syndrome, 169

Labeling, 85-86
Laboratories, 76-77, 91, 106, 195; advantages of, 100, 123
Language, 16, 20, 37, 43, 53, 90, 95, 173; in animals, 74, 147, 176; associations in, 77; brain localization of, 168; influence over thought, 193; nature-nurture issue and, 116-17
Language universals, 117
Las Vegas, 55
Latent learning. *See* Learning, latent
Latin, 7, 117
Law of parsimony, 53, 54, 93, 140, 155, 164, 177, 180, 185
Laws. *See* Psychology, laws in; Science, laws in
Lawyers, 137, 148
Learned helplessness, 63, 79, 123
Learning, 33, 41, 42, 57; avoidance, 63, 64, 79, 189-90; behaviorist views of, 17-18, 129; constraints on, 79-80, 108, 117, 196; to discriminate, 22, 191; effects on brain chemistry of, 170-71; from errors, 192; Gestalt views of, 129, 185; as a hobby, 80; imagery and, 139; incremental accounts of, 185-

86; latent, 33-34, 133, 185-86; to
learn, 22, 68; love of, 192; motor,
89; paired-associate, 22-24, 77, 78,
128, 139, 159-60, 164, 188, 192;
place, 133; serial, 21, 22-24, 156-
57, 163-64; Skinner's account of, 57-
59, 105-7, 156, 164, 184; S-R
accounts of, 17-18, 130, 131, 133,
147, 156-57, 163-64, 184-91, 193;
theories of, 107, 184-91; Tolman's
account of, 132-33; verbal, 20-24,
36, 66-68, 116-17, 131-32, 159-60,
184. *See also* Conditioning; Nature-
nurture issue
Learning disability, 73
Learning-performance distinction, 33-
34
Le Sacre de Printemps (Stravinsky), 40
Level of aspiration, 146-147
Levels of processing, 134
Libraries, 135
Life-lie, 125-26
Life space, 146
Linguistics, 117, 131, 196
Literature, 110, 118, 142, 168, 196,
198, 199
Literature of freedom, 105
Lithium, 82, 171
Localization of function. *See* Brain,
localization of function in
Logical positivism, 1, 7, 44, 95, 196
Logotherapy, 145
Love, 20, 107; romantics' view of, 165;
Sartre's account of, 152; and spring,
101
Lower Depths, The (Dostoevsky), 196
LSD (Lysergic acid diethylamide), 172

Magnitude estimation, method of, 57
Make-do methodology, 146
Manhattan project, 48
Marriage, 147
Mars, 181
Masochism, 77, 142, 151-52
Mathematics, 7, 12, 15, 21, 40, 42, 52,
91, 154, 166, 200; Hull's use of, 184;
models using, 191-92; sex difference
in, 118
McCarthyism, 133

McGill University, 171
Meaningfulness, 77, 159-60
Measles, 64, 84
Measurement. *See* Operational
definitions
Mechanics, 165, 183
Mechanism-vitalism issue, 172-73,
177-78
Mediation, 131
Medical model. *See* Psychology,
medical model in
Medicine, 60, 61-62, 64-65, 83, 86,
116, 124, 138, 144, 174
Melancholy Baby, 58
Memory, x, 17, 25, 36, 55, 62, 66-68,
71, 77-78; autobiographical, 77; for
childhood experiences, 169;
components of, 165; and encoding,
134; episodic, 90; excessive analysis
of, 165; flashbulb, 78; implicit, 42,
90; for interrupted tasks, 145; long-
term, 169, 170-71; models of, 179;
for odors, 89; photographic, 138;
procedural, 90; for prose, 136;
reconstruction in, 136-37, 176;
recovered, 41; requirements for, 134;
semantic, 90; for sentences, 136-37;
for sequence, 163-64; short-term, 88,
89, 169; storage in brain of, 167-71,
176; in structure of intellect model,
161-62; tests of, 134; textbooks of,
157-58; visual, 89-90, 137-41. *See
also* Coding; Interference; Learning;
Organization
Mental retardation, 62, 65, 88, 171
Mental telepathy, 11
Mescalin, 138
Mesomorph, 27-28
Metaneeds, 117, 148-49, 190
Metaphors, 51, 94, 129
Method of additive factors, 156
Metrication, 1
Middle Ages, the, 96
Militant enthusiasm, 114-15
Mind, x, 5, 8, 17-19, 36-37, 50, 59;
analysis of, 155; bicameral, 148-49;
empiricist views of, 128; frames of,
91, 122, 168; idols of, 51, 54; Kant's
view of, 128; Mills's view of, 162;

psychology's loss of, 193; reductionist denials of, 172-73, 177-78; romantic views of, 70; Skinner's views of, 105-7, 123; unconscious, 16, 40, 41-43, 64, 103-4, 175

Mind-body problem, 19, 36, 46, 56, 165, 172-73

Misanthrope, The (Molière), 33

Mnemonic devices, 89, 134, 137-38

Mnemonists, 137-38

Mobs, 114

Models: in psychology, 191-93; in science, 179-81

Morals, 47-50, 88, 106-7, 125-26, 170, 175-76, 197; development of, 69, 92

Morphine, 174

Motivation, 2, 33; in avoidance learning, 189-90; Chein's view of, 143; effect of reinforcement on, 185-86; extrinsic, 76; Hull's view of, 184-89; incentive, 147; intrinsic, 76, 141; and performance efficiency, 187-88; reductionistic approaches to, 185

Motorcycles, 165-66

Mrs. Dalloway (Woolf), 196

Multiple choice examinations, 31-32, 134

Murphy's law, 53

Music, 25, 36, 40, 58-59, 70, 91, 92, 99, 197; perception of, 163; sex difference in, 118

Mutations, 57; behavioral, 58

Muzak, 124

My Brilliant Career, 196

My Fair Lady, 20

Myths, 44

National Socialism. *See* Fascism

Nature-nurture issue, 79, 107-119, 191, 195; moral issues and, 126-27. *See also* Aggression; Heredity; Intelligence

Neptune, 2

Neuropsychology. *See* Psychology, physiological

Neurosis, 44, 46, 65, 82, 124, 144, 148, 150. *See also* Psychopathology

Neurotransmitter substances, 169-70, 171

New puritanism, 47

1984 (Orwell), 87, 88, 107

Nobel Prize, 7, 15, 99, 175

Nobility, 106

Noise, 123-24

Nomothetic methods, 54, 72

Nonsense syllable, 20, 78, 89, 131, 156

Norepinephrine, 171

North America, 81, 92, 107, 108, 109, 110, 153

Nuclear power, 40, 49, 106

Nuremberg trials, 92

Nutrition. *See* Hunger drive

Obedience, 49-50, 88

Objectivity, 2, 5, 8, 11-13, 16-18, 32-33, 39, 48, 74, 166

Occipital lobe, 168

Ode on a Grecian Urn (Keats), 39

Oedipus complex, 122-23

Oligarchies, 106

Olympic Games, 114

One Flew Over the Cuckoo's Nest (Kesey), 88

Operational definitions, 1-2, 11-12, 18, 32, 36, 37, 40, 43, 55, 56-57, 71-72, 92-93, 133, 195; of creativity factors, 162; of imagery, 139; justification of using, 164; of teaching, 113

Operationism, 1, 7, 13, 33, 92

Order of the Golden Fleece, 3

Organization, 134-36. *See also* Memory

Orient, the, 94

Originality. *See* Creativity

Original Sin, 102

Othello (Shakespeare), 198

Overmen, 75, 97

Pandora's box, 95, 164

Panty raids, 199

Paradigms, 9, 18, 35, 43, 46; in psychology, 122, 190, 193. *See also* Generative ideas; Theories

Paranoia, 83, 84

Parapsychology, 11

Passive subjects. *See* Behaviorism,
    passive view of subjects
Passover Plot, The, 183
Peak experiences, 45, 142, 144
Peg-word system, 89
Penis envy, 103
Pep rallies, 199
Perception, x, 129-30, 131, 175, 195;
    object of, 151. *See also* Attention
Periodic table, 52, 53
Personal equations. *See* Individual
    differences
Personality, attributes of, 72;
    application of Hull's theory to, 184;
    authoritarian, 94; development of,
    69; theorizing about, 190; types of,
    26-27; 80
Ph.D., 145
Phenothiazines, 83
Phenylketonuria, 171
Philosophy, 21, 75, 113, 128, 149,
    155, 159, 162, 177, 196
Phi phenomenon, 163
Phobias, 19-20, 62, 63, 80, 81
Photographs, 167
Physics, 1, 5, 9, 42, 43, 120, 146, 154,
    164, 166, 167, 200
Physiology, 154
Pineal gland, 19
Pioneers, 108
Placebo effect, 174
Plans, 147
Play, 191
Playboy, 47
Poetry, 12, 34, 40, 43, 44, 70-71, 74,
    79, 142, 165, 176
Politics, 149, 155, 166
Polygamy, 196
Pompeii, 151
Power, 151-52
Pragmatism, 21, 62
Predestination, doctrine of, 102
Prejudice, 146
Principle of gradualness, 52, 73
Principle of mass action, 167-68
Priority disputes, 15
Prisons, 124-25
Problem finding, 28-29, 193

Problem solving, 9, 129, 176, 181,
    188, 192, 195
Procrastination, 141
Procrustean methods, 32-34, 40, 177,
    192
Propaganda, 74
Proteins, 170-71
Protestant schism. *See* Reformation
Prototype, 65, 193
Providence, 196
Prozac, 83
Psyche. See Mind
Psychedelic drugs, 174. *See also* LSD;
    Mescalin
Psychiatry, 84
Psychoanalysis, 41-43, 44, 62, 63, 75,
    83, 88, 103-4, 127, 144, 166, 196;
    Adler's version of, 130; analysis in,
    155; emphasis on early childhood,
    109; Popper's view of, 181
Psychological tests: biases in, 109; of
    creativity, 40, 71-72; of
    development, 68; history of, 155; of
    intelligence, 1, 2, 12, 24-25, 28, 33,
    72, 93, 108-110, 160-62; of
    personality, 25-28, 55
Psychologists, accreditation of, 102,
    122, 145; beliefs concerning ESP,
    11; biases of, 159, 157, 195, 198;
    errors made by, 121; ignoring of
    Sartre by, 152; imagery in, 141;
    inferiority complex of, 200-1;
    insistence on studying animals, 74;
    laypeople's suspicion of, 85;
    mathematical skills in, 102; religious
    faith in, 197; surplus of, 145; writers
    as, 196
Psychology: absence of agreed
    paradigm in, 167; applied, 21, 25,
    49, 59-60, 73, 95, 131, 195;
    clinical, 84, 102, 143-45, 195, 197;
    cognitive, 17, 166; competitive
    motives in, 127; concern for being
    scientific, 8, 164, 194; dangers of,
    183; as dead, 35; definition of, ix-
    xiv, 15-19, 54, 198-99;
    developmental, 26, 68-69, 91-92,
    104; difficulty of, 200; diverse

content of, 122, 167, 190, 200;
eminent practitioners of, xiii;
enrollments in, ix, 199; esoteric, 38;
Gestalt, 127, 128-29, 132-33, 136,
145-48, 159, 163-64, 165, 167, 173,
175, 200; history of, 15-19, 20-23,
24-25, 132, 140, 155, 162-63, 168,
171, 184, 190-91, 193, 194-96, 198;
as a historical undertaking, 95;
humanistic, 47, 71, 75, 117, 127,
165, 191, 196; importance of, ix;
interest of, ix, 200; laws in, 55, 57-
59, 79-82, 92-95, 121, 187-88, 195;
medical model in, 62, 64-65, 82-85,
171-72, 174; methods in, 30-36, 95;
morals and, 49-50, 85-88, 125-27;
myths about, x, 199-200; need for
breadth in, 167, 195, 196; North
American, 107; physiological, 158,
167-73, 195; pop, 75, 200;
preconceptions of, 8-9; problems of
measurement in, 12-13, 24-29;
progress of, 34-35, 52, 73, 139, 198,
200; pure, 49, 73; rejection of, 177;
as a revolutionary science, 49; social,
49-50, 60-61, 78, 94-95, 107, 145-
48, 190; textbooks of, 157-58, 181,
191, 199; value judgments in, 94; as
a young science, 36, 73. *See also*
Analysis, in psychology; Conceptual
devices, in psychology;
Determinism, in psychology;
Empiricism, in psychology;
Generalization, in psychology;
Reductionism, in psychology
Psychopathology, 61-65, 107, 196; in
artists, 71; classification of, 64-65;
82-85; definition of, 84, 87-88;
psychoanalytic explanation of, 103-
4; reductionistic explanations of,
171-72. *See also* Neurosis
Psychopaths, 26
Psychophysics, 56-57, 89
Psychosis, 62, 64-65, 86, 108, 124,
144. *See also* Bipolar mood disorder;
Schizophrenia
Psy.D. (Doctor of psychology), 145
Publish or perish syndrome, 30-31, 35,
112-13, 166

Punishment, 107
Puritan work ethic, 187
Puromycin, 170
Pyrrhic victory, 190

Quality, 32, 35, 39, 48, 166, 175, 192
Quantum mechanics, 120. *See also*
Indeterminism

Radio, 153
Random assignment of subjects, 100-
101
Random selection of subjects, 100
Rational emotive therapy. *See* Therapy,
rational emotive
Reaction potential, 184-89
Recentering, 129
Receptive field, 168
Reductionism: approaches to therapy
of, 144; criticisms of, 173-78;
definition of, xiv; explanations of
homosexuality, 126; explanations of
sex differences, 118; Freud's views
on, 175; Lewin's attitude toward, 146;
in psychology, 8, 35, 62, 87, 95,
154-55, 167-73; in science, 154-55.
See also Psychology, physiological
Reformation, 4, 102, 105
Regret, 196-97
Rehearsal, elaborative, 134;
maintenance, 134
Reincarnation, 177
Reinforcement: and aggression, 115-
16; in avoidance learning, 189-90;
Bandura's view of, 141-43, 187; in
brain areas, 171, 187; circularity of;
123; definition of, 56; history of, 58,
146; Hull's explanation of, 185-86;
in laboratory and naturalistic
settings, 77; limitations on, 79-80,
82, 94; magnitude of, 81; partial, 56,
64, 93; Premack's view of, 187;
secondary, 58, 64; Skinner's views
of, 57-59, 61, 105-7, 116-17, 123,
124, 141-42, 185; types of, 57
Relativity, theory of, 3, 10, 177, 179,
182
Reliability, 2, 11, 16, 32, 39, 41, 43,
93, 199; of diagnosis, 65, 82

Religion, 7, 8, 43, 44-46, 50, 74, 149, 173, 177, 197, 199; as analogous to creativity, 191; contrasted to science, 181, 183; history of, 166
Renaissance, 190
Repentance, 125
Repression, 41, 46-47, 62, 94
Reserpine, 171, 172
Response integration, 164
Response produced cues, 157, 158, 163-64
Responsibility, 102, 105, 106, 125, 127, 143, 144, 176; variations in, 148. *See also* Free will
Reticular formation, 185
Retina, 168
Retrieval, 134-35, 167. *See also* Memory
Reverberation, 169
Revolution, 74
Rhetoric, 137
RNA (Ribonucleic acid), 170
Roadrunner, 116
Role-playing technique, 61, 81
Roman Catholicism, 102
Romanticism, 70-71, 75, 92, 103, 127, 140, 149, 150, 165, 173, 191, 196
Romantic understanding, 165-66
Rome/Romans 96, 149
Rorschach test, 11, 150
Rosencrantz and Guildenstern are Dead (Stoppard), 150
Rotation experiments, 139
Rules, 147

Saccharine, 186
Sadism, 152
Salauds, 150
Salzburg, 59
San Francisco, 84
SAT (Scholastic Aptitude Test), 118
Schizophrenia, xi, 62, 65, 82, 86, 152, 167, 171, 172, 191. *See also* Psychosis
Scholars, 110, 112-13, 122, 133, 158, 170, 198, 200; existentialist attitude toward, 150; reinforcers for, 142; specialization of, 166

Science: aesthetic criteria in, 9, 13, 40; aims of, 98-100, 122; applied, 3-4, 48-49, 113; ascending tree of, 154; as cautious, 165; characteristics of, xii-xiv; in clinical training, 145; collaboration in, 79; as cumulative, 52; effectiveness of, 99; in the Enlightenment, 70; faith in, xiv, 54, 98, 99, 154; financing of, 48-49; fraud in, 10, 31; as a game, 1; generalization in, 49-54; history of, 9-11, 15, 18, 153, 158, 196; as a hobby, 4; importance of timing in, 158; laws in, 53, 54, 93, 179-80; limitations of, 174, 194, 196; linear thought in, 37; mechanism-vitalism issue and, 172-73; mind-body problem and, 36; need to broaden, 195; normal, 9, 46; peak experiences in, 45-46; philosophy of, xii; problem finding in, 28; progress in, 10, 36, 103, 158, 182, 183, 190, 200; psychoanalysis and, 41, 103, 181; psychology of, xi, 38; publications in, 30-31; publish or perish syndrome in, 112-13; pure, 3-4, 48-49, 113, 195; as release for aggression, 114; religion and, 6-7, 10, 183; revolutionary, 9, 35, 46, 158, 194; as a sacred cow, 72, 113, 198; similarity to art, 49; specialization in, 166-67; symbols in, 44; tacit knowledge in, 11-12, 163; Taoistic, 47; theories in, 2-3; totalitarianism and, 48; value judgments in, 39-40, 166; values in, 47-50, 78, 92, 110-11, 125, 126-27, 170, 175-76; views of, x, xi
Scientism, 194, 198
Scientist-practitioner model, 102, 145
Scientists, xi; attitudes of, 3-7, 53, 54, 71, 78, 107, 110-13, 121, 141, 157-59, 166, 172, 182-84, 197, 200; attributes of, 114, 181; beliefs concerning ESP, 11; existentialist attitude toward, 150; imagery in, 141; motives of, 3-5, 15; other abilities of, 201; psychology of, 9-11, 45-46;

reinforcers for, 142; sex difference in, 118; tender and tough-minded, 5

Search: parallel, 156; self-terminating, 156; serial-exhaustive, 156

Self: concept of, 60, 85, 94; existential views of, 150-51; ideal, 41; real, 75

Self-actualization, 75, 148-49, 190

Self-consciousness, 152

Self-fulfilling prophecies, 85-86, 123-26, 142, 148, 193

Self-interest, 106

Self-monitoring, 147

Sensation. See Stimulus

Serial position hypothesis, 22-24, 157

Serotonin, 171, 172

Sex, 41, 42, 46, 47, 63, 87, 104; Sartre's account of, 152; as test of Hull's theory, 186

Sex differences, 74, 92, 94, 108, 115, 118-19, 142, 152, 196

Shame, 151

Shaping, 58, 60, 61, 64, 80, 160

Shotgun marriages, xii, 196

Signs, 42

Sin, 125

Sinai, Mount, 106

Skepticism, 5-6

Skinner box, 58, 106

Smell, 36

Smoking, 61, 81, 82, 83; and cancer, 101

Soccer, 114

Social constructionism, 95

Social interest, 130

Socialization. See Education

Social sciences, 154, 196

Solar eclipse, 182

Solar system, 179

Sophists, 166

Soul. See Mind

South Africa, 12

South Pacific, 60

Soviet Union, 78, 126

Species-specific defense reaction, 79

Split brain studies, 38, 139, 173, 175

Spontaneous generation, 10

Sports, 4, 45, 93, 114, 147

SPSSI (Society for the Psychological Study of Social Issues), 111

Stages of development, 68-69, 91

Stanford-Binet Test. See Psychological tests, of intelligence

Stanford prison experiments, 124-25

Statistical methods, 25, 45, 71-72, 101-2, 110, 121-22, 145, 191, 197, 198

Steam engines, 179

Stevens's Power Law, 57

Stereotyping, 53

Stimulus, 12, 18, 25, 43, 53, 57, 70; analysis of, 155-56; as different from perception, 163-64; functional, 22-24, 131-32, 157, 163; nominal, 22, 131; phobic, 63; produced by responding, 156-57; standard, 56; unconditioned, 58, 130-31

Stimulus generalization, 64

Stimulus selection, 131

Stimulus similarity, 66

Stock market, 74

Stress, 174

Structuralism, 155, 162

Structure of intellect model, 160-62, 164

Style of life, 41, 130

Subject variable experiments. See Experiments, subject variable

Sublimation, 41

Subtraction method, 155-56

Successive approximations. See Shaping

Sufism, 38

Super males, 115

Surgery. See Medicine

Swan Lake, 58

Symbols, 42-44, 70, 74, 124, 173

Synapse, the, 169, 172, 175

Synesthesia, 138

Syphilis, 62

Tabula rasa, 17, 128, 193

Tacit knowledge, 11-12, 38, 42, 163, 193, 199

Taxi Driver, 116

Teaching, in universities, 112-13. *See also* Education
Teaching machine, 60
Technology, 3, 10, 15, 35, 57, 82, 106, 131
Telephones, 124
Telescope, 6
Television, 116
Temporal lobe, 169
Tennis, 105, 156
Tenure, 110, 112-13
Theatre, xiii
Theories: compared to other conceptual devices, 179; definition of, xiv; of development, 68-69; dogma and, 6, 10; empirical rule and, 2-3, 13, 182; hypothetico-deductive approach to, 185-86; Popper's description of, 181-82; Skinner's attitude toward, 59, 104, 123, 179, 190; as source of deductions, 52; truth of, 10; uses of, 179-81. *See also* Conceptual devices; Science, theories in
Theories of learning. *See* Learning, theories of
Therapy, 61-64, 81-83, 86; Adler's methods of, 130; cognitive behavior, 143-45; factors influencing success of, 122, 124; moral, 144; moral problems of, 87-88; rational emotive, 143-44; reductionistic approaches to, 171-72, 174
Third Reich, 48, 96
Thirst drive, 180, 185
Thought, 195; abstract, 74, 195; application of Hull's theory to, 184-85; control over behavior of, 105, 142-43; divergent, 161-62; influence of language over, 193; linear, 37-38, 39, 165-66; nonlinear, 37-38, 39, 165-66; relation to brain function, 172-73. *See also* Cognition
Tip-of-the-tongue phenomenon, 78
Token economies, 63, 81, 82
Tolerance for ambiguity, 4
Tower of Babel, the, 183
Traits, 26, 55, 93, 146, 161-62
Transfer, 20-24, 42, 135-36
Trivial Pursuit, 32, 134

True believers, 182
24 Sussex Drive, 105
Two-stage analysis, 159-60, 164
Typing, 163, 164

Ulcers, 174
Ulysses (Joyce), 110
Unconscious. *See* Mind, unconscious
United States, 88, 133, 145
Universities, 30-32, 110-13, 124, 145, 167, 199. *See also* Academic Freedom
University of Alberta, 56
University of California, 133
University of Chicago, 21
University of Western Ontario, 111
Uranus, 2
Urine, 115
Utopia, 103, 107

Validity, 32, 83, 93; ecological, 76-79, 100, 147, 191, 192, 195; of Guilford's tests, 162
Valium, 144, 174
Value. *See* Quality
Values. *See* Morals
Vienna, 59
Vienna circle, 1
Viet Nam war, 110
Violence. *See* Aggression
Vision, 168
Visual imagery, 25, 89, 137-41
Vitalism, 172-73. *See also* Mechanism-vitalism issue

WAIS (Wechsler Adult Intelligence Scale). *See* Psychological tests, of intelligence
Waiting for Godot (Beckett), 150
Walden II (Skinner), 59, 107
War of the Ghosts, The, 136
Watergate scandal, 176
Weapons, 114
Weather forecasting, 99
Weber's Law, 56, 93
Western thought, 165-66, 197
West Side Story, 125
White House, 105
Wichita, KS, 84
Wild Duck, The (Ibsen), 125-26

Women, psychology of, 152
World War I, 103, 104, 128
World War II, 149
World within the skin. *See* Mind,
    Skinner's view of
Worm Runner's Digest, The, 170
Writing. *See* Literature

Yerkes-Dodson function, 187-88

Zeigarnik effect, 145
Zeitgeist, 158, 172
*Zen and the Art of Motorcycle
    Maintenance* (Pirsig), 39

About the Author

JOCK ABRA is Professor of Psychology at the University of Calgary.